Responsible AI Integration in Education

Juan J. Araujo
Texas Woman's University, USA

Sharla Snider
Texas Woman's University, USA

IGI Global
Scientific Publishing
Publishing Tomorrow's Research Today

Vice President of Editorial Melissa Wagner
Director of Acquisitions Mikaela Felty
Director of Book Development Jocelynn Hessler
Production Manager Mike Brehm
Cover Design Jose Rosado

Published in the United States of America by
IGI Global Scientific Publishing
701 East Chocolate Avenue
Hershey, PA, 17033, USA
Tel: 717-533-8845
Fax: 717-533-7115
Website: https://www.igi-global.com E-mail: cust@igi-global.com

Library of Congress Cataloging-in-Publication Data

Names: Araujo, Juan Jose, 1971- editor | Snider, Sharla, 1964- editor
Title: Responsible AI integration in education / [edited by] Juan J. Araujo, Sharla Snider.
Description: Hershey, PA : IGI Global Scientific Publishing, [2026] | Includes bibliographical references and index. | Summary: "This book explores the consequences of integrating AI into education. This book delves into the transformative potential of AI, as well as the risks associated with its unchecked advancement"-- Provided by publisher.
Identifiers: LCCN 2025031518 (print) | LCCN 2025031519 (ebook) | ISBN 9798337360072 hardcover | ISBN 9798337360089 paperback | ISBN 9798337360096 ebook
Subjects: LCSH: Artificial intelligence--Educational applications | Educational technology
Classification: LCC LB1028.43 .R479 2026 (print) | LCC LB1028.43 (ebook)
LC record available at https://lccn.loc.gov/2025031518
LC ebook record available at https://lccn.loc.gov/2025031519

British Cataloguing in Publication Data
A Cataloguing in Publication record for this book is available from the British Library.

Table of Contents

Detailed Table of Contents

This study aims to introduce the AI-Evaluation Quadrant Model (AI-EQM) proposed for evaluating AI-supported student work. The AI-EQM model takes into account ethical and social challenges such as students' usage behavior, fairness in the evaluation process, and the development of students' unique skills. In addition, the AI-EQM model focuses on practical applications of AI in education, such as teaching, curriculum, literacy, and language. Focusing on supporting individuals' efforts in both teaching and learning processes through the use of AI, this study emphasizes the importance of the integration of AI in the aim of responsible innovation. The AI-EQM model proposed in this study also offers an approach to measure, evaluate, and identify possible risks for the transformative effect of artificial intelligence in education. model is proposed where the effects can be seen in many dimensions such as creating a curriculum that will reduce inequality in education, increase original outcomes, and ensure responsible use of AI, increasing literacy rates, special and vocational education.

This chapter explores the integration of artificial intelligence (AI) in early childhood lesson planning through the lens of Developmentally Appropriate Practice (DAP). It examines how generative AI tools respond to varying levels of instructional prompting, and how these responses align with DAP core considerations: commonality, individuality, and context. Through case studies and critical evaluations of AI-generated lesson plans, the chapter highlights the potential and limitations of AI as a collaborative planning partner. The findings reveal that front-loading AI with specific information about a classroom's demographics, children's individual needs, and DAP core considerations improves lesson quality. While AI can support educators in designing engaging, differentiated, and standards-aligned lessons, its effectiveness depends on educators' ability to guide, critique, and adapt its outputs. The chapter concludes with recommendations for leveraging AI to enhance—rather than replace—professional expertise in the creation of joyful, inclusive, and play-based learning environments

This chapter explores the developmental implications of artificial intelligence (AI) in contemporary educational settings. Employing a dual-methodological approach that combines interdisciplinary expertise with an integrative literature review, the chapter explores how AI technologies are reshaping student identity, emotional regulation, motivation, autonomy, and interpersonal relationships. Drawing on developmental psychology, educational theory, and empirical research, it interrogates the unintended consequences of algorithmic surveillance, pedagogical automation, and AI-mediated social interactions. The analysis highlights both the affordances and risks of AI in education, including its impact on emotional resilience, self-directed learning, and the construction of academic identity. Reframing the discourse away from purely technical efficiency toward developmental integrity makes visible the deeper human stakes of AI integration in education. The chapter consequently calls for ethical, inclusive, and human-centered approaches to AI design and implementation in schools.

Artificial Intelligence (AI) is no longer a distant concept confined to theoretical discourse; it has become a transformative force within classrooms across the globe. This chapter critically explores the evolution of AI in education, tracing its journey from speculative theory to practical deployment. With a reflective lens, it examines how AI-driven systems have reshaped pedagogical methodologies, from personalized

This chapter delves into the complex relationship between artificial intelligence (AI) and its influence on contemporary classrooms, examining this through the dual lenses of cognitivism and constructivism. The integration of AI technologies is explored as a transformative force that is reshaping pedagogical approaches, streamlining administrative tasks, and offering personalized learning experiences. While acknowledging the concerns about AI potentially replacing teachers, the chapter emphasizes AI's role as a tool to augment teaching practices, enhance learning outcomes, and address equity and accessibility challenges. By analyzing case studies and theoretical frameworks, the chapter aims to provide a balanced perspective on AI's implications, highlighting both its potential benefits and the importance of thoughtful implementation to foster effective, equitable, and ethical learning environments.

This chapter examines the ethical challenges posed by integrating artificial intelligence in early childhood education (birth through age 8), highlighting research that reveals unintended consequences, including algorithmic bias that perpetuates discrimination, privacy erosion through surveillance technologies, and developmental risks that can impair children's social-emotional growth. Young children are especially vulnerable because they cannot understand AI's implications, consent to data collection, or resist technological influence during critical developmental periods when their capacity for moral reasoning is still forming. Drawing from research on child development, moral philosophy, and educational ethics, it is demonstrated that AI implementation with young children is fundamentally a moral endeavor that shapes children's understanding of truth, authentic relationships, and development as ethical beings. To address these needs, the illuminED Framework is introduced—a comprehensive, human-centered, rights-based model providing practical guidance for teachers and caregivers.

Preface

In recent years, artificial intelligence (AI) has become more than a futuristic concept. It is now an active and evolving presence in the everyday practices of education. From adaptive learning platforms to AI-powered writing assistants, the technology is transforming how we teach, learn, and engage with knowledge. Yet, with this transformation comes a profound responsibility: to ensure that the integration of AI into educational systems is thoughtful, equitable, and ethically sound.

Responsible AI Integration in Education was conceived as a response to this challenge. As editors, researchers, and educators, we have witnessed both the promise and the perils of AI in our own classrooms and institutions. This book brings together scholars, researchers, and practitioners who recognize that AI is not just a technical tool rather a way to make education more accessible and transformative. It is a social force with the potential to reshape the educational landscape in ways that can either empower or marginalize learners.

This volume offers a comprehensive and critical examination of how AI intersects with key areas of educational practice, including bilingual education, curriculum and instruction, early childhood education, language and literacy, and special education. Our contributors explore not only the innovative uses of AI but also the unintended consequences that may arise, such as biases embedded in algorithms, inequities in access, and the erosion of human-centered pedagogies.

We believe that theory must walk hand in hand with practice. Therefore, this collection balances conceptual frameworks with real-world applications, providing preservice and inservice teachers, administrators, and policymakers with both the understanding and the tools to navigate this evolving terrain. Readers will find chapters that delve into the pedagogical models guiding AI integration, practical case studies of AI in classroom environments, and critical analyses of the broader implications for policy and practice.

Perhaps most importantly, this book underscores the importance of responsibility in every aspect of AI implementation. As educators, we must ask difficult questions. Who benefits from AI? Who is left out? What values are embedded in the technologies we adopt? And how do we ensure that our embrace of innovation does not come at the cost of equity, privacy, or pedagogical integrity?

As you read the eight chapters, we ask that you consider taking a look, think, act approach (Patterson et al, 2010; Stringer, 1996). Look (and read) the chapters and carefully consider what patterns, trends, and ideas you notice as you read the author's works. Think about why these ideas might be bubbling into the surface, and what factors might you consider as a educator. Take action to adjust or implement some of these ideas, tools, strategies, or frameworks in your day-to-day activities.

To that end, each chapter in this volume offers a unique lens on the evolving relationship between AI and education:

Chapter 1 introduces the AI-Evaluation Quadrant Model (AI-EQM), a practical framework for assessing AI-supported student work. With a focus on ethics, equity, and individual growth, this model provides guidance for responsible curriculum design, language instruction, and inclusive education practices, while also emphasizing the importance of measuring and mitigating AI's risks in schools.

Chapter 2 explores the use of AI in early childhood lesson planning through the lens of Developmentally Appropriate Practice (DAP). Through critical evaluations and classroom case studies, the chapter demonstrates how educators can use AI to support, rather than substitute, pedagogical expertise and ensure that technology contributes to joyful, inclusive, and culturally responsive learning.

Chapter 3 takes a developmental perspective on AI's presence in schools, spotlighting its effects on student motivation, autonomy, identity formation, and emotional well-being. The chapter challenges readers to consider the psychological consequences of algorithmic surveillance and automation, urging a shift toward human-centered AI design in education.

Chapter 4 charts AI's evolution from theory to classroom practice. This chapter critically examines adaptive technologies, intelligent tutoring systems, and learning analytics, while also raising concerns about ethical blind spots and the overreliance on automation. It calls for AI deployment that respects the relational and transformative nature of teaching and learning.

Chapter 5 turns to higher education, where AI is shifting classroom dynamics and redefining the roles of professors and students. The chapter presents a thoughtful analysis of how AI invites new forms of collaboration and participation, while also introducing tensions around authority, agency, and educational values.

Chapter 6 emphasizes the importance of ethical leadership in the age of AI. As digital technologies reshape educational decision-making, this chapter provides a framework for school leaders to ensure transparency, privacy, and fairness in their institutions' use of AI. It helps leaders navigate the complex terrain of policy and implementation.

Chapter 7 revisits foundational learning theories, cognitivism and constructivism, to examine how AI technologies influence teaching strategies and learner outcomes. By anchoring AI's potential in established pedagogical principles, the chapter offers a roadmap for equitable, personalized, and thoughtful AI integration.

Chapter 8 offers a deeply humanistic and ethical reflection on AI use with young children. Highlighting the unique vulnerabilities of early learners, this chapter introduces the illuminED Framework, a rights-based model designed to protect children's developmental, emotional, and moral growth. It urges educators and caregivers to approach AI in early childhood with care, intentionality, and unwavering attention to ethical impact.

Together, these chapters form a cohesive and timely exploration of responsible AI integration. Each contribution reinforces our central conviction that technology must remain a tool in the service of human values, not a force that overrides them. We invite readers to engage critically, reflect deeply, and join us in shaping a future where AI serves as a partner in advancing equity, creativity, and care in education.

REFERENCES

Patterson, L., Baldwin, S. C., Araujo, J. J., Shearer, R., & Stewart, M. (2010). Look, think, act: Using critical action research to sustain reform in complex teaching/learning ecologies. *Journal of Inquiry and Action in Education, 3*(3). https://digitalcommons.buffalostate.edu/jiae/vol3/iss3/4

Stringer, E. T. (1996). *Action research: A handbook for practitioners*. Sage Publications.

Chapter 1
Measuring the Role of AI-Enhanced Learning: A Responsible Framework for Educational Innovation

Magdalini Vlami
https://orcid.org/0009-0005-9671-5194
University of Alicante, Spain

Serdar Yener
https://orcid.org/0000-0003-1413-7422
Sinop University, Turkey

ABSTRACT

This study aims to introduce the AI-Evaluation Quadrant Model (AI-EQM) proposed for evaluating AI-supported student work. The AI-EQM model takes into account ethical and social challenges such as students' usage behavior, fairness in the evaluation process, and the development of students' unique skills. In addition, the AI-EQM model focuses on practical applications of AI in education, such as teaching, curriculum, literacy, and language. Focusing on supporting individuals' efforts in both teaching and learning processes through the use of AI, this study emphasizes the importance of the integration of AI in the aim of responsible innovation. The AI-EQM model proposed in this study also offers an approach to measure, evaluate, and identify possible risks for the transformative effect of artificial intelligence in education. model is proposed where the effects can be seen in many dimensions such as creating a curriculum that will reduce inequality in education, increase original outcomes, and ensure responsible use of AI, increasing literacy rates, special and vocational education.

DOI: 10.4018/979-8-3373-6007-2.ch001

INTRODUCTION

Artificial Intelligence (AI) creates significant transformations in many fields, especially in education. AI increases the learning opportunities of individuals at all ages, spreads personalized education, and increases efficiency with inclusive evaluation methods (Kizilcec, 2023). Many applications such as AI-supported learning content creators, flexible-smart teaching tools, spelling-meaning-grammar correctors, curriculum design, foreign language education, and education in a foreign language are adopted in almost every field (Luckin et al., 2021; Akinwalere et al., 2022). In addition, there are difficulties in measuring the role of AI in measuring student effort, measuring learning outcomes, and measuring AI contribution or role. In this context, it is seen that both educators and students need practical methods and tools that can measure the impact of AI. In this study, analytical information is presented regarding the use of AI in both the contribution to learning and the measurement of learning level. The spread of AI (AI) has led to unpredictable changes, especially in the field of education. Its impact on personalized learning systems in particular is felt more today. In addition, automatic content production that will meet personal needs eliminates the disadvantages of traditional education and increases the efficiency and effectiveness of education (Luckin, Jones, & Cukurova, 2021; Wang et al., 2024). Especially during the pandemic period, individuals' interaction with information and communication tools has gradually increased, and AI applications have further increased this interaction. Difficulties and obstacles such as educational inequalities encountered in traditional education, limited access to education, high class sizes, and differences in learning speeds have facilitated the acceptance and dissemination of AI (Owoc, Sawicka, & Weichbroth, 2021). However, the uncontrolled spread of AI in the field of education and its unpredictable effects require individual or institutional measures. In particular, it is necessary to measure learning with AI, to measure the role of AI in learning, to increase awareness about students' dependence and trust on AI, and to develop which skills and abilities AI is used in particular (Akinwalere & Ivanov, 2022). To give examples of the surprising use of AI, the learning method and model compatible with the student's learning speed and performance, natural language processing (NLP) tools that facilitate writing and reading, tools that can perform instant language translation, writing speech recognition software, curriculum designers, and microcredit catalogs show promising results (Abushariah et al., 2023; Marzuki et al., 2023). Applications called Intelligent Learning Systems (ITS) provide real-time feedback supported by AI and produce positive results in STEM fields (Woolf, 2010).

These applications and transformations brought about by AI lead to paradigm shifts in the evaluation of student performances in all stakeholders, especially policy makers. While traditional assessment methods take into account factors such as students' motivation, effort, and originality of performance, the role of AI in these factors and the measurement of its impact on student development in AI-supported education emerge as a major problem area. This change and transformation increases concerns in all stakeholders on the subject (Luckin et al., 2021).

LITERATURE REVIEW

In general, we see the increasing impact of AI in many areas such as learning, foreign language learning, curriculum development, special education, and vocational training.

1. Language and Literacy Education

AI-supported NLP systems, etc. software are increasingly used in language and literacy education. Examples of AI-supported software in language and literacy education include Grammarly and GPT. These software provide continuity and consistency in education by providing instant feedback according to the users' learning speed, performance and level thanks to AI. It is observed that users who use these software make progress in a short time, improve their writing and speaking skills, and find continuous practice opportunities (Wang et al ., 2024). On the other hand, it is also emphasized that individuals learning English as a Foreign Language (EFL), one of the most difficult education areas, gain language proficiency using valid and reliable methods (Marzuki et al., 2023). While these applications and users' experiences increase the interest of other users in AI, the uncontrolled overconfidence that occurs also prevents users from making objective and critical evaluations. As a result, users use AI-supported software without evaluating it, and research and critical thinking efforts decrease (Kasneci et al., 2023).

2. Bilingual Education AI

Many opportunities for the use of AI have emerged, especially in bilingual education. Before AI technology, speech recognition and language translation software were widely used. While AI increases the capacities of these systems, it has also begun to offer individualized opportunities by taking into account the readiness, learning speed and learning styles of individuals. AI-supported speech recognition and language translation systems have increased students' word memory, pronunciation and comprehension skills (Abushariah et al., 2023). However, one of the important factors in bilingual education and language learning is the existence of contexts in which the language will be used. For example, there is a need to create AI-supported contexts for the use of language in the health field and in commerce. It is known that studies are being conducted on this subject and it is thought that such software can be developed in the near future. In language learning and bilingual education, there are concerns in areas such as measuring the effect of AI, controlling the use of AI, unconditional acceptance of students, and feeling the cultural effect of the target language (Chen et al., 2020).

3. Special Education

In special education, another area where AI is used, AI-supported personal solutions are produced for the education of individuals with different disabilities. AI tools that produce inclusive learning solutions for the varying needs of disabled students eliminate many obstacles or reduce their effects. In this way, many opportunities that cannot be provided in traditional educational environments are created thanks to AI-supported applications (Owoc et al., 2021). For individuals with dyslexia, motor disorders, speech, hearing and vision disorders, the use of AI provides benefits that will increase equal opportunities. While there are some clear benefits to AI in special education, there are some potential disadvantages. Among the most prominent is the retention of systemic bias and discrimination in AI algorithms. If the information that underwrites the algorithms is biased or reflective of social injustice, then its applications will codify and exonerate those injustices, especially for marginalised or underprivileged students. The potential harm of AI in special education is also that it may lead to an invasion of privacy and security for students. AI-powered tools harvesting student data causes ethical concerns about the protection of confidential information. Furthermore, dependence on AI-based assessment and feedback systems can narrow down the syllabus and prevent students from having access to diverse learning sources (Ma & Jiang, C., 2023)

4. STEM and Curriculum Design

STEM (Science, Technology, Engineering and Mathematics)-focused education is a recently popular field of education that focuses on special abilities. In this method, which emphasizes the association of students' learning topics with STEM dimensions, AI-supported intelligent teaching systems (ITS) make a unique contribution. ITS provides real-time flexible curricula according to students' individual performance, learning performance, readiness and learning needs (Woolf, 2010). ITS tools increase the effectiveness of learning by providing students with real-time feedback during the learning process. However, controlled use of ITS tools is not possible without the teacher's intervention and contribution. The teacher's interventions during the process will increase the effectiveness of learning (Nithiyanandam et al., 2022).

In the learning areas mentioned above, AI-supported applications, which generally take into account many factors such as students' performance, readiness, learning efforts, learning needs, individual obstacles, etc., represent a transformation in education, while on the other hand, they push students into a passive role. In order for students to take on a role that intervenes in the process from a passive position, they need to criticize and evaluate the impact of AI (Akinwalere & Ivanov, 2022).

On the one hand, incorporating AI-based tools into vocational training could yield huge benefits. The cooperation between academia and industry, as well as the correct balance between human and machine learning, can lead to more efficient learning and teaching. AI-powered platforms can deliver adaptive and tailored learning, depending on the specific student's needs and learning preferences. Furthermore, AI-based simulations and virtual reality environments can enable students to perform the skills they have learned in a controlled environment and transfer knowledge from theory to practice (Yang, 2021). But AI in vocational education doesn't come without obstacles and risks. The acculturation of many researchers and professors to the concept of AI and big data might hinder successful use of these tools. Moreover, an over-reliance on AI in vocational training might deprive humans of human skills and expertise, and undermine vocational education altogether.

MEASUREMENT CHALLENGES IN AI-SUPPORTED LEARNING

While the use of AI in different areas of education increases efficiency and productivity, it has also brought with it many challenges regarding both learning and measuring the impact of AI. The fact that AI offers personalized learning opportunities that take into account student differences in particular necessitates the use of personalized measurement methods in measuring learning and demonstrating the impact of AI.

1. Difficulties in Measuring Cognitive Effort and Real Participation

The primary problem in AI-supported education and training is the difficulty of measuring the cognitive effort shown by the student. While the time spent by the student is used to measure student participation in traditional education and training methods, unfortunately, the use of student task durations can be problematic in the use of AI. In addition to task duration, critical thinking is also a variable that is difficult to measure in the use of AI (Akinwalere & Ivanov, 2022). Because it is very difficult to measure the time spent by students using AI for lessons and homework, and it becomes almost impossible to measure the critical dimension of the outputs.Within this framework, it is recommended that students who use AI keep self-assessment/process diaries, and these diaries should be structured in a way that reflects students' participation and applications (Luckin et al., 2021). Self-assessment/process diaries that students will fill out and the teacher will follow can show how AI is used in assignments, what gains students have achieved, and how it contributes to the result.

2. Difficulties in Measuring the Contribution of AI and the Scope of Assistance

The difficulties experienced in measuring students' performance are another problem area in AI-supported education. In this context, determining a framework by teachers regarding the use of AI in education and training, and having clear instructions on which stage and under what conditions AI will be used can facilitate performance measurement. Luckin et al. (2021) recommend the creation of framework structures that will facilitate the monitoring of the use of AI in education and training. Some examples of such applications are presented below:

- Supportive AI: In such applications, AI is recommended as a moderator that will increase the student's performance, not as the main purpose or tool. In grammar lessons, AI-supported models that will correct students' mistakes can be given as an example.
- Collaborative AI: In such applications, where students gain critical thinking skills in any subject, the student is expected to make inputs and the AI responds to these inputs, allowing the student to gain critical/critical thinking skills by making more inputs. AI-supported brainstorming or AI-supported fishbone problem-solving methods can be given as examples.
- Productive AI: In some assignments and tasks where the student has no knowledge or experience, AI can productively give clues about basic inputs and students can develop the process based on these clues. In these very sensitive conditions, measures should be taken to prevent a decrease in student participation.

The situations suggested above for measuring the contribution of AI can be developed in different ways. What is important is to create reliable, valid, fair and equal evaluation models in AI measurement.

3. Difficulties in Measuring Result Quality and Skill Development

Another measurement challenge in AI-supported education is the difficulty of measuring the quality of results and quality/skill development. The indicator of the results of education is seen as the change in the development of students' qualifications and skills and the quality of the outputs. In this respect, it is difficult to measure whether positive changes have occurred in students in the long term. This difficulty also makes it difficult to measure the effect of AI. When we look at observations and research, while AI creates positive changes in the quality of output and student performance in the short term, valid and reliable results have not yet been obtained in the long term. In fact, some studies have observed that AI negatively affects creativity, critical thinking, and knowledge acquisition (Nithiyanandam et al., 2022). In some studies, although AI has been observed to increase linguistic accuracy in instant feedback in language education, it has been observed to have negative effects on students' writing skills (Marzuki et al. 2023). In this context, longitudinal AI-supported education and training studies are needed for reliable results (Luckin et al., 2021).

RESPONSIBLE INNOVATION APPROACH IN THE USE OF AI

The responsible innovation approach in education and training requires the use of innovation tools in accordance with the interests of all stakeholders. In this context, controlling the unpredictable and uncontrolled spread of AI use in education, assessing the risks it may pose in the short-medium-long term, and taking preventive measures are among the fundamental responsibilities of policy makers and users. From this perspective, inclusive, fair, and transparent methods need to be used in measuring the use of AI in education (Akinwalere and Ivanov, 2022; Wang et al., 2024).

1. Equity and Access

Equity and access, which is a dimension of the responsible innovation approach, should prioritize the access of schools with insufficient resources and low-income families to AI-supported opportunities. Because schools with insufficient resources and low-income families, and the opposite situations, create gaps in society in many ways (Abushariah et al., 2023). For example, some regions may be isolated due to insufficient resources and students' access to education may be restricted. This situation creates both social conflicts and dissatisfaction in the medium and long term.

2. Transparency and Academic Integrity

Another dimension of the responsible innovation approach is transparency and reliability in the use of AI. The spread of AI creates problems and concerns in the reliability of academic outputs. Since there are no clear guidelines and limits that determine the framework in the use of AI, it becomes almost impossible to measure student contribution. Even AI determinants often fail to provide reliable results. Guidelines and restrictions to be created in the use of AI can provide a separation of student and AI contributions (Luckin et al., 2021). On the other hand, students' moral identity levels can also enable them to self-assess and explain the use of AI. Policies that will increase trust in society can produce positive results in the long term.

3. Developing and Protecting Students' Skills

The process of developing skills and talents is directly based on to the difficulties experienced and the challenging environmental conditions. Expecting students' skills to develop in education and training processes without challenging conditions can produce misleading results. In this respect, the use of AI-supported software that will improve students' skills can support the responsible innovation approach by facilitating adaptation to the current situation. Because current studies reveal that the use of AI reduces speaking-writing, critical thinking skills (Wang et al., 2024). In this respect, the AI evaluation quadrilateral model, as suggested in this study, can provide a reference for the integration of the use of AI in education within the framework of the responsible innovation approach. This framework can enable students to establish a balance between the use of AI and skill development.

AI IN EDUCATION

The endless functions of AI have found many areas of use in the field of education, as in every sector. We can use the functions of AI in many areas, from learning tools that can be adapted to the person to eliminate personal learning differences to content creation tools that will meet the needs of the individual. Especially the most well-known tools, Natural Language Processing (NLP) and Intelligent Learning Systems (ITS), Foreign Language Learning Tools can be given as examples of these functions. These functions can be used in the creation of many tools such as learning content, course curriculum, learning development tracking tools, study tools. Classes integrated with AI-supported tools have begun to be used to ensure that students learn effectively and efficiently (Marzuki et al., 2023).

- Adaptive Learning Platforms: Personalized learning platforms that will meet the different needs of students arising from their individual differences make learning both effective and enjoyable. Knewton and DreamBox can be given as examples of tools used in this context. Real-time learning platforms that can be adapted according to both student differences and the characteristics of the educational subject can be seen as a revolution of AI in the field of education. In addition, while some platforms do not require a teacher, policy makers also consider different alternatives. Platforms are being developed, especially in the USA and some countries, where families who do not want to send their children to school can follow their children's education. Personalized and adaptable platforms of AI offer enjoyable experiences to many students (Owoc et al., 2021).
- AI-Supported Writing Tools: AI-supported writing tools provide incredible convenience to teachers and students, especially in education-training subjects where writing performance is required. For example, Grammarly is widely used in foreign language education. ChatGPT, on the other hand, offers writing support to students in almost every field with its many functions. These programs provide real-time feedback to students and increase the effectiveness of individual work (Wang et al., 2024).
- Speech Recognition Systems: Speech recognition systems provide convenience to students, especially in the early stages of foreign language and primary education. Since speech recognition systems must have different features for different languages and accents, they are very difficult to develop. In fact, even for the English language alone, several different versions are needed. This would require hundreds of versions when considered for other languages and local accents. AI-supported speech recognition systems offer great opportunities for acquiring multi-literacy skills in many languages (Abushariah, et al., 2023).

As can be seen, while AI has led to many revolutions in education, monitoring and evaluating learning development has become one of the fundamental problems. Many evaluation issues such as determining the student's contribution to student outcomes or learning processes, correctly evaluating skill development, and determining appropriate learning variables make the job of teachers and relevant stakeholders difficult and complicated. One of the most important reasons for this can be seen as the ability of AI to imitate human talents and skills almost perfectly. For this reason, it is very difficult to predict the role of AI (Wang et al., 2024). Measuring students' ability to work independently, their autonomy, their contribution to the outcomes, and their performance has become complicated.

THE ROLE OF RESPONSIBLE INNOVATION IN THE USE OF AI IN EDUCATION

It is seen that many stakeholders, from students to policy makers, are affected by the use of AI in education. Therefore, cooperation is required between all stakeholders. In this context, an approach that will balance the expectations of each stakeholder is required. Luckin et al. (2021) suggest a three-stage approach:

1. Teacher Education: Teachers have the main role in the use of AI in education. Teachers are seen as both responsible for the process and have a great responsibility as educators. Perhaps the most important stage in the process is for teachers to gain the ability to use AI in roles such as implementing the curriculum, creating course content, and evaluating learning. In this respect, teachers' competence and awareness in using AI should be increased.
2. Policy Development: The development of national policies in the use of AI in education enables the analytical evaluation of the process. National policies also accelerate the formation of national awareness. National policies also accelerate regional activities. The content of national policies should also be determined in accordance with the needs. Many variables such as the integration of AI, usage guidelines, evaluation criteria, evaluation and usage tools need to be determined. On the other hand, ethical use and reliability-validity of the evaluation need to be determined.
3. Inclusive AI Tools: Inclusivity in education requires taking many precautions. Especially in the special education of individuals with special needs and in bilingual education, inclusivity can be provided with AI tools. In this respect, precautions may be required for the integration of AI into problematic areas of education.

AI IN EDUCATION

AI technology has revolutionized the world of a lot of industries like education. Both scientists and practitioners are searching for ways in which AI-driven tools and systems can be used to enhance the student and teacher experience (AalSaud, 2021; Shen, 2020; Fahimirad & Kotamjani, 2018; Kamalov et al., 2023). The purpose of this research paper is to consider the mixed role of AI in education, its uses, benefits, and barriers, as well as the ethical issues and routes for long-term adoption.

Revolutionary Uses of AI in the Classroom

AI applications in education have been the fruit of several bold and reorienting trends. The first area for AI applications will be the collaborative teacher-student learning, where intelligent tutoring platforms can give individual guidance and feedback to make learning relevant to students. (Kamalov et al.,2023) Moreover, AI-based test platforms can even automate grading to provide timely and relevant results to students as well as feedback to the teachers to adjust their teaching practices. (Kamalov et al.,2023)

The second of the most visible uses of AI for education is the development of personalised learning spaces where the technology is used to tailor the content, pace and delivery of the lesson according to the individual student's strengths, weaknesses and interests. This individualized service could result in higher levels of student participation, motivation and learning.

Benefits and Potential of AI in Learning.

This is just one of the many positives and negatives associated with AI in education. Using AI systems, administrative tasks can be automated — from allocation of resources to enrollment and scheduling, for better and more effective control over schools. Moreover, AI can also help in the detection of learning trends and learning barriers that will be identified in time and given support early on to the students. (Kamalov & Gurrib, 2023)

The greatest contribution of AI-based education technology lies in the capacity to bridge the geographical divide and bring access to high-quality education to those who otherwise would be denied access (Kamalov & Gurrib, 2023). Thanks to the scale and international reach of AI-based learning products, learners across socio-economic and cultural divides have access to individualized learning environments and intelligent tutoring platforms they didn't otherwise have.

Challenges and Ethical Considerations

AI could be so much more useful for learning, but there are a lot of challenges and moral issues that have to be overcome. Data privacy and data security of the students' information are front and center in these considerations. What is more, algorithmic bias – the possibility that AI systems reinforce and deepen existing societal biases and injustices – is also a concern that must be addressed early on (Akgün & Greenhow, 2021).

But others worry that AI will affect the teacher profession – some believe that intelligent tutoring platforms and automated tests will eventually supersede or displace human teachers. For the adoption of AI in schools to work and stay sustainable, we need to invest in teacher training and professional development programmes that equip educators to use AI-based devices in ways that support not substitute for how they teach.

AI's integration in the classroom is a revolutionary and a complicated phenomenon. AI applications could improve education, administrative efficiency, and quality education in many parts of the world. But there are many issues that the responsible and ethical use of AI in education must address, to ensure the gains can be realised and the risks and difficulties mitigated. If education can be mindful of the ethical issues, invest in teacher education and make good protections, AI could enable the sector to propel a lasting and fair change in education and teaching.

Theoretical Backframe

The AI Evaluation Quadrant Model provides an efficient way to evaluate the advantages and disadvantages of AI interventions in education (Elstad, 2024). Taking the model into consideration alongside some of the other learning theories and frameworks will allow us to better understand how AI can support or supplement different methods of teaching and learning (Elstad, 2024; Gillani et al.,2023; Sajja et al.,2023; Simhadri & Swamy,2023)

Constructivist Learning Theory

Constructivist learning theory suggests that students should be actively involved in continuous experience in the learning process and that they create knowledge through interaction and reflection on learning. Constructivist theory suggests that education is contextual and the effects of contextual factors should be taken into account (Vygotsky, 1978; Jonassen, 1999). From a constructivist theory perspective, AI should increase the student's experience, interaction and reflection processes. In AI-supported learning environments, the role of technology should ideally not replace the student's active participation, but rather enhance it. Tools such as AI-powered writing aids or adaptive learning systems are most effective when they encourage students to reflect, engage in critical interaction, and apply higher-order thinking skills (Luckin, Holmes, Griffiths, & Forcier, 2021).

- Zone of Proximal Development (ZPD) (Vygotsky, 1978):

From a ZPD perspective, AI systems are thought to contribute by providing facilitating references and clues for tasks that students cannot accomplish on their own. From this perspective, it can be seen that AI can be used as a direction or guide. In addition, it can be used without negatively affecting students' cognitive, psychological, or behavioral efforts. Doing this without control also makes it difficult to measure (Luckin et al., 2021).

- Application to AI-EQM:

The AI-Evaluation Quadrant Model (AI-EQM) can be used to evaluate student cognitive effort in the use of AI and reveal collaboration that will increase positive outcomes. AI can be used to ensure that students develop basic abilities and skills before moving on to complex tasks. Examples of supportive AI tools can be speech recognition tools, grammar correction tools. In this way, students gain basic skills and become ready for complex tasks (Akinwalere & Ivanov, 2022).

BLOOM'S TAXONOMY AND HIGHER-ORDER THINKING

Bloom's Taxonomy (1956) was developed by Bloom and divides the cognitive process of learning into different levels. In this framework, it divides learning into cognitive levels such as remembering, understanding, applying, analyzing, evaluating and reconstructing. After Bloom, the theory was revised by Anderson and Krathwohl (2001). Within the framework of Bloom's taxonomy, AI can provide integration into learning in a way that will facilitate different cognitive processes. It can be checked whether the low-level cognitive processes of remembering and applying and the high-level cognitive processes of analyzing and reconstructing are developed through AI (Wang et al., 2024).

- **AI and Bloom's Taxonomy:**

AI tools can be used effectively in reinforcing low-level tasks such as directing remembering and applying and correcting grammar. In this respect, as the effect of AI increases, the student's function and role will decrease, and critical thinking ability may not develop (Kasneci, Sessler, & Kortemeyer, 2023). While it can be used to reinforce basic grammar and semantic knowledge in writing skills, it can negatively affect creativity in creatively writing ideas (Marzuki, Widiati, Rusdin, & Indrawati, 2023).

- Application to AI-EQM:

It is considered that AI-EQM may have problems especially in evaluating students' performances. It may be difficult to reveal whether students' contribution levels or sufficient participation in high-level cognitive tasks. Evaluating the quality of the results is another problem. Students' work should be evaluated in different dimensions. For example, AI can be used as a good tool to evaluate studies in dimensions such as innovation, originality, creativity, and usefulness. In this respect, the facilitating role of AI should be emphasized (Nithiyanandam et al., 2022).

Cognitive Load Theory (CLT)

Cognitive Load Theory (CLT), which suggests that the intensity of individuals' cognitive processes affects learning (Sweller, 1988), suggests that cognitive load should be low for learning to occur. It is thought that appropriate references that will facilitate individuals' regulation of their cognitive processes will facilitate learning. In this way, students can focus and construct meaningful knowledge.

- From a CLT perspective, AI prevents cognitive load by personalizing learning processes according to the characteristics of the student and can facilitate learning. Applications such as Dreambox can adapt learning processes in accordance with personal characteristics (Owoc, Sawicka, & Weichbroth, 2021). The effect of AI should be limited. Excessive use of AI can negatively affect student skill acquisition (Luckin et al., 2021; Wang et al., 2024).
- Application to AI-EQM:

Evaluating the use of AI in AI-EQM in a way that prevents cognitive load can increase student participation. The use of AI that prevents cognitive workload should be encouraged. AI software that produces only output should not be used. Student participation should be facilitated. The balance of AI use should also be included in the evaluation (Akinwalere & Ivanov, 2022).

Technological Pedagogical Content Knowledge (TPACK)

TPACK (Mishra & Koehler, 2006) recommends the integration of technology for effectiveness in education. The balanced integration of technology, pedagogy, curriculum and content knowledge is seen as the basic condition for learning. It is important how to integrate AI tools between curriculum, content knowledge and pedagogy. Therefore, decision-making processes should be established with the participation of all stakeholders of the subject.

- Pedagogical Integration:

AI tools should be used in a way that increases teacher-student interactions and contributes to the increase in learning outcomes (Luckin et al ., 2021). These issues should be taken into account in the integration of AI. AI tools used with the STEM approach can personalize teaching. Teaching processes should be carried out with the active participation of the teacher in the process and shaping the strategies (Nithiyanandam et al ., 2022).

- Application to AI-EQM:

With AI-EQM, evaluators can determine whether the use of AI is compatible with the objectives of education and determine the gaps. The role of AI in reflective tasks in students' cognitive processes can be revealed. It can be revealed whether students use AI for content generation or facilitative purposes (Marzuki et al., 2023).

Self-Regulated Learning Theory (SRL)

Self-Regulated Learning (SRL) theory explains the process of individuals determining their own goals, monitoring development, and gaining critical thinking skills in the learning process (Zimmerman, 2002). With the effective use of AI tools, students can draw the framework of learning, think analytically, make comparisons, and exhibit autonomous behaviors. In addition, educational conditions that will increase student development can be created thanks to AI (Chen et al., 2020).

- AI and SRL:

AI tools provide personalized feedback according to individuals' learning differences and provide the necessary repetition for learning, supporting the development of individuals. In addition, as in other theories, the main problem is that individuals create performance with their own efforts. AI tools should be used in a way that does not negatively affect individuals' performance. Individuals should use AI tools only as facilitators in processes such as setting goals in learning, monitoring learning and development, and gaining critical thinking skills (Wang et al., 2024).

- **Application to AI-EQM:**

AI-EQM focuses on improving student performance while supporting students' self-assessment and critical thinking. In this respect, SRL supports the functions of the AI-EQM model to improve students' performance. The AI EQM model includes the evaluation of students' self-assessment/reflection journals, which meets the recommendations of SRL. Students' interaction with AI tools, their limits and guidelines, monitoring their progress, and performance evaluation processes are supported by SRL.

Contribution to the Field

1. Balanced AI Integration Framework

AI is being implemented in education as well, researchers and educators have been experimenting on how AI can be used to facilitate learning and teaching (Ojha et al., 2023). The AI-Evaluation Quadrant Model is a model that could help with this. This is an organized way to assess how well AI interventions work in education by considering factors such as the level of AI integration, the kind of education goals, and human-AI cooperation (Malik et al., 2018; Gillani et al., 2023; Paek & Kim, 2021; al-Zyoud, 2020).

The Balanced AI Integration Framework, in contrast, is designed to support the responsible and ethical use of AI in education, so that the adoption of AI follows the mission of education, does not compromise learner privacy, and does not undermine human values to be more specific. The AI-Evaluation Quadrant Model could contribute Balanced AI Integration Framework in several dimensions (al-Zyoud, 2020; Alzahrani, 2022; Kamalov & Gurrib, 2023). First, because the model gives us a method for quantifying the effectiveness of AI interventions, it could lead to AI being integrated into education in a manner that aligns with educational purposes and beliefs. This may include a review of how well AI tools are performing against certain learning goals, and the effects of AI on equity, accessibility, and student wellbeing.

In the second place, AI-Evaluation Quadrant Model can help us develop strategies for using AI in education successfully. If teachers knew the scale of AI integration and its implications for students' agency and autonomy, they could more effectively design how to implement AI into their classroom in a way that empowers and captivates students (Darvishi et al, 2023) (Tan & Subramonyam, 2023).

This might be especially so under the Balanced AI Integration Framework, which highlights the importance of keeping student agency and encouraging interactivity between humans and AI (Darvishi et al., 2023).

Taking all together, the AI-Evaluation Quadrant Model and the Balanced AI Integration Framework could complement each other in ensuring that AI in education is compatible with learning objectives, equitable and accessible, and sustainable for learners.

2. Focus on Authentic Learning

AI in education has presented new avenues for learning and teaching. The most recent of these, AI-Evaluation Quadrant Model, is intended to help with more authentic learning (al-Zyoud, 2020; Zhou et al., 2021;Ojha et al., 2023).

AI-Evaluation Quadrant Model: This is a model for the whole school system that provides a systematic method to implement AI tools to transform different aspects of the learning process. Leveraging AI-based evaluation, this model provides more accurate assessment of teaching quality and student learning outcomes for teachers, providing them with the data to make informed decisions and ultimately improve the quality of education (Ojha et al., 2023; Zhou et al., 2021). It is the AI-Evaluation Quadrant Model's main strength that it covers a broad spectrum of student activity, such as boredom, focus, and engagement. With this level of granular student behaviour and performance, instructors can then modify their instruction to better address individual students and create a more individualized and personal learning environment.

In addition, AI-Evaluation Quadrant Model can enhance students' self-assessment, critical thinking and problem solving ability. With AI-based intelligent tutoring tools and adaptive classrooms, the model can offer tailored feedback, take students through challenging tasks and create a dynamic learning environment. This belief in the possibility of AI-Evaluation Quadrant Model as a tool for authentic learning in the real world is also borne out by the increasing research in the area. (Malik et al., 2018; Zhai et al., 2021; Ojha et al.,2023). Researches cited in sources (Zhai et al., 2021; Ojha et al., 2023; Malik et al., 2018) has shown how AI-powered technologies could lead to higher grades, lighter load on teachers, and more personalized and interactive learning environments. (Bulathwela et al., 2021)

But there are some potential issues and drawbacks to the AI-Evaluation Quadrant Model. This model has a lot to recommend it, but must also be undertaken cautiously and with great moral emphasis (Kamalov & Gurrib, 2023; Ojha et al, 2023). Algorithmic bias, lack of transparency in AI decision-making, fairness and equity: all these issues should be addressed so that using AI for education doesn't reinforce and exaggerate the existing inequalities.

Achieving these fears will require ongoing dialogue between educators, policymakers and AI scientists. With clear rules, standards and strong systems of evaluation, AI-Evaluation Quadrant Model can be used in a safe and fair way to ensure genuine learning in education can be improved. (Kamalov et al., 2023; Bulut et al., 2024; Kamalov & Gurrib, 2023)

3. Bridging the Digital Divide

Science and especially the invention of AI brought hope for a more just and equal education system. But the truth is that these advances do not always reap the full fruits and we are left with a digital divide. The AI-Evaluation Quadrant Model provides an opportunity to close the gap and set the course for using AI-based technologies to close the gap so that everyone gains equally from the educational revolution that AI brings.

The digital divide, the difference between how and where digital technologies are being used, accessed and what they do, has been an educational issue for years (Wang & Cheng, 2021). These opportunities come at the risk of further exacerbated inequality by the adoption of AI-driven instruments, for technological change has always been known to raise between-country inequality. (Bulathwela et al, 2021) To address this risk, the AI-Evaluation Quadrant Model goes further by advising educators and policymakers to design intelligent integration of AI-based technologies in a way that ensures equity and accessibility for all students, regardless of their socioeconomic status, geographical position or other demographic characteristics.

AI-Evaluation Quadrant Model: Accessibility, Adaptability, Accountability, and Adaptivity are the four foundations of AI-Evaluation Quadrant Model. By considering AI-enabled learning technologies in this way, we can as educators make sure these tools are not only technologically innovative but also socially conscious, and that students of all backgrounds have an opportunity to enjoy the transformative possibilities of AI-enabled learning. The first principle of the model deals with accessibility providing equal access for students to access and use AI-based educational resources. Focusing on inclusive design, multilingualism and assistive technologies, the model will dismantle walls that had traditionally been barriers to a marginalised community's inclusion in the digital learning environment. The AI-Evaluation Quadrant Model's focus on adaptability keeps in mind the different learners' learning styles and interests. Creating AI-enabled systems that are dynamically capable of changing their delivery, content and speed to meet the needs of each student means that the gains of AI-enabled learning are not only shared with a selected subset of individuals (Bulathwela et al., 2021). Reputation is also an important factor, since it takes AI-powered learning tools to task for their effects on students and the wider education system. Through a comprehensive approach to transparency, fairness and ethical AI, the model hopes to tackle concerns about algorithmic bias, data privacy and ethical AI use in education. Adaptability requires constant testing and improvements in AI-based learning technologies. This model allows teachers to actively participate in the creation and use of AI-based tools, making them agile enough to change with learners' and the wider education community's demands, and reducing the digital divide through a collaborative, ongoing process. (Bulut et al., 2024; Kizilcec, 2023; Tan & Subramonyam, 2023)

4. Practical Application Across Disciplines

The adoption of AI in education has created new avenues for teaching and learning. A model with potential to be useful in this area is the AI-Evaluation Quadrant that provides an overview of how to apply AI tools and strategies to different fields of education. This is where the AI-Evaluation Quadrant contribute a lot: in language and literacy education. With the help of AI-powered feedback and assessment, teachers can offer dynamic, adaptive learning, based on each student's needs and pace. AI writing assistants, for instance, can review student essays, suggest corrections and suggestions, in turn increasing the students' linguistic and communication abilities. In addition, in bilingual learning, AI-Evaluation Quadrant has great potential for creating intelligent tutoring systems that are able to adapt adaptively to the students' linguistic abilities and provide content and tests in their own languages.

In the same way, the use of AI-Evaluation Quadrant in STEM education could completely change how students learn and apply difficult concepts. Teachers can create personalized learning experiences with AI-powered simulations, interactive visualizations and adaptive assessment tools that provide the foundations for more detailed learning and problem solving. This AI-Evaluation Quadrant has much to offer also in special education, where the versatility and personalisation of AI-powered systems can be crucial. Intelligent tutoring algorithms can also offer individual instruction and consistent feedback to students with learning differences in order for them to overcome challenges and reach their potential.

Lastly, in the vocational schooling industry, AI-Evaluation Quadrant could help training and evaluating hands-on skills. AI based simulations and virtual environments could also help students do tasks relevant to the work, in a safe and collaborative way, with the AI system giving immediate feedback and tips on how to achieve more. comment on the work in special education. Since the AI-Evaluation Quadrant Model is ubiquitously applicable to language and literacy, bilingual education, STEM, special education, and vocational education, it stands a chance of changing the way education is delivered and outcomes are achieved in many different settings. In using the AI to design personalized, flexible, data-driven learning experiences that reflect the individual student's needs and strengths, a more inclusive and adaptive education system can be built.

FUTURE RESEARCH DIRECTIONS

The AI Evaluation Quadrant Model is a functional tool to assess the impact of AI systems (Pierson et al., 2023). It takes into account the AI intelligence (Narrow to General) and task difficulty (Simple to Complex) in order to calculate the probable impact of using AI. This model is promising, but in several key respects future work could be expanded on this model. First, there would be the case of longitudinal studies looking at how long-term AI systems play out (Brundage, 2015). As AI becomes more powerful and applies to a wider spectrum of applications, the impact of AI systems will likely shift with it. Analyzing the AI Evaluation Quadrant Model against other evaluation methods would also be informative in revealing both what is different about this model and what needs to be refined or extended (Brundage, 2015). Second, more needs to be discovered about the equity and access effects of AI infrastructures. The use of AI is likely to only increase current social and economic inequality if not properly planned and executed (Kusters et al, 2020). In future research, we may examine how AI intelligence and tasks might differentially impact underrepresented groups, and how to achieve more equal AI development and application.

If we can follow these research avenues, we can advance from the AI Evaluation Quadrant Model into a deeper sense of what the social impacts of AI might be (Kusters et al., 2020; Brundage, 2015; Davenport et al., 2019). AI Evaluation Quadrant Model (a systematic way of evaluating the various dimensions of AI systems) finds growing applications in industries, such as education. The model has much to offer for enhancing the evaluation of educational resources, spaces and outcomes. The next steps of research for The AI Evaluation Quadrant Model should be to apply it in education. It's an investigation that might transform assessment processes in education through the strengthening of critical thinking and the synthesis of innovative pedagogical approaches.

The deployment of AI Evaluation Quadrant Model into a classroom is about understanding both the model design and how it can be used to meet the educational requirements. Effective implementation requires it to be adopted into existing institutional frameworks in which its quadrants (ethics, accuracy and impact vs. scaleability) can align with learning objectives. This convergence enables the AI instruments in the classroom to meet performance and ethical requirements so that it is possible to measure the quality of the education.

Integrating the AI Evaluation Quadrant Model in learning environments is a sophisticated operation that involves iterative test and adaptation. By using this framework, school leaders can see what's merely an alternative to the old way and what is beneficial for students. Making sure these AI tools do good for students' learning is crucial and the Quadrant Model allows you to determine the educational value of tech apps. The model itself creates an environment of continual improvement in which education technologies adapt to the dynamic needs of learning.

Adapting the AI Evaluation Quadrant Model for educational purposes is changing its previous uses to school measurement. The model can be used by teachers to find student comprehension gaps, distinguish different learning pathways, and tailor instruction. With fine-grained testing, teachers can use AI tools to analyse student data to match the objectives of the course with the needs of the student. This fosters a learning-at-the-student level that moves teaching in the direction of adaptive and personalized strategies based on student needs and results.

AI Evaluation Quadrant Model to improve education evaluation: The aim is to improve the analysis processes in which AI tools are evaluated. And that means questioning not only the learning products, but also the moral value of AI in education. Educators can make sure these technologies respect educational integrity and play an responsible role in student development by focusing on the assessment of AI's effects on instruction and learning. The model therefore acts as an intermediate, between academic goals on the theoretical level and data-driven classroom applications.

How the AI Evaluation Quadrant Model works for education will need longitudinal and judgment studies. Those researches should quantify the effectiveness of the model for students, teacher and student satisfaction. It's good to review some case studies where you have used the model in practice to learn what works and what doesn't. By deeply recognising these dynamics, scholars and teachers can tweak the use of the Quadrant Model so that it is a robust, adaptive system capable of meeting the heterogeneous needs of today's schools.

AI Evaluation Quadrant Model opens numerous doors for changing how people teach and take tests. The possibilities of using it to support classrooms well align themselves with the pursuit of educational excellence. Researchers would still need to refine and further delineate the model's role in pedagogy what it could, could work, could be ethically responsible for. In a world where our learning practices have become increasingly technologically enmeshed, the Quadrant Model offers a framework for how AI can be safely and usefully used in education.

CONCLUSION

AI Evaluation Quadrant Model (CEQM), created by a group of renowned scientists including [Author(s)] is a rigorous, and revolutionary way to evaluate the efficiency and potential of AI systems, unlike any other current methods in the field. But rather than taking aggregate metrics, or instance-by-instance assessments, the Quadrant Model is a holistic and more sophisticated approach, weighing four dimensions — task complexity, task diversity, task specificity, and system generality (Burnell et al., 2023). Such a three-dimensional rating model lets researchers and practitioners see an AI system more closely, without having to compare it to other AI systems on a small sample of tasks. What's more, the Quadrant Model also takes into account the possibility of an AI system generalizing its skills and knowledge beyond the domains in which it was trained, something that other frameworks neglect. As opposed to the Quadrant Model, some scholars have proposed different solutions based on more narrow definitions of AI performance. The "Rethink Reporting of Evaluation Results in AI" study, for example, mentions that the aggregate metrics are inadequate and instances-level evaluation results need to be more openly reported with fine-grained detail, which fits with the Quadrant Model's focus on fine-grained assessment (Burnell et al., 2023). Moreover, the "BetterBench" methodology of quality and accessibility of AI benchmarks points out that good and well-designed evaluation tools are necessary to be created and it's also a component of the Quadrant Model methodology. These insights together make the AI Evaluation Quadrant Model a richer and more comprehensive way to evaluate AI systems, and ultimately help provide a better understanding of the advances and limits of AI beyond existing assessments.

The AI Evaluation Quadrant Model stands out from other AI evaluation methods because it is specifically designed for education and caters to the specific problems of AI adoption in education. There are various generic AI evaluation methods (Brundage, 2015; Hernández Orallo, 2014)) but it doesn't tend to be as rich in rigour that is needed for educational purposes. The AI-EQM's focus on student learning, cognitive development and ethical thinking is especially timely for educators.

Broader AI Testing: Researches (Brundage, 2015; HernándezOrallo, 2014) mention broad AI testing procedures such as task-based and ability-based testing. These methods are valuable for measuring general AI but can be incomplete to measure AI's educational effect. A score measuring whether an AI could solve complex equations, for instance, might not measure whether the AI helped students acquire knowledge about mathematics.

AI in Enterprise: Studies (Ben-Bassat, 2018) focus on the evaluation of AI software in enterprise environment with a focus on the output and automation metrics. Some principles may be similar but the educational environment asks for different criteria for evaluation, such as student involvement or ethical issues related to student data privacy.

Human-AI Interaction: Research (Lai et al., 2021) is focused on human-AI decision making, but from the perspective of human performance and experience. Although it applies to education, the AI-EQM extends the challenge to specifically introducing AI in education, as well as monitoring its effects on student learning and development.

It's hard to draw any comparison between the outputs of these studies and the AI-EQM since they tend to study very different aspects of AI and use very different evaluation procedures. But the AI-EQM can learn a lot from these larger research fields. For instance, the focus on human-AI collaboration from (Lai et al., 2021) can inform the planning of AI-enabled learning tasks that successfully use both human and AI.

REFERENCES

Abushariah, H., Ting, H., Mustafa, M. B. P., Khairuddin, A. S. M., Abushariah, A. M., & Tan, T. (2023). Bilingual Automatic Speech Recognition: A Review, *Taxonomy and Open Challenges. IEEE Access : Practical Innovations, Open Solutions*, *11*, 5944–5954. DOI: 10.1109/ACCESS.2022.3218684

Akgün, S., & Greenhow, C. (2021). AI in education: Addressing ethical challenges in K-12 settings [Review of AI in education: Addressing ethical challenges in K-12 settings]. *AI and Ethics*, 2(3), 431. Springer Nature. DOI: 10.1007/s43681-021-00096-7

Akinwalere, S., & Ivanov, V. (2022). AI in Higher Education: Challenges and Opportunities. *Border Crossing*, *12*, 1–15. DOI: 10.33182/bc.v12i1.2015

al-Zyoud, H. M. M. (2020). The Role of AI in Teacher Professional Development. In *Universal Journal of Educational Research, 8(11)* (p. 6263). Horizon Research Publishing., DOI: 10.13189/ujer.2020.082265

Alzahrani, A. (2022). A systematic review of AI in education in the arab world. *Revista Amazonia Investiga*, *11*(54), 293. DOI: 10.34069/AI/2022.54.06.28

Ben-Bassat, M. (2018). AIQ: Measuring Intelligence of Business AI Software. In arXiv (Cornell University). Cornell University. https://doi.org//arxiv.1808.03454DOI: 10.48550

Brundage, M. (2015). Modeling Progress in AI. In arXiv (Cornell University). Cornell University. https://doi.org/DOI: 10.48550/arXiv.1512

Bulathwela, S., Pérez-Ortiz, M., Holloway, C., & Shawe-Taylor, J. (2021). Could AI Democratise Education? Socio-Technical Imaginaries of an EdTech Revolution. In arXiv (Cornell University). Cornell University. https://doi.org//arxiv.2112.02034DOI: 10.48550

Bulut, O., Beiting-Parrish, M., Casabianca, J. M., Slater, S. C., Jiao, H., Song, D., Ormerod, C. M., Fabiyi, D. G., Ivan, R., Walsh, C., Rios, O., Wilson, J. M., Yildirim-Erbasli, S. N., Wongvorachan, T., Liu, J. X., Tan, B., & Morilova, P. (2024). The Rise of AI in Educational Measurement: Opportunities and Ethical Challenges. In arXiv (Cornell University). Cornell University. https://doi.org//arxiv.2406.18900DOI: 10.48550

Burnell, R., Schellaert, W., Burden, J., Ullman, T., Martínez-Plumed, F., Tenenbaum, J. B., Rutar, D., Cheke, L. G., Sohl-Dickstein, J., Mitchell, M., Kiela, D., Shanahan, M., Voorhees, E. M., Cohn, A. G., Leibo, J. Z., & Hernández-Orallo, J. (2023). *Rethink reporting of evaluation results in AI.* In Science (Vol. 380, Issue 6641, p. 136). American Association for the Advancement of Science. DOI: 10.1126/science.adf6369

Darvishi, A., Khosravi, H., Sadiq, S., Gašević, D., & Siemens, G. (2023). Impact of AI assistance on student agency. In *Computers & Education* (Vol. 210, p. 104967). Elsevier BV., DOI: 10.1016/j.compedu.2023.104967

Darvishi, A., Khosravi, H., Sadiq, S., Gašević, D., & Siemens, G. (2023). Impact of AI assistance on student agency. In *Computers & Education* (Vol. 210, p. 104967). Elsevier BV., DOI: 10.1016/j.compedu.2023.104967

Elstad, E. (2024). AI in Education: Rationale, Principles, and Instructional Implications. In arXiv (Cornell University). Cornell University. https://doi.org//arxiv.2412 .12116DOI: 10.48550

Fahimirad, M., & Kotamjani, S. S. (2018). A Review on Application of AI in Teaching and Learning in Educational Contexts [Review of A Review on Application of AI in Teaching and Learning in Educational Contexts]. *International Journal of Learning and Development*, *8*(4), 106. DOI: 10.5296/ijld.v8i4.14057

Gillani, N., Eynon, R., Chiabaut, C., & Finkel, K. A. (2023). Unpacking the "Black Box" of AI in Education. In arXiv (Cornell University). Cornell University. https://doi.org//arxiv.2301.01602DOI: 10.48550

Hernández-Orallo, J. (2014). AI Evaluation: past, present and future. In arXiv (Cornell University). Cornell University. https://doi.org//arxiv.1408.6908DOI: 10.48550

Kamalov, F., Calonge, D. S., & Gurrib, I. (2023). New Era of AI in Education: Towards a Sustainable Multifaceted Revolution. In Sustainability (Vol. 15, Issue 16, p. 12451). Multidisciplinary Digital Publishing Institute. DOI: 10.3390/su151612451

Kizilcec, R. F. (2023). To Advance AI Use in Education, Focus on Understanding Educators. In International Journal of AI in Education (Vol. 34, Issue 1, p. 12). Springer Science+Business Media. https://doi.org/DOI: 10.1007/s40593-023-00351-4

Lai, V., Chen, C., Liao, Q. V., Smith, A., & Tan, C. (2021). Towards a Science of Human-AI Decision Making: A Survey of Empirical Studies. In arXiv (Cornell University). Cornell University. https://doi.org/DOI: 10.48550/arXiv.2112

Luckin, R., Jones, K., & Cukurova, M. (2021). *AI for School Teachers*. Routledge.

Malik, G., Tayal, D. K., & Vij, S. (2018). An Analysis of the Role of AI in Education and Teaching. In *Advances in intelligent systems and computing* (p. 407). Springer Nature., DOI: 10.1007/978-981-10-8639-7_42

Marzuki, W., Widiati, U., Rusdin, D., Darwin, , & Indrawati, I. (2023). The impact of AI writing tools on the content and organization of students' writing: EFL teachers' perspective. *Cogent Education, 10*(2), 2236469. Advance online publication. DOI: 10.1080/2331186X.2023.2236469

Nithiyanandam, N. Dhanasekaran, A., Kumar.,S. Gobinath, D., Vijayakarthik, P. Vinoth, G.and Rajkumar (2022). AI Assisted Student Learning and Performance Analysis using Instructor Evaluation Model, 2022 3rd International Conference on Electronics and Sustainable Communication Systems (ICESC), Coimbatore, India, 2022, pp. 1555-1561, DOI: 10.1109/ICESC54411.2022.9885462

Ojha, S., Narendra, A., Mohapatra, S., & Misra, I. (2023). From Robots to Books: An Introduction to Smart Applications of AI in Education (AIEd). In arXiv (Cornell University). Cornell University. https://doi.org//arxiv.2301.10026DOI: 10.48550

Owoc, M., Sawicka, A., & Weichbroth, P. (2021). *AI Technologies in Education: Benefits*. Challenges and Strategies of Implementation., DOI: 10.1007/978-3-030-85001-2_4

Paek, S., & Kim, N. (2021). Analysis of Worldwide Research Trends on the Impact of AI in Education. In Sustainability (Vol. 13, Issue 14, p. 7941). Multidisciplinary Digital Publishing Institute. DOI: 10.3390/su13147941

Sajja, R., Sermet, Y., Cikmaz, M., Cwiertny, D. M., & Demir, İ. (2023). AI-Enabled Intelligent Assistant for Personalized and Adaptive Learning in Higher Education. In arXiv (Cornell University). Cornell University. https://doi.org//arxiv.2309.10892DOI: 10.48550

Shen, J. (2020). *The Innovation of Education in the Era of AI.*, DOI: 10.3390/proceedings2020047057

Simhadri, N., & Swamy, T. N. V. R. (2023). Awareness among teaching on AI and ML applications based on fuzzy in education sector at USA. In Soft Computing. Springer Science+Business Media. https://doi.org/DOI: 10.1007/s00500-023-08329-z

Tan, M., & Subramonyam, H. (2023). More than Model Documentation: Uncovering Teachers' Bespoke Information Needs for Informed Classroom Integration of ChatGPT. In arXiv (Cornell University). Cornell University. https://doi.org//arxiv.2309.14458DOI: 10.48550

Tan, M., & Subramonyam, H. (2023). More than Model Documentation: Uncovering Teachers' Bespoke Information Needs for Informed Classroom Integration of ChatGPT. In arXiv (Cornell University). Cornell University. https://doi.org//arxiv.2309.14458DOI: 10.48550

Wang, S., Wang, F., Zhu, Z., Wang, J., & Tran, T. And Du, Z. (2024). AI in education: A systematic literature review. Expert Systems with Applications, 252, ISSN 0957-4174, https://doi.org/DOI: 10.1016/j.eswa.2024.124167

Woolf, B. P. (2010). *Building Intelligent Interactive Tutors*. Elsevier.

Yang, H. (2021). Explore How AI and VR Technology will Change the Development of Future Education. In Journal of Physics Conference Series (Vol. 1744, Issue 4, p. 42146). IOP Publishing. https://doi.org/DOI: 10.1088/1742-6596/1744/4/042146

Zhai, X., Chu, X., Chai, C. S., Jong, M. S., Starčič, A. I., Spector, M., Liu, J., Jing, Y., & Li, Y. (2021). A Review of AI (AI) in Education from 2010 to 2020 [Review of A Review of AI (AI) in Education from 2010 to 2020]. Complexity, 2021(1). Hindawi Publishing Corporation. DOI: 10.1155/2021/8812542

Zhou, H., Lu, J., Huang, Y., & Chen, Y. (2021). Research on key Technology of Classroom Teaching Evaluation Based on AI. In Journal of Physics Conference Series (Vol. 1757, Issue 1, p. 12014). IOP Publishing. DOI: 10.1088/1742-6596/1757/1/012014

Chapter 2
Integrating AI in Lesson Planning Within an Early Childhood Developmentally Appropriate Framework:
ECE, Special Education, and Cultural Contexts

Jennifer Quong
https://orcid.org/0009-0008-7649-3194
Texas Woman's University, USA

Sara Matthews
https://orcid.org/0009-0002-1515-8604
University of Idaho, USA

ABSTRACT

This chapter explores the integration of artificial intelligence (AI) in early childhood lesson planning through the lens of Developmentally Appropriate Practice (DAP). It examines how generative AI tools respond to varying levels of instructional prompting, and how these responses align with DAP core considerations: commonality, individuality, and context. Through case studies and critical evaluations of AI-generated lesson plans, the chapter highlights the potential and limitations of AI as a collaborative planning partner. The findings reveal that front-loading AI with specific information about a classroom's demographics, children's individual needs, and DAP core considerations improves lesson quality. While AI can support

DOI: 10.4018/979-8-3373-6007-2.ch002

educators in designing engaging, differentiated, and standards-aligned lessons, its effectiveness depends on educators' ability to guide, critique, and adapt its outputs. The chapter concludes with recommendations for leveraging AI to enhance—rather than replace—professional expertise in the creation of joyful, inclusive, and play-based learning environments.

INTRODUCTION

In the 21st century, the early childhood classroom is an exciting place to be. Research and technology are confirming fundamental principles about how children grow and develop. For example, in physical development research, x-ray technology has been used to study pencil grip. Four-year-old hands versus nine-year-old hands demonstrate that younger children have more cartilage and physically cannot hold a pencil in the same way, necessitating alternative writing approaches in order to be developmentally appropriate in supporting the evolution of a pencil grip. Furthermore, technological advancement in brain imaging has allowed us to actually see the architecture of the brain, revealing the rate at which new neural connections are formed the first few years of life, by far the fastest of any other period of the life span (Shonkoff & Phillips, 2000). These advancements give scientific validity to the field of early childhood development and fundamentally shift how we understand development in the early years. Experiences in the early years matter. In addition, play, the conduit of learning in the early years, allows children to process new information in context while attaching to current schema, enabling differentiation based on individual needs and knowledge (Piaget, 1962). Early childhood educators can use technology along with knowledge of child development and learning to develop high-quality curriculum for children.

Highly trained and effective teachers are a strong predictor of student success (Darling-Hammond, 2000), with children flourishing in high-quality research and evidence-based programs. Darling-Hammond examined data from all 50 states and found that teacher preparation and certification were the strongest correlates of student achievement in reading and mathematics. The study also demonstrated that teacher qualifications accounted for more of the variance in student achievement than other factors such as class size, overall spending, or teacher salaries.

The classroom has incorporated the current technology of its time throughout educational history (Figure 1). For example, writing allowed thoughts to be immortalized; chalkboards brought a technological shift to instruction in the early 1800s that allowed for spontaneous writing and allowed for more group learning (Krause, 2000) and since the latter half of the 20th century, electronic technology has been integrated into education (e.g., calculators, desktop computers, tablets, and laptops).

Although existing since the 1950s, Artificial intelligence (AI), the latest innovation, has only been actively incorporated into education over the last 20 years (Stone et al., 2016), with exponential growth in the last 3 years through large language models and generative AI (Sheehan, 2023). In other words, technology and education have seemingly always gone hand in hand.

Figure 1. Technology timeline

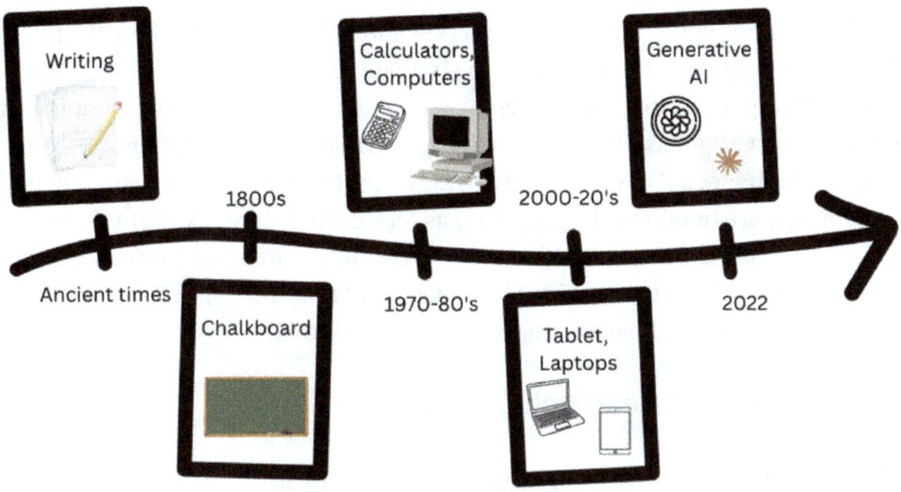

Purpose of the Chapter

This chapter examines the integration of artificial intelligence (AI) tools in early childhood lesson planning through the lens of Developmentally Appropriate Practice (DAP), providing early childhood educators and teacher preparation programs with evidence-based guidance for the ethical and effective use of AI as a collaborative tool.

The primary purpose of the chapter is to evaluate how AI-generated lesson plans align with the three core considerations of DAP (commonality, individuality, and context) and NAEYC's principles of child development and learning, demonstrating that AI can support but not replace educator expertise in creating developmentally appropriate curricula.

In addition, this chapter explores how generative AI tools, when used with effective prompting strategies and critical assessment, create high-quality lesson plans demonstrating the direct relationship between prompt specificity and quality outcomes.

The overarching goal is to position AI as a collaborative partner rather than a replacement for professional judgment, ensuring that technology enhances rather than diminishes the human-centered, relationship-based foundations of quality early childhood education while maintaining the centrality of play-based, joyful learning experiences.

Understanding Artificial Intelligence in Education

Artificial intelligence is defined by Stryker and Kavlakoglu (2024) as "technology that enables computers and machines to simulate human learning, comprehension, problem solving, decision making, creativity and autonomy." This technology has begun to impact all areas of education. In response to AI in education, the National Artificial Intelligence Act of 2020, the U.S. Department of State created their own definition that artificial intelligence (AI) as "a machine-based system that can, for a given set of human-defined objectives, make predictions, recommendations, or decisions influencing real or virtual environments" (para. 3). Educators have an immediate response and partner to lighten the workload.

Current State of AI Research in Education

With the integration of artificial intelligence in education, the field is researching its impacts and effectiveness (AbuSahyon et al., 2023; Adams et al., 2023; Akgun & Greenhow, 2022; Cooper, 2023; Gayatri & Pau, 2022; Kanders et al., 2024; Lammert et al., 2024; Lozano et al., 2024; McCormack, 2024; Park & Park, 2024; Pearce, 2024; Powell & Courchesne, 2024; Rice & Dunn, 2023; Setyaningsih et al., 2024, Tunjera & Chigona, 2023; Weiner et al., 2024; Yilmaz Can & Durmus, 2024). Literature has started reviewing AI in higher education and educator preparation programs down into K-12 public education. Educational research on AI in higher education, teacher education has examined pre-service teachers' attitudes towards AI (Park & Park 2024), in-service teachers' attitudes (Gayatri & Pau, 2022) creating and tailoring lesson plans (Powell & Courchesne, 2024, McCormack, 2024; Yilmaz Can & Durmus, 2024) and how to collaborate with AI (Park & Park 2024).

In the K-12 setting, recent advancements in artificial intelligence are transforming English language education through two primary innovations: AI-driven tools for learners and AI assistance for teachers' lesson planning. For language learners, AI-powered chatbots offer personalized learning experiences with immediate feedback, authentic conversational practice, and 24/7 accessibility (AbuSahyon et al., 2023). These technologies adapt to individual strengths and weaknesses, making language acquisition more efficient while reducing anxiety through low-pressure practice environments. However, they face challenges including technical limitations in understanding context, privacy concerns regarding data collection, and the inability to fully replicate human cultural sensitivity and emotional support.

For teachers, AI tools like MagicSchool AI enhance lesson planning efficiency, support differentiated instruction, and inspire creative teaching approaches (Setyaningsih et al., 2024). Indonesian EFL teachers reported that AI streamlines material creation and assessment design while enabling the tailoring of content for diverse student needs. However, teachers emphasized that AI-generated content typically requires significant refinement to meet pedagogical standards, particularly for classroom-specific contexts.

Both studies conclude that the most effective implementation comes from viewing AI as a complementary resource rather than a replacement for human instruction – a collaborative partnership where technology enhances rather than replaces the essential human elements of language teaching and learning (AbuSahyon et al., 2023; Setyaningsih et al., 2024).

However, there remains a paucity of research on AI with children ages four and below and their teachers, and even less on early childhood educators using AI to design developmentally appropriate lessons. As the field of education establishes AI usage guidelines, one critical thread runs throughout the research: ethics.

Ethical Considerations in AI Use in Early Childhood Education

The use of AI in education is an ethical issue as much as a technological one. Key questions include: Are teachers using AI to create lesson plans, and if so, is AI providing quality learning experiences for students? Is it unethical to use AI as an educational material source if its effectiveness in the classroom has not been fully researched? Ethical considerations for AI use in the classroom include "pedagogical appropriateness" (Adams et al., 2023), which can be interpreted both from the standpoint of what we teach and how we teach. Can AI truly understand and plan for the learning needs of children?

Maintaining confidentiality of children's and families' information is a cornerstone of ethics in education. The integration of AI requires early childhood educators to navigate important legal frameworks such as the Children's Online Privacy Protection Act (COPPA) and the Family Educational Rights and Privacy Act (FERPA). Early childhood educators must ensure data privacy by implementing strategies such as limiting student data collection, using secure platforms, and obtaining parental consent for AI tools.

Though little has been written specifically on the ethical principles of AI in early childhood education, organizations such as the National Association for the Education of Young Children (NAEYC) (2024), the Division of Early Childhood (DEC) (2022), and the Council for Exceptional Children (CEC) (2015) provide codes of ethical conduct for early childhood educators and adult educators in professional preparation programs. Principles in these codes invoke questions regarding the ethical use of AI in curriculum development, instructional design, and teacher-child interactions (Table 1).

Table 1. Ethical principles and AI considerations

Source	Ethical Principle	AI Considerations
NAEYC	"Early childhood educators base professional practice on current and accurate knowledge of how to understand and support children's development and learning." (1)	How accurate are AI curriculum creators and chatbots at applying this knowledge to instructional design? Are educators adequately prepared to analyze the quality of these practices in AI-generated materials?
NAEYC	"Only utilize and integrate technology, interactive media, and artificial intelligence when it is done intentionally, responsibly, and within the framework of developmentally appropriate practice, and particularly to support learning goals established for individual children, strengthen family relationships, and provide equitable access for children with special needs." (1)	Are early childhood educators equipped to use AI tools intentionally and responsibility? Can AI support educators in setting relevant learning goals and connecting with families?
NAEYC	"Respect and support diversity among individuals, within and across groups, in terms of backgrounds and lived experiences." (1)	Is AI able to recognize and incorporate diversity and individuality among humans into learning experiences for children? What kinds of potential bias might appear?
NAEYC	Maintain confidentiality of children's and families' sensitive information. (1)	Does inputting children's information in an AI tool breach confidentiality? What guidelines should be in place to protect children's information while still using the AI tools to their most useful capacity?
DEC	"Remain current in knowledge of evidence-based practices that support effectiveness within their role and discontinue use of practices no longer supported by evidence." (2)	How capable is AI of filtering out outdated practices and adopting current evidence-based practices?
CEC	"Using evidence, instructional data, research, and professional knowledge to inform practice." (3)	Is there evidence that AI is incorporating these elements in guidance to educators and in curriculum design?

Note.

1. National Association for the Education of Young Children. (2024). Code of ethics for early childhood educators (Draft Revision). NAEYC. https://www.naeyc.org/sites/default/files/globally-shared/downloads/PDFs/2024_code_of_ethics_for_early_childhood_educators_final_3.pdf

2. Division for Early Childhood. (2022). Position statement on ethical practice. Council for Exceptional Children. https://divisionearlychildhood.egnyte.com/dl/KAh4cOFBZ8

3. Council for Exceptional Children. (2015). What every special educator must know: Professional ethics and standards (7th ed.). Arlington, VA: CEC. https://exceptionalchildren.org/sites/default/files/2020-07/Code%20of%20Ethics.pdf

Early Childhood Education Best Practices

There are many excellent organizations, foundations, agencies that research, advocate and have best and research-based practices for children birth to age eight. In the field of early childhood education and child development, the National Association for the Education of Young Children is a cornerstone. "The National Association for the Education of Young Children (NAEYC) is a professional membership organization that works to promote high-quality early learning for all young children, birth through age 8, by connecting early childhood practice, policy, and research. We advance a diverse, dynamic early childhood profession and support all who care for, educate, and work on behalf of young children" (NAEYC, 2024, para. 1).

NAEYC has set guidelines and standards used as industry standards. Early childhood educators use these to guide evidence-based practices of AI in lesson planning in early childhood education. These guidelines include developmentally appropriate practices, principles of child development and learning, and professional standards and competencies for early childhood educators.

Developmentally Appropriate Practice (DAP) Framework

The National Association for the Education of Young Children (NAEYC) defines developmentally appropriate practice as "methods that promote each child's optimal development and learning through a strengths-based, play-based approach to joyful, engaged learning" (NAEYC, 2020). Developmentally appropriate practice provides guidelines for early childhood educators compiled from evidence-based practices and research on child development and learning. It has been used in the field of early childhood development since its first published position statement in the mid-eighties.

Figure 2. Three core considerations for developmentally appropriate practices

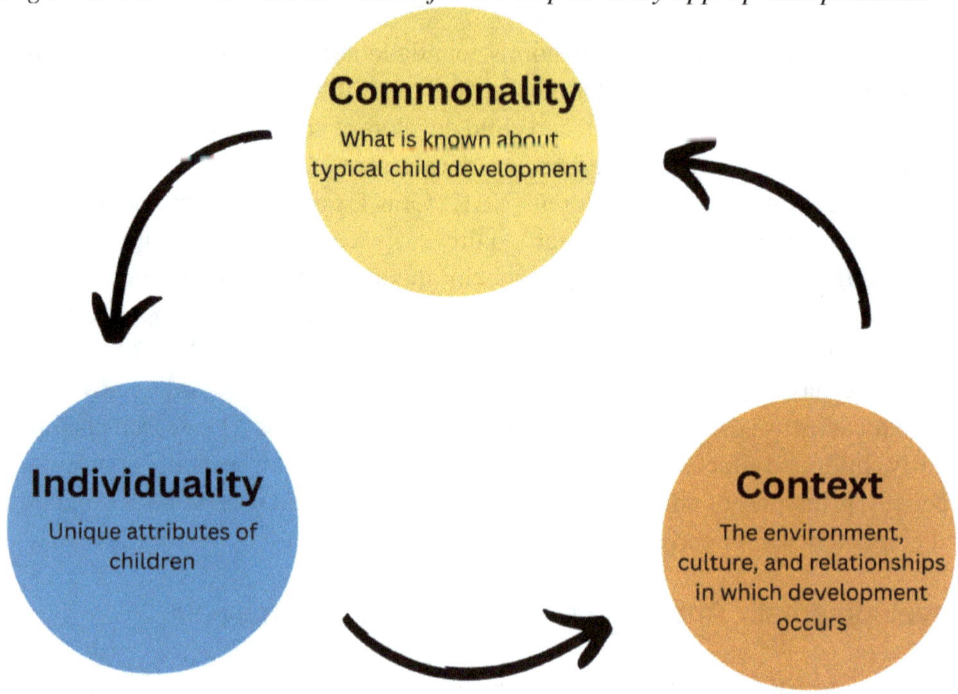

The framework comprises three core evidence-based considerations to inform practice (Figure 2):

1. Commonality: What is known about typical child development
2. Individuality: Unique attributes of children
3. Contexts: The environment, culture, and relationships in which development occurs

Commonality

What is known about typical child development is based upon decades of research on the growth and development of children. From the extensive observations of researchers such as Dr. Arnold Gesell (1925) who helped to identify and define known developmental milestones and sequences, to educational experts such as Maria Montessori, who developed the Montessori method of education and Loris Malaguzzi, founder of the Reggio Emilia approach, the consideration of commonality seeks to incorporate the vast body of knowledge on best practice in early childhood education for typically developing children. This knowledge is used as a foundation for teaching young children according to what can reasonably be expected of children at certain ages. Though updated as new research and technologies emerge, much of our understanding of development has remained unchanged. Using assessment and diagnostic tools developed in the 1920's and revised periodically, children appear to perform much at the same level over the decades (Guddemi et al., 2014).

State early learning standards, also known as early learning guidelines (ELGs), provide guidance on the common developmental characteristics of children. Though there are no federally outlined ELGs, as of 2016 all 56 States and Territories had adopted their own ELGs (National Center on Early Childhood Quality Assurance, 2016). These early learning guidelines are particularly useful in determining what children should know and be able to do by kindergarten entry. These guidelines are not meant to be a curriculum guide, rather a place to gain knowledge and ideas to implement into early childhood programs and to ensure accurate up-to-date information about child development and progressions of learning.

Considering what is commonly known about young children's learning, a teacher of four-year-olds, using her state's early learning guidelines, looks at the typical physical development of children who are 48-60 months old. The teacher then selects materials and activities that support and align with this age group. Knowing the average size of four-year-olds, the teacher selects child-sized furniture and materials that the children can competently utilize.

Outdoors, the teacher plans an obstacle course that promotes the growth of physical skills such as running, jumping forward with both feet, balancing and hopping on one foot, throwing with some accuracy, and kicking a ball forward. The teacher does not incorporate skipping with alternate feet into the obstacle course, because that skill does not typically develop until after 60 months or 5 years of age (Idaho Department of Health and Welfare, 2021b).

Individuality

Just as no two adults are the same, no two young children are the same. The consideration of individuality recognizes the uniqueness of each child and intentionally plans to meet these individual differences. NAEYC charges early childhood educators to learn about these differences through reliable and authentic observation and assessment, as well as information gained from each child's family. These differences are "the children's various social identities, interests, strengths, and preferences; their personalities, motivations, and approaches to learning; and their knowledge, skills, and abilities related to their cultural experiences, including family languages, dialects, and vernaculars" (NAEYC, 2020, Core Considerations to Inform Decision Making).

Differing Abilities and Special Education.

Children's strengths, developmental delays, and disabilities are also taken into consideration. Teachers may use Individualized Education Plans (IEP) to support children's education when they have identified disabilities (U.S. Department of Education, 2019). These plans outline children's individual needs and support to ensure academic success and overall developmental growth. IEPs are protected under federal law. Additionally, early childhood teachers at times serve as the first line in identifying possible delays and disabilities as they interact with and assess children at such young ages. In a study by Sanders et al. (2022), it was found that around 5% of referrals for developmental assessments in order to identify delays and disabilities came from childcare or early childhood school settings. This number does not include teachers who recognize developmental concerns and encourage parents to follow up with their pediatricians, so in actuality, the number of early childhood educators who initiate the process is likely higher.

In a preschool setting, a teacher may make modifications to a lesson plan to ensure each child can fully participate in learning activities. For example, a teacher may recognize that certain children are particularly sensitive to the sensory experience of getting paint on their hands. When planning a finger-painting activity, the teacher provides latex gloves for those children to wear so that they may still gain the developmental benefits of the activity.

Contexts

The interaction of family dynamics, values, relationships, neighborhoods, educational settings, culture, and societal events each play a role in the complexity of human development (Bronfenbrenner, 1979). The importance of context in child development has been interwoven into early childhood education for many decades, notably in the creation of Head Start, a federally funded school readiness program for low-income families, established in 1965, which provides not only preschool but also supports family development through goals and resources (U.S. Department of Health & Human Services, 2025). Head Start is an expansive program serving 799,901 children from birth to five years of age in fiscal year 2023.

In developmentally appropriate practice, educators must consider the context of the children and families they serve. This becomes even more important when the teacher does not share the same cultural backgrounds as the children they serve. Teachers may incorporate cultural practices, foods or languages of the families into the classroom. Understanding that knowledge is built upon previous knowledge (Piaget, 1962), the teacher may choose to provide pretend foods and utensils that represent the cultures of each of the children in the class. For example, if a child is known to use chopsticks at home, the teacher places chopsticks along with child-safe forks, spoons, and knives in the pretend play area of the classroom. Additionally, the teacher may ask families to bring in empty boxes of foods they eat at home that can also be placed in the pretend play area. This enhances the level of pretend play for all children as they expand their play themes with these familiar items. For cultural practices, a teacher who knows which cultures encourage downward eye-gaze as a sign of respect and listening rather than direct eye contact will navigate conversations with their students more effectively.

Dual Language Learning

Society is in the time of recognizing the value of children's first language pivoting from terms like English Language Learners to Dual Language Learners to honor the families and cultures, and while this reason is sufficient, when educators understand that maintaining the home language actually facilitates rather than hinders English acquisition, they can create inclusive environments where multilingualism is viewed as an asset rather than a deficit (Escobar, 2013).

Dual Language Learners are "young children who have at least one parent who speaks a language other than English in the home". The Migration Policy Institute (Giang & Park, 2022) notes that approximately one-third of U.S. children ages 0-5 and growing. In early childhood classrooms across the United States, bringing richness through their varied linguistic and cultural backgrounds. These young children, who are simultaneously developing proficiency in their home language and English, face unique challenges that require thoughtful pedagogical approaches. DLLs need consistent support for both their home language development—which provides the foundation for cognitive growth and cultural identity—and their emerging English skills.

Effective early childhood programs for DLLs incorporate several essential elements: language-rich environments that validate and incorporate home languages; culturally responsive teaching practices that connect learning to children's lived experiences; intentional vocabulary development in both languages; opportunities for meaningful peer interactions; and strong family partnerships that recognize parents as valuable resources in the educational process.

Principles of Child Development and Learning

In addition to the three core considerations, NAEYC (2020) provides nine principles of child development and learning (Table 2). These principles incorporate research-based knowledge of child growth and development as a foundational part of effective practice, including understanding developmental sequences, recognizing the interrelatedness of developmental domains, and acknowledging the essential role of play in enhancing learning. DAP includes hands-on explorations, supportive environments for learning, and positive relationships. The educational opportunities of technology are recognized and its thoughtful, intentional use in the early childhood classroom is encouraged. The position statement also recognizes that though much of development is common among children, individual and cultural differences also impact development and must be considered.

Table 2. 9 principles of child development and learning

Principle	Description
1. Development is dynamic	A child's growth results from the interaction of biology and environment. Early experiences, including responsive caregiving, shape brain development and future learning.
2. Development is holistic	Physical, cognitive, social, emotional, and linguistic development are interconnected. Support in one area enhances growth in others.
3. Play is essential	Play fosters joy, self-regulation, problem-solving, and learning across all domains. Guided play enhances engagement and deepens understanding.
4. Development varies	Children grow at different rates based on individual traits, cultural contexts, and experiences. Progress should be seen as waves rather than fixed stages.
5. Children construct knowledge	From birth, children actively seek meaning through relationships, exploration, and observation. Educators provide rich, play-based learning experiences to support this process.
6. Motivation grows with belonging	A secure, inclusive environment enhances learning. Connections between school, home, and community foster agency and engagement.
7. Learning is interdisciplinary	Knowledge is best acquired through integrated experiences rather than isolated subjects. Early education lays the foundation for future learning.
8. Challenge supports growth	Children thrive when engaged in learning just beyond their current abilities, with opportunities to practice and reflect.
9. Technology can be a tool	When used intentionally, technology supports communication, inclusion, and learning. However, hands-on experiences remain crucial for development.

Note. Adapted from National Association for the Education of Young Children. (2020). Developmentally appropriate practice: A position statement of the National Association for the Education of Young Children. NAEYC. https://www.naeyc.org/resources/position-statements/dap

NAEYC Professional Standards and Competencies for Early Childhood Educators

The last component of NAEYC standards considered in this topic applies to early childhood education with teacher education programs. The six NAEYC Professional Standards and Competencies for Early Childhood Educators (Table 3) seeks to provide guidelines for the teacher educators in the knowledge base all highly-qualified EC educators need to have. Institutions of higher learning have guideposts and accreditation standards for training the teachers. The first standard:

Standard 1: Child Development and Learning in Context. Early childhood educators must be steeped in the knowledge and research of the developmental period from birth through age 8 across domains of development (i.e., physical, cognitive, social and emotional). This standard emphasizes recognizing each child as an individual with unique developmental variations, trajectories, strengths, challenges, and approaches to learning. Educators recognize that children develop within interconnected spheres of influence—from family structures and cultural backgrounds to linguistic environments, community settings, and broader societal frameworks. Drawing upon this layered understanding, they craft evidence-based approaches and environments tailored to support the unique developmental journey and learning requirements of each child.

For example, in a childcare setting, a teacher might notice that a 3-year-old child struggles with transitions between activities but excels in small group settings. Understanding typical development and this child's unique profile, the teacher implements a visual schedule with timely warnings before transitions and incorporates the child's strengths by assigning them special helper roles during small group activities, demonstrating how developmental knowledge informs individualized teaching strategies.

Standard 2: Family-Teacher Partnerships and Community Connections This standard acknowledges that effective early childhood education hinges on collaborative partnerships between educators and the young children's families. Educators need to comprehend, appreciate, and honor the rich variety of family structures and characteristics while leveraging this insight to foster mutually respectful and reciprocal connections and partnerships. They actively involve families as essential collaborators in their children's growth and education through regular, purposeful exchanges and joint efforts. Educators also seek to use local community resources to support both the learners and their families. A synergistic relationship is developed between families, community, and the school community.

For instance, a childcare facility might develop a family participation initiative where caregivers introduce cultural practices and heritage languages within the learning environment, utilize daily correspondence logs linking educators and families, and coordinate regular evening gatherings featuring activities that children have found engaging at the center. Moreover, the facility might establish connections with neighborhood resources such as public libraries for reading programs and arrange visits from healthcare specialists for oral health education.

Standard 3: Child Observation, Documentation, and Assessment "Early childhood educators understand that the primary purpose of assessment is to inform instruction and planning" (NAEYC, 2020, p. 9). Educators need to have and effectively use a toolbox of assessments and instruments ranging from screening to diagnostic, formal to informal, developmental to authentic assessments. Educators know how to use observation, documentation, and various assessment approaches and tools in ways that are ethically grounded and developmentally, culturally, and linguistically appropriate for "positive outcomes for each child". In addition, educators need to develop collaborative assessment relationships with both families and fellow education professionals.

In an ECE setting, teachers might maintain individual portfolios for each child containing work samples, photographs of projects, observation notes, and developmental checklists that track progress over time. During parent-teacher conferences, educators share these portfolios, discussing the child's development across domains and collaboratively setting goals with families. When a teacher notices through regular observations that several children show interest in construction and building, they might document this interest with photos and anecdotal notes, then plan a curriculum unit on architecture and engineering that builds on the children's natural curiosity, demonstrating how assessment directly informs responsive curriculum planning.

Standard 4: Developmentally, Culturally, and Linguistically Appropriate Teaching Practices. This standard acknowledges the intricate nature of educating young learners including knowing and incorporating varieties of methodologies and adapting them according to children's developmental stages, individual traits, and learning environments. Also, educators need to cultivate nurturing, compassionate, and encouraging connections and exchanges are the cornerstone of their professional practice.

For example, within an early childhood center, a teacher will get on the child's eye level for a conversation or could establish predictable daily rhythms that foster a sense of safety and stability for the children. Another example is a classroom could feature learning centers with materials at various levels of difficulty to accommodate different developmental stages, such as puzzles ranging from simple three-piece options to complex 20-piece challenges. Additionally, the teacher might incorporate diverse cultural elements in dramatic play areas, display books and labels in all languages represented in the classroom, and use visual supports alongside verbal instructions to accommodate different learning styles and language proficiencies, exemplifying culturally and linguistically responsive teaching.

Standard 5: Knowledge, Application, and Integration of Academic Content. Early childhood educators must also possess a working knowledge of academic disciplines (e.g., literacy, arts, mathematics, social studies, science) and pedagogical methods for teaching each subject, and most importantly teachers need to be able to scaffold to the next level of learning for each learner.

In an early childhood education setting, this might be demonstrated through thoughtfully designed learning centers that integrate multiple content areas where a child can play at their own level—for example, during a cooking activity, children might follow picture recipes (literacy), measure ingredients (mathematics), discuss food traditions from different cultures (social studies), and observe how ingredients change when mixed or heated (science). The educator understands the science concepts behind these transformations and uses appropriate vocabulary (dissolve, evaporate, solidify) while asking open-ended questions that prompt children to predict, observe, and explain what's happening, showing deep content knowledge integrated with effective teaching strategies.

Standard 6: Professionalism as an Early Childhood Educator. This standard focuses on professional identity and practice. Early childhood educators actively engage within the early childhood field. They champion the interests of young children, their families, and the profession through informed advocacy. These educators apply ethical standards and professional guidelines in their practice. They utilize effective communication strategies that strengthen their connections with children, families, and fellow professionals. Early childhood educators commit to ongoing, cooperative learning while continuing to grow through professional development. This might be exemplified by a teacher who attends regular professional development workshops to learn current best practices, maintains professional certifications, and participates in early childhood education associations. The educator might advocate for high-quality early learning by speaking at community events about the importance of early education.

Table 3. 6 NAEYC professional standards and competencies for early childhood educators

Standard	Explanation
1. Child Development and Learning in Context	Early childhood educators understand child development from birth through age 8 across all domains, recognize each child's uniqueness, acknowledge that development occurs within multiple contexts (family, culture, community), and use this knowledge to make evidence-based decisions
2. Family-Teacher Partnerships and Community Connections	Educators value family diversity, build respectful reciprocal relationships with families as partners in children's development, and utilize community resources to support children and families.
3. Child Observation, Documentation, and Assessment	Educators understand that assessment primarily informs instruction, know various observation and assessment tools, use them ethically and appropriately, and collaborate with families and colleagues to document progress and plan learning experiences.

continued on following page

Table 3. Continued

Standard	Explanation
4. Developmentally, Culturally, and Linguistically Appropriate Teaching Practices	Educators build positive relationships with children, use teaching approaches responsive to children's learning trajectories and individual needs, and employ a broad repertoire of developmentally appropriate, culturally relevant, and evidence-based teaching strategies
5. Knowledge, Application, and Integration of Academic Content	Educators understand content knowledge across disciplines, know how children learn this content, and apply this knowledge to create meaningful, challenging curriculum experiences
6. Professionalism as an Early Childhood Educator	Educators identify as members of the early childhood profession, serve as advocates, uphold ethical guidelines, use effective communication skills, engage in continuous learning, and develop reflective and intentional practice

Note. Adapted from National Association for the Education of Young Children. (2020). Professional Standards and Competencies for Early Childhood Educators. https://www.naeyc.org/sites/default/files/globally-shared/downloads/PDFs/resources/position-statements/standards_and_competencies_ps.pdf

Artificial Intelligence and DAP Core Considerations

Since its release in 2022, AI large language models such as ChatGPT have become more intelligent, more customizable, and better at producing useful results. When examined under the lens of developmentally appropriate practice, a mix of findings have emerged from the limited research available.

Commonality

Utilizing known child development information appears to be an area where AI can support educators, though research in this area is limited. Early learning standards and developmental milestones factor into commonality, which is readily available through a variety of online sources, and certainly accessible to artificial intelligence programs. Even so, AI may misinterpret or give information that is not in alignment with our understanding of child development. In January 2023, when prompted to provide a lesson plan for 24-month children, ChatGPT offered this instructional strategy, "Praise their efforts and remind them that they have worked on improving their fine motor skills." Many teachers may find this suggestion laughable, as the concept of fine motor skills is above most two-year-old comprehension, leaving this statement meaningless.

Individuality

The uniqueness of the individual in qualities such as strengths, challenges, temperament, interest, and learning style is an important consideration in education, particularly for young children (NAEYC, 2020). The field of special education offers some insight into AI lesson planning and individual needs. When compared to the Universal Design for Learning and Transition (UDL/UDT) framework, commonly used in special education settings, AI-generated lesson plans "show minimal alignment with these frameworks and required teacher modifications to enhance the learning environment" (Lammert et al., 2024). This suggests that while AI might prove valuable for beginning educators, it is likely less useful for experienced ones who already have expertise in differentiation.

Rice & Dunn (2023) in a systematic review of the use of AI with students with disabilities, found that AI has been used primarily to support an individual's emotion, communication, social skills, and reading and language needs. AI was used to support teacher and specialist decision making as well as a time-saving tool. The review brought to light concerns that research on AI thus far had consistently positioned students with disabilities to be burdens on teachers and parents that could be relieved by AI rather than focusing on how AI can empower students and remove administrative burdens. Rice and Dunn (2023) argue that while AI offers support for children with disabilities, how children are viewed and how disability is conceptualized should be examined. AI should be a tool to support children, rather than primarily supporting teachers.

Research by Setyaningsih et al. (2024) supports this finding in language education contexts. While AI tools can help generate differentiated content, teachers reported that significant refinement is typically required to truly meet diverse student needs, especially in classroom-specific contexts.

Context

Context considerations within DAP recognize the influence of individual, social, and cultural contexts in which the child develops. NAEYC offers a broader definition of context: "Context includes both one's personal cultural context (that is, the complex set of ways of knowing the world that reflect one's family and other primary caregivers and their traditions and values) and the broader multifaceted and intersecting (for example, social, racial, economic, historical, and political) cultural contexts in which each of us live. In both the individual- and societal- definitions, these are dynamic rather than static contexts that shape and are shaped by individual members as well as other factors." (NAEYC position statement, 2020, p. 7). Context considerations are also supported by the Council for Exceptional Children

(2015), which includes in its code of ethics. Principle 1 states that educators ensure instruction aligns with each student's culture, language, and background.

Research regarding AI and contextual factors shows promising developments in second language acquisition. AbuSahyon et al. (2023) found that AI-powered chatbots can provide personalized learning experiences for language learners. However, these technologies face limitations in understanding cultural context and providing culturally sensitive support. This aligns with broader concerns about AI's ability to effectively address the contextual dimensions of early childhood education.

Play

Play is essential to children's learning and warrants its own recognition. Play is a driving force for children's learning, allowing them to act beyond their current abilities and develop higher mental functions such as self-regulation, abstract thinking, and voluntary attention (Bodrova & Leong, 2015). Play as a mechanism by which children learn about their world, emphasizing hands-on exploration and imaginary play (Piaget, 1962). Play is also the vehicle for demonstrating knowledge and mastery of learning (Bruner, 1983).

Play is the natural language of children. It "bridges the gap between concrete experience and abstract thought," (Landreth, 2002, p.529). It creates an environment where children can organize and be "in control of life experiences in ways that are not possible in the world of reality outside of play." (Landreth, 2002, p.529) It empowers children to rework their environment into their own understanding (Vygotsky, 2004) while engaging in play for the "mere pleasure of mastering them [the activities] and acquiring thereby a feeling of virtuosity or power." (Piaget, 1962, p. 89). In play, children have power and are in control of their own learning. They meet the content at the level they need to. Unstructured play is the precursor to academic learning. (Elkind, 2007).

On the surface, play may seem like a simple concept; however, Moses (2022) offers a caveat: "It takes professional knowledge, experiences, and beliefs to recognize what play is, to interpret what play means, and to respond in ways that foster play and playful learning" (para. 1). She also encourages educators to consider whether their play-based approaches truly include all children.

Accurately defining play has been an issue that scholars have pursued for over 100 years. Rather than a single definition, it might serve better to look at the common characteristics that most scholars include in play discussions. Hendricks (2008) in a broad interdisciplinary exploration of play, offers common characteristics that support our understanding of this universal phenomenon.

- Voluntary – Play is freely chosen.

- Intrinsically Motivated – The activity is enjoyable in itself.
- Separated from Real Life – Often occurs in a special time and space.
- Rule-Bound Yet Flexible – Involves structured or emergent rules.
- Imaginative & Transformative – Encourages creativity and role exploration.
- Social or Solitary – Can involve collaboration or individual engagement.

Can AI create early learning experiences that enhance the very human experience of play? Can AI correctly interpret what is play and what isn't? Research on AI and early childhood education suggests that AI could be a tool to create games and materials to support children's learning (Kanders et al., 2024). This raises questions about the quality of these materials to provide play-based and joyful learning experiences for young children.

Lesson Plans

Lesson plans serve as essential roadmaps that guide educational practices in early childhood settings, providing educators with structured approaches to facilitate children's learning journeys. These frameworks establish clear learning objectives, outline appropriate teaching strategies, and identify necessary resources to support children's developmental trajectories across cognitive, social-emotional, physical, and linguistic domains. When teachers create intentional learning opportunities through thoughtful planning, they ensure curriculum alignment and pedagogical coherence while making sure activities are developmentally appropriate for each child's unique stage.

Well-designed lesson plans create flow and purpose for both educators and young learners in practical ways. For teachers, having structured plans enhances instructional efficiency, promotes reflective practice, designs effective environments and creates more time for meaningful assessment and interaction rather than impromptu planning. For children, these plans create predictable learning routines that foster security and confidence while still encouraging exploration and creativity. Intentional teaching through systematic planning correlates positively with improved learning outcomes, deeper engagement, and stronger foundations for future academic success.

Advantages and Disadvantages of AI in Lesson Planning

As artificial intelligence tools become increasingly integrated into educational settings, their role in lesson planning in the K-12 school setting has garnered both excitement and caution. AI platforms like ChatGPT and Claude offer significant potential to support teachers by streamlining the planning process, reducing workload, and enhancing creativity (Pearce, 2024). These tools can generate lesson outlines, quizzes, and instructional materials in a fraction of the time traditionally required, offering a powerful starting point for educators. However, the use of AI in lesson planning also introduces important challenges, such as ensuring content accuracy, addressing privacy concerns, and navigating the limitations of AI in understanding context and cultural nuance (Akgun & Greenhow, 2022). The following table (Table 4) explores both the advantages and disadvantages of using AI in lesson planning, drawing on recent studies in the K-12 setting to highlight its practical implications in the classroom.

Table 4. Advantages and disadvantages of using AI in lesson planning

Advantages	Disadvantages
● Saves time with lesson planning and creation of supporting materials like quizzes and worksheets (reducing planning time from a median of 5 hours to potentially 30 minutes per day) ● Decreases teacher burnout ● Provides a starting point for teachers to plan ● Offers real-time peer-like support ● Enhances lesson planning efficiency and supports differentiated instruction (McCormack, 2024; Setyaningsih et al., 2024) ● Inspires creative teaching approaches through varied suggestions ● Streamlines material creation and assessment design (Setyaningsih et al., 2024)	● Potential for inaccurate information ● The learning curve for effective AI system use ● Teachers must develop skills to effectively prompt AI systems. ● Technical limitations in understanding contextual nuances (AbuSahyon et al., 2023) ● Privacy concerns regarding data collection and use ● Inability to fully replicate human cultural sensitivity (AbuSahyon et al., 2023) ● Generated content typically requires significant refinement to meet pedagogical standards (Setyaningsih et al., 2024)

AI-Generated Lesson Plans in Use

Powell and Courchesne (2024) created and examined a first-grade science lesson plan on heredity and traits using the 5E lesson plan model and Massachusetts educational standards in ChatGPT. They front-loaded ChatGPT with two prompts: learning the 5E lesson planning model and specific information about the standards and students.

In the first iteration, ChatGPT created all steps in the 5E process (Engagement, Exploration, Explanation, Elaboration, and Evaluation) with half the lesson teacher-driven and half student-driven. The lesson plans included active learning opportunities that were age-appropriate, but no specific guiding questions, prompts, or examples for novice teachers to build upon. Additionally, no ancillary materials like books to further learning were provided.

In the second iteration, seven additional prompts were used to further tailor the lesson plan to be more developmentally appropriate. Prompts asked for more time for questions and answers, literacy materials, photos, and a KWL chart. In the output, guiding questions were provided, students were asked to write questions, but no specific time for questions and answers was allocated, and a book was provided that the researchers couldn't verify as an original AI creation or a published work.

ChatGPT created time efficiency by generating and substantially refining a lesson plan within 30 minutes that aligned with curriculum frameworks. However, teachers needed to know to refine for more research-based practices like increased literacy opportunities and time for individual processing. In addition, ChatGPT "ended with a recommendation to, 'Remember to adapt the lesson plan to the specific needs and abilities of the students, and feel free to incorporate any additional resources or media that may enhance the learning experience,' but didn't provide a list of specific strategies.

Powell and Courchesne (2024) emphasize that while generative AI can serve as a helpful starting point for lesson planning, teachers must critically evaluate and adapt the outputs. ChatGPT should be viewed as a tool to assist in creating initial drafts of lesson plans, but teachers' expertise remains essential for adapting lessons to meet curriculum standards and students' diverse needs.

Similar findings emerge in language education research. Setyaningsih et al. (2024) found that tools like MagicSchool AI can enhance lesson planning efficiency for EFL teachers, but AI-generated content typically requires significant refinement to meet pedagogical standards, particularly for classroom-specific contexts.

Teacher Preparation and AI

Teacher preparation programs are beginning to instruct on how to use AI in the classroom. As with all technology, there is a learning curve while higher education faculty adopt, learn, and practice AI themselves before they can effectively teach future teachers. Some programs are asking their students to explore this world so it could become part of effective practice, but questions remain about what constitutes effective and ethical practice.

The findings of AbuSahyon et al. (2023), Park and Park (2024) and Setyaningsih et al. (2024) underscore the importance of preparing teachers to view AI as a collaborative tool—a partnership where technology enhances rather than replaces the essential human elements of teaching and learning. "Humans and AI can improve each other's capabilities through collaboration and can perform tasks more effectively when they perform tasks independently to achieve a common goal through a cooperative network" (Park & Park, p.216). This perspective aligns well with early childhood education's emphasis on relationships and individualized approaches.

Park and Park (2024) conducted a study on 15 elementary pre-service teachers composing a physics lesson plan for the first time with no guidance. Then the 15 students put their lesson plans through ChatGPT and were asked to "revise and supplement the lesson plan" (p. 217). The analysis was done through two prongs, looking at the revisions and the lesson plan offered by ChatGPT and the interactions of the student with ChatGPT. AI offered changes from 2 aspects: the content of the material or the structure of the lesson, the organization of topics or activities to include. Most of the changes were to the structure of the lesson plan.

Three groups of collaboration emerged: low level, mid-level, and high-level (Figure 3). In the low-level of collaboration (13.3%) no changes were made to lesson plans. Students did not trust or have confidence in ChatGPT. ChatGPT was not accepted as a collaborative partner. In the intermediate level collaboration (53.4%), students did view ChatGPT as a collaborative partner and changed or added new content. Suggested changes related to the structure of the lesson plan, but no modifications in the content. All changes were accepted without critical review and there were no second iterations or clarifications to ChatGPT. Students didn't perceive AI as fallible. In the high level of collaboration group (33.3%), students accepted ChatGPT as a collaborative partner peer and mentor, but critically reviewed, selected and accepted some of the revisions based on students' evaluations of the changes and asked for more iterations and clarifications. The students viewed AI as a collaborator, a peer, and a mentor. Park and Park (2024) concluded that students must first accept AI as appearing first, and then the successful use of AI as a collaborative tool could be reached.

Figure 3. Preservice teachers' levels of collaboration with AI (Park & Park, 2024)

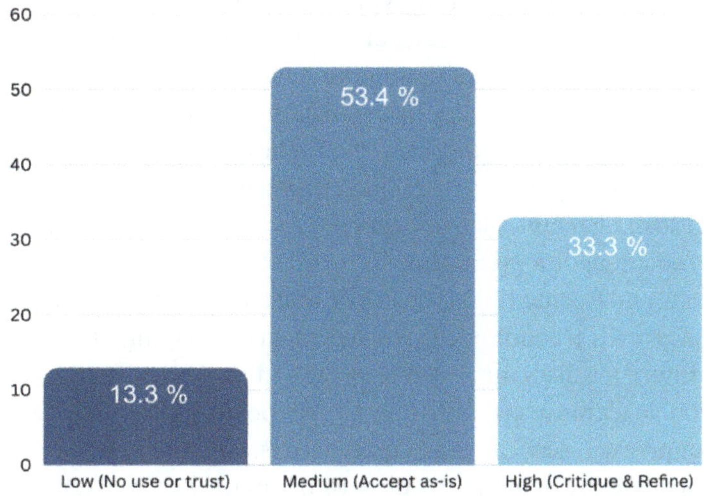

*Park, H. K., & Park, J. (2024). Lesson plan development for pre-service elementary school teachers through collaboration with AI: Focused on ChatGPT. New Physics: Sae Mulli. https://doi.org/10.3938/NPSM.74.215

Park and Park's (2024) article illustrates the strong connection between NAEYC Professional Standards and Competencies for Early Childhood Educators four and five and skills teachers need to know if competently use generative AI. For competency 4: Developmentally, Culturally, and Linguistically Appropriate Teaching Practices teachers need to be able to review the structure of the chatbot's lesson plan activity and pedagogy changes to know if they are appropriate for the make-up of their specific classroom to accept, or prompt for a new applicable strategy.

Moreover, Competency 5: Knowledge, Application, and Integration of Academic Content is addressed. Teachers need to know the specific content in the academic areas to evaluate the suggestions and modifications of content of the lesson plan to either accept, modify the AI suggestions or prompt for more specific content information. Teachers need to know how to use technology effectively, understanding the when and where to use in lesson planning and incorporation within the classroom. "In order to successfully collaborate with ChatGPT it is necessary to not only develop the ability to collaborate with ChatGPT but also have prior knowledge of the relevant field in which you wish to collaborate" (Park & Park, 2024, p. 225).

The Center for Reinventing Public Education (CRPE) released a report in October 2024 examining how teacher preparation programs are adapting to the emergence of AI in education. Based on interviews and surveys of 500 U.S. education school leaders with a 14% response rate, the report revealed that most institutions are in the early stages of integrating AI into their curricula, with the primary focus being on preventing plagiarism rather than preparing future teachers to use AI as an educational tool. About 59% of programs provide some AI-related instruction, but only 25% offer training on integrating AI into teaching practices.

The report shows that only 10% of faculty feel confident using AI themselves and this really limits teaching teachers in training how and when to use AI effectively and ethically. The instructors who are using artificial intelligence to improve student creativity and personalize learning have the highest percentage of incorporation. Whereas the lowest incorporation is teaching how to use AI to assess students. With regards to the use of chat bots such as chat GBT, a little over 25% of faculty felt that they used it a moderate or a great deal.

Weiner, Lake, and Rosner (2024) conclude that teacher preparation programs are not keeping pace with technological advancements reshaping classrooms, potentially leaving future teachers unprepared for AI's impact on education. While most education school leaders are optimistic about AI's positive potential, they expressed concerns about privacy, security, and equity issues.

It appears that we are again at the crux of the place that we were 15 years ago with online learning where the teachers and the students have about the same amount of knowledge of AI, whereas in education with Vygotsky's ideas of scaffolding, we do not currently have a more knowledgeable other in the use of AI in teacher education programs. More concerted efforts are needed to provide training for faculty members to teach the teacher trainers to support effective use with their students for the maximum benefit. NAEYC (2024) supports the integration of ethical and responsible AI instruction in teacher education programs; however, in the constantly evolving landscape of AI, faculty continue to grapple with how to define and apply those principles in practice.

The Power of Prompts: AI as a Collaborator

The real linchpin in lesson planning with AI appears to be the prompts provided by the user (Lammert et al., 2024). The more specific the instructions provided, the more customized the response. Rather than a curricular guide, AI should be seen as a colleague or collaborator, using AI to supplement educator expertise (Cooper, 2023; Park & Park, 2024; Lammert et al., 2024; Kanders et al.; 2024; Yilmaz Can & Durmus, 2024).

With growing success and research of AI in lesson planning in the K-12 settings, the focus can now turn to how AI can help design lesson plans for children in early childhood settings. How do generative AIs align with developmentally appropriate strategies?

Scenario: Lesson Plan on the Five Senses

Ms. Meroudjie is a teacher at a public prekindergarten class at a large urban classroom. Her class is composed of 14 students ages 3 turning 4 years old. Two students are from families whose first language is Spanish, and one family has recently moved from China and the student speaks Mandarin at home. In addition one student has speech delays and tends to point rather than use words and one student has large sensory needs and ADHD.

One morning during recess, Ms. Meroudjie notices that most of the children are in the sandbox full of buckets, shovels and sieves. Henry pours sand on his feet and says, "Oh that tickles!" The friends around him notice and begin to pour sand on their hands and feet. Lola takes the sieve and sprinkles sand on McKenzie's legs. "It looks like rain."

"It sounds like rain too!" McKenzie replies. Ms. Meroudjie as she listens begins to think of how she can use their interest in using their senses to design the next weeks' lessons. During her planning time, she sits at her computer and pulls up ChatGPT. Ms. Meroudjie begins with a minimal prompt for designing the early childhood lesson plan.

Prompt: Minimal Prompt (ChatGPT): Create a Preschool Lesson Plan

OUTPUT: Here's a Preschool Lesson Plan that focuses on Exploring the Five Senses through hands-on activities. This lesson is designed to be engaging, developmentally appropriate, and interactive.

Lesson Plan: Exploring the Five Senses

Age Group: 3-5 years

Time Duration: 45-60 minutes

Theme: The Five Senses (Sight, Sound, Smell, Taste, and Touch)

Learning Objectives:

- *Children will identify and describe the five senses.*
- *Children will explore their senses through hands-on activities.*
- *Children will engage in conversations about their observations.*

Materials Needed:

- *Sight: Magnifying glasses, picture cards, kaleidoscope, mirrors*
- *Sound: Shakers, bells, different musical instruments, sound bottles*

- *Smell: Cotton balls with essential oils (lavender, lemon, cinnamon, peppermint)*
- *Taste: Small samples of sweet (banana), salty (pretzels), sour (lemon), and bitter (dark chocolate) foods (ensure no allergies)*
- *Touch: Texture bags with soft cotton, rough sandpaper, smooth fabric, bumpy plastic*

Lesson Outline:

1. Circle Time Introduction (10 minutes)
    - *Greeting & Warm-up Song: "If You're Happy and You Know It"*
    - *Discussion:*
        - *Ask: "What parts of our body help us learn about the world?"*
        - *Show a visual of the five senses (eyes, ears, nose, mouth, and hands).*
        - *Briefly introduce each sense and what it does.*
2. Five Senses Exploration Stations (30 minutes total)

Children rotate through five stations, spending about 5-6 minutes per station.

1. Sight Station
    - *Look through magnifying glasses at objects.*
    - *Use mirrors to look at facial expressions.*
    - *Explore a kaleidoscope.*
    - *Play a quick game of "I Spy."*
2. Sound Station
    - *Listen to different sounds (bells, shakers, rain stick).*
    - *Guess the sound from mystery sound bottles.*
    - *Play an instrument and listen for differences.*
3. Smell Station
    - *Smell different cotton balls with familiar scents.*
    - *Match scents to pictures (e.g., cinnamon picture of cinnamon sticks).*
4. Taste Station
    - *Try a tiny sample of each taste (sweet, salty, sour, bitter).*
    - *Talk about how each one makes their tongue feel.*
5. Touch Station
    - *Feel mystery objects in a bag and describe them.*
    - *Sort items by texture (soft, rough, smooth, bumpy).*

3. Group Discussion & Reflection (10 minutes)

- *Gather children and ask:*

- *"What was your favorite station?"*
- *"What surprised you the most?"*
- *"Which sense do you think you use the most every day?"*

- *Read a book related to the five senses (e.g., My Five Senses by Aliki).*

4. Closing Activity (5-10 minutes)

- *Song: "The Five Senses Song" (to reinforce learning).*
- *Goodbye Ritual: Each child shares one thing they learned before leaving.*

Assessment & Extensions:

Assessment:

- *Observe if children can name at least three of their senses.*
- *Listen for descriptive words as they engage in activities. Extensions:*
- *Take a Five Senses Nature Walk outside.*
- *Do a "What's That Smell?" Guessing Game another day.*
- *Use finger painting to explore touch and sight together.*

This lesson plan provides structured, hands-on learning while keeping it fun and engaging for preschoolers! Let me know if you need any modifications.

Critique of Lesson Plan with Minimal Prompt

The first lesson plan ChatGPT picks a topic that is appropriate for 3 to 5-year-olds. Helping children learn to explore the environment through their five senses will teach how to use them for future exploration and learning. The learning objectives do use concrete verbs that allow for observation of mastery of the learning goals. In the materials list, a variety of materials are provided, however in the smell and the touch materials, cotton balls in essential oils are listed. Real objects with smells are not used. For example, you could have a real lemon rather than a cotton ball with lemon essential oils. When reviewing the direct teaching lesson plan, it starts with an engaging song, however, rotating students through five sensations where children are only allowed to explore for 5 to 6 minutes is not developmentally appropriate in order to make it more appropriate having the stations and allowing the children to engage as interested would alter this part of the lesson plan.

In the group discussion and reflection, a well-known book, *My Five Senses* by Aliki, is used to increase literacy opportunities. However, no writing is present in the lesson plan. The teacher could easily incorporate it by writing on a whiteboard. The extension activities are age-appropriate and allow the children to use multiple senses at the same time in order to explore their environment. At the end ChatGPT asks if you would like modifications rather than providing them without prompting.

When applying the lens of the core considerations of DAP and principles of learning, this plan shows elements of DAP. Commonality is considered in that the child development research shows that children do indeed learn from hands-on experiences (Piaget, 1962). However, it is easy to note that this plan is missing the DAP considerations of individuality and context. The individual needs of varying language needs and the diversity of families are not included.

Play appears to be incorporated in songs and a story, though whether these activities genuinely reflect play is debatable. ChatGPT claims this plan is developmentally appropriate, it lacks two of the core considerations.

In order to make the lesson plan more developmentally appropriate, Ms. Meroudjie inputs an adapted prompt to specifically include the 3 core considerations: commonality, individuality, and context. ChatGPT offers these changes.

Expanded Prompt (ChatGPT): Please modify this plan to include the 3 core considerations of developmentally appropriate practice (commonality, individuality, context).

OUTPUT: Preschool Lesson Plan: Exploring the Five Senses
Aligned with Developmentally Appropriate Practice (DAP)
Age Group: 3-5 years
Time Duration: 45-60 minutes
Theme: The Five Senses (Sight, Sound, Smell, Taste, and Touch)
Developmentally Appropriate Practice (DAP) Alignment

1. Commonality – This lesson is based on what is universally known about how young children develop and learn. It incorporates hands-on, sensory-based experiences, which are crucial for preschoolers' cognitive and language development.
2. Individuality – Activities allow for individual exploration and differentiation based on each child's preferences, sensory sensitivities, and developmental level. Children can engage at their own comfort level and express their observations in different ways.
3. Context – The lesson considers children's backgrounds, cultures, and experiences. Some children may have different sensory experiences at home or cultural preferences related to taste and smell. The teacher will facilitate discussions that respect and incorporate diverse perspectives.

Learning Objectives

- *Children will identify and describe the five senses.*
- *Children will explore their senses through hands-on activities.*
- *Children will engage in conversations about their observations.*
- *Children will make connections between sensory experiences and their own lives.*

Materials Needed

- *Sight: Magnifying glasses, picture cards, kaleidoscope, mirrors*
- *Sound: Shakers, bells, different musical instruments, sound bottles*
- *Smell: Cotton balls with essential oils (lavender, lemon, cinnamon, peppermint)*
- *Taste: Small samples of culturally diverse sweet, salty, sour, and bitter foods (adjust for allergies and preferences)*
- *Touch: Texture bags with soft cotton, rough sandpaper, smooth fabric, bumpy plastic*

Lesson Outline

1. Circle Time Introduction (10 minutes)

DAP Considerations: This group time respects individual differences in attention span and engagement by allowing movement, visuals, and songs.

- *Greeting & Warm-up Song: "If You're Happy and You Know It" (includes movement).*
- *Discussion:*
    - *Ask: "What parts of our body help us learn about the world?"*
    - *Show a visual of the five senses (eyes, ears, nose, mouth, hands).*
    - *Invite children to share personal experiences (e.g., "What is your favorite smell? How do you know when food is yummy?").*

2. Five Senses Exploration Stations (30 minutes total)

DAP Considerations: These activities allow children to explore at their own pace, follow their interests, and engage in developmentally appropriate sensory play.

1. Sight Station
    - *Look through magnifying glasses at objects.*
    - *Use mirrors to look at facial expressions.*
    - *Explore a kaleidoscope.*

- *Play a quick game of "I Spy."*

2. Sound Station
   - *Listen to different sounds (bells, shakers, rain stick).*
   - *Guess the sound from mystery sound bottles.*
   - *Play an instrument and listen for differences.*
3. Smell Station
   - *Smell different cotton balls with familiar scents.*
   - *Match scents to pictures (e.g., cinnamon picture of cinnamon sticks).*
   - *Invite children to share if they recognize any smells from home.*
4. Taste Station
   - *Try a tiny sample of culturally diverse flavors (sweet, salty, sour, bitter).*
   - *Respect individual differences (some children may opt out or prefer to describe rather than taste).*
   - *Discuss how different foods are enjoyed in different families.*
5. Touch Station
   - *Feel mystery objects in a bag and describe them.*
   - *Sort items by texture (soft, rough, smooth, bumpy).*
   - *Allow children to describe how different textures make them feel.*

3. Group Discussion & Reflection (10 minutes)

DAP Considerations: Acknowledges individual differences in communication skills by allowing children to express themselves in multiple ways (verbal responses, gestures, pointing).

- *Gather children and ask:*
  - *"What was your favorite station?"*
  - *"What surprised you the most?"*
  - *"Which sense do you think you use the most every day?"*
- *Read a book related to the five senses (e.g., My Five Senses by Aliki).*

4. Closing Activity (5-10 minutes)

DAP Considerations: Children process new concepts best through play and repetition, so a song reinforces learning in an engaging way.

- *Song: "The Five Senses Song"*
- *Goodbye Ritual: Each child shares one thing they learned before leaving.*

Assessment & Extensions

DAP Considerations: Assessment is informal, observation-based, and respects individual learning paces.

Assessment:

- *Observe if children can name at least three of their senses.*
- *Listen for descriptive words as they engage in activities.*

Extensions:

- *Take a Five Senses Nature Walk outside.*
- *Do a "What's That Smell?" Guessing Game another day.*
- *Use finger painting to explore touch and sight together.*

This DAP-aligned lesson ensures that activities are meaningful, individualized, and contextually relevant, while still being fun and engaging! Let me know if you'd like any additional modifications.

Critique of the Lesson Plan with Expanded Prompt

At first glance, ChatGPT adds the DAP alignments with the definition of each of the core considerations. An additional learning objective that ties to individuality and context where "children will make connections between sensory experiences and their lived lives". In the material and exploration stations, core considerations were added only to the sense of taste/ ChatGPT offers direction to add culturally diverse food, however, does not give specific examples of what that would look like. Moreover, in the taste station ChatGPT asks the teacher to discuss how different foods are enjoyed in different families to deepen the incorporation of the core consideration. In the lesson plan outline DAP considerations are explained at the top of each step, but no suggestions are embedded within the step-by-step directions, the assessments and extensions have no incorporation of more individuality or context.

While all the core considerations are addressed, minimal adjustments to the actual plan are made. Another limitation is the limited scope of AI's interpretation of lesson plan, creating a whole-group, teacher-directed plan. Hands-on exploration is included, though a short period of teacher-structured time is allowed at each activity. Contexts are broadly discussed, but guidance on the application of the specific children's contexts is very limited.

This leads to the question, when front-loaded with very specific information can the AI created lesson plan become more developmentally appropriate and serve teachers to enhance their curriculum? Providing the AI with specifics about commonality (such as early learning guidelines, age range of children, and group size), individuality (such as disabilities, preferences and strengths or needs of the children), and contextual information (such as dual language learners and cultural considerations) may be an effective way to gain the most from the AI tool.

In the third iteration, Ms. Meroudjie decides to see what more than one AI chatbot can do. She inputs the expanded lesson plan into ChatGPT and Claude for the comprehensive prompt to explore the level of incorporation of DAP would be provided. For the purposes of this demonstration, Texas PK Guidelines (Texas Education Agency, 2022) and the Idaho Early Learning eGuidelines (Idaho Department of Health and Welfare, 2021) are included to prompt the chatbot's response.

When Ms. Meroudjie reviews both outputs of the two AI-created plans; she notices many similarities, though ChatGPT's plan was less detailed and more condensed. Some elements of the ChatGPT plan are not as rich in play-based activities and omit reflection and extension activities. After reviewing both lesson plans, Ms. Meroudjie decides on the Claude lesson planning with AI.

Prompt: Comprehensive Prompt (Claude)

Design a lesson plan over the 5 senses with these 2 standards:

Texas PK Guidelines PK4.VI.A.1 Child observes, investigates, describes, and discusses characteristics of common objects.

Idaho Early Learning eGuidelines: Goal 42: Children observe, describe, and collect information by exploring the world around them.

For an early childhood classroom class of 14 students ages 3 turning 4 years old has 2 students whose first language is Spanish and Spanish is the language spoken at home. One student speaks Mandarin at home. One student has speech delays and tends to point rather than use words. One student has large sensory needs and ADHD.

Includes principles of DAP and the core considerations of commonality, individuality and context. Include a large group lesson plan, activities for outdoor learning, and activities for centers including: Art center Dramatic play Math/manipulatives Science center Blocks center

OUTPUT: Five Senses Lesson Plan

Age Group: 3-4 years old (14 students)

Standards Addressed:

- *Texas PK Guidelines PK4.VI.A.1: Child observes, investigates, describes, and discusses characteristics of common objects.*
- *Idaho Early Learning eGuidelines: Goal 42: Children observe, describe, and collect information by exploring the world around them.*

Core DAP Considerations

- *Commonality: All children develop through predictable patterns of growth*
- *Individuality: Each child has unique characteristics, strengths, and needs*
- *Context: Development is influenced by social and cultural contexts*

Accommodations for Diverse Needs

- *Dual Language Learners (Spanish): Visual supports, key vocabulary in Spanish, partnering*
- *Dual Language Learner (Mandarin): Visual supports, pictorial instructions, partnering*
- *Speech Delays: Visual choice cards, nonverbal participation options, peer modeling*
- *Sensory Needs/ADHD: Sensory breaks, fidget tools, movement opportunities, clear boundaries*

Unit Overview (1 Week)

Each day will focus on one sense while integrating previously learned senses: 1. Sight (Monday) 2. Hearing (Tuesday) 3. Touch (Wednesday) 4. Smell (Thursday) 5. Taste (Friday)

Large Group Lesson Plan: Introduction to the Five Senses

Materials

- *Poster with images of five senses*
- *Picture book about senses (suggestions: "My Five Senses" by Aliki or "You Can't Taste a Pickle With Your Ear" by Harriet Ziefert)*
- *Five sensory items in mystery box:*
  - *Sight: Colorful pinwheel*
  - *Sound: Small musical instrument (egg shaker)*
  - *Touch: Textured ball*
  - *Smell: Scented marker (mint)*
  - *Taste: Small container of honey*

Vocabulary (English/Spanish)

- *Senses/sentidos*
- *See/ver*
- *Hear/oír*
- *Touch/tocar*
- *Smell/oler*
- *Taste/saborear*

- *Eyes/ojos*
- *Ears/orejas*
- *Hands/manos*
- *Nose/nariz*
- *Mouth/boca*

Preparation

- *Have visual cards for each sense*
- *Create a simple visual schedule*
- *Place a quiet area with sensory tools nearby*
- *Prepare visuals for transition to centers*

Introduction (5 minutes) 1. Gather children in a circle on the carpet 2. Introduce the concept of five senses using the poster 3. Point to each body part and say the corresponding sense in English and Spanish 4. Use gestures for each sense that children can imitate

Story Time (5-7 minutes) 1. Read a picture book about the five senses 2. Pause frequently to ask open-ended questions 3. Invite children to point to the body part used for each sense

Mystery Box Exploration (10 minutes) 1. Present the mystery box and explain that it contains objects for each sense 2. One by one, invite children to explore an item from the box 3. Guide the discussion:

- *"What do you notice about this object?"*
- *"Which sense are you using?"*
- *"What body part helps you use this sense?" 4. Allow children with speech delays to point to visual cards to indicate which sense 5. Provide movement breaks between items for the child with sensory needs*

Closing and Transition (3 minutes) 1. Review the five senses using the poster and gestures 2. Sing a simple song about the five senses 3. Show the center activity cards and explain transitions

Outdoor Learning Activities

Sensory Scavenger Hunt

Materials: Paper bags, clipboards with picture checklists, magnifying glasses Setup: Prepare a visual checklist of items to find using different senses Activity: Children search for items that engage different senses (something rough, something that makes noise, something colorful)

Accommodations:

- *Pair Spanish/Mandarin speakers with English-speaking buddies*
- *Allow the child with speech delays to collect items rather than describe them*
- *Give the child with sensory needs extra space and a fidget tool*

Nature Sound Map

Materials: Large paper with a simple map of the playground, stickers Setup: Create a basic map showing key features of the playground Activity: Children sit quietly in different spots, listen for sounds, then place stickers on the map where they heard sounds Accommodations:

- *Use color-coded stickers for different types of sounds*
- *Allow pointing and nonverbal communication*
- *Provide a quiet zone option for sensory breaks*

Texture Walk

Materials: Various textured materials (carpet squares, bubble wrap, sandpaper, foam) Setup: Create a path with different textures Activity: Children walk barefoot across different textures and describe how they feel Accommodations:

- *Have cards with texture words in multiple languages*
- *Allow children to use gestures to show if they like/dislike textures*
- *Make participation optional for children with sensory sensitivities*

Center Activities

Art Center: Sensory Art Station

Materials:

- *Textured materials (sandpaper, bubble wrap, corrugated cardboard)*
- *Scented markers/paint*
- *Musical painting (painting while listening to different types of music)*
- *Colorful tissue paper and glue*

Activities: 1. Texture rubbings with crayons 2. Scented marker drawings 3. Musical paintings (changing movements based on tempo) 4. Collage with textured materials

Accommodations:

- *Visual step-by-step instructions with pictures*
- *Vocabulary cards in multiple languages*
- *Allow choices between materials for sensory-sensitive children*
- *Provide clean-up visual schedule*

Dramatic Play Center: Five Senses Restaurant
Materials:

- *Play food with different textures and colors*
- *Plastic utensils, plates, and cups*
- *Chef hats and aprons*
- *Menus with pictures*
- *Pretend spice containers with different scents*
- *Play kitchen tools that make sounds*

Activities: 1. Setting up a restaurant 2. Creating "sensory meals" with different textures and colors 3. Taking orders using picture menus 4. Serving food and describing tastes
Accommodations:

- *Label items in English, Spanish, and simple Mandarin characters*
- *Picture-based order forms for nonverbal communication*
- *Defined spaces with clear boundaries for the child with ADHD*
- *Quiet corner within the center for sensory breaks*

Math/Manipulatives Center: Sensory Sorting
Materials:

- *Sorting trays*
- *Objects with different properties (sizes, colors, textures, sounds)*
- *Sorting mats with pictures of the five senses*
- *Counting bears with scented/textured modifications*

Activities: 1. Sort objects by sense (things we see, hear, touch, etc.) 2. Match textured items to feel bags 3. Count and sort by color and size 4. Pattern creation with sensory items
Accommodations:

- *Number cards in multiple languages*
- *Textured numbers for tactile learners*
- *Clear, defined spaces for materials*
- *Visual timers for transitions*

Science Center: Sensory Exploration Station
Materials:

- *Magnifying glasses*
- *Listening tubes/devices*
- *Feely boxes with mystery objects*
- *Scent jars (spices, extracts)*
- *Light table with colored transparencies*
- *Collection of items with different properties*

Activities: 1. Using magnifying glasses to observe details 2. Making and recording sounds with different objects 3. Mystery box guessing game (identifying objects by touch) 4. Matching scents in containers 5. Light table color mixing

Accommodations:

- *Picture-based recording sheets*
- *Headphones for sound-sensitive children*
- *Vocabulary cards with pictures and multiple languages*
- *Flexible participation options*

Blocks Center: Sensory Building Challenge

Materials:

- *Various types of blocks (wooden, foam, textured)*
- *Colored cellophane for "windows"*
- *Small musical instruments to place in structures*
- *Scented play dough to use as "mortar"*
- *Pictures of buildings from different cultures*

Activities: 1. Build structures that incorporate sensory elements 2. Create "sound walls" that make noise when touched 3. Design buildings with textured pathways 4. Make structures based on cultural pictures

Accommodations:

- *Clear boundaries for building areas*
- *Pictures of step-by-step building ideas*
- *Fidget tools available*
- *Choice board for participation levels*

Assessment Strategies

Observation Checklist

- *Documents each child's engagement with sensory activities*

- *Notes vocabulary used to describe sensory experiences*
- *Records preferences and aversions*

Documentation

- *Photos of children engaged in sensory exploration*
- *Work samples from sensory art activities*
- *Dictated descriptions of sensory experiences*

Family Connection

- *Send home "Five Senses Scavenger Hunt" to complete as a family*
- *Request family recipes that engage multiple senses*
- *Share key vocabulary in all home languages*

Daily Reflection Questions for Teachers 1. Which sensory experiences engaged children most deeply today? 2. What accommodations were most effective for each child? 3. How did children communicate their observations? 4. What adjustments are needed for tomorrow's activities? 5. Which children might benefit from additional support or challenge?

Extensions

- *Add sensory elements to literacy activities (textured letters, scented books)*
- *Incorporate sensory breaks throughout the day*
- *Create a "sensory journal" where children document discoveries*
- *Invite family members to share sensory experiences from their cultural traditions*

Critique of the Comprehensive Prompt Lesson Plan

Based on the prompt the lesson plan went from a one day, direct-teach lesson to a weeklong exploration of the five senses. The engagement with the content over an extended period of time in multiple manners, like direct teaching and centers, indoor and outdoor environments allow for a more natural, play-based exploration. In addition, accommodations for dual language learners and special needs were incorporated throughout the lesson plan though culturally sustaining materials were not directly incorporated. Vocabulary was given for English and Spanish. The outdoor learning activities were hands-on and kinesthetic for each of the centers,

In the assessment strategies, there is a family connection section that includes ideas for sending home a senses scavenger hunt to involve families in the classroom activities and to request family recipes to have the different cultures incorporated into the classroom. The lesson plan ended with reflective questions and extensions that included literacy activities.

Table 5 reviews each lesson plan under the lens of the NAEYC six educator standards and competencies looking at which lesson plan prompts incorporated the pre-service teachers being able to practice the standards. The minimal prompt incorporated three of the six standards, and the expanded prompt incorporated four of the six standards. The comprehensive prompt lesson plan with front-loading details of the children, their needs and specific requirements for an evidence-based DAP classroom provided a connection to five of the six standards. In this one lesson plan, generative AI has the beginning of developmentally appropriate strategies but the highly-trained early childhood educators have the strong presence to make effective research-based lesson plans and environments. Educator Preparation Programs and professional developments can support developing this knowledge base.

Table 5. Comparison of professional standards and competencies with level of prompting

Standard	**Minimal prompt**	**Expanded prompt**	**Comprehensive prompt**
Child Development and Learning in Context	Commonality	Commonality Individuality Context	Commonality Specific strategies for Individuality Context
Family-Teacher Partnerships and Community Connections:			Included direct family connection
Child Observation, Documentation, and Assessment	Includes assessment strategies through observation	Includes assessment strategies through observation	Included observation, documentation and assessment
Developmentally, Culturally, and Linguistically Appropriate Teaching Practices		Brief mention of cultural and families in taste	Specific strategies for differentiation and learning preferences
Knowledge, Application, and Integration of Academic Content	Academic comment was correct	Academic comment was correct	Academic comment was correct
Professionalism as an Early Childhood Educator			

After the human review of the comprehensive lesson plan, how will ChatGPT critique an AI-generated lesson plan? As a collaborator, can it identify areas for improvement?

ChatGPT was then prompted to critique the lesson plan and address how it aligns with DAP. This evaluation is fascinating as it outlines how the AI chose activities and interpreted core considerations and principles of child development and learning. ChatGPT also provides strengths and areas of improvement on this AI-generated plan.

PROMPT: PROVIDE A DAP EVALUATION FOR THIS LESSON PLAN

DAP Evaluation: Five Senses Lesson Plan (Claude, Comprehensive Prompt)

Overview

This lesson plan demonstrates thoughtful alignment with Developmentally Appropriate Practice (DAP) by explicitly addressing the **three core considerations—commonality, individuality**, and **context**—as well as applying several of NAEYC's **nine principles of child development and learning**. It is also aligned to state early learning standards and includes rich, meaningful, and engaging learning opportunities across various domains.

Core Considerations of DAP

Commonality

- *The lesson plan reflects widely accepted developmental expectations for 3- to 4-year-old children (e.g., sensory exploration, guided play, whole group and center-based learning).*
- *Activities like mystery box exploration, sorting by texture, and identifying sensory experiences match cognitive and language abilities typical for this age group.*
- *The plan integrates hands-on, sensory-rich experiences, which are known to support development at this stage (NAEYC, 2020; Piaget, 1962).*

Individuality

- *Accommodations for children with speech delays, sensory processing needs, ADHD, and dual language learners are embedded throughout.*
- *Visual aids, flexible participation options, fidget tools, peer modeling, and multilingual vocabulary supports allow for differentiated access.*
- *Activity choices and sensory variations (e.g., texture walk, sensory art) offer multiple entry points and respect different learning styles and preferences.*

Context

- *The plan incorporates cultural responsiveness by including family languages, familiar foods, and opportunities for families to contribute.*
- *Reflects an understanding of classroom dynamics (e.g., 14 children, varying languages spoken at home).*
- *Suggestions for home connections (e.g., family scavenger hunt, family recipes) and use of multilingual materials make learning relevant to children's lived experiences.*

Table 6 reviews how the comprehensive lesson plan aligns with NAEYC's nine principles of child development and learning.

Table 6. Lesson plan alignment with child development and learning principles

Principle	*Evidence in the Lesson Plan*
1. Development is dynamic	*The plan acknowledges that children's development results from interactions between biology and the environment by embedding flexible supports like sensory tools, fidget options, and visual aids. Daily teacher reflection questions guide adaptation based on emerging needs and observations.*
2. Development is holistic	*Physical (texture walk), cognitive (sorting, predicting), social (group activities), emotional (safe routines), and language (multilingual vocabulary) domains are all addressed in integrated ways.*
3. Play is essential	*Children engage in imaginative and guided play through dramatic play (restaurant), sensory art, block building, and exploration stations. Play-based learning is embedded throughout the plan.*
4. Development varies	*The plan accounts for individual differences in learning styles, sensory needs, and language background. Children can engage at their own pace, and options for support or challenge are built into each activity.*
5. Children construct knowledge	*Open-ended questions, mystery exploration, hands-on investigation, and meaningful materials (like culturally relevant pretend food) foster active learning and meaning making.*
6. Motivation grows with belonging	*Visual cues, multilingual materials, and family connections create inclusive, safe environments. Children's cultural and linguistic backgrounds are reflected and celebrated.*

continued on following page

Table 6. Continued

Principle	*Evidence in the Lesson Plan*
7. Learning is interdisciplinary	*Content areas such as literacy, math, science, social studies, and art are woven into centers and group activities under the common theme of the five senses.*
8. Challenge supports growth	*Tasks are scaffolded (e.g., sorting complexity, vocabulary levels) and responsive to children's needs. Teachers are encouraged to reflect daily on adjustments needed to support continued growth.*
9. Technology can be a tool	*Technology is not used in this lesson, which aligns with recommendations for this age group. The plan appropriately focuses on hands-on and relational learning, which are essential for preschoolers.*

Strengths

- *Holistic, hands-on learning across multiple domains*
- *Clear DAP alignment with evidence-based accommodations*
- *Culturally sustaining elements built into both classroom and family connections*
- *Predictable routines and visual supports to foster self-regulation and security*

Recommendations for Enhancement

- *Consider increasing the role of child-led inquiry (e.g., allowing children to design their own sensory stations or choose order of exploration).*
- *Add explicit time for unstructured, imaginative play beyond themed centers (e.g., open-ended materials or dramatic play not tied to the five senses).*
- *Include opportunities for teacher reflection on how play and DAP principles were observed and supported during the week.*

ChatGPT does a decent job analyzing the comprehensive prompt lesson plan. It looks for the three core considerations of DAP, and the nine principles of learning. The critique offers strength of the lesson plan and recommendations for enhancement. This critique offers a valuable starting point for pre-service teachers learning evidence-based practice. Generative AI learns over time and is growing to be a better collaborator with early childhood educators to design research-based lessons and environments.

Discussion

The lesson plan aligns with the core considerations and principles of child development and learning more richly and comprehensively than the previous two plans. ChatGPT was able to evaluate the Claude-created plan with attention to key elements of developmentally appropriate practice, highlighting both strengths and areas for improvement. One notable recommendation is the inclusion of more opportunities for unstructured, imaginative play, which supports creativity, social-emotional development, and problem-solving skills. Additionally, the plan could be strengthened by incorporating more child-led inquiry, which fosters autonomy, critical thinking, and engagement through exploration and discovery.

In the created scenario, Ms. Meroudjie offers a template for evaluating lesson plans and thinking about specificity and assessment of prompts and outputs (Figure 4).

Figure 4. Steps to collaborate with AI in lesson design

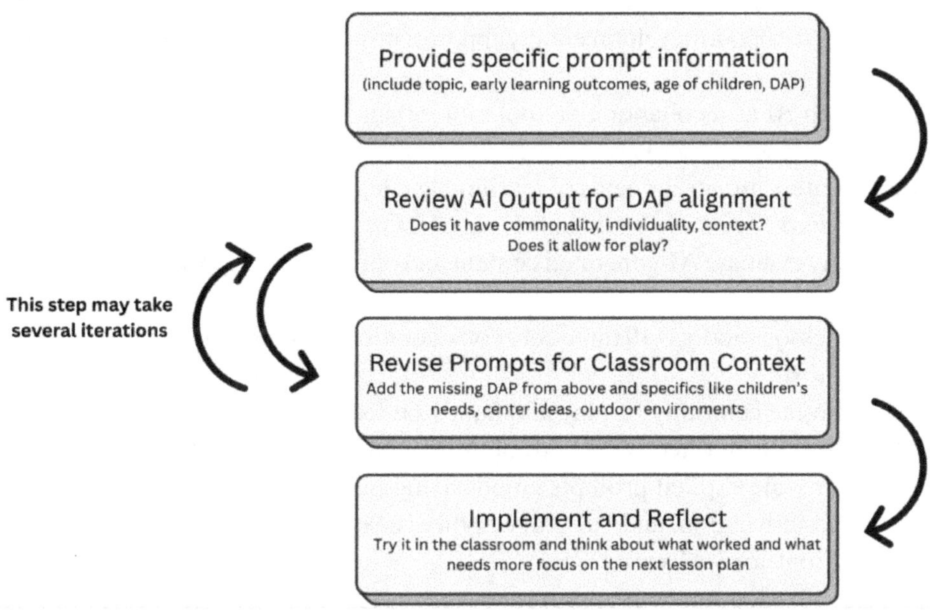

In addition, in Appendix A, the authors have created a *Rubric for Evaluating AI Lesson Plans for Developmentally Appropriate Practices* for both preservice and in-service teachers to begin the application of the core considerations in ECE lesson planning. Each consideration is assessed individually and the teacher is asked to reflect on specific aspects of each consideration. This reflection makes explicit key ideas in each consideration that can be internalized over time when reviewing teacher-generated and AI-generated lesson plans.

It is important to recognize that different AI platforms—such as Claude and ChatGPT—can vary significantly in their output and recommendations, even when given similar prompts. These differences stem not only from the design and training data of the AI models themselves but also from the way users interact with them. The language used in prompts, the specificity of instructions, and the background knowledge of the user can all shape the final product. Therefore, educators using AI for lesson planning or evaluation must approach AI-generated content with a critical lens, understanding both its potential and its limitations. As the field of generative AI continues to evolve, so too must our strategies for using it ethically, responsibly, and effectively in educational settings.

Recommendations

Integrating AI into early childhood lesson planning offers both opportunities and challenges. To maintain developmentally appropriate practices (DAP), educators must:

1. Approach AI as a collaborative tool rather than a replacement for professional expertise. The teacher is the expert. Technology enhances rather than replaces the essential human elements of teaching and learning (AbuSahyon et al., 2023; Park & Park, 2024; Setyaningsih et al., 2024).
2. Critically evaluate AI-generated content and outputs thoroughly through a DAP lens.
3. Ensure lessons address all three core considerations: commonality, individuality, and context.
4. Maintain the centrality of play and hands-on learning experiences.
5. Develop skills in effective AI prompting and iterative refinement:
    - Provide explicit prompts emphasizing play-based learning, differentiated instruction, and cultural responsiveness.
    - Front-load AI with:
        i. developmentally appropriate principles
        ii. specific content for lesson plan creation
        iii. standards and classroom demographics
    - Be prepared for multiple iterations of lesson plans.
6. Recognize the limitations of AI in understanding cultural context and providing culturally sensitive support.

7. Take steps to maintain confidentiality and privacy of children's and families' information by omitting names and any other identifying information in AI prompts and uploaded data. Obtain parental consent before uploading any child's data into AI and use a secure platform.

Further research is needed to establish best practices for AI use in early childhood lesson planning, particularly regarding play-based learning and addressing diverse needs within multicultural and special education contexts. The emerging research in language education (AbuSahyon et al., 2023; Setyaningsih et al., 2024) provides valuable models for how to study and evaluate AI's effectiveness in early childhood educational settings.

Professional Development and Trainings

The final recommendation is to increase the knowledge base and expertise of teachers of essential skills (Figure 5) in two areas: developmentally appropriate practices and strategies and Artificial Intelligence. Developmentally appropriate strategies include: developmental knowledge (understanding how children grow and learn), differentiation strategies (adapting for diverse learners), and reflection and refinement (the process of analyzing and adjusting curriculum to best suit the learners). Essential artificial intelligence skills include: prompting skills (how to ask AI clear and specific questions), ethical awareness (understanding privacy, confidentiality and responsible AI use), and adopting a collaboration mindset (using AI as a tool rather than a replacement).

Through professional development, teacher education programs and training, educators can become grounded in developmentally appropriate practices and research and evidence-based strategies so they can be able to develop high-quality curriculum and environments, create effective prompts, and critically assess AI lesson plans. Teacher education programs should incorporate explicit training on AI collaboration, ethics, privacy laws, as well as, intentional, effective practices for AI lesson planning in early childhood classrooms. Partnering with state professional development systems to offer training in these essential skills would be beneficial in supporting educators already in the workforce as they explore and integrate AI tools into their classroom practices.

Figure 5. Essential skills for AI use for educators

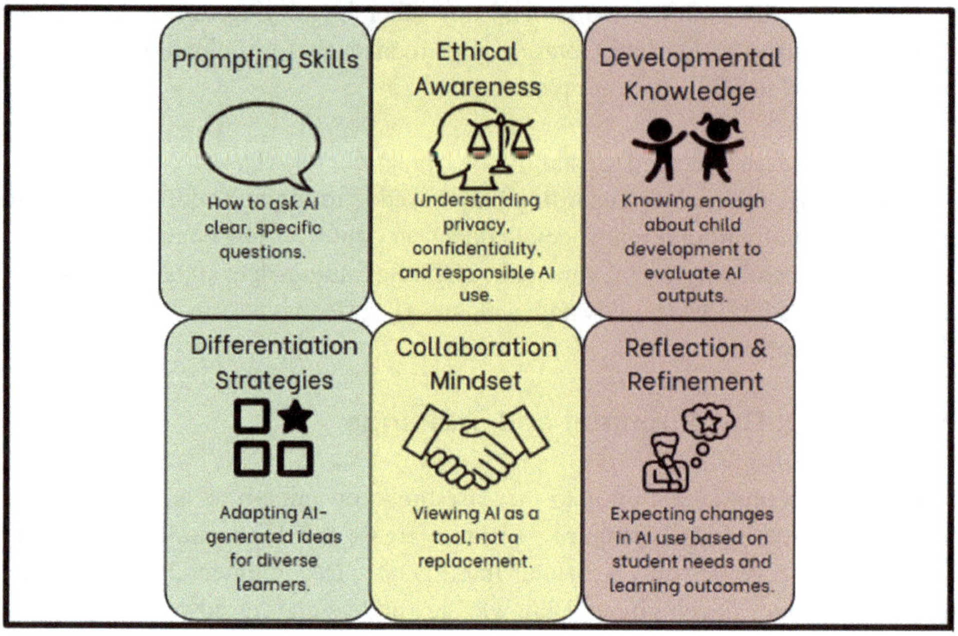

What's Next?

As the field of education is expanding to embrace and integrate generative AI into lesson planning, this chapter ends offering an exciting next step for educator preparation programs to help pre-service teachers develop the NAEYC professional standards and competencies, create responsive classrooms and develop ethical and reflective use of chatbots.

In March 2025, Myers and Jeter (A. Myers, personal communication, March 29, 2025) created a chatbot called Joy Junction. Joy Junction is designed to help teachers make their pre-existing lesson plans more culturally responsive based on Goldie Muhammad's Equity Framework for Culturally and Historically Responsive Literacy. In the design, Myers and Jeter programmed the chatbot not to use euro-centric algorithms, to be encouraging to the learner, and create inclusive, culture sustaining, and interdisciplinary lesson plans.

The impetus for the creation of this Chatbot was to provide a reflective collaborator for students designing their lesson plans. As the learner begins to use Joy Junction, the chatbot states "Welcome to Joyful Junction! Are you ready to make your classroom be more inclusive and equitable to all your learners?" This positions the learner to be inclusive of all learners in the classroom including those with diagnosed exceptionalities and dual language learners.

Next, the chatbot prompts for demographic questions of individual learners and their needs in order to focus the lesson and then create the lesson plan. Joy Junction then provides an analysis based on the Equity Framework highlighting the pillars (Identity, Skills, Intellect, Criticality, and Joy) already embedded and strategies to incorporate the ones not included. Specific examples like "create a sensory break option with a fidget tool" students can ask Joy Junction to explain what a sensory break is if it's a new concept.

Joy Junction helps to translate key phrases to languages of all learners in the classroom. It also asks if you would like to see all the learning standards (Texas standards: PK guidelines, TEKS and ELPS (English Language Proficiency Standards are preloaded) to broaden the interdisciplinary impact of the lesson.

After tailoring the lesson, Joy Junction asks students with reflective questions focused on the accuracy of the modifications and the reasoning behind why it is culturally responsive. In addition, the Chatbot gives specific activities and student prompts and questions that other researchers have found lacking in general generative AI. At the end the chatbot asks how accurate the recommendations are for better feedback for the next lesson plan.

This will be a powerful tool for educator preparation programs to effectively train teachers in the collaborative use of AI and as more faculty become trained and skilled, more chatbots can be created for these reflective, inclusive lesson planning experiences. This is a new frontier where teacher educators can create chatbots to provide more individualized, age-appropriate in context, specific activities and questions for our youngest learners to ensure that all core considerations are addressed and make sure learning is play-based.

CONCLUSION

As this chapter demonstrates, integrating artificial intelligence into early childhood lesson planning presents both promising opportunities and important responsibilities. When guided by the principles of Developmentally Appropriate Practice (DAP), AI can support educators in creating meaningful, individualized, and culturally relevant learning experiences. However, this potential is only realized when teachers remain at the center of decision-making, applying their professional judgment to evaluate and adapt AI-generated content.

AI does not replace the educator's expertise in child development, family partnerships, and ethical practices. It is a collaborator that can amplify effective planning when prompted with care and intention. This partnership relies on educators' ability to front-load AI tools with detailed information about children's developmental stages, individual needs, classroom contexts, and curricular goals. As seen in the case studies, the specificity and quality of prompts directly impact the developmental appropriateness of AI-generated lesson plans.

To fully harness the benefits of AI in early childhood education, teacher preparation programs must take the lead. Future educators need training not only in how to use generative AI but also in how to critique its outputs, integrate DAP principles, and uphold ethical standards. The development of culturally responsive tools like the Joy Junction chatbot signals a promising direction—one in which AI is purpose-built to support equity, inclusion, and joy in early learning environments.

Ultimately, the integration of AI in early childhood education should be approached with both optimism and caution. The goal is not simply to modernize lesson planning, but to enrich it—ensuring that all children receive play-based, joyful learning experiences that honor who they are, how they learn, and the communities they come from. As the field evolves, early childhood educators will continue to be essential in shaping how technology serves the youngest learners, grounding innovation in developmental science, cultural competence, and the human connections at the heart of teaching.

REFERENCES

AbuSahyon, A. S. A. E., Alzyoud, A., Alshorman, O., & Al-Absi, B. (2023). AI-driven technology and Chatbots as tools for enhancing English language learning in the context of second language acquisition: A review study. *International Journal of Membrane Science and Technology*, *10*(1), 1209–1223. DOI: 10.15379/ijmst.v10i1.2829

Adams, C., Pente, P., Lemermeyer, G., & Rockwell, G. (2023). Ethical principles for artificial intelligence in K-12 education. *Computers & Education*, *4*, 1–10. DOI: 10.1016/j.caeai.2023.100131

Akgun, S., & Greenhow, C. (2022). Artificial intelligence in education: Addressing ethical challenges in K-12 settings. *AI and Ethics*, *2*(3), 431–440. DOI: 10.1007/s43681-021-00096-7 PMID: 34790956

Bodrova, E., & Leong, D. J. (2015). Vygotskian and post-Vygotskian views on children's play. *American Journal of Play*, *7*(3), 371–388.

Bruner, J. (1983). Play, Thought, and Language. *Peabody Journal of Education*, *60*(3), 60–69. https://www.jstor.org/stable/1492180. DOI: 10.1080/01619568309538407

Cooper, G. (2023). Examining Science Education in ChatGPT: An exploratory study of generative artificial intelligence. *Journal of Science Education and Technology*, *32*(3), 444–452. Advance online publication. DOI: 10.1007/s10956-023-10039-y

Council for Exceptional Children. (2015). What every special educator must know: Professional ethics and standards (7th ed.). Arlington, VA: CEC. https://exceptionalchildren.org/sites/default/files/2020-07/Code%20of%20Ethics.pdf

Darling-Hammond, L. (2000). Teacher quality and student achievement. *Education Policy Analysis Archives*, *8*(1), 1–44. DOI: 10.14507/epaa.v8n1.2000

Division for Early Childhood. (2022). Position statement on ethical practice. Council for Exceptional Children. https://divisionearlychildhood.egnyte.com/dl/KAh4cOFBZ8

Elkind, D. (2007). *The power of play: How spontaneous imaginative activities lead to happier, healthier children*. Da Capo Press.

Escobar, A. (2013). *The home language advantage: Using children's primary language to build literacy skills*. English Language Learning ReSource. https://inside.isb.ac.th/nativelanguage/files/2016/03/home-language-advantage.pdf

Gayatri, M., & Pau, N. (2022). Teacher reflective perceptions on artificial intelligence integrated science lesson plans. *The Educational Beacon*, *11*, 12–23.

Gesell, A. (1925). *The mental growth of the pre-school child: A psychological outline of normal development from birth to the sixth year, including a system of development diagnosis*. Macmillan.

Giang, I. T. N., & Park, M. (2022). *Dual language learners: Key characteristics and considerations for early childhood programs*. https://www.migrationpolicy.org/research/dual-language-learner-characteristics

Guddemi, M., Sambrook, A., Wells, S., Randel, B., Fite, K., Selva, G., & Gagnon, K. (2014). Arnold Gesell's developmental assessment revalidation substantiates child-oriented curriculum. *SAGE Open*, *4*(2), 2158244014528918. Advance online publication. DOI: 10.1177/2158244014528918

Idaho Department of Health and Welfare. (2021a). *About Idaho Early Learning eGuidelines*. Idaho Early Learning eGuidelines. https://healthandwelfare.idaho.gov/services- programs/about-idaho-early-learning-eguidelines

Idaho Department of Health and Welfare. (2021b). *Sub-domain: Motor development*. Idaho Early Learning eGuidelines. https://healthandwelfare.idaho.gov/services-programs/sub-domain-motor-development

Kanders, K., Stupple-Harris, L., Smith, L., & Gibson, J. L. (2024). Perspectives on the impact of generative AI on early-childhood development and education. *Infant and Child Development*, *33*(4), e2514. DOI: 10.1002/icd.2514

Krause, S. D. (2000). "Among the greatest benefactors of mankind": What the success of chalkboards tells us about the future of computers in the classroom. *The Journal of the Midwest Modern Language Association*, *33*(2), 6–16. DOI: 10.2307/1315198

Lammert, C., DeJulio, S., Grote-Garcia, S., & Fraga, L. M. (2024). Better than nothing? An analysis of AI-generated lesson plans using the Universal Design for Learning & Transition frameworks. *The Clearing House: A Journal of Educational Strategies, Issues and Ideas*, *97*(5), 168–175. DOI: 10.1080/00098655.2024.2427332

Landreth, G. L. (2002). Therapeutic limit setting in the play therapy relationship. *Professional Psychology, Research and Practice*, *33*(6), 529–535. DOI: 10.1037/0735-7028.33.6.529

Lozano, J. R., Ramos, Y., Tecnologia, E., & Cruz, C. E. C. (2024). *Enhancing English language teaching through AI: The case of Magic School AI*. https://www.researchgate.net/profile/Jean-Paul-Rojas-2/publication/388757322_ Enhancing_English_Language_Teaching_Through_AI_The_Case_of_Magic_School_AI/ links/67a4eb53461fb56424cc7bbc/Enhancing-English-Language-Teaching-Through-AI- The-Case-of-Magic-School-AI.pdf

McCormack, V. (2024). Employing AI for instructional planning, teaching, and learning. *Proceedings from SITE conference*.

Moses, A. (2022). DAP and playful learning: Equitable approaches. *Young Children, 77*(2). https://www.naeyc.org/resources/pubs/yc/summer2022/dap-and-playful-learning

National Association for the Education of Young Children. (2020). *Developmentally appropriate practice: A position statement of the National Association for the Education of Young Children*. NAEYC. https://www.naeyc.org

National Association for the Education of Young Children. (2020). Professional Standards and Competencies for Early Childhood Educators. https://www.naeyc.org/sites/default/files/globally-shared/downloads/PDFs/ resources/position-statements/standards_and_competencies_ps.pdf

National Association for the Education of Young Children. (2024). *About us*. https://www.naeyc.org/about-us

National Association for the Education of Young Children. (2024). Code of ethics for early childhood educators (Draft Revision). NAEYC. https://www.naeyc.org/sites/default/files/globally-shared/downloads/PDFs/ 2024_code_of_ethics_for_early_childhood_educators_final_3.pdf

National Center on Early Childhood Quality Assurance. (2016). *Early learning standards and guidelines*. U.S. Department of Health & Human Services. https://childcareta.acf.hhs.gov

Park, H. K., & Park, J. (2024). Lesson plan development for pre-service elementary school teachers through collaboration with AI: Focused on ChatGPT. New Physics: Sae Mulli. DOI: 10.3938/NPSM.74.215

Pearce, N. (2024). Revolutionising modern teaching with AI technology. *Education Journal Review, 29*(3), 148–154.

Piaget, J. (1962). *Play, dreams, and imitation in childhood* (Gattegno, G., & Hodgson, F. M., Trans.). W. W. Norton.

Powell, W., & Courchesne, S. (2024). Opportunities and risks involved in using ChatGPT to create first grade science lesson plans. *PLoS One, 19*(6), e0305337. Advance online publication. DOI: 10.1371/journal.pone.0305337 PMID: 38885244

Rice, M. F., & Dunn, S. (2023). The use of artificial intelligence with students with identified disabilities: A systematic review with critique. *Computers in the Schools, 40*(4), 370–390. DOI: 10.1080/07380569.2023.2244935

Sanders, B., Zuckerman, K., Ash, J.S., Kopstick, A.J., Rivas Vazquez, L., Gorman, P. N. (2022). Early intervention referral information, transmission, and sources—A survey of state Part C Coordinators and Analysis of Referral Forms. *Journal of Developmental & Behavioral Pediatrics 43*(3), 153-161, | DOI: DOI: 10.1097/DBP.0000000000001004

Setyaningsih, E., Asrori, M., Ngadiso, , Sumardi, , Zainnuri, H., & Hariyanti, Y. (2024). Exploring high school EFL teachers' experiences with Magic School AI in lesson planning. *Voices of English Language Education Society, 8*(3). Advance online publication. DOI: 10.29408/veles.v8i3.27700

Sheehan, T. (2023). Generative AI in education: Past, present, and future. *Educause Review*. https://er.educause.edu/articles/sponsored/2023/9/generative-ai-in-education-past-present-and-future

Shonkoff, J. P., & Phillips, D. A. (Eds.). (2000). *From neurons to neighborhoods: The science of early childhood development*. National Academies Press., https://www.ncbi.nlm.nih.gov/books/NBK225562/

Stone, P., Brooks, R., Brynjolfsson, E., Calo, R., Etzioni, O., Hager, G., Hirschberg, J., Kalyanakrishnan, S., Kamar, E., Kraus, S., Leyton-Brown, K., Parkes, D., Press, W., Saxenian, A., Shah, J., Tambe, M., & Teller, A. (2016, September). *Artificial intelligence and life in 2030*. One Hundred Year Study on Artificial Intelligence: Report of the 2015-2016 Study Panel, Stanford University. https://ai100.stanford.edu/2016-report

Stryker, C., & Kavlakoglu, E. (2024, August 9). *What is AI?* IBM. https://www.ibm.com/think/topics/artificial-intelligence

Texas Education Agency. (2022). *Texas prekindergarten guidelines: PK3 and PK4 comprehensive guide*. https://tea.texas.gov

U.S. Department of Education. (2019). *Individuals with Disabilities Education Act, Section 1414(d)(3): Individualized education programs—Development of IEP*. https://sites.ed.gov/idea/statute-chapter-33/subchapter-ii/1414/d/3

U.S. Department of Health & Human Services. (2025). *Head Start programs.* Head Start. https://headstart.gov

U.S. Department of State. (2020). National Artificial Intelligence Act of 2020. https://www.state.gov/artificial-intelligence/

Vygotsky, L. S. (2004). Imagination and creativity in childhood. *Journal of Russian & East European Psychology*, *42*(1), 7–97. DOI: 10.1080/10610405.2004.11059210

Weiner, S., Lake, R., & Rosner, J. (2024, October). *AI is evolving, but teacher prep is lagging: A first look at teacher preparation program responses to AI.* Center on Reinventing Public Education. https://crpe.org

Yilmaz Can, D., & Durmus, C. (2024). From AI-generated lesson plans to the real-life classes: Explored by pre-service teachers. *10th International Conference on Higher Education Advances (HEAd'24)*, Valencia, June 18-21, 2024. https://doi.org/DOI: 10.4995/HEAd24.2024.17060

APPENDIX A

Rubric for Evaluating AI Lesson Plans for Developmentally Appropriate Practices

Created by Quong & Matthews, 2025

For each item, give a score 1-4: 1 = Not there at all 2 = Kind of there 3 = Definitely there 4 = Well done.

Part 1: Commonality (Things True for All Children)

Table 7. Physical and Brain Development

1	**Lesson doesn't match how children this age typically develop.**
2	Lesson somewhat matches typical development but misses some important things.
3	Lesson fits well with how children this age typically develop.
4	Lesson perfectly matches typical development patterns and helps children grow.

Table 8. Body, Mind, Feelings, and Social Skills

1	**Lesson only focuses on one part of the child (like just their mind).**
2	Lesson includes different parts but doesn't connect them.
3	Lesson connects different parts of development (body, mind, feelings, social).
4	Lesson weaves together all parts of development in a way that makes sense.

Table 9. Learning Through Play and Experience

1	**Lesson is all sitting and listening with no active learning or play.**
2	Lesson has some active parts but they don't seem meaningful.
3	Lesson includes hands-on learning that helps children understand.
4	Lesson perfectly balances active learning, play, and direct teaching.

Part 2: Individuality (Every Child is Unique)

Table 10. Different Abilities and Learning Styles

1	**Lesson treats all children the same with no room for differences.**
2	Lesson mentions differences but doesn't really adjust for them.
3	Lesson includes specific ways to help different kinds of learners.
4	Lesson has many flexible ways for children with different abilities to succeed.

Table 11. Personal Interests and Strengths

1	**Lesson ignores children' personal interests and strengths.**
2	Lesson briefly mentions interests but doesn't build on them.
3	Lesson connects to things children might be interested in.
4	Lesson allows children to use their unique strengths and follow their interests.

Table 12. Choice and Voice

1	**Lesson gives children no choices or ways to express themselves.**
2	Lesson gives a few simple choices but they don't matter much.
3	Lesson includes meaningful choices and ways for children to share ideas.
4	Lesson empowers children to make important decisions and express their unique thoughts.

Part 3: Context (The World Around the Child)

Table 13. Family and Community Connections

1	**Lesson has no connection to families, communities, or real life.**
2	Lesson makes a few general connections but they feel forced.
3	Lesson connects learning to families and communities in meaningful ways.
4	Lesson integrates family and community knowledge and experiences.

Table 14. Cultural Responsiveness

1	**Lesson shows no awareness of cultural differences.**
2	Lesson mentions culture but in a surface-level or stereotypical way.
3	Lesson respects and includes different cultural perspectives.
4	Lesson authentically integrates diverse cultural knowledge and practices.

Table 15. Real-World Application

1	**Lesson teaches skills with no connection to how they're used in real life.**
2	Lesson mentions real-world connections but they feel artificial.
3	Lesson shows how learning applies to real situations children understand.
4	Lesson makes learning meaningful by connecting directly to children' lives and communities.

Your Final Thoughts

What's good about this lesson?
What could be better?
How would you make it better?

Think about how you could improve this lesson plan by adding:

- Connections to your own culture and community
- Things that match children' specific interests in your class
- Local resources you know about
- Changes that would help specific children you know

Total Score: _____ / 36

Table 16. Overall Rating

Score	What It Means
32-36	Awesome! This lesson plan is really good for children
27-31	Pretty Good - This lesson plan works well but needs a few small fixes
18-26	Needs Work - This lesson plan shows some understanding but needs big changes
Below 17	Start Over - This lesson plan needs to be completely redone to be good for children

APPENDIX B

Glossary of Key Terms

The following glossary defines key terms used throughout this chapter. It is designed to support readers in understanding the essential concepts related to artificial intelligence, early childhood education, and developmentally appropriate practice. These definitions aim to make the content accessible to a broad audience, including educators, families, and students who are new to the field.

Table 17.

Term	Definition
Artificial Intelligence (AI)	Technology that enables machines to perform tasks that typically require human intelligence, such as learning, problem-solving, decision-making, and understanding language.
Large Language Model (LLM)	A type of AI trained on large datasets of text to generate human-like responses and assist with tasks like writing, translating, and answering questions. Examples include ChatGPT and Claude.
lesson plan	A teacher's guide that outlines what students will learn, how they will learn it, and how progress will be assessed. Lesson plans support intentional teaching aligned with developmental goals.
Developmentally Appropriate Practice (DAP)	Teaching methods that promote each child's optimal development based on age, individual needs, and cultural background. DAP includes three core considerations: commonality, individuality, and context.
commonality	The general knowledge about how children typically develop across ages and stages. This guides educators in understanding what is generally appropriate for each developmental level.
individuality	Recognizing and planning for each child's unique strengths, needs, interests, and learning styles. Part of the DAP framework.
context	The social, cultural, and environmental factors that shape a child's learning experiences. Educators consider context to ensure culturally and linguistically responsive teaching.
COPPA (Children's Online Privacy Protection Act)	A U.S. law that protects children's privacy online by requiring parental consent for collecting data from children under the age of 13.
FERPA (Family Educational Rights and Privacy Act)	A U.S. law that protects the privacy of student education records and gives families rights over their child's information.
confidentiality	The ethical and legal responsibility to keep private and sensitive information, such as child records and family date, secure and protected from unauthorized access or disclosure.
Dual Language Learner (DLL)	A child who is learning two or more languages at the same time, often speaking a home language and learning English in an educational setting.

continued on following page

Table 17. Continued

Term	Definition
Culturally Responsive Teaching	Teaching practices that recognize and honor students' cultural identities, languages, and lived experiences as valuable resources in learning.
differentiation	Adjusting instruction to meet the diverse needs, strengths, and interests of individual learners, ensuring all students can access the curriculum meaningfully.
ethics in education	The principles and standards guiding professional behavior in teaching, including fairness, respect, responsibility, and adherence to codes such as those by NAEYC, DEC, and CEC.
prompting (AI)	The process of giving specific instructions or questions to an AI system to generate a desired response or outcome. Prompting is key to effectively using AI tools like ChatGPT for lesson planning.
privacy	The protection of personal information from unauthorized access, use, or disclosure, especially important when using technology with children.
accessibility	Designing content and tools so they can be used by all learners, including those with disabilities or different learning needs.
professional development (PD)	Ongoing learning opportunities that help educators improve their knowledge and skills, such as developing AI literacy or integrating technology effectively in the classroom.
collaborative planning	A teaching approach where educators—and potentially AI tools—work together to design and improve learning experiences that are responsive to children's needs.

*terms are grouped by topic and chapter organization rather than alphabetically

Chapter 3

Psychological and Developmental Repercussions of Pervasive AI Usage in Schools:

A Review of Educational Benefits and Challenges

Manuel B. Garcia
https://orcid.org/0000-0003-2615-422X
FEU Institute of Technology, Philippines

Ahmed Hosny Saleh Metwally
https://orcid.org/0000-0002-9545-5870
Helwan University, Egypt

Tianchong Wang
Flinders University, Australia

Kingsley Ofosu-Ampong
https://orcid.org/0000-0003-0561-6376
Heritage Christian University, Ghana

Rena Alasgarova
Baku-Oxford School, Azerbaijan

Chrissi Nerantzi
University of Leeds, UK

James Nixon
Arden University, UK

Aras Bozkurt
https://orcid.org/0000-0002-4520-642X
Anadolu University, Turkey

ABSTRACT

This chapter explores the developmental implications of artificial intelligence (AI) in contemporary educational settings. Employing a dual-methodological approach

DOI: 10.4018/979-8-3373-6007-2.ch003

that combines interdisciplinary expertise with an integrative literature review, the chapter explores how AI technologies are reshaping student identity, emotional regulation, motivation, autonomy, and interpersonal relationships. Drawing on developmental psychology, educational theory, and empirical research, it interrogates the unintended consequences of algorithmic surveillance, pedagogical automation, and AI mediated social interactions. The analysis highlights both the affordances and risks of AI in education, including its impact on emotional resilience, self-directed learning, and the construction of academic identity. Reframing the discourse away from purely technical efficiency toward developmental integrity makes visible the deeper human stakes of AI integration in education. The chapter consequently calls for ethical, inclusive, and human-centered approaches to AI design and implementation in schools.

INTRODUCTION

Once reserved for science fiction and Silicon Valley demos, artificial intelligence (AI) is now marking attendance, grading essays, and whispering answers in students' ears. In just a few short years, AI has evolved from an educational accessory to an embedded agent in everyday school life. Across classrooms, learning platforms, and assessment systems, AI technologies are being deployed to personalize instruction, automate feedback, and optimize learning pathways (Mittal et al., 2024; Pitrella et al., 2024). No longer confined to niche pilot programs, AI now plays a structural role in shaping how curricula are delivered and how learning is experienced. These advances are reshaping pedagogical norms and transforming how students interact with knowledge, authority, and even themselves. The discourse surrounding AI in education often highlights its efficiency and potential to democratize learning, but much less attention is given to its latent effects on the psychological and developmental fabric of the learner (Ali et al., 2024).

As these AI-powered systems become more affectively responsive, more socially performative, and more integrated into the rhythms of schooling, they transform from supportive tools into active shapers of the learning experience. What was once a tool has become a co-participant in the learning process that is capable of influencing students' emotional states, self-perception, and motivation (Hulus, 2025; N. Wang et al., 2024; Wiese et al., 2025). Their presence can influence how students perceive success, engage with struggle, and construct academic identity over time. In environments where digital agents offer constant feedback and predictive guidance, learners may internalize different conceptions of effort, mastery, and autonomy than in traditionally human-led settings (Bilquise et al., 2022; Garcia, 2025; Venter et al., 2024). These systems, in their pursuit of optimization, may inadvertently signal to students that ambiguity, failure, or slow progress is undesirable. Unfortunately, these subtle yet persistent messages risk undermining key dispositions such as persistence, curiosity, and self-regulation. Over time, such conditioning could contribute to diminished tolerance for uncertainty, reliance on machine authority, or even attenuated interpersonal empathy in peer interactions.

This shift raises profound questions about how AI may be influencing not just academic outcomes but the cognitive, emotional, and social development of students across age groups. What kind of learners, and ultimately, what kind of people, are we cultivating in an AI-mediated environment? As students increasingly engage with machine agents in place of, or in addition to, human teachers and peers, they may be absorbing new models of interaction, authority, and relational dynamics. For instance, consider students who turn to an AI chatbot instead of a classmate for clarification, or who rely on automated praise rather than developing self-assessment skills. When the relational dynamics of learning are increasingly governed by algorithms, we must ask what we are gaining, and what might we be losing. Therefore, this chapter calls for a shift in focus from merely quantifying AI's instructional effectiveness to interrogating its deeper developmental consequences. It seeks to reframe the conversation around AI in education by asking not only what these systems can do, but what kind of learners and learning cultures they help create. By elevating this dimension of inquiry, we aim to foreground student well-being, identity, and emotional integrity as central concerns in the evolving relationship between AI and education. Against this backdrop, it becomes essential to examine the broader developmental consequences of pervasive AI use in educational contexts.

MAIN FOCUS OF THE CHAPTER

AI, like previous waves of technological innovation in education, presents both opportunities and unintended consequences. As AI tools become increasingly embedded in the everyday functioning of schools, they begin to shape not only pedagogical practices but also the psychological and developmental trajectories of students. While the educational benefits of AI are often emphasized, there is growing concern about its pervasive and potentially intrusive role in shaping students' behavior, cognition, and social interactions. Technologies, especially those that mediate learning and assessment, inevitably influence the ways students engage with knowledge, perceive themselves, and interact with peers and authority figures. Despite the accelerating integration of AI in educational environments, there remains a notable research gap regarding its broader developmental and psychological repercussions. Existing studies often focus on technical efficacy, learning outcomes, and teacher adoption, with far less attention to the socio-emotional and cognitive implications for students across different age groups and learning contexts. As such, there is a need for a more comprehensive understanding of how pervasive AI usage affects identity formation, motivation, attention spans, critical thinking abilities, and emotional resilience. This chapter addresses this gap by providing a critical review of the psychological and developmental implications of AI's presence in educational settings. Specifically, this chapter explores both the benefits and risks associated with widespread AI implementation in schools, with an emphasis on long-term student well-being and developmental integrity.

METHODS

This chapter adopts a dual methodological approach to examine the developmental implications of AI in educational contexts. The first component of the methodology involves leveraging interdisciplinary expertise, drawing from the collective knowledge of contributing researchers across the domains of artificial intelligence, educational technology, developmental psychology, and pedagogy (Xiao et al., 2025). This collaborative, cross-disciplinary lens aligns with the principles of transdisciplinary research (Max-Neef, 2005), which emphasizes the integration of multiple knowledge systems to address complex societal challenges (e.g., the psychological and pedagogical impacts of emerging technologies). The second component is a comprehensive review of existing literature. This includes an integrative analysis of empirical studies, theoretical frameworks, and policy-oriented discussions related to AI in education. The literature review follows the guidance of Torraco (2016), who advocates for integrative reviews as a means of synthesizing diverse bodies of work to advance understanding and generate new conceptual insights. To ensure both breadth and depth, the review includes sources drawn from peer-reviewed journal articles, conference proceedings, and scholarly book chapters, with a focus on contributions from educational and psychological scholarship. This dual approach is particularly well-suited to the rapidly evolving nature of AI in education, where technological advancement often outpaces ethical and developmental understanding (Gantalao et al., 2025; Mangubat et al., 2025). By combining technical and theoretical perspectives, this methodology supports a more holistic and developmentally grounded analysis of AI's impact on learners.

PSYCHOLOGICAL AND DEVELOPMENTAL REPERCUSSIONS

Learning Engagement and Inclusion

Education is about awakening minds, triggering curiosity and wonder, and making a difference (Freire, 2007). There is evidence that young people want to contribute to solving some of the wicked challenges of our times, and that this desire serves as a strong motivator for learning. Triggering criticality and creativity in students is vital for inspiring their learning, enabling meaningful connections, and supporting their positive contributions to society and the planet during volatile and unpredictable times. This process also involves the thoughtful integration of AI. The activation of minds and hearts happens when learning is authentic, purposeful, and engaging and when flexibility is built into the learning experience to stimulate growth and transformation. Critical self-reflection on one's assumptions and the reframing of one's positionality, beliefs, and actions are key (Mezirow, 1978). Therefore, questioning and (self-)criticality are key for transformative learning experiences. Slee (2018) emphasized inclusive education is grounded in the pursuit of fairness, justice, and equity. It represents both a political commitment and an educational strategy. Achieving an inclusive society requires teaching practices that accommodate all students, including those with disabilities. The structure of the curriculum, pedagogy, assessment methods, and physical learning spaces can either foster inclusion or create barriers. How can we create powerful learning opportunities for all students (UNESCO, 2020)? How can we ensure an inclusive approach that enables critical and creative engagement in learning for everyone? Diverse and varied learning and teaching approaches, including multimedia, tools, and resources, are vital to inclusive pedagogy. These approaches create fertile spaces for critical and creative self-expression, offer choice, and support flexible engagement that suits individual learners while also stretching them.

However, there is currently limited evidence that AI has had a significant impact on inclusive practice (Díaz & Nussbaum, 2024). For some time, the opportunities for flexible connection and self-expression have been abundant, thanks to participatory pedagogies, digital networked technologies, the social web, multimedia, and open learning with people, ideas, resources, and tools. Does AI turn this offer into a superabundance? Not for all and certainly not by itself. AI does not automatically democratize education. In fact, digital inequality has grown, as access to AI remains uneven across the world (Bulathwela et al., 2024). Knowing how to harness the power of AI for learning is crucial. AI does not understand the truth or possess knowledge itself, and it struggles with complex reasoning. Its outputs are based on data, algorithms, and the prompts users provide. This is why learner criticality is essential, as well as understanding what AI can and cannot do and what responsible and ethical AI use looks like. Atenas et al. (2025) illuminated the importance of data and AI literacies. Participation and co-creation are key strategies to protect vulnerable individuals and groups and to mitigate the data asymmetries deeply rooted in existing power structures. For school students, AI literacy is particularly important, as it enables them not only to understand complex concepts but also to engage fully with AI and better prepare them for the job market and for life. Superficial use of AI can lead to the meaningless generation of outputs that mislead, miscommunicate, and hold little or no educational value. The two UNESCO AI competency frameworks, one for educators (Miao & Cukurova, 2024) and one for students (Miao et al., 2024) provide scaffolds for responsible AI integration into education that progressively develops deeper understanding and expands competencies for educators and students through the effective use and application of AI.

Support for Flexible Learning

A review of empirical and conceptual pedagogical frameworks for blended, fully online, and open settings revealed that four dimensions are particularly important when learning and teaching in technology-rich environments: choice, activity, facilitator support, and community (Nerantzi, 2018). These dimensions enable learning that is varied, flexible, and tailored to individuals' needs and aspirations. However, autonomy must be carefully balanced with appropriate scaffolding to ensure that too much choice does not become overwhelming. Bringing learners together into a community acknowledges the critical role of learning relationships and collaborative learning, both within and beyond formal courses, where diversity is valued as enrichment (OECD, 2023). Such space fosters growth and flourishing for all learners when psychological safety is present, where all voices are heard and respected, and where learning with and from each other is made possible. Learning is socially constructed, and it is through interactions, conversations, debates, and co-creation that individuals not only learn from others but also reduce power asymmetries, discover themselves, and deepen their understanding (Vygotsky, 1978). Conversation, dialogue, and co-creation remain central to the learning process. The deeper the engagement in learning, the more questions naturally emerge.

The pandemic revealed a dependency, and perhaps even over-reliance, on tutors for feedback and access to learning materials. Now, students increasingly turn to AI. Educators are not always available when learners have urgent questions, nor are peers always accessible for idea exchanges. Personalized learning supported by AI is becoming a reality. AI acts as a new learning companion that is available 24/7, ready to engage in conversation, provide feedback, and respond to unlimited queries without judgment. For some students, especially those less confident in sharing work-in-progress with others, this may be seen as a significant advantage. However, there are concerns. Could overuse and over-reliance on AI create new forms of dependency (Bozkurt et al., 2024)? Could it harm human-to-human relationships and reduce learners' comfort and confidence in dealing with interpersonal conflict, debate, and collaboration? Furthermore, if students are not critically engaging with AI-generated outputs, there is a risk of bypassing deep learning altogether, completing tasks and assessments strategically without meaningful cognitive development. Educators thus play a vital role in designing opportunities for flexible, AI-supported learning within the curriculum. This requires developing their own understanding and competencies in AI grounded in sound pedagogical principles (Díaz & Nussbaum, 2024). Educators must model the responsible and transparent use of AI, experiment thoughtfully, and design learning experiences that prioritize choice, responsibility, meaningful engagement, and assessment practices that foster agency, motivation, and a genuine desire to learn.

Figure 1. Sample math lessons from the DreamBox grades 6–8 environment

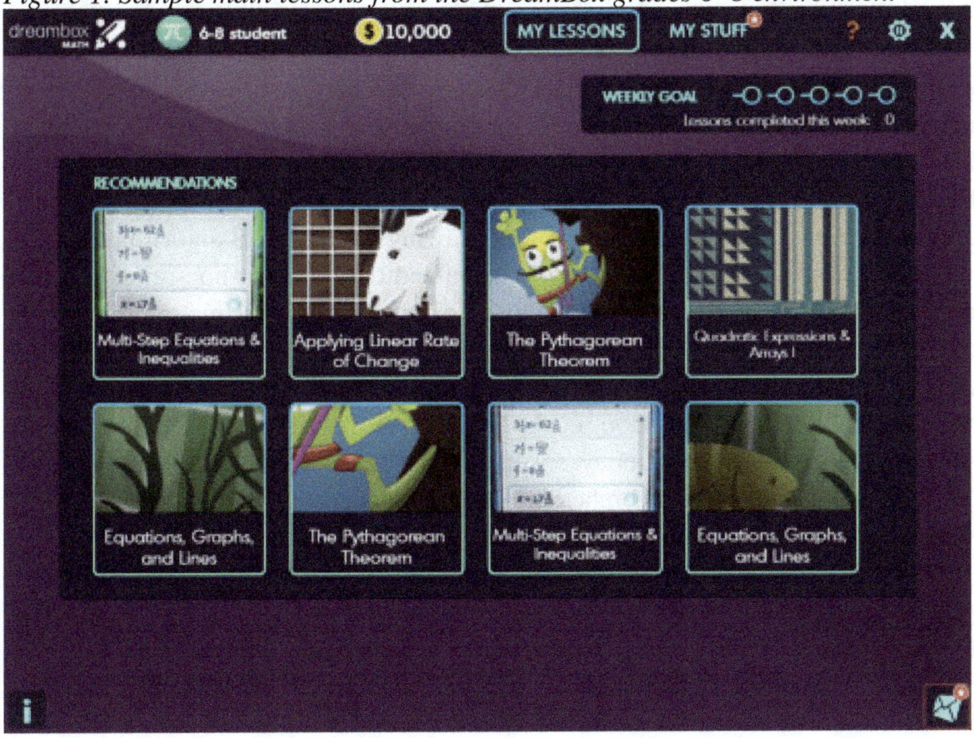

Feedback and Performance Monitoring

Amid the accelerating integration of AI into educational practice, few areas are as double-edged or as fundamentally transformative as feedback and performance monitoring. In line with behaviorist learning models, AI provides granular feedback that helps students identify errors and adjust their strategies in real time (Hulus, 2025). For instance, platforms such as *Khanmigo* now offer real-time corrective prompts during problem-solving tasks. Yet, while the promise of immediacy is substantial, the psychological risks are equally pronounced. According to the Self-Determination Theory, over-reliance on external feedback may undermine intrinsic motivation. Particularly in creative or subjective domains, instantaneous AI critiques may inadvertently stifle divergent thinking by encouraging conformity to algorithmic standards (Garcia, 2024). Thus, the pedagogical imperative is clear: AI-generated feedback must be strategically delayed or mediated in certain contexts to preserve critical self-assessment capacities and creative resilience. In terms of personalization, AI's ability to tailor feedback to individual learner profiles aligns with differentiated instruction models and universal design for learning (Sewell et al., 2022). By analyzing patterns in student work, AI systems can diagnose specific misconceptions and offer bespoke scaffolding. A case in point is adaptive learning platforms like *DreamBox* (Figure 1), which modulate mathematical instruction dynamically based on real-time learner performance. However, the promise of personalization is accompanied by significant equity risks. Drawing from critical algorithm studies, we must recognize that if AI systems are trained on biased or non-representative datasets, feedback could systematically disadvantage certain demographic groups (Acut, Malabago, et al., 2025; Bozkurt et al., 2024). In one real-world example, automated essay scoring algorithms were found to penalize essays written in non-standard dialects (Ofosu-Ampong et al., 2024). To mitigate these risks, policies must mandate algorithmic transparency, ensure diverse training datasets, and require that AI feedback mechanisms be embedded within broader dialogic feedback cultures where human educators contextualize and challenge AI outputs.

Another important point of consideration is that while AI's capacity for detailed performance monitoring enables unprecedented insights into learning trajectories (Yampolskiy, 2025), this constant surveillance simultaneously introduces psychosocial hazards. Continuous tracking can produce a "*panopticon effect*," where students internalize the sense of being constantly observed, leading to heightened anxiety, performance pressure, and strategic compliance rather than authentic engagement. Empirical studies have documented increased rates of academic stress in environments utilizing AI-based proctoring and monitoring tools (Seo et al., 2021), suggesting that surveillance undermines both well-being and genuine learning orientation. For example, students subjected to persistent biometric tracking during online examinations reported feelings of dehumanization and distrust toward educational institutions. Thus, any implementation of AI monitoring must adhere to strict principles of proportionality, consent, and psychological safety. AI-driven performance data should be used primarily for formative, not punitive, purposes, and students must be given an explicit agency over how their data is collected, interpreted, and used. Therefore, the deployment of AI in schools must be meticulously anchored to educational theory, critical ethics, and a commitment to preserving learner autonomy, equity, and well-being. A human-centered AI feedback ecosystem where immediacy, personalization, and tracking are used judiciously rather than ubiquitously remains essential to fostering empowered learners in the age of pervasive intelligent technologies.

Social Interaction and Collaboration

Consistent with sociocultural theories of development (Vygotsky, 1978), the integration of AI into educational settings demands a reexamination of how social interaction and collaboration are constituted, mediated, and potentially disrupted. Peer collaboration, once predominantly nurtured through direct interpersonal engagement, is increasingly mediated by intelligent systems that scaffold group dynamics, monitor participation, and algorithmically optimize group compositions (Ofosu-Ampong et al., 2024). For instance, platforms like *Disco* (Figure 2) can now automatically assemble student groups based on complementary skill profiles and interaction histories. While this offers a powerful mechanism for expanding learning opportunities across geographic and socioeconomic boundaries, it risks reducing the unpredictability and friction integral to authentic collaborative learning. Moreover, persistent mediation by AI interfaces attenuates the micro-social cues fundamental to socio-cognitive development, including gesture, tone, and proxemics (Sethi & Jain, 2024). Without intentional design promoting high-fidelity interaction modes (e.g., live video or virtual reality-based collaboration), students may experience "social deskilling" or the erosion of their capacity for empathy, negotiation, and non-verbal attunement (Miranda et al., 2025). A poignant example arises in international virtual classrooms, where AI translation tools remove language barriers but simultaneously strip away cultural nuance, leading to miscommunication despite linguistic clarity. Therefore, the recommendation is not mere technological enhancement but pedagogical re-engineering. AI tools must be mandated to simulate, rather than supplant, the messy, situated nature of real-world collaboration.

Figure 2. Disco AI platform for automated group formation based on profiles history

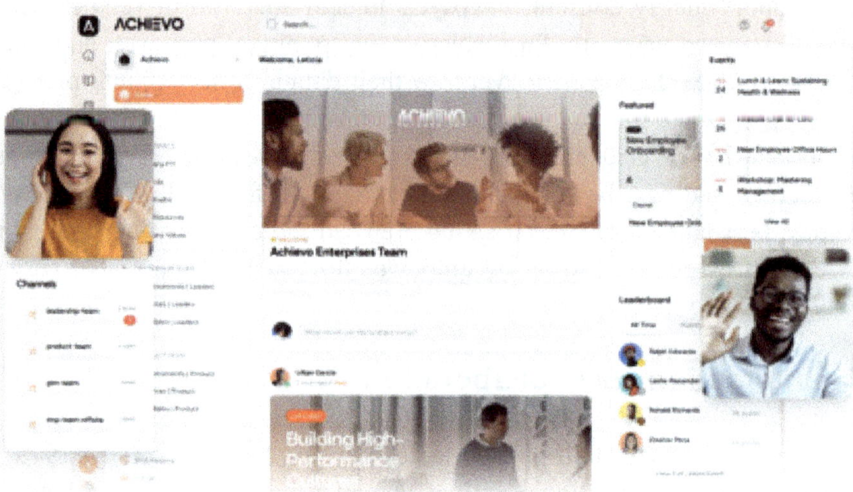

Turning to teacher-student interaction, the affordances of AI-driven personalization can potentially realize the vision of differentiated instruction championed by educational psychologists (Xie et al., 2023). For example, AI platforms can detect when a student's cognitive load exceeds optimal thresholds and adjusts the difficulty accordingly. Yet, critical developmental theories highlight that students' academic risk-taking and motivation are deeply contingent on relational trust and perceived emotional support from teachers. Overemphasis on AI-mediated feedback can dilute these relational anchors, fostering an instrumentalist view of learning devoid of emotional resonance. A real-world illustration is seen in AI-based homework systems, where students increasingly prefer algorithmic feedback over teacher consultation, leading to a measurable decline in classroom participation rates (Ofosu-Ampong et al., 2023). To counteract this trend, blended learning designs must deliberately preserve and even elevate the salience of human teacher-student bonds through structured "relational check-ins" and dialogical pedagogy (Zhang, 2025). In another facet, AI's role in facilitating social-emotional learning (SEL) must be approached with acute theoretical and ethical caution. While machine learning algorithms can detect emotional states through sentiment analysis or facial recognition, the epistemological basis of emotion itself poses a fundamental challenge to algorithmic interpretation. A vivid case emerges in AI-driven SEL programs in U.S. middle schools, where automated mood trackers misinterpreted cultural expressions of respect (e.g., avoiding direct eye contact) as indicators of social withdrawal. As Vygotskian perspectives emphasize, emotional regulation is co-constructed through authentic social interactions, not computational approximations (Vygotsky, 1978). Therefore, while AI can assist in early detection and resource recommendation, comprehensive SEL must remain grounded in human facilitation, narrative approaches, and culturally responsive pedagogy. Integration should prioritize scenario-based simulations, participatory role-play, and reflective discussions where AI tools act as supplements for human mentorship.

Emotional Development

As AI extends its reach into the most intimate domains of education, perhaps nowhere is its influence more ethically and psychologically fraught than in the domain of emotional development. AI-driven emotional learning systems are increasingly integrated within SEL frameworks. These tools offer interactive simulations, role-playing environments, and real-time feedback mechanisms aimed at cultivating emotional competencies (Hsu & Chaudhary, 2023; Indellicato, 2024). These interventions resonate with the model of emotional intelligence, wherein perceiving, using, understanding, and managing emotions are seen as critical for adaptive functioning. Intelligent tutoring systems (ITS) analyze emotional cues, which include but are not limited to expressions of frustration, signs of disengagement, moments of anxiety, and adjust their responses to provide personalized guidance. Researchers have found that AI-powered empathetic agents can enhance motivation and provide emotional support, fostering emotional engagement and empathy in educational settings (Jamaluddin & Mokhtar, 2025; Mayrene et al., 2024). Some argue that this kind of tailored support helps students build emotional confidence in ways traditional methods cannot (Zong & Yang, 2025). Llurba and Palau (2024) found that real-time emotion recognition software enhances students' emotional awareness by analyzing their facial expressions and engagement levels, enabling teachers to adjust instructional strategies in real time to create a more emotionally responsive learning environment. Unlike a classroom setting where a single teacher must manage the varied emotional needs of many students, AI can focus on the individual, offering support tailored to a specific emotional state.

However, while these technologies can facilitate skill acquisition within controlled environments, they fall short of replicating the emergent, reciprocal nature of authentic human emotional interaction (Vistorte et al., 2024). The ability to recognize patterns in emotional expression is different from truly understanding emotions. Artificial intelligence processes vast amounts of behavioral data and responds based on predefined models, but its reactions remain scripted, even when they appear natural. This fundamental gap between imitation and understanding raises concerns about what students are learning when they engage with AI-driven SEL tools. One of the most well-documented psychological phenomena in human-

AI interaction is the ELIZA effect, named after an early chatbot designed in the 1960s. Although ELIZA functioned on simple pattern-matching algorithms, many users believed it genuinely understood them (Eisenmann et al., 2023). This tendency to ascribe human-like emotional intelligence to artificial systems persists in modern AI. Over time, it can lead to over-reliance on artificial emotional support and reduced opportunities to practice the kind of dynamic, reciprocal engagement that real-world relationships require. Developers are aware of these limitations and have taken steps to reduce the risk of AI being mistaken for a true emotional presence (Garcia et al., 2025). Some AI-driven educational programs emphasize transparency to ensure students understand they are interacting with a tool rather than a sentient entity (Raza et al., 2024). Regulatory frameworks are beginning to reflect these concerns. The European Union Artificial Intelligence Act, which began its phased implementation in February 2025, places strict controls on AI systems that influence human behavior. Emotion recognition technology is now prohibited in educational settings except for medical or safety purposes, with concerns about privacy, reliability, and the ethical implications of such systems playing a role in this decision. AI tools that assess student learning, influence admission decisions, or monitor behavior during exams are now classified as high-risk, subject to stringent transparency and accountability measures.

Autonomy and Self-Directed Learning

AI is reshaping education by enabling self-paced and personalized learning experiences. Moving away the traditional one-size-fits-all curriculum, AI analyzes student interactions to tailor content, helping learners reinforce strengths while revisiting challenging concepts with adaptive guidance (Jian, 2023). This adaptability ensures a tailored educational experience, allowing students to take ownership of their learning. The benefits of AI-driven learning extend beyond convenience; it actively cultivates a deeper, more engaged educational experience. By continuously assessing student progress and adjusting instruction accordingly, AI ensures that no student is left behind or held back by rigid curricula. AI-driven tools analyze student performance in real time, dynamically adjusting content to provide targeted instruction (Izzat Ruslim & Khalid, 2024) while delivering personalized feedback to enhance learning outcomes (Venter et al., 2024). Platforms like *Knewton* (Figure 3) exemplify this approach using adaptive learning technologies to tailor instruction to individual learners' needs. This real-time feedback fosters a responsive learning environment that caters to individual needs to ensure continuous improvement. By offering individualized pathways, AI fosters greater student autonomy and empowers learners to develop critical thinking and problem-solving skills without constant teacher intervention. With AI-driven learning, students are encouraged to take a more active role in their education, leading to increased motivation, engagement, and long-term learning retention. The flexibility of AI-driven learning systems also accommodates diverse learning styles and paces, making education more accessible and inclusive for students with different abilities and backgrounds.

Figure 3. Knewton displaying real-time student performance across active courses

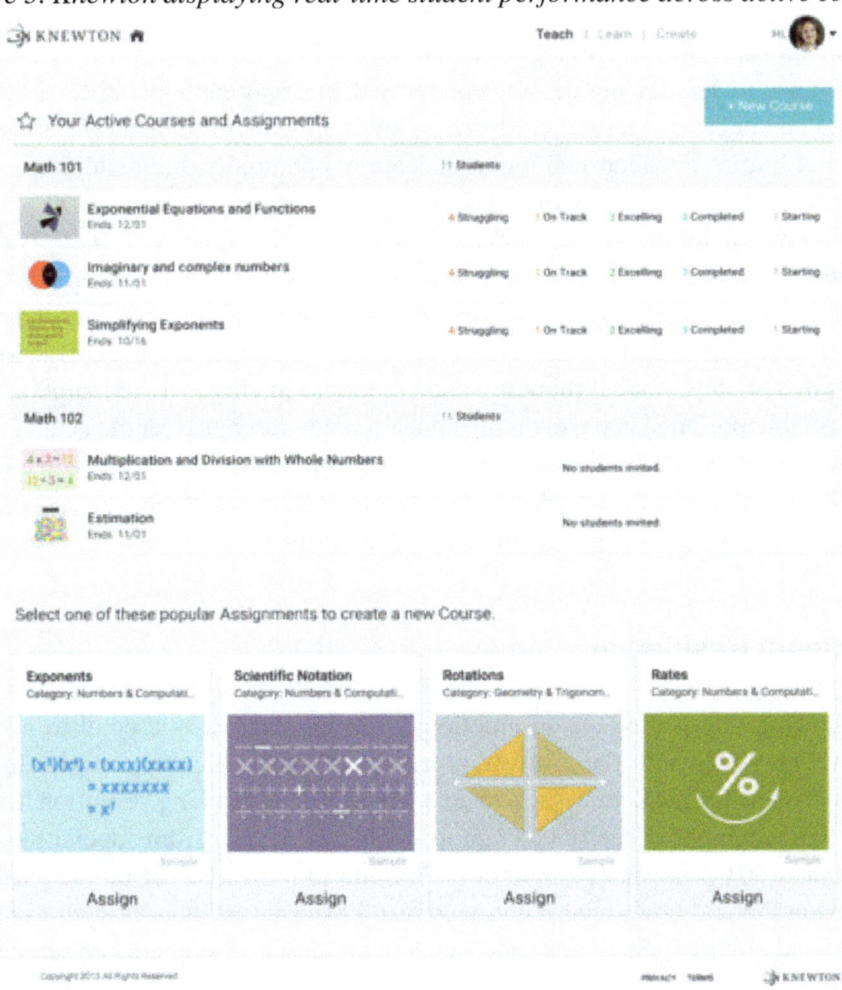

However, the increasing autonomy afforded by AI also challenges the traditional role of educators. As students become more reliant on AI-generated feedback and support, they may decrease their engagement with teachers, shifting their perception of academic success away from human mentorship (Gupta et al., 2024). While AI enhances individualized learning, it may inadvertently weaken the student-teacher relationship, a critical component of academic and emotional development. Studies suggest that students often trust AI-generated content more than their teachers' explanations, which can weaken the student-teacher relationship (Alasgarova & Rzayev, 2024). This over-reliance on AI risks diminishing the value of human interaction in learning, potentially leading to a lack of interpersonal skills and emotional intelligence. The efficiency of AI in offering quick solutions may also reduce students' willingness to seek deeper discussions or collaborate with educators in their learning process. By prioritizing efficiency over dialogue, students may develop a surface-level understanding of subjects rather than engaging in the critical inquiry that human educators facilitate. AI-driven environments raise concerns about the erosion of human decision-making in education, potentially diminishing teachers' influence over curriculum design and student development (Ahmad et al., 2023). If AI assumes a dominant role in determining educational content, there is a risk of homogenization, where diverse perspectives and pedagogical approaches are sidelined in favor of algorithmically optimized instruction. This shift highlights the need for educators to adapt their roles, emphasizing the human aspects of learning, such as mentorship, critical thinking, and emotional intelligence, to maintain their indispensable presence in the evolving educational landscape (Gentile et al., 2023). As AI continues to shape education, it is crucial to strike a balance between technological efficiency and the irreplaceable benefits of human guidance, ensuring that AI remains a tool for enhancement rather than a substitute for human interaction in learning.

Emotional Resilience

Following the discussion on emotional development, it is crucial to address how AI intersects with the cultivation of emotional resilience, a psychological construct vital for academic success and long-term well-being. Emotional resilience, defined as the capacity to adapt to stress and recover from adversity (Grant & Kinman, 2014), is shaped by a complex interplay of internal factors, such as self-regulation and emotional intelligence, and external influences such as social support and environmental stressors. In educational settings, resilience serves as a protective factor against burnout, academic failure, and mental health challenges, particularly during periods of heightened uncertainty or transition. Effective coping strategies are central to resilience as they empower students to reframe challenges and maintain psychological equilibrium (Diaz et al., 2025). Emotional intelligence further enhances resilience by promoting self-awareness, emotional regulation, and adaptive interpersonal skills. Empirical studies corroborate that students with higher emotional intelligence exhibit more robust coping mechanisms, leading to superior academic performance and psychological health (e.g., Guo et al., 2024). In this context, AI offers powerful tools for supporting emotional resilience by facilitating personalized emotional support, real-time monitoring, and adaptive interventions (Vistorte et al., 2024). Through sophisticated pattern recognition and data analysis, AI systems can detect signs of emotional distress, track physiological markers such as heart rate variability, and provide tailored resilience-building exercises (Mishra et al., 2024). For example, wearable devices combined with AI-powered emotional coaching have shown promise in enhancing emotional regulation among graduate students by correlating biometric data with emotional states and tailoring interventions accordingly (Liu & Zoghi, 2024). Similarly, AI-driven platforms now offer virtual therapy sessions and real-time coaching that deliver cognitive-behavioral techniques and stress-management strategies at scale (Garcia, 2023; Olawade et al., 2024; Tomé & Coelho, 2023).

However, despite these benefits, significant theoretical and ethical concerns persist. AI, by its nature, lacks genuine emotional experience as its empathy remains a simulation based on probabilistic pattern matching (Xiao et al., 2025). From a phenomenological perspective, authentic emotional support is not merely the delivery of appropriate responses but emerges from embodied and reciprocal presence that AI fundamentally cannot replicate. Excessive reliance on AI for emotional support risks commodifying and dehumanizing the learning process, as educators and institutions may increasingly delegate relational responsibilities to algorithmic systems (Acut, Gamusa, et al., 2025; Naseer et al., 2025). This detachment could lead to a diminution of the rich, trust-based human relationships essential for genuine emotional resilience. Moreover, AI's interpretation of human emotion remains vulnerable to misclassification and cultural bias. Subtle emotional cues influenced by cultural background, individual neurodiversity, or personal history may be misunderstood or flattened into reductive models of emotional expression. Such misinterpretations can exacerbate alienation rather than foster resilience. Consequently, a human-AI collaboration model is imperative (Huang et al., 2023). AI should serve as an augmentative resource, offering preliminary support, early detection, and personalized scaffolding while preserving the primacy of human-to-human emotional interaction. Educators must be trained to integrate AI tools ethically and critically, ensuring that they complement rather than replace authentic relational work. After all, Emotional resilience is cultivated through shared vulnerability, authentic dialogue, and human solidarity within educational communities.

Identity and Personal Development

Building upon prior discussions of emotional and social competencies, the intersection of AI and personal identity development warrants a critical examination. AI technologies offer novel pathways for fostering self-awareness, skill development, and lifelong learning. At the center of these innovations is the principle of personalization, allowing educational content to be dynamically adapted to individual cognitive profiles, learning styles, and career aspirations (S. Wang et al., 2024). For instance, AI platforms like *Degreed* (Figure 4) use real-time analytics to recommend targeted upskilling interventions, which enables students to align their learning trajectories with evolving labor market demands (Bösl & Achtenberg, 2024). Moreover, AI-driven reflective tools (e.g., emotionally intelligent chatbots) enable students to engage in iterative self-assessment and goal-setting processes (Bilquise et al., 2022). ITS that adapt to learning rhythms provide formative feedback that scaffolds not only knowledge acquisition but also metacognitive development (Lin et al., 2023). Students are thus empowered to construct evolving self-concepts grounded in evidence-based reflections on their strengths and areas for improvement. Generative AI extends this potential by simulating complex real-world scenarios, enhancing students' strategic planning, leadership capabilities, and decision-making skills (Yan et al., 2024; Yusuf et al., 2024). Such applications are particularly salient in higher education contexts, where identity formation intersects with professional readiness. However, as identity formation is a social and existential process, AI-mediated personal development also introduces significant conceptual and ethical tensions. The creation of digital selves, such as AI-driven avatars in the metaverse (Tabassum et al., 2025), blurs the distinction between authentic and constructed identities. Anthropomorphic avatars designed to mirror physical and behavioral realism can facilitate novel modes of social interaction (Garcia, 2025), yet they also risk commodifying personal identity and distorting authentic self-expression. The dynamic interplay between human inputs and AI outputs complicates traditional understandings of selfhood, authenticity, and representation.

Figure 4. Degreed AI-powered skill assessment showing real-time skill gap analysis

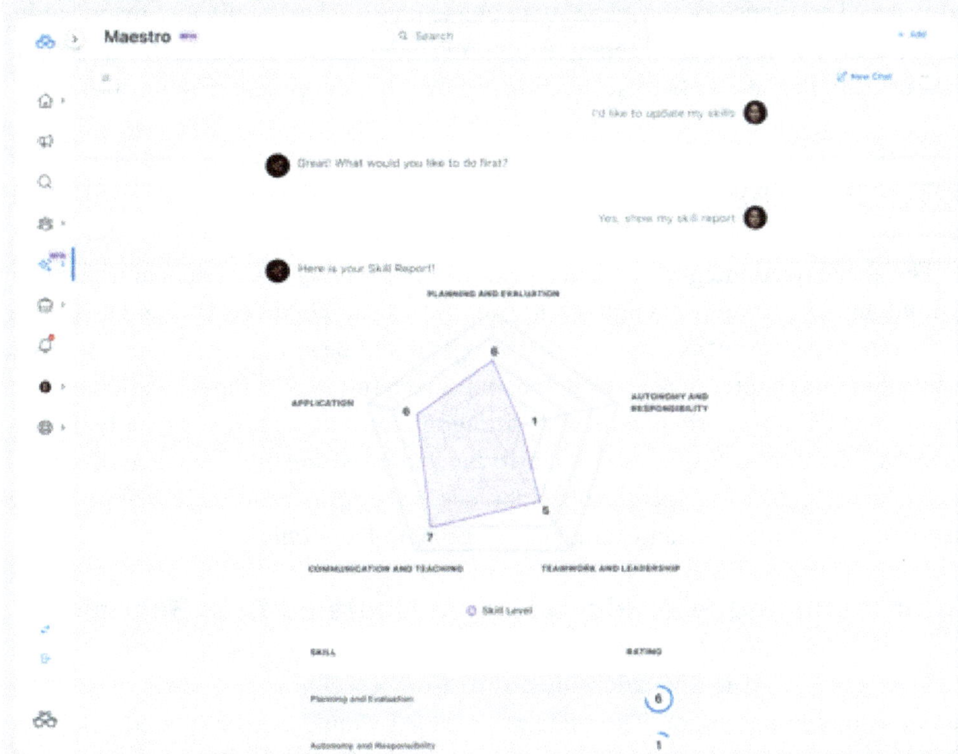

Empirical findings further reveal that the psychological correlates of AI use are complex and sometimes troubling. Rodríguez-Ruiz et al. (2025) found that lower self-control and self-efficacy predict higher reliance on AI tools, while higher self-esteem inversely correlates with dependence on AI-mediated interaction. These findings suggest that while AI can support personal development, it may simultaneously entrench vulnerabilities in self-concept and autonomy, particularly among students with pre-existing psychological fragilities. Moreover, challenges related to data privacy, algorithmic bias, and identity manipulation must not be understated. Biases embedded in AI agents can reinforce stereotypes, marginalize certain groups, and compromise the inclusivity of digital learning environments (Hasanah et al., 2025; Mittal et al., 2024). Furthermore, the potential for unauthorized appropriation or alteration of personal identities necessitates robust legal and ethical protection. Without deliberate safeguards, AI systems may inadvertently erode the very authenticity they seek to empower. The over-dependence on generative AI tools for academic tasks, if left unchecked, risks stunting the development of critical 21st century skills such as creative problem-solving, analytical reasoning, and reflective judgment (N. Wang et al., 2024). Educational strategies must, therefore, explicitly cultivate AI resilience or the capacity to engage with AI critically and responsibly. This entails fostering digital literacy, promoting independent cognitive development, and ensuring that students retain authorship over their own learning journeys.

FUTURE PERSPECTIVES

The accelerated integration of AI in education presents a paradoxical trajectory. It simultaneously empowers and disrupts, nurtures and alienates, and enhances and undermines. As we reflect on the psychological and developmental repercussions outlined in this chapter, it becomes evident that the future of AI in education cannot be approached as a purely technical or pedagogical challenge. It is a deeply human issue that demands foresight, ethical clarity, and inclusive design. This section aims to chart a forward-thinking agenda that embraces the benefits of AI while safeguarding the cognitive, emotional, and social development of students.

From Technology-Centric to Human-Centered AI in Schools

The future of AI in education must shift from a technology-centric model to a human-centered paradigm. The integration of AI should not be guided solely by efficiency metrics or algorithmic precision but should prioritize learner well-being, identity formation, autonomy, and emotional resilience. Initiatives like the iSTAR framework (Huang et al., 2023) emphasize the importance of designing intelligent systems that foster human-AI collaboration rather than substitution. In this future, AI will not replace teachers, mentors, or social structures but will become a silent partner that is working behind the scenes to amplify human potential.

In doing so, educational institutions must critically assess the hidden curriculum embedded in AI systems—the subtle messages about behavior, achievement, and identity that learners internalize through prolonged exposure. Future AI tools must be co-designed with students, educators, and communities, drawing on principles of participatory design and epistemic justice to ensure equity, transparency, and contextual relevance (Atenas et al., 2025).

AI Literacy and Resilience as Core Competencies

To navigate AI-rich learning environments responsibly, students must be equipped not only with AI literacy but also with AI resilience, a values-based competency that enables learners to maintain agency in the face of automation and algorithmic authority (Garcia et al., 2024; Zhao, 2025). As AI becomes more pervasive, the risk of dependency and diminished human criticality increases. Future-ready learners will require cognitive tools to question, contextualize, and reinterpret AI outputs rather than accept them as infallible.

Institutional efforts must go beyond technical training. Curricula must embed AI ethics, bias recognition, emotional intelligence, and human-machine boundary awareness as fundamental learning outcomes. The dual AI competency frameworks developed by UNESCO for educators and students (Miao & Cukurova, 2024; Miao et al., 2024; Wiese et al., 2025) offer a robust roadmap for scaling such efforts globally. National education systems should formally adopt and localize these frameworks to align with regional needs and digital access realities.

Mitigating Algorithmic Harm and Data Colonialism

One of the most pressing concerns for the future is the algorithmic harm that AI systems may perpetuate, especially when trained on data that encode societal biases, reinforce stereotypes, or marginalize vulnerable learners (Xiao et al., 2025). The challenge is compounded by data colonialism, wherein learner data is extracted, processed, and commodified by global tech entities often far removed from local accountability mechanisms.

Educational ecosystems must implement transparent data governance frameworks that ensure student data is treated as a public good, not a commercial asset. This includes mandatory explainability protocols, third-party audits, and student data ownership rights. Policies must ensure that AI tools in schools undergo rigorous ethical evaluation, especially when deployed in contexts that involve behavioral monitoring, emotional analysis, or identity shaping. Following the EU's Artificial Intelligence Act, educational systems worldwide may benefit from establishing "red lines", which are explicit prohibitions on certain high-risk applications of AI in schools.

Designing for Developmental Integrity

The next phase of AI adoption in education must respect what can be termed developmental integrity, or the protection of students' holistic growth across cognitive, emotional, social, and moral domains. This means AI must never replace authentic learning experiences that depend on ambiguity, struggle, empathy, and human connection. The future of AI in schools should be invitational and not prescriptive—designing systems that prompt exploration, curiosity, and collaborative meaning-making rather than mechanistic task completion.

Such integrity can be safeguarded by anchoring AI implementation in transformative learning theories (Mezirow, 1978) that emphasize critical reflection, perspective-taking, and consciousness development. As AI tools evolve, future educational environments must resist the temptation to over automate (Karamuk, 2025). Instead, they should curate a hybrid space where technological augmentation and human mentorship coexist, each complementing the other in promoting deep and meaningful learning (Molenaar, 2022).

Equitable Futures and the Risk of Educational Stratification

Perhaps one of the gravest risks facing the future of AI in schools is educational stratification—a scenario where well-resourced schools benefit from advanced AI systems while underfunded institutions fall further behind. Without proactive intervention, AI could become a tool of exclusion rather than inclusion, exacerbating digital divides across socioeconomic, geographic, and linguistic lines (Bulathwela et al., 2024).

Equity-focused design must be embedded at every level—from infrastructure to pedagogy to policy. Governments and international organizations must commit to digital justice frameworks that ensure universal access to AI tools and AI education. Open-source AI platforms, localized content, multilingual interfaces, and community-based AI literacy programs will be crucial in democratizing the benefits of educational AI.

A New Social Contract for AI in Education

The road ahead demands the drafting of a new social contract between learners, educators, institutions, developers, and policymakers—a contract rooted in transparency, accountability, and care. This social contract must recognize students as not merely users of AI but as rights-bearing individuals whose mental health, identity, and agency must be protected.

In crafting this contract, we must ask:

- What kind of citizens are we shaping through AI-enabled schooling?
- Whose interests are embedded in the algorithms that shape learning pathways?
- How do we ensure that AI promotes dignity, curiosity, and civic responsibility rather than conformity, surveillance, or instrumentalism?

In answering these, we must remember AI is not neutral. As emphasized in *The Manifesto for Teaching and Learning in a Time of Generative AI* (Bozkurt et al., 2024), the narratives and metaphors we use to frame AI matter. Whether we view it as a tool, partner, threat, or mirror, AI challenges us to rethink not only how we teach and learn but also what it means to be human in an algorithmic age. It is not a question of whether we adopt AI, but how—critically, inclusively, and with unwavering commitment to education as a deeply human endeavor.

CONCLUSION

The pervasive integration of AI into educational ecologies is fundamentally recalibrating the psychosocial and cognitive development trajectories of students. This review underscores that while AI-mediated instructional systems afford opportunities for hyper-personalized learning pathways and optimized academic performance, they concurrently introduce significant developmental perturbations. Chief among these developmental concerns are the implications of algorithmic surveillance, pedagogical automation, and the erosion of organic peer interaction. These issues have consequences for identity formation, self-efficacy, and socioemotional resilience. In this evolving context, students increasingly navigate teaching and learning environments where adaptive systems modulate content delivery, scaffold attention, and mediate performance feedback. While such affordances may bolster engagement and learner persistence through tailored cognitive stimuli, they risk engendering maladaptive dependencies on extrinsic reinforcement mechanisms. This dynamic may attenuate the cultivation of metacognitive autonomy, emotional regulation, and intrinsic motivation.

The engagement with AI interlocutors necessitates that learners acquire not only digital fluency but also critical interpretive frameworks to navigate algorithmic authority, mitigate epistemic passivity, and preserve agency in data-saturated contexts. In parallel, educators must assume a translational role, one who interprets AI affordances through a developmental lens, curates hybrid pedagogical modalities that foreground relational pedagogy, and safeguards the affective dimensions of schooling. Empirical inquiry is urgently required to interrogate the longitudinal impact of AI-powered tools on developmental constructs such as identity coherence, adaptive functioning, and social-emotional connectedness across diverse learner demographics. Policymakers, in turn, must articulate regulatory architectures that embed psychological safeguards, mandate transparency in algorithmic design, and ensure that AI serves as an adjunct for human-centric educational praxis. With deliberate planning, ethical oversight, and a focus on student development, AI technologies can serve as a powerful complement to inclusive and emotionally intelligent education. Without these guiding principles, however, the risks to student well-being and developmental integrity may outweigh the intended benefits.

REFERENCES

Acut, D. P., Gamusa, E. V., Pernaa, J., Yuenyong, C., Pantaleon, A. T., Espina, R. C., & Garcia, M. B. (2025). AI Shaming Among Teacher Education Students: A Reflection on Acceptance and Identity in the Age of Generative Tools. In *Pitfalls of AI Integration in Education: Skill Obsolescence, Misuse, and Bias*. IGI Global., DOI: 10.4018/979-8-3373-0122-8.ch005

Acut, D. P., Malabago, N. K., Malicoban, E. V., Galamiton, N. S., & Garcia, M. B. (2025). "ChatGPT 4.0 Ghosted Us While Conducting Literature Search:" Modeling the Chatbot's Generated Non-Existent References Using Regression Analysis. *Internet Reference Services Quarterly*, *29*(1), 27–54. DOI: 10.1080/10875301.2024.2426793

Ahmad, S. F., Han, H., Alam, M. M., Rehmat, M. K., Irshad, M., Arraño-Muñoz, M., & Ariza-Montes, A. (2023). Impact of Artificial Intelligence on Human Loss in Decision Making, Laziness and Safety in Education. *Humanities & Social Sciences Communications*, *10*(1), 1–14. DOI: 10.1057/s41599-023-01787-8 PMID: 37325188

Alasgarova, R., & Rzayev, J. (2024). The Role of Artificial Intelligence in Shaping High School Students' Motivation. *International Journal of Technology in Education and Science*, *8*(2), 311–324. DOI: 10.46328/ijtes.553

Ali, O., Murray, P. A., Momin, M., Dwivedi, Y. K., & Malik, T. (2024). The Effects of Artificial Intelligence Applications in Educational Settings: Challenges and Strategies. *Technological Forecasting and Social Change*, *199*, 1–18. DOI: 10.1016/j.techfore.2023.123076

Atenas, J., Havemann, L., & Nerantzi, C. (2025). Critical and Creative Pedagogies for Artificial Intelligence and Data Literacy: An Epistemic Data Justice Approach for Academic Practice. *Research in Learning Technology*, *32*, 1–16. DOI: 10.25304/rlt.v32.3296

Bilquise, G., Ibrahim, S., & Shaalan, K. (2022). Emotionally Intelligent Chatbots: A Systematic Literature Review. *Human Behavior and Emerging Technologies*, *2022*(1), 9601630. DOI: 10.1155/2022/9601630

Bösl, D. B. O., & Achtenberg, T. (2024, 6-8 Nov. 2024). Lifelong Learning Companion: Development Milestones in an AI-Based, Cross-Platform Companion App for Lifelong Learning Optimization 2024 21st International Conference on Information Technology Based Higher Education and Training (ITHET)

Bozkurt, A., Xiao, J., Farrow, R., Bai, J. Y. H., Nerantzi, C., Moore, S., & Asino, T. I. (2024). The Manifesto for Teaching and Learning in a Time of Generative AI: A Critical Collective Stance to Better Navigate the Future. *Open Praxis, 16*(4), 487–513. DOI: 10.55982/openpraxis.16.4.777

Bulathwela, S., Pérez-Ortiz, M., Holloway, C., Cukurova, M., & Shawe-Taylor, J. (2024). Artificial Intelligence Alone Will Not Democratise Education: On Educational Inequality, Techno-Solutionism and Inclusive Tools. *Sustainability (Basel), 16*(2), 1–20. DOI: 10.3390/su16020781

Díaz, B., & Nussbaum, M. (2024). Artificial Intelligence for Teaching and Learning in Schools: The Need for Pedagogical Intelligence. *Computers &amp. Computers & Education, 217*, 1–19. DOI: 10.1016/j.compedu.2024.105071

Diaz, F. C. B., Trinidad, I., Agustin, M. J., Panganiban, T. P., & Garcia, M. B. (2025). Mindfulness for Health and Well Being: An Innovative Physical Education Course in the University of the Philippines Diliman. In Garcia, M. B. (Ed.), *Global Innovations in Physical Education and Health* (pp. 139–168). IGI Global., DOI: 10.4018/979-8-3693-3952-7.ch006

Eisenmann, C., Mlynář, J., Turowetz, J., & Rawls, A. W. (2023). "Machine Down": Making Sense of Human–Computer Interaction—Garfinkel's Research on ELIZA and LYRIC from 1967 to 1969 and Its Contemporary Relevance. *AI & Society, 39*(6), 2715–2733. DOI: 10.1007/s00146-023-01793-z

Freire, P. (2007). Pedagogy of the Heart. *Continuum.*

Gantalao, L. C., Calzada, J. G. D., Capuyan, D. L., Lumantas, B. C., Acut, D. P., & Garcia, M. B. (2025). Equipping the Next Generation of Technicians: Navigating School Infrastructure and Technical Knowledge in the Age of AI Integration. In *Pitfalls of AI Integration in Education: Skill Obsolescence, Misuse, and Bias*. IGI Global., DOI: 10.4018/979-8-3373-0122-8.ch009

Garcia, M. B. (2023). Can ChatGPT Substitute Human Companionship for Coping with Loss and Trauma? *Journal of Loss and Trauma, 28*(8), 784–786. DOI: 10.1080/15325024.2023.2240697

Garcia, M. B. (2024). The Paradox of Artificial Creativity: Challenges and Opportunities of Generative AI Artistry. *Creativity Research Journal*, •••, 1–14. DOI: 10.1080/10400419.2024.2354622

Garcia, M. B. (2025). Teachers in the Metaverse: The Influence of Avatar Appearance and Behavioral Realism on Perceptions of Instructor Credibility and Teaching Effectiveness. *Interactive Learning Environments*, •••, 1–17. DOI: 10.1080/10494820.2025.2462144

Garcia, M. B., Arif, Y. M., Khlaif, Z. N., Zhu, M., de Almeida, R. P. P., de Almeida, R. S., & Masters, K. (2024). Effective Integration of Artificial Intelligence in Medical Education: Practical Tips and Actionable Insights. In *Transformative Approaches to Patient Literacy and Healthcare Innovation* (pp. 1-19). IGI Global. DOI: 10.4018/979-8-3693-3661-8.ch001

Garcia, M. B., Goi, C.-L., Shively, K., Maher, D., Rosak-Szyrocka, J., Happonen, A., . . . Damaševičius, R. (2025). Understanding Student Engagement in AI-Powered Online Learning Platforms: A Narrative Review of Key Theories and Models. In *Cases on Enhancing P-16 Student Engagement With Digital Technologies* (pp. 1-30). IGI Global. DOI: 10.2139/ssrn.5074608

Gentile, M., Città, G., Perna, S., & Allegra, M. (2023). Do We Still Need Teachers? Navigating the Paradigm Shift of the Teacher's Role in the AI Era. *Frontiers in Education*, *8*, 1–14. DOI: 10.3389/feduc.2023.1161777

Grant, L., & Kinman, G. (2014). Emotional Resilience in the Helping Professions and How It Can Be Enhanced. *Health and Social Care Education*, *3*(1), 23–34. DOI: 10.11120/hsce.2014.00040

Guo, W., Zhao, X., Lee, P. G., & Ke, L. (2024). Bridging Heart and Mind: Exploring Emotional Intelligence among Undergraduates in the Age of Artificial Intelligence. *Environment-Behaviour Proceedings Journal*, *9*(29), 13–20. DOI: 10.21834/e-bpj.v9i29.6009

Gupta, D. P., Sreelatha, D. C., Latha, A., Raj, D. S., & Singh, D. A. (2024). Navigating The Future Of Education: The Impact Of Artificial Intelligence On Teacher-Student Dynamics. *Educational Administration: Theory and Practice*, 6006-6013. DOI: 10.53555/kuey.v30i4.2332

Hasanah, N. A., Aziza, M. R., Junikhah, A., Arif, Y. M., & Garcia, M. B. (2025). Navigating the Use of AI in Engineering Education Through a Systematic Review of Technology, Regulations, and Challenges. In *Pitfalls of AI Integration in Education: Skill Obsolescence, Misuse, and Bias*. IGI Global., DOI: 10.4018/979-8-3373-0122-8.ch016

Hsu, A., & Chaudhary, D. (2023). AI4PCR: Artificial intelligence for practicing conflict resolution. *Computers in Human Behavior: Artificial Humans*, *1*(1), 1–11. DOI: 10.1016/j.chbah.2023.100002

Huang, R., Tlili, A., Xu, L., Chen, Y., Zheng, L., Metwally, A. H. S., & Bonk, C. J. (2023). Educational Futures of Intelligent Synergies Between Humans, Digital Twins, Avatars, and Robots-The iSTAR Framework. *Journal of Applied Learning & Teaching*, *6*(2), 28–43.

Hulus, A. (2025). A Systematic Review of Educators' Overreliance and Misuse of AI in Student Feedback: Introducing the ETHICAL-FEED Framework. In *Pitfalls of AI Integration in Education: Skill Obsolescence, Misuse, and Bias*. IGI Global., DOI: 10.4018/979-8-3373-0122-8.ch015

Indellicato, R. (2024). Artificial Intelligence and Social-Emotional Learning: What relationship? *Journal of Modern Science*, *60*(6), 460–470. DOI: 10.13166/jms/196765

Izzat Ruslim, M., & Khalid, F. (2024). The Use of Artificial Intelligence in Differentiated Instruction Classrooms. *International Journal of Academic Research in Business & Social Sciences*, *14*(8), 680–695. DOI: 10.6007/IJARBSS/v14-i8/22435

Jamaluddin, N. S., & Mokhtar, M. (2025). Teaching Empathy: How AI Can Support the Development of Soft Skills in Education. *International Journal of Academic Research in Business & Social Sciences*, *15*(3), 704–713. DOI: 10.6007/IJARBSS/v15-i3/24469

Jian, M. J. K. O. (2023). Personalized Learning Through AI. *Advances in Engineering Innovation*, *5*(1), 16–19. DOI: 10.54254/2977-3903/5/2023039

Karamuk, E. (2025). The Automation Trap: Unpacking the Consequences of Over-Reliance on AI in Education and Its Hidden Costs. In *Pitfalls of AI Integration in Education: Skill Obsolescence, Misuse, and Bias*. IGI Global., DOI: 10.4018/979-8-3373-0122-8.ch007

Lin, C.-C., Huang, A. Y. Q., & Lu, O. H. T. (2023). Artificial Intelligence in Intelligent Tutoring Systems Toward Sustainable Education: A Systematic Review. *Smart Learning Environments*, *10*(1), 1–22. DOI: 10.1186/s40561-023-00260-y

Liu, Y., & Zoghi, B. (2024). AI-Powered Strategies for Alleviating Graduate Student Burnout Through Emotional Intelligence and Wearable Technology 16th International Conference on Education and New Learning Technologies

Llurba, C., & Palau, R. (2024). Real-Time Emotion Recognition for Improving the Teaching–Learning Process: A Scoping Review. *Journal of Imaging*, *10*(12), 1–15. DOI: 10.3390/jimaging10120313

Mangubat, J. C., Mangubat, M. R., Uy, T. B. L., Acut, D. P., & Garcia, M. B. (2025). Safeguarding Educational Innovations Amid AI Disruptions: A Reassessment of Patenting for Sustained Intellectual Property Protection. In *Pitfalls of AI Integration in Education: Skill Obsolescence, Misuse, and Bias*. IGI Global., DOI: 10.4018/979-8-3373-0122-8.ch013

Max-Neef, M. A. (2005). Foundations of Transdisciplinarity. *Ecological Economics*, *53*(1), 5–16. DOI: 10.1016/j.ecolecon.2005.01.014

Mayrene, F. H. E., Basantes, A. C., Martínez, M. F. C., Salas, F. P. P., & Jose, M. V. D. (2024). Emotional Interaction and Artificial Intelligence in Educational Research. *Journal of Ecohumanism*, *3*(8), 4858–4871. DOI: 10.62754/joe.v3i8.5131

Mezirow, J. (1978). Perspective Transformation. *Adult Education*, *28*(2), 100–110. DOI: 10.1177/074171367802800202

Miao, F., & Cukurova, M. (2024). AI Competency Framework for Teachers. *UNESCO*, 1-52. DOI: 10.54675/ZJTE2084

Miao, F., Shiohira, K., & Lao, N. (2024). AI Competency Framework for Students. *UNESCO*, 1-80. DOI: 10.54675/JKJB9835

Miranda, J. P. P., Cruz, M. A. D., Fernandez, A. B., Balahadia, F. F., Aviles, J. S., Caro, C. A., & Gaña, E. P. (2025). Erosion of Critical Academic Skills Due to AI Dependency Among Tertiary Students: A Path Analysis. In *Pitfalls of AI Integration in Education: Skill Obsolescence, Misuse, and Bias*. IGI Global., DOI: 10.4018/979-8-3373-0122-8.ch002

Mishra, N., Garcia, P. S., Habal, B. G. M., & Garcia, M. B. (2024). *Harnessing an AI-Driven Analytics Model to Optimize Training and Treatment in Physical Education for Sports Injury Prevention* Proceedings of the 8th International Conference on Education and Multimedia Technology, Tokyo, Japan. https://manuelgarcia.info/publication/sports-injury-prevention

Mittal, U., Sai, S., Chamola, V., & Sangwan, D. (2024). A Comprehensive Review on Generative AI for Education. *IEEE Access : Practical Innovations, Open Solutions*, *12*, 142733–142759. DOI: 10.1109/ACCESS.2024.3468368

Molenaar, I. (2022). Towards Hybrid Human-AI Learning Technologies. *European Journal of Education*, *57*(4), 632–645. DOI: 10.1111/ejed.12527

Naseer, A., Ahmad, N. R., & Chishti, M. A. (2025). Psychological Impacts of AI Dependence: Assessing the Cognitive and Emotional Costs of Intelligent Systems in Daily Life. *Review of Applied Management and Social Sciences*, *8*(1), 291–307. DOI: 10.47067/ramss.v8i1.458

Nerantzi, C. (2018). The Design of an Empirical Cross-Boundary Collaborative Open Learning Framework. *Open Praxis, 10*(4), 325–341. DOI: 10.5944/openpraxis.10.4.907

OECD. (2023). *Equity and Inclusion in Education: Finding Strength through Diversity*. OECD Publishing., DOI: 10.1787/e9072e21-

Ofosu-Ampong, K., Acheampong, B., Kevor, M.-O., & Amankwah-Sarfo, F. (2023). Acceptance of Artificial Intelligence (ChatGPT) in Education: Trust, Innovativeness and Psychological Need of Students. *Information and Knowledge Management, 13*(4), 37–47. DOI: 10.7176/IKM/13-4-03

Ofosu-Ampong, K., Atebawone, E., Mustafa, A. S., & Koomson, A. (2024). The Shift to Artificial Intelligence, ChatGPT, and Emerging Technologies in Education: A Review on Dominant Issues. In *Empowering Digital Education with ChatGPT*. CRC Press., DOI: 10.1201/9781032716350-2

Olawade, D. B., Wada, O. Z., Odetayo, A., David-Olawade, A. C., Asaolu, F., & Eberhardt, J. (2024). Enhancing Mental Health with Artificial Intelligence: Current Trends and Future Prospects. *Journal of Medicine, Surgery, and Public Health, 3*, 1–10. DOI: 10.1016/j.glmedi.2024.100099

Pitrella, V., Perna, S., Allegra, M., Gentile, M., Ottaviano, S., Re, A., Tosto, C., & Città, G. (2024). Artificial Intelligence for Personalized Learning in K-12 Education. A Scoping Review. *Communications in Computer and Information Science, 2076*, 372–382. Advance online publication. DOI: 10.1007/978-3-031-67351-1_25

Raza, S., Fatima, I., Arif, S., Sharif, M., Jalal, M. S., & Muhammad, Z. (2024). The Future of Learning: Building Trust and Transparency in AI Education. *Journal of Management Practices. Humanities and Social Sciences, 8*(3), 1–13. DOI: 10.33152/jmphss-8.3.6

Rodríguez-Ruiz, J., Marín-López, I., & Espejo-Siles, R. (2025). Is Artificial Intelligence Use Related to Self-Control, Self-Esteem and Self-Efficacy Among University Students? *Education and Information Technologies, 30*(2), 2507–2524. DOI: 10.1007/s10639-024-12906-6

Seo, K., Tang, J., Roll, I., Fels, S., & Yoon, D. (2021). The Impact of Artificial Intelligence on Learner–Instructor Interaction in Online Learning. *International Journal of Educational Technology in Higher Education, 18*(1), 1–23. DOI: 10.1186/s41239-021-00292-9 PMID: 34778540

Sethi, S. S., & Jain, K. (2024). AI Technologies for Social Emotional Learning: Recent Research and Future Directions. *Journal of Research in Innovative Teaching & Learning*, *17*(2), 213–225. DOI: 10.1108/JRIT-03-2024-0073

Sewell, A., Anastasia, K., & Pugh, V. (2022). Universal Design for Learning as a Theory of Inclusive Practice for Use by Educational Psychologists. *Educational Psychology in Practice*, *38*(4), 364–378. DOI: 10.1080/02667363.2022.2111677

Slee, R. (2018). *Defining the Scope of Inclusive Education: Think Piece Prepared for the 2020 Global Education Monitoring Report, Inclusion and Education*. UNESCO.

Tabassum, A., Elmahjub, E., Padela, A. I., Zwitter, A., & Qadir, J. (2025). Generative AI and the Metaverse: A Scoping Review of Ethical and Legal Challenges. *IEEE Open Journal of the Computer Society*, *6*, 348–359. DOI: 10.1109/OJCS.2025.3536082

Tomé, A., & Coelho, J. L. (2023). Physiotherapy Education in the Digital Era: A Roadmap of Educational Technologies for Allied Health Educators. In *Handbook of Research on Instructional Technologies in Health Education and Allied Disciplines*. IGI Global., DOI: 10.4018/978-1-6684-7164-7.ch002

Torraco, R. J. (2016). Writing Integrative Literature Reviews: Using the Past and Present to Explore the Future. *Human Resource Development Review*, *15*(4), 404–428. DOI: 10.1177/1534484316671606

UNESCO. (2020). Global Education Monitoring Report, 2020: Inclusion and Education: All Means All. *UNESCO*, 1-502. DOI: 10.54676/JJNK6989

Venter, J., Coetzee, S. A., & Schmulian, A. (2024). Exploring the Use of Artificial Intelligence (AI) in the Delivery of Effective Feedback. *Assessment & Evaluation in Higher Education*, •••, 1–21. DOI: 10.1080/02602938.2024.2415649

Vistorte, A. O. R., Deroncele-Acosta, A., Ayala, J. L. M., Barrasa, A., López-Granero, C., & Martí-González, M. (2024). Integrating Artificial Intelligence to Assess Emotions in Learning Environments: A Systematic Literature Review. *Frontiers in Psychology*, *15*, 1–13. DOI: 10.3389/fpsyg.2024.1387089 PMID: 38966729

Vygotsky, L. S. (1978). *Mind in Society: Development of Higher Psychological Processes*. Harvard University Press., DOI: 10.2307/j.ctvjf9vz4

Wang, N., Xiao, W., & Su, Y.-S. (2024). Critical Analysis of the Technological Affordances, Challenges and Future Directions of Generative AI in Education: A Systematic Review. *Asia Pacific Journal of Education*, *44*(1), 139–155. DOI: 10.1080/02188791.2024.2305156

Wang, S., Wang, F., Zhu, Z., Wang, J., Tran, T., & Du, Z. (2024). Artificial Intelligence in Education: A Systematic Literature Review. *Expert Systems with Applications*, *252*, 1–19. DOI: 10.1016/j.eswa.2024.124167

Wiese, L. J., Patil, I., Schiff, D. S., & Magana, A. J. (2025). AI Ethics Education: A Systematic Literature Review. *Computers and Education: Artificial Intelligence*, *8*, 1–22. DOI: 10.1016/j.caeai.2025.100405

Xiao, J., Bozkurt, A., Nichols, M., Pazurek, A., Stracke, C. M., Bai, J. Y. H., Farrow, R., Mulligan, D., Nerantzi, C., Sharma, R. C., Singh, L., Frumin, I., Swindell, A., Honeychurch, S., Bond, M., Dron, J., Moore, S., Leng, J., van Tryon, P. J. S., & Themeli, C. (2025). Venturing into the Unknown: Critical Insights into Grey Areas and Pioneering Future Directions in Educational Generative AI Research. *TechTrends*, *69*(3), 1–16. DOI: 10.1007/s11528-025-01060-6

Xie, Y., Huang, Y., Luo, W., Bai, Y., Qiu, Y., & Ouyang, Z. (2023). Design and Effects of the Teacher-Student Interaction Model in the Online Learning Spaces. *Journal of Computing in Higher Education*, *35*(1), 69–90. DOI: 10.1007/s12528-022-09348-9 PMID: 36618325

Yampolskiy, R. V. (2025). On Monitorability of AI. *AI and Ethics*, *5*(1), 689–707. DOI: 10.1007/s43681-024-00420-x

Yan, L., Greiff, S., Teuber, Z., & Gašević, D. (2024). Promises and Challenges of Generative Artificial Intelligence for Human Learning. *Nature Human Behaviour*, *8*(10), 1839–1850. DOI: 10.1038/s41562-024-02004-5 PMID: 39438686

Yusuf, A., Pervin, N., Román-González, M., & Noor, N. M. (2024). Generative AI in Education and Research: A Systematic Mapping Review. *Review of Education*, *12*(2), e3489. DOI: 10.1002/rev3.3489

Zhang, A. (2025). Human Computer Interaction System for Teacher-Student Interaction Model Using Machine Learning. *International Journal of Human-Computer Interaction*, *41*(3), 1817–1828. DOI: 10.1080/10447318.2022.2115645

Zhao, J. (2025). The Role of Learners' AI Literacy and Resilience in Boosting Their Engagement and Motivation in AI-Based Settings: From an Achievement Goal Theory Perspective. *Learning and Motivation*, *91*, 1–11. DOI: 10.1016/j.lmot.2025.102152

KEY TERMS AND DEFINITIONS

Artificial Intelligence: It refers to machine-based systems capable of performing tasks that typically require human intelligence.

Student Development: It encompasses the cognitive, emotional, and social growth of learners, which can be shaped by sustained interactions with AI technologies in educational settings.

Emotional Resilience: The ability of students to adapt to stress and adversity, potentially supported or undermined by AI-driven emotional feedback and monitoring tools.

Identity Formation: The process through which students develop a sense of self, which may be influenced by AI systems that mediate learning experiences and performance evaluation.

Socioemotional Learning: Learning that fosters emotional intelligence, empathy, and interpersonal skills, increasingly mediated by AI tools that support emotional interactions.

Human-Centered Education: An educational philosophy prioritizing student well-being, relational dynamics, and holistic development.

Algorithmic Surveillance: The use of AI systems to monitor student behavior and performance, which raises ethical and psychological concerns related to autonomy and privacy.

Developmental Integrity: A guiding principle that emphasizes the need to preserve the full spectrum of students' developmental needs when integrating AI into educational environments.

Chapter 4

The Evolution of Artificial Intelligence in Education: From Theory to Practice

Mustafa Kayyali
https://orcid.org/0000-0003-3300-262X
Maaref University of Applied Sciences, Syria

ABSTRACT

Artificial Intelligence (AI) is no longer a distant concept confined to theoretical discourse; it has become a transformative force within classrooms across the globe. This chapter critically explores the evolution of AI in education, tracing its journey from speculative theory to practical deployment. With a reflective lens, it examines how AI-driven systems have reshaped pedagogical methodologies, from personalized learning environments and adaptive assessments to the nuanced roles of intelligent tutoring and learning analytics. Beyond the promise of efficiency and customization, the chapter grapples with ethical dilemmas, pedagogical dependencies, and the socio-emotional implications of AI-mediated instruction. Ultimately, it argues for a more human-centered, ethically conscious path forward—one where technology supports, rather than supplants, the relational and transformative essence of education.

INTRODUCTION

There are moments in the arc of human progress that feel both subtle and seismic. The integration of artificial intelligence (AI) into the fabric of education is one such moment (Pedro et al, 2019). It didn't arrive all at once, with dramatic flair or thunderous announcements. Rather, it seeped quietly into the corners of classrooms, into the dashboards of teachers, and into the curious fingertips of students tapping

DOI: 10.4018/979-8-3373-6007-2.ch004

on smart devices—shaping, shifting, and sometimes unsettling the very essence of how we learn and teach. Once relegated to science fiction or speculative research papers, AI is now a tangible presence in schools across the globe. But this transition from theory to practice did not occur in a vacuum. It emerged from decades of interdisciplinary work in computer science, cognitive psychology, linguistics, and education, converging toward the dream of creating systems that could not just process data, but understand and respond to learners. It has been a journey from early aspirations of replicating human intelligence to more nuanced approaches that seek to augment human capacities rather than replace them.

At its core, education is not simply about information transfer—it is about transformation (Williams, 2023). It is about connection, growth, and the development of critical consciousness. The promise of AI in this realm was, and still is, immense. Proponents envisioned intelligent tutoring systems that could adapt to every learner's needs, virtual agents that could provide around-the-clock support, and platforms that could analyze student behavior with unprecedented precision. In many ways, these dreams have materialized. In others, they remain unfulfilled, complicated by technical, ethical, and pedagogical challenges. This chapter does not merely celebrate the technological advancements AI has brought to education; rather, it interrogates them. It considers the implications of deploying learning algorithms that may know how a student thinks but not how they feel. It questions what is gained and what is lost when we prioritize personalization over collective experience or efficiency over empathy. It reflects on the educator's evolving role—not as a transmitter of knowledge, but as a guide, interpreter, and sometimes even a counterbalance to automated systems.

The transition from theory to practice has been neither linear nor universally embraced. In some contexts, AI tools have enhanced learning outcomes and freed up educators to focus on more meaningful interactions (Alam & Mohanty, 2023). In others, they have widened inequalities, introduced new forms of surveillance, or simplified the complexity of learning into mere metrics. The stories of AI in education are as diverse as the learners it touches. And that is precisely why this moment demands careful thought, critical inquiry, and deep reflection. To understand where we are headed, we must first trace where we have been. This chapter begins with a historical overview of AI in education, moves through key theoretical and pedagogical frameworks, and then examines concrete applications currently shaping classrooms. Throughout, it returns to the human questions: What does it mean to learn? What should be the role of a teacher? Can machines support not just the acquisition of knowledge, but the cultivation of wisdom? As we stand at this intersection of innovation and introspection, it becomes clear that the evolution of AI in education is not just a technological journey—it is a profoundly human one.

And like all human journeys, it is marked by hope, contradiction, and the enduring desire to create a better future for the generations to come.

From Vision to Reality: Tracing the Historical Trajectory of AI in Education

The story of artificial intelligence in education is not just a tale of algorithms and innovations—it is a reflection of our changing beliefs about what it means to learn, to teach, and to know (Tedre et al, 2021). For decades, educators, philosophers, technologists, and dreamers have pondered how machines might one day understand us—not just process our words, but respond with relevance, perhaps even with empathy. What began as a theoretical vision—sometimes utopian, sometimes dystopian—has, over time, become something far more real, complex, and unpredictable. In the early stages, the vision of AI in education emerged at the crossroads of two distinct yet deeply interconnected disciplines: computer science and cognitive psychology. In the 1950s and 1960s, as researchers like Alan Turing posed questions about machine intelligence, others began to wonder: if a machine can simulate human reasoning, could it also simulate the way a child learns? These early years were marked more by philosophical inquiry than practical application, yet they planted seeds that would later bloom into real-world experimentation (Gonçalves, 2020).

By the 1970s, pioneers such as Seymour Papert began shifting the conversation. Papert, a student of Piaget and one of the creators of the programming language LOGO, believed deeply in constructivist learning. He envisioned computers not as replacements for teachers but as intellectual companions—tools that could help children think, explore, and express themselves (Lachney & Foster, 2020). Papert's ideas gave birth to the concept of learners programming computers, not the other way around. It was a radical departure from passive instruction and a move toward active, student-driven engagement with technology. These early attempts were imaginative but limited. Computers were bulky, expensive, and inaccessible to most schools. But the ambition to personalize learning through intelligent systems persisted. In the 1980s and 1990s, research into intelligent tutoring systems (ITS) gained momentum (Gobert et al, 2023). These systems aimed to simulate the guidance of a human tutor by adapting feedback to a student's performance in real time. They represented a significant leap forward—not just machines delivering information, but machines interacting with learners, monitoring errors, and adjusting the content accordingly.

Yet even then, the dream was larger than the reality. ITS were often expensive to develop, difficult to scale, and confined to narrow subjects like mathematics and physics. They worked best in structured domains with clear right-or-wrong answers. The human complexity of open-ended thinking, emotional intelligence, or collaborative learning remained out of reach. But still, progress continued—quietly, steadily. The 2000s brought a wave of optimism. With the rise of the internet and increasingly powerful computing systems, educational technology began to evolve more rapidly. Learning management systems, digital assessments, and online courseware laid the groundwork for more advanced, AI-driven tools. At the same time, machine learning—especially with the development of neural networks—offered a new approach. Unlike earlier rule-based systems, machine learning models could improve through exposure to data. The implications for education were profound. A system could now potentially "learn" how students learn.

Around this time, adaptive learning platforms began to take root. These systems promised something revolutionary: personalized pathways through content based on real-time analysis of a student's knowledge, pace, and preferences. Products like Knewton, DreamBox, and ALEKS became examples of this new generation of learning tools (Annuš, 2024). For the first time, large numbers of students could engage with content tailored to their individual needs. Teachers could gain insight into student performance through dashboards and analytics, allowing for targeted intervention. Still, the excitement was tempered by caution. As platforms expanded and data collection increased, questions began to surface. Who owned the data? Were the algorithms fair? Could personalization unintentionally reinforce existing inequalities by pigeonholing students into predefined learning tracks? The vision was becoming reality, yes—but not without shadows. As we entered the 2010s, the pace quickened. Voice assistants, speech recognition tools, and natural language processing became part of the educational landscape (Sayers et al, 2021). Virtual teaching assistants like Georgia Tech's "Jill Watson"—an AI built on IBM Watson—began answering student questions in online forums, sometimes without students even realizing they were interacting with a machine. The boundary between human and machine blurred further.

Massive Open Online Courses (MOOCs), once hailed as the future of higher education, began integrating AI tools to manage and scale instruction (Mutawa, 2023). Automated grading, plagiarism detection, and predictive analytics became commonplace. Some universities explored AI-generated content recommendations, while others tested systems that could predict student dropout risk based on behavioral patterns. These developments were not mere add-ons—they were quietly changing the infrastructure of education. Yet, alongside these technical advancements, a deeper philosophical shift was unfolding. Education was no longer just a human endeavor aided by tools—it was becoming a shared space, a partnership, between human judgment and machine intelligence (Luckin, 2018). Teachers were no longer just providers of knowledge but curators of content, interpreters of data, and guides through algorithmically shaped learning paths. The nature of pedagogy itself was evolving. And then, of course, came a turning point no one could have predicted:

the COVID-19 pandemic. When schools around the world shut their doors, digital learning platforms became lifelines. AI-driven tools—once optional—became necessary. Systems that could assess students remotely, offer immediate feedback, or guide independent learning were suddenly not just useful, but essential. The crisis fast-tracked adoption, exposing both the strengths and weaknesses of AI in education. Some students thrived with the autonomy and flexibility, while others floundered in the absence of social connection and human guidance. Equity gaps widened. The digital divide became a chasm. And once again, we were reminded: technology alone cannot save education.

Figure 1. Timeline of AI Milestones in Education

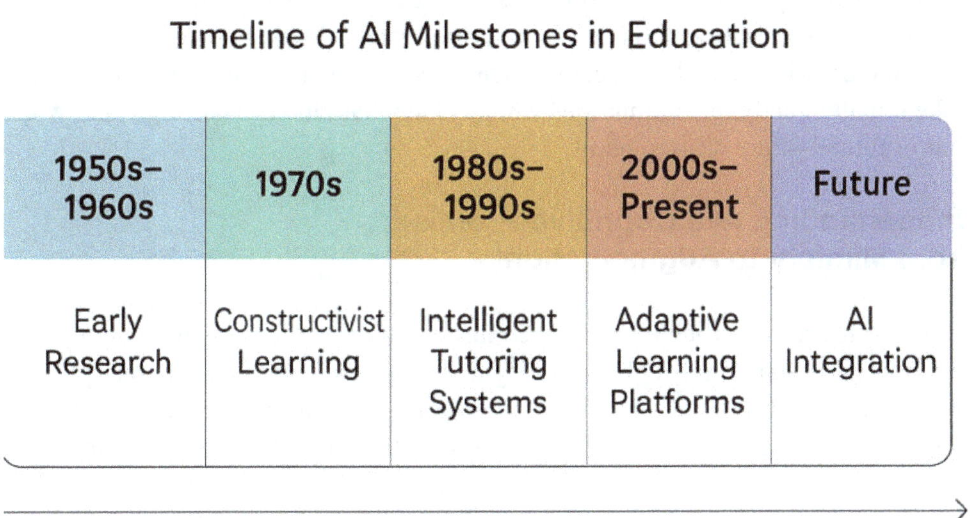

Yet the post-pandemic world didn't turn away from AI. If anything, the momentum continued. New tools emerged, and older ones matured. AI chatbots began offering writing assistance, emotional support, and content recommendations (Chew, 2022). Platforms started incorporating affective computing, attempting to detect student emotion through facial recognition or keyboard behavior. The idea was simple but ambitious: not just to track what students know, but how they feel as they learn. But this brings us to a crossroads—a moment where we must reflect on the distance traveled and the direction ahead. The dream of AI in education was never just about efficiency. It was about possibility. About the belief that learning could be more responsive, more inclusive, more human, paradoxically, through machines. And yet, as we move forward, we must ask ourselves whether we are designing systems that honor that vision, or simply chasing the next innovation. Because somewhere along this trajectory—from LOGO turtles to neural networks, from tutoring systems to predictive analytics—we risk losing sight of the learner. Not as a data point or a user, but as a person. A child struggling to find their voice. A teenager asking questions that don't have neat answers. A curious mind that learns not just by consuming content, but by connecting with others, by reflecting, by failing, by growing.

The history of AI in education is not a straight line. It is a braided thread of hope, experimentation, contradiction, and renewal. It has always danced between what is possible and what is meaningful. And perhaps that is the most important lesson of all. That even as our tools become more powerful, our responsibility deepens. To remember that education is not a problem to be solved, but a relationship to be nurtured. In tracing this trajectory—from early visions to present realities—we are not just mapping technological progress. We are telling a human story, one that is still unfolding. The next chapter is unwritten, and it belongs to all of us: to the programmers who write the code, the teachers who bring it to life, the students who make it matter, and the communities who decide what kind of learning—and what kind of future—they want to build.

Understanding AI's Cognitive Promise: From Mimicry to Augmentation

At the heart of artificial intelligence lies a centuries-old human yearning: the desire to understand and replicate thought. Long before AI had a name, philosophers and scientists were already imagining mechanical minds, theorizing how reason, memory, language, and learning might be deconstructed and simulated. This impulse—to mimic the mind—has always walked a fine line between wonder and caution. In education, where the mind is both the subject and the instrument, the implications are particularly profound.

AI's early cognitive ambitions were rooted in mimicry. The goal was to replicate human reasoning, to encode logic into machines that could solve problems, make decisions, and respond intelligently to stimuli. In the context of education, this meant designing systems that could act like tutors—guiding students, posing questions, assessing answers, and delivering tailored responses (Chang et al, 2023). At first, these systems were rigid and predictable. They followed scripts, applied rules, and made inferences based on structured data. They were impressive in their logic but limited in their scope. They mimicked cognition in narrow bands, often succeeding in formal tasks like solving algebra problems or guiding vocabulary acquisition, but faltering when confronted with ambiguity, emotion, or context. Despite their limitations, these early systems carried with them a quiet revolution. They challenged the assumption that learning must always be mediated by a human. They opened the door to a new kind of cognitive partnership—one where machines might share in the work of understanding. Over time, as the field evolved, the emphasis began to shift. The question was no longer just how to mimic the mind, but how to augment it. What if AI could extend our cognitive capacities? What if it could help us think more deeply, more clearly, more creatively? This shift—from mimicry to augmentation—marked a turning point in both AI research and educational philosophy. Augmentation reframes the role of technology not as a substitute for human thinking, but as a companion to it. The goal is no longer replication, but resonance. Machines don't need to be "just like us" to be useful. In fact, their difference—their tireless capacity for pattern recognition, their indifference to fatigue, their ability to process vast amounts of information in milliseconds—can be their greatest gift, if aligned with human needs and values.

Figure 2. Theories of AI in Education

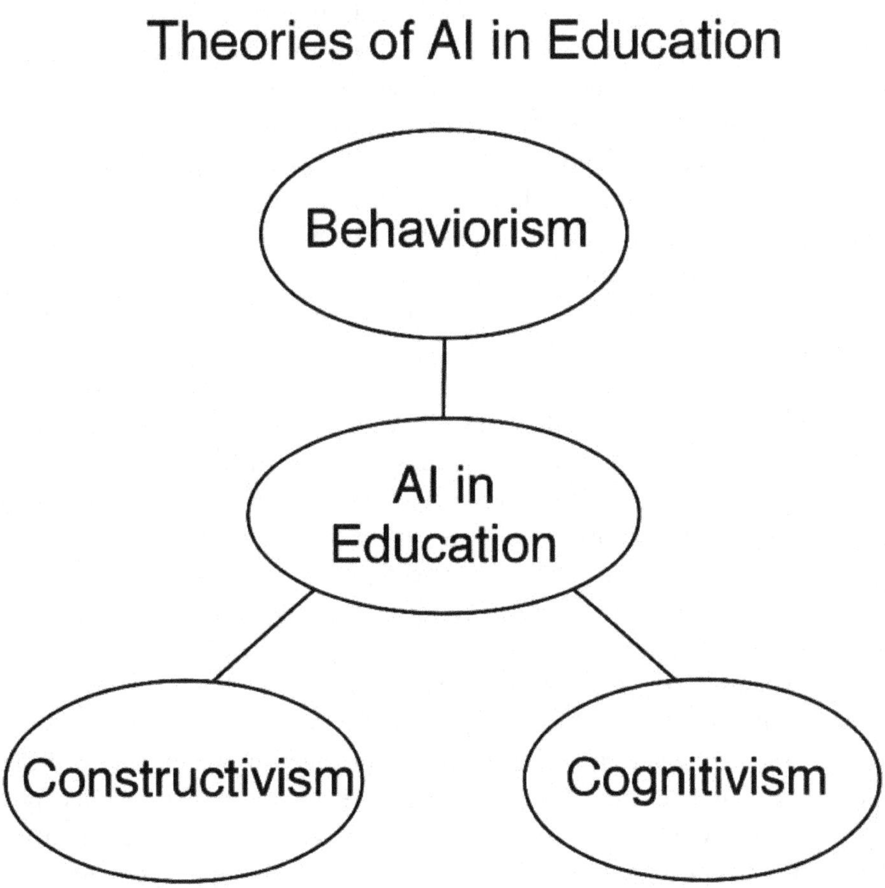

In classrooms, this promise begins to materialize in subtle but powerful ways. Consider the case of adaptive learning platforms that analyze a student's performance and tailor the difficulty, pacing, and type of content in real-time. These systems do not merely mimic a tutor's responses; they create entirely new feedback loops that would be impossible for a human alone to manage. They spot trends across cohorts, surface misconceptions before they become entrenched, and allow learners to progress at a personalized rhythm that respects their unique journey. But the promise of cognitive augmentation extends far beyond efficiency (Kayyali, 2024 A). AI can provoke reflection. It can challenge assumptions. It can serve as a mirror that helps students—and teachers—see their own thinking more clearly. For instance, writing assistants powered by natural language processing can help learners revise their arguments, offering suggestions not just on grammar, but on tone, structure, and clarity. These tools encourage metacognition—thinking about one's own thinking—a cornerstone of deep learning. When used thoughtfully, they do not diminish the role of the writer; they elevate it.

In scientific discovery and project-based learning, AI is beginning to play a generative role (Attaluri & Mudunuri, 2025). Tools that analyze large datasets can support students in asking better questions, exploring patterns, and testing hypotheses. AI can simulate ecosystems, model historical scenarios, or visualize abstract concepts in ways that spark curiosity and deepen understanding (Kayyali, 2025 D). These are not acts of mimicry. They are acts of amplification—moments where machine intelligence catalyzes human insight. The teacher's role in this landscape is not diminished; it is redefined. With AI taking on certain cognitive functions—sorting, predicting, responding—the educator is freed to focus on the relational and interpretive dimensions of teaching. They can attend more closely to student well-being, foster critical dialogue, and help learners navigate not just the content, but the context of what they are learning. Teachers become curators of experience, mentors in the art of discernment, and guides in the ethical use of powerful tools.

Still, the promise of cognitive augmentation comes with its tensions. There is a danger in offloading too much thinking to machines. Convenience can lead to complacency. If students begin to rely on AI to generate ideas, organize thoughts, or evaluate arguments, they may forgo the struggle that often precedes true understanding (Aymen et al, 2024). Learning is not always efficient, nor should it be. It is often slow, messy, nonlinear. There is something deeply human about wrestling with uncertainty, about making sense of complexity without shortcuts. Not all forms of augmentation are equal. A tool that helps a student brainstorm ideas is different from one that completes their assignment. A system that visualizes a concept may deepen understanding, while one that simplifies it may dilute it. The line between support and substitution is thin, and easy to cross. It requires careful thought, transparent design, and an unwavering commitment to preserving the learner's agency.

Another tension lies in the way AI systems learn. Their cognitive "insight" is not born of understanding, but of statistical association (Haugeland, 2023). They do not know what they know; they recognize patterns. This distinction matters. A human teacher might infer a student's confusion based on subtle cues—hesitation, frustration, a furrowed brow. An AI might infer it based on response time or accuracy. Both can be useful, but they are not the same. The richness of human cognition, with its emotional undercurrents, intuitive leaps, and ethical reflexes, remains beyond the reach of even the most advanced algorithms. Yet even with these limitations, the path of augmentation holds more promise than peril—if navigated with wisdom. It invites us to reimagine the cognitive ecology of the classroom. What if students had access to intelligent systems that helped them learn how to learn? What if teachers had tools that illuminated not just what students got wrong, but why? What if the learning process itself became more transparent, more responsive, more reflective?

These questions are not hypothetical. They are already shaping the design of emerging AI tools. Some platforms are beginning to integrate affective computing, attempting to detect student emotions and adjust content accordingly (Wang et al, 2022). Others are exploring conversational agents that engage learners in Socratic dialogue, prompting them to explain, elaborate, and defend their thinking. These efforts aim not just to mimic thought, but to foster it. In this context, the cognitive promise of AI is not about creating perfect thinkers, but about creating more thoughtful learning environments. It's about expanding the space in which ideas can grow. It's about offering scaffolds, not crutches; provocations, not prescriptions. It's about using the precision of machines to enhance the depth of human thought. But perhaps most importantly, the real power of AI lies not in what it does, but in what it makes possible. It invites educators to rethink the architecture of learning, to design experiences that are more adaptive, more inclusive, and more attuned to the diverse ways people make sense of the world. It challenges old hierarchies, blurs the boundary between teacher and learner, and opens new pathways for discovery.

As we continue to explore this terrain, we must remember that cognition is not just a technical process—it is a profoundly human one. It is shaped by culture, emotion, experience, and values. Augmenting cognition, therefore, is not just a technical challenge—it is a moral one. It requires us to ask not only what is possible, but what is desirable. Not only what AI can do, but what we want education to become. We are still in the early stages of this journey. The systems we have today are crude compared to what will emerge tomorrow. But already, we see glimpses of a future where AI and human intelligence are not in competition, but in conversation. A future where the goal is not to make machines think like us, but to use machines to help us think more clearly, more creatively, and more compassionately. The cognitive promise of AI is not about machines becoming human. It is about humans becoming more fully themselves—with the help of machines that understand, not in the way we do, but in ways that can still support our learning, our growth, and our collective flourishing.

Pedagogical Shifts in the Age of Intelligent Systems

Something subtle yet fundamental is happening in education. It is not always visible in the lesson plans or the classroom walls, and it doesn't announce itself with fanfare. It slips in quietly—through recommendation engines, adaptive assessments, chatbot tutors, and predictive dashboards. What's shifting is not just the tools, but the very nature of pedagogy itself. With the steady rise of intelligent systems, the foundations of how we teach, how students learn, and how knowledge is structured are beginning to shift beneath our feet. And while the surface may still look familiar, the dynamics underneath are transforming in ways that demand both deep reflection and careful reimagining. Pedagogy has always evolved in conversation with the technologies of its time (Ali, 2019). The printing press democratized knowledge, the blackboard enabled group instruction, and the internet reshaped access to information. But artificial intelligence introduces something different. Unlike previous tools, AI doesn't merely serve as a passive conduit; it actively processes, interprets, responds. It makes decisions—often in real time—about what content to deliver, when, and how. This makes it more than just a medium; it becomes a participant in the learning process. And that changes everything.

In traditional classrooms, pedagogy often followed a relatively fixed rhythm: content delivery by the teacher, engagement through practice, and assessment to measure retention (Semel, 2019). The teacher was the planner, the provider, the evaluator. But intelligent systems are disrupting this structure. AI-driven platforms can now analyze a student's behavior and performance at granular levels, providing insights that were once hidden or assumed. They can suggest the next topic based on mastery, recommend revision material for forgotten concepts, and even adjust the pace to match individual cognitive patterns. In this environment, the teacher's role is no longer to deliver knowledge, but to orchestrate a learning experience that is increasingly mediated by algorithms. This shift—from direct instruction to orchestration—requires a redefinition of pedagogical identity. Teachers must become interpreters of data, designers of meaningful engagement, and facilitators of ethical technology use. They must decide when to lean into the machine's capabilities and when to pull back. They must ask not just what students are learning, but how and why—and what they might be missing in the process. In this new ecology, professional judgment becomes more essential, not less.

One of the most noticeable changes lies in how learning paths are structured. AI systems allow for hyper-personalized experiences, where each student can follow a different trajectory based on their current knowledge, interests, and needs (Singh &

Kaunert, 2024). This flexibility is a powerful antidote to the one-size-fits-all approach that has long plagued formal education. Students who struggle can receive immediate, targeted support; those who excel can move ahead without waiting. Learning becomes more responsive, more dynamic, and potentially more humane. But this individualized approach also disrupts the collective nature of traditional classrooms. When each student is interacting with a different version of the curriculum, guided by different algorithms, what happens to the shared experience of learning? What happens to the conversations, the disagreements, the group struggles that often shape understanding? AI systems can optimize instruction for the individual, but they may inadvertently erode the communal dimension of education—the messy, social process through which ideas are challenged and refined in dialogue with others. This is not an argument against personalization.

Rather, it is a reminder that pedagogy is more than delivery. It is a set of values, assumptions, and relationships. And while AI can make learning more efficient, it cannot—on its own—make it more meaningful. That task still falls to the human architect of the learning environment: the teacher. Another shift is emerging in assessment. Traditional testing has long been critiqued for its rigidity, its focus on recall over reasoning, and its failure to capture deeper forms of understanding (Stewart, 2021). Intelligent systems offer new possibilities—formative assessments that adapt in real time, dashboards that visualize progress, and analytics that predict risk. These tools can support more timely and targeted interventions, allowing teachers to move from reactive to proactive support. But they also raise new questions. When performance becomes a stream of data points, do we risk reducing learning to what is easily measurable? Do we start to value what we can track over what we should cultivate?

Some of the most important outcomes of education—curiosity, resilience, ethical reasoning—are not easily quantifiable. Yet they are essential for human flourishing. If pedagogy becomes too closely tied to what AI systems can monitor, we may unintentionally shift our priorities (Kayyali, 2025 E). We may begin designing learning experiences that optimize for engagement metrics or time-on-task rather than critical thinking or joy. This is where pedagogy must push back—asserting its deeper purposes in the face of technological pressures. In the age of intelligent systems, pedagogy must also become more ethically conscious. Decisions that were once made intuitively—what content to teach, how to group students, how to provide feedback—are now increasingly informed by algorithmic recommendations. These systems are not neutral. They are shaped by the data they are trained on, the assumptions encoded in their models, and the design choices of their creators. Educators must develop new literacies—not just digital, but ethical. They must learn to interrogate AI tools, ask about transparency, bias, and privacy, and advocate for systems that align with their values and their students' needs. This is a difficult balancing act. Teachers are already stretched, managing not only the curriculum but also the emotional and developmental well-being of their students. Adding AI to the mix can feel like both a gift and a burden. It promises support but demands vigilance. It offers insight but can also overwhelm. For pedagogy to thrive in this context, teachers must be supported—not just with training, but with time, space, and professional autonomy to explore these tools thoughtfully.

Amid all this change, something else is shifting—something less discussed, but equally important. It is our very imagination of what education is and what it could be. Intelligent systems invite us to reconsider the boundaries of the classroom. Learning no longer needs to be confined to a physical space or a fixed schedule. Students can engage with content at any time, collaborate with peers across the world, and access mentors through digital interfaces (Carvalho & Santos, 2022). The classroom becomes porous, extending into homes, communities, and digital platforms. But this expanded access is not automatically equitable. It depends on infrastructure, digital literacy, and support systems. As pedagogy evolves, it must address these disparities head-on. Intelligent systems can widen opportunities, but they can also widen gaps if deployed without attention to context. This is not just a technical issue—it is a pedagogical one. Who is included? Who is left out? What assumptions are baked into the design of our learning tools, and whose voices are shaping those designs?

Pedagogical shifts in the age of intelligent systems are not just about technology (Lorenzo & Gallon, 2019). They are about re-centering the human. They are about reclaiming the teacher's role as a thoughtful guide in an increasingly automated world. They are about ensuring that learning remains a relational, purposeful, and transformative endeavor. We stand at a threshold. The tools at our disposal are more powerful than ever. But the question remains: what kind of education do we want to create with them? Will we pursue efficiency at the cost of empathy? Will we automate instruction but forget inspiration? Or will we find ways to use intelligent systems not as replacements, but as extensions of our deepest pedagogical commitments? There are no easy answers. But there is, perhaps, a guiding principle: that every technological shift is also a moral one. Every new tool forces us to ask again what matters most. And in education, what matters most has never changed. It is the learner's growth, the teacher's care, and the fragile, beautiful process through which knowledge becomes meaning. In this new age, pedagogy must not just adapt—it must lead. It must shape the use of intelligent systems, not be shaped by them. It must hold fast to its core purpose: not to train compliant minds, but to nurture questioning, connected, and courageous ones. Only then can we ensure that the systems we build serve not just our classrooms, but our humanity.

Practical Applications in the Classroom: Tools, Platforms, and Personalized Learning

In the modern classroom, technology is no longer a supplemental tool, but an integral part of the learning environment (Hamilton, 2022). The advent of AI and intelligent systems has introduced a shift in how education is structured, allowing for greater flexibility, adaptability, and personalization. For decades, educators have dreamed of being able to address the unique needs of each student, but the tools to do so were limited by time, resources, and sheer scale. Now, with AI-powered platforms and intelligent tools, these dreams are being realized in new and innovative ways. However, the true potential of these systems lies not only in the technology itself but in how they are integrated into everyday teaching practices.

One of the most notable and promising applications of AI in the classroom is personalized learning (Mahmoud & Sørensen, 2024). Personalized learning has long been a goal in education, yet achieving it at scale has remained an elusive challenge. Traditional classroom structures often operate under the assumption that all students should progress at the same pace, through the same material, in the same manner. This model works for some students, but for others, it fails to meet their individual needs. With AI, the barriers that have traditionally hindered personalized learning are slowly being dismantled. AI-powered platforms, such as adaptive learning tools, provide the ability to cater to each student's pace and level of understanding (Kayyali, 2025 A). These systems can track a learner's progress in real time, identify areas where the student may be struggling, and adjust the content accordingly. The result is a dynamic learning environment where the curriculum is constantly shifting to meet the student where they are, offering both support and challenge in equal measure. For example, tools like DreamBox Learning and Knewton have revolutionized the way math and reading are taught in schools (Rajput, 2025). These platforms use complex algorithms to assess students' knowledge and learning styles, providing personalized learning paths. If a student struggles with a particular concept, the system will automatically adjust and provide additional practice or explanations. This instant feedback loop, powered by AI, is one of the most valuable aspects of these platforms. It allows students to progress at their own pace, without feeling the pressure of keeping up with the rest of the class.

However, personalization through AI is not limited to adaptive learning tools alone (Gligorea et al, 2023). Other platforms focus on offering tailored content recommendations. AI systems can analyze a student's interests, past performance, and engagement with the material to suggest additional resources that align with their unique learning needs. This goes beyond simply providing more practice; it opens up opportunities for students to explore topics they may not have otherwise encountered in a traditional curriculum. For instance, AI-powered content recommendation engines can offer students videos, articles, and interactive simulations that relate to their current lessons, but also extend to other areas of curiosity. This broader approach to personalization helps foster deeper learning and a more intrinsic motivation to explore. While adaptive learning and content recommendation are perhaps the most talked-about AI applications in the classroom, AI tools also offer significant benefits in more traditional forms of assessment. Grading has long been one of the most time-consuming tasks for teachers, often taking hours to provide detailed feedback. AI tools like Gradescope and Turnitin can assist in grading, freeing up time for teachers to focus on more meaningful interactions with their students (Giri, 2025). AI-driven grading platforms can evaluate both objective tests, such as multiple-choice questions, and more subjective assignments like essays. They offer instant, accurate assessments, providing students with feedback in real time. This feedback helps students adjust their approach to learning before they move too far down the wrong path, ultimately leading to more effective and efficient learning. Yet, as beneficial as these tools are, the integration of AI into the classroom is not without its challenges. The first and most obvious hurdle is ensuring that AI tools are accessible to all students. While AI-powered platforms have the potential to enhance learning, they can also widen the gap for students who lack access to the necessary technology or internet infrastructure (Kayyali, 2025 B). The digital divide, a problem that has existed for years, is exacerbated in the age of AI. Many schools, particularly those in underserved communities, struggle to provide the devices and internet access that would allow students to fully take advantage of AI-powered learning (Mathai, 2024). The potential of AI in education will only be realized when all students have equal access to these tools.

The second challenge lies in the implementation of AI systems themselves. Teachers, the primary users of these platforms, must be adequately trained in how to use AI tools effectively. If a teacher is not comfortable with the technology or lacks the knowledge of how to interpret the data these systems generate, the benefits of AI can quickly be lost. Teacher professional development must be an integral part of the rollout of AI tools, ensuring that educators are equipped not only with the technical skills but also the pedagogical knowledge to integrate AI meaningfully into their teaching practices (Fakhar et al, 2024). While AI has the ability to personalize learning at an unprecedented scale, it is essential to remember that AI is not a replacement for human teachers. The role of the educator remains critical in creating a supportive learning environment, fostering student relationships, and helping students develop the critical thinking and emotional intelligence necessary for navigating the complexities of the world. AI can assist in delivering content and offering immediate feedback, but it cannot replace the human touch that is central to effective education. The best results will be achieved when AI is used as a complementary tool to support, rather than replace, the teacher.

Another significant concern is the ethics of using AI in the classroom (Tang & Su, 2024). AI systems rely on vast amounts of data to function effectively, and this raises serious questions about privacy, security, and the potential for bias. How is student data being collected, stored, and used? Who owns this data? Are the algorithms that power these systems transparent, and do they perpetuate existing biases? These questions are not just technical—they are ethical. As AI systems become more integrated into classrooms, it is crucial that educators, policymakers, and technologists work together to ensure that these systems are designed with student privacy and fairness in mind (Khan, 2024). Despite these challenges, the potential for AI to revolutionize education remains immense. One of the most promising applications of AI in the classroom is in the area of formative assessment. Rather than waiting for a final exam or test to gauge a student's understanding, AI can provide ongoing feedback, allowing teachers to identify areas of struggle and offer support in real-time. This shift from summative assessment to formative assessment changes the way learning is approached. Students no longer work in isolation until the final exam; instead, they receive continuous guidance and support, making learning more fluid and responsive.

Furthermore, AI's potential to assist in administrative tasks cannot be overlooked. Teachers often spend countless hours on administrative work—grading papers, organizing schedules, communicating with parents, and managing student data. AI tools can help streamline many of these tasks, allowing teachers to spend more time doing what they do best: teaching. AI can automate scheduling, assist with class management, track student progress, and even help with personalized communications to parents. By taking over these time-consuming tasks, AI gives teachers more time to focus on the creative, interpersonal, and critical aspects of teaching. AI also holds the potential to foster greater collaboration between students. With AI-powered tools like collaborative platforms and interactive simulations, students can work together on projects, share ideas, and engage in dynamic learning experiences (Bianchi, 2024). These tools allow for deeper, more meaningful collaboration, as AI systems can provide real-time feedback to students as they work together. This is particularly beneficial for developing skills like teamwork, communication, and problem-solving, which are critical in today's interconnected world. AI-powered tools and platforms are offering exciting new opportunities for personalized learning, but the successful implementation of these systems requires careful attention to ethical, pedagogical, and practical considerations. While AI has the potential to revolutionize the way we teach and learn, it must be implemented thoughtfully, with an eye toward equity, accessibility, and human interaction. Teachers must be supported and empowered to use AI tools effectively, and AI must be viewed as a complement to, rather than a replacement for, the invaluable role of the human teacher. As we move forward, the integration of AI into the classroom has the potential to transform education in ways that we are only beginning to understand. The tools are powerful, but their true potential lies in how we use them to create better learning experiences for all students.

Bridging the Gap Between Theory and Impact: Successes and Shortcomings

The journey of artificial intelligence in education is as much a story of ambition and hope as it is one of caution and reflection. From its inception as an abstract idea, AI has evolved into a tangible presence within schools and universities. Its potential to revolutionize education is widely acknowledged, and yet the path from theory to tangible impact has been neither linear nor smooth. As much as AI promises to tailor learning to the individual, to reduce educational inequalities, and to enhance the efficacy of teaching, it also brings with it challenges, ethical dilemmas, and limitations that cannot be ignored.

In examining the successes and shortcomings of AI in education, we find ourselves at the intersection of optimism and realism (Sargent, 2024). For every breakthrough that demonstrates AI's capacity to personalize learning, there are instances where its deployment has fallen short, raising questions about its scalability, accessibility, and true impact. The gap between theory—the vision of a perfectly tailored, data-driven educational system—and reality—the challenges faced in classrooms around the world—is where much of the conversation lies.

Successes: Personalization, Efficiency, and Engagement

The most celebrated success of AI in education has been its ability to personalize learning (Rane et al, 2023). Traditional educational models have often struggled to accommodate the diverse needs, abilities, and learning styles of students. In a typical classroom, one teacher must cater to a wide variety of learners, each with different paces of understanding, strengths, and weaknesses. Personalized learning has always been the ideal, but achieving it at scale has proven difficult. AI, however, has demonstrated its capacity to meet this challenge in remarkable ways. Through adaptive learning technologies, AI systems are able to assess a student's knowledge in real time and adjust the learning path accordingly (Demartini et al, 2024). These tools do not merely repeat content until it is understood; they respond dynamically, providing scaffolding where needed and offering more advanced material when appropriate. Students who struggle can receive targeted interventions, while those who excel can bypass content they already understand, progressing at a pace that suits them. In this way, AI has the potential to ensure that no student is left behind and that all students can work at their own level of competence and confidence.

AI-powered platforms such as DreamBox, Knewton, and Duolingo have demonstrated this potential in real-world classrooms. DreamBox, for instance, offers adaptive math lessons that respond to students' actions in real time, adjusting content based on their input, errors, and successes. Duolingo, an AI-driven language learning platform, allows learners to practice vocabulary, grammar, and pronunciation at their own pace, offering personalized feedback that helps students improve (Rajput, 2025). These platforms not only reduce the time teachers spend on remedial work but also ensure that learning is personalized and responsive to individual needs. Another success of AI in education is the efficiency it brings to administrative tasks. Teachers often spend a disproportionate amount of time on tasks that have little to do with teaching itself—grading, scheduling, managing student data, and communicating with parents. AI has the potential to significantly reduce the burden of these tasks, giving teachers more time to focus on their students. Grading platforms powered by AI, such as Gradescope, allow teachers to automate the grading process for a wide range of assessments, from multiple-choice quizzes to short-answer essays. These platforms not only speed up the grading process but also offer more consistent and objective evaluations.

AI's ability to handle data also enhances the way teachers monitor student progress. Analytics dashboards can provide real-time insights into student performance, highlighting areas of improvement and potential risks. This data-driven approach allows teachers to identify struggling students before they fall too far behind, ensuring that interventions can be made early. Furthermore, these insights enable teachers to design more targeted and effective lessons, using the data to understand which teaching methods work best for different groups of students. The capacity to gather and analyze data at scale represents a significant advantage in terms of teaching efficacy and student success. AI also has the potential to increase engagement in learning (Huang et al, 2023). Traditional classrooms can sometimes struggle to maintain student interest, especially when the material feels disconnected from the students' lives or when the pace is too fast or too slow. AI-powered learning tools, such as gamified platforms or virtual tutors, have the ability to engage students in ways that traditional methods cannot. These tools can provide immediate feedback, encourage competition, and make learning feel more like an interactive experience than a passive activity. For example, platforms like Kahoot! use game mechanics to engage students in learning, while intelligent tutors provide personalized guidance and support, making learning feel less like a chore and more like an exciting challenge.

Shortcomings: Equity, Data Privacy, and Unintended Consequences

Despite these successes, there are significant shortcomings that must be addressed in the ongoing implementation of AI in education (Kayyali, 2025 C). The first and most glaring of these is the issue of equity. While AI has the potential to level the playing field for students, it also risks exacerbating existing inequalities. Access to the technology necessary to benefit from AI-driven education is not equally distributed. In many parts of the world, schools struggle with outdated infrastructure, limited internet connectivity, and a lack of devices for students to use. In these contexts, AI becomes a luxury, not a tool available to every student. This divide between students who have access to AI-powered learning platforms and those who do not threatens to deepen existing educational inequities (Li, 2023). Students in low-income areas, rural regions, or developing countries may find themselves further behind their peers simply because they do not have access to the technology that could help them succeed. The promise of personalized learning, so central to AI's appeal, becomes irrelevant if students are unable to engage with the systems that offer it (Mahmoud & Sørensen, 2024). Thus, the digital divide remains a significant barrier to AI's potential to transform education for all.

Another major concern is data privacy. AI systems rely on vast amounts of data to function, and this data often includes highly sensitive information about students—such as their academic performance, behavior patterns, and even personal information. This raises serious questions about how that data is stored, who has access to it, and how it is used. While many AI platforms claim to adhere to privacy laws, the complexity of data-sharing agreements, the potential for data breaches, and the lack of transparency in some AI systems make this a difficult issue to address (Mbah, 2024). Parents, educators, and students must be assured that their data is secure and being used ethically. The data-driven nature of AI-powered systems can lead to unintended consequences. For example, algorithms that rely on past performance data to predict future outcomes can inadvertently reinforce biases. If a system is trained on data that reflects historical inequalities—such as lower academic performance among certain demographic groups—it may perpetuate these biases, providing less favorable outcomes for those students. This "algorithmic bias" is a growing concern in many fields, not just education, as AI systems begin to make decisions about everything from college admissions to job applications. In education, such biases could disproportionately affect minority or marginalized students, reinforcing stereotypes and limiting their opportunities.

Another issue lies in the potential for AI to undermine the role of human educators (Yang et al, 2021). While AI can provide personalized learning, it cannot replicate the nuanced understanding and emotional intelligence that teachers bring to the classroom. A machine may be able to identify that a student is struggling with a particular concept, but it cannot understand why the student is struggling, nor can it offer the empathy or encouragement needed to help them through a difficult time. The human connection between teacher and student remains a vital component of the learning process, and AI should be seen as a tool to enhance, not replace, that connection. Relying too heavily on AI could lead to a depersonalization of education, where students are seen as data points rather than individuals.

Bridging the Gap: Moving from Vision to Reality

To bridge the gap between the theoretical promise of AI and its real-world impact, several steps must be taken. First, efforts must be made to ensure that AI tools are accessible to all students. Governments, educational institutions, and technology companies must work together to ensure that every student has access to the devices, internet connections, and AI-powered platforms that can help them succeed (Goel, 2020). This will require significant investment in infrastructure, particularly in underserved areas. It will also require a commitment to ensuring that AI tools are designed to be inclusive, addressing the needs of students with disabilities, language barriers, and varying levels of technological literacy. Second, greater attention must be paid to data privacy and security. Schools must ensure that AI systems adhere to the highest standards of data protection, safeguarding students' personal information and ensuring that data is only used in ways that are ethical and transparent (Muli, 2024). There must be clear guidelines and regulations around the use of student data, and schools must be transparent about how AI systems collect, store, and use that data. We must acknowledge the limitations of AI and recognize that it cannot replace human educators. Teachers should be seen as essential partners in the implementation of AI systems, with their insights, judgment, and emotional intelligence remaining central to the learning process. AI should be used to augment the teacher's ability to support students, not to replace the teacher's role in building relationships, fostering critical thinking, and creating a sense of community in the classroom.

While the success of AI in education is undeniable, its shortcomings are equally significant. The challenge lies in bridging the gap between these two extremes: ensuring that the theoretical benefits of AI translate into tangible, equitable, and meaningful impacts on students' lives. By addressing issues of access, data privacy, and the irreplaceable role of the human teacher, we can ensure that AI fulfills its promise to transform education for the better. But this will require ongoing collaboration, critical reflection, and an unwavering commitment to the values that underpin education itself.

Ethical Considerations: Navigating the Moral Landscape

To ensure that AI's integration into education is both effective and just, it is essential to navigate the complex ethical landscape that accompanies technological innovation. First, a clear framework must be established to address algorithmic bias—the risk that AI systems can perpetuate or even exacerbate existing inequalities in education. Schools, policymakers, and technology developers must work collaboratively to audit AI models regularly, ensuring that they are fair, transparent, and inclusive of diverse student populations (Tang & Su, 2024). This means diversifying training data, testing for bias in outputs, and involving educators in the design process to identify potential blind spots. Second, student data privacy must be treated as a cornerstone of ethical AI implementation. AI systems rely on vast amounts of data to function effectively, yet without strong safeguards, this data can be misused or exposed. Educational institutions must develop rigorous data governance policies that protect students' personal information, ensure informed consent, and maintain clear lines of accountability for how data is collected, stored, and utilized. Transparency is essential—students and parents must know how their data is used and who has access to it. The role of the teacher in ethical AI integration cannot be overlooked.

Teachers are not just facilitators of content but stewards of the learning environment and guardians of student well-being. AI should be viewed as a tool to empower teachers, not to replace them. Educators must have a voice in shaping how AI is used in the classroom, ensuring it aligns with pedagogical values and supports—not undermines—critical thinking, creativity, and empathy (Kayyali a, 2025). While AI's potential in education is undeniable, so too are the ethical challenges it raises. Balancing innovation with responsibility demands an ongoing commitment to dialogue, reflection, and adaptation. By addressing issues of bias, privacy, and the evolving role of educators, we can ensure that AI serves as a force for equity, trust, and human flourishing in education. Achieving this will require unwavering vigilance and a collective commitment to placing ethical principles at the heart of every technological advancement.

Charting the Future: Towards a More Human-Centered Integration of AI in Education

The future of education is, by all accounts, an exciting one. As we stand on the precipice of a new era, driven by the rapid development of artificial intelligence, we are confronted with both immense opportunities and profound challenges. The promise of AI in education is clear: personalized learning, efficient assessment, and enhanced student engagement (Bhatia et al, 2024). But as the technology continues to evolve, so too must our understanding of its role in shaping the future of education. It is no longer enough to simply adopt AI for its own sake or to pursue the latest technological advancements without a clear sense of purpose. What is needed now, more than ever, is a shift towards a more human-centered integration of AI—one that prioritizes the well-being, growth, and potential of students over mere efficiency or novelty. At its best, AI can be a powerful ally in the educational process. It can provide tools for teachers, allowing them to focus more on teaching and less on administrative tasks. It can offer personalized learning paths that cater to the unique needs of each student, ensuring that everyone has the opportunity to succeed at their own pace. It can even provide insights into student behavior, enabling early interventions and supporting students who may be struggling. Yet, for all its potential, AI in education cannot and should not be a replacement for the human elements that make education meaningful. It must work alongside, not replace, the fundamental relationship between teacher and student.

This relationship is at the heart of a human-centered approach to AI integration in education (Topali et al, 2025). Teachers do more than convey information—they inspire, challenge, and guide their students. They provide emotional and social support, helping students navigate not only academic challenges but personal and emotional ones as well. AI, while powerful, cannot replicate the empathetic understanding, intuition, and emotional intelligence that teachers bring to their classrooms. A truly human-centered integration of AI in education recognizes this, using technology not to replace the teacher, but to empower them—to give them the tools they need to build stronger, more meaningful relationships with their students. But how do we ensure that AI serves this purpose? How do we chart a future in which AI's role is aligned with the values we hold dear in education—values like equity, empathy, and growth? The first step is to recognize that AI, like all technology, is a tool. Its impact is determined not by its capabilities alone but by the way it is used. In education, AI should never be about simply automating tasks or delivering content more efficiently; it should be about enriching the learning experience. This means that, instead of focusing on what AI can do on its own, we must focus on how it can support teachers in fostering deeper, more engaging learning experiences.

Personalized learning, for example, is one of the most powerful ways in which AI can support students (Kaswan et al, 2024). But for personalization to truly be effective, it must go beyond simply adjusting the pace or difficulty of content. It must take into account the individual needs, interests, and aspirations of each student. AI can help identify where a student is struggling, but it can also help uncover their unique strengths and interests, creating opportunities for deeper exploration. AI-driven platforms that recommend resources based on a student's learning profile, interests, and behaviors can help students connect more meaningfully with the content (Singh, 2024). However, this must always be done in a way that respects the student's autonomy, allowing them to take an active role in their learning process.

Personalization is not just about the delivery of content—it is about fostering a sense of ownership and agency in the learner. AI can help facilitate this by providing feedback that is specific, timely, and actionable, guiding students toward mastery in a way that is tailored to their needs. But the ultimate goal of personalization should always be to empower students, helping them become self-directed learners who can navigate the complexities of the world around them. This is where the teacher's role becomes crucial—teachers are the ones who can help students interpret and apply the insights provided by AI, offering guidance on how to use this information to enhance their learning.

Moreover, the integration of AI into education must prioritize inclusivity. One of the great promises of AI is its ability to make education more accessible to a broader range of students, including those with disabilities or learning challenges (Habib, 2022). AI tools that offer real-time translations, speech recognition, or assistive technologies can provide vital support to students who might otherwise struggle in a traditional classroom setting. But for these tools to be effective, they must be designed with the needs of all students in mind. This includes ensuring that AI systems are flexible, adaptable, and sensitive to the cultural and linguistic diversity of the classroom. In the future, AI must not be used as a tool for reinforcing existing educational inequalities. It must be used to level the playing field, offering every student the opportunity to succeed, regardless of their background, learning style, or personal circumstances. To achieve this, policymakers, educators, and technologists must work together to ensure that AI tools are accessible, transparent, and equitable. This means addressing the digital divide, ensuring that all students have access to the technology they need, and making sure that AI systems are trained on diverse datasets to avoid biases and ensure fair outcomes for all learners.

Beyond personalization and inclusivity, AI can also play a vital role in fostering collaboration (Shireesha, M., & Jeevan, 2024). In traditional classrooms, students often work individually, completing assignments and assessments in isolation. AI can change this dynamic by creating more opportunities for collaborative learning. For instance, AI systems can facilitate group projects, offering suggestions for how students can divide tasks, collaborate on problem-solving, and share resources. By leveraging AI to enhance collaboration, we can move away from the traditional model of competition and toward a more cooperative learning environment, where students learn not just from their teachers but from each other as well. AI can also be a valuable tool for promoting social and emotional learning SEL (Sethi & Jain, 2024). Emotional intelligence, self-regulation, and empathy are crucial skills for success in today's world. AI systems that monitor students' emotional responses to learning materials—such as their frustration, excitement, or confusion—can provide valuable insights into how students are engaging with the content. This can help teachers better understand the emotional needs of their students and tailor their teaching strategies accordingly. Furthermore, AI can be used to develop tools that support emotional well-being, such as virtual counselors or chatbots that offer guidance and support when students are struggling with stress or anxiety (Al-Sayed et al, 2024). However, AI must always be used in conjunction with human support in this area. Teachers, counselors, and caregivers must remain at the forefront of emotional guidance, using AI insights to inform their interactions with students rather than replace them. As we look to the future, it is also essential that we remain vigilant in our ethical considerations. The integration of AI into education raises numerous ethical questions, particularly around privacy, consent, and data security. Students' data is incredibly sensitive, and AI systems rely on vast amounts of personal information to function effectively. For AI to be implemented in a way that is truly human-centered, we must ensure that the data collected is protected, used ethically, and kept transparent. Students, parents, and educators must have control over how their data is used and must be able to trust that AI systems are designed with their best interests in mind.

One of the most crucial aspects of a human-centered approach to AI in education is ensuring that the technology is designed with empathy and understanding at its core. Developers, designers, and technologists must be mindful of the social and emotional context in which AI tools will be used (Kayyali, 2024 B). This requires a collaborative approach, with input from educators, students, and communities, to ensure that AI systems are not only effective but also respectful of the humanity they aim to serve. Technology must be seen as a tool to enhance human connection, not to diminish it (Barbosa Neves et al, 2019). Charting the future of AI in education requires more than just technological innovation—it requires a fundamental rethinking of the role of technology in our lives. A more human-centered approach to AI integration in education is essential to ensuring that the technology serves the needs of all learners. This means using AI not to replace teachers, but to support them in creating more personalized, inclusive, and collaborative learning environments. It means prioritizing the emotional and social aspects of learning, recognizing that AI has a role to play in fostering not just intellectual growth, but personal and social development as well (Kayyali, 2024 C). And most importantly, it means ensuring that AI is deployed in a way that is ethical, transparent, and respectful of the students it is meant to serve. In the end, AI should enhance the human experience of education, not replace it—working alongside teachers, students, and communities to create a future where learning is more accessible, engaging, and meaningful than ever before.

CONCLUSION

To look at the trajectory of AI in education is to look at a mirror reflecting our aspirations, fears, and values as a society. We began this journey with the belief that artificial intelligence could bring precision, equity, and insight into the most human of practices—teaching and learning. And in many ways, it has. From the automation of feedback to the fine-tuning of instructional strategies, AI has brought a level of scalability and responsiveness that human-centered education alone could not achieve. Yet alongside these advancements lies a more complex, less comfortable truth: intelligence—however artificial—does not guarantee understanding, and data—however vast—does not equal wisdom.

The evolution of AI in education has highlighted both the possibilities and limitations of relying on machines to shape minds. On one hand, adaptive learning platforms have enabled differentiated instruction at unprecedented scale, helping students from diverse backgrounds to learn at their own pace. Natural language processing has facilitated language learning and writing development. Predictive analytics have helped identify students at risk before failure becomes irreversible. These achievements are not trivial; they are meaningful, and in many cases, life-changing. But we must also acknowledge what AI cannot yet do, and perhaps should never be expected to do. It cannot replace the relational depth of a teacher who sees a student struggling and responds with compassion, or the spark of a mentor who recognizes a gift the student didn't know they had. It cannot model curiosity, nor can it foster resilience in the face of failure through a knowing glance or a well-timed word of encouragement. AI, at its best, can support learning. But only humans can truly inspire it.

Moreover, the adoption of AI has surfaced difficult ethical questions. Who owns the data collected in classrooms? What biases are encoded in the algorithms that shape learning experiences? How do we ensure transparency, accountability, and consent in the use of these tools? And most importantly, are we at risk of narrowing education to what is quantifiable, and in doing so, abandoning the rich, messy, and beautifully human aspects of learning? The conclusion of this chapter is not a final word, but an open invitation—to educators, policymakers, technologists, parents, and learners alike—to engage more critically and creatively with the role of AI in education. This is not a moment to passively adopt, but to actively shape. To decide not only how AI is used, but why it is used, and in whose interest. The goal should never be to replace teachers, but to reimagine their role in ways that empower both educators and learners to thrive. The road ahead is uncertain, and that's precisely why we must walk it with clarity, humility, and a commitment to values that transcend the latest software update. Let us not confuse progress with purpose. Let us not mistake efficiency for equity. And let us not allow the dazzling power of AI to distract us from the quiet, enduring truth that at the heart of all learning is a relationship—between teacher and student, between knowledge and curiosity, between the world as it is and the world as it could be. Artificial intelligence will continue to evolve. The real question is whether we, as educators and as a society, will evolve with it—not by surrendering to its logic, but by using it wisely, humanely, and with a sense of shared responsibility for the kind of future we want to build.

REFERENCES

Al-Sayed, S., Assayed, S. K., Alkhatib, M., & Shaalan, K. (2024). Impact of Artificial Intelligence Chatbots on Student Well-being and Mental Health: A Systematic Review. *People and Behavior Analysis*, *2*(2), 10–31098.

Alam, A., & Mohanty, A. (2023). Educational technology: Exploring the convergence of technology and pedagogy through mobility, interactivity, AI, and learning tools. *Cogent Engineering*, *10*(2), 2283282. DOI: 10.1080/23311916.2023.2283282

Ali, W. (2019). The efficacy of evolving technology in conceptualizing pedagogy and practice in higher education. *Higher Education Studies*, *9*(2), 81–95. DOI: 10.5539/hes.v9n2p81

Annuš, N. (2024). EDUCATIONAL SOFTWARE AND ARTIFICIAL INTELLIGENCE: STUDENTS'EXPERIENCES AND INNOVATIVE SOLUTIONS. *Information Technologies and Learning Tools*, *101*(3), 200–226. DOI: 10.33407/itlt.v101i3.5479

Attaluri, V., & Mudunuri, L. N. R. (2025). Generative AI for Creative Learning Content Creation: Project-Based Learning and Art Generation. In Smart Education and Sustainable Learning Environments in Smart Cities (pp. 239-252). IGI Global Scientific Publishing.

Aymen, D. I. F., & Zakarya, B. O. U. S. I. O. U. D. (2024). The Influence of Artificial Intelligence on Students' Critical Thinking (Doctoral dissertation, university center of abdalhafid boussouf-MILA).

Barbosa Neves, B., Franz, R., Judges, R., Beermann, C., & Baecker, R. (2019). Can digital technology enhance social connectedness among older adults? A feasibility study. *Journal of Applied Gerontology*, *38*(1), 49–72. DOI: 10.1177/0733464817741369 PMID: 29166818

Bhatia, A., Bhatia, P., & Sood, D. (2024). Leveraging AI to transform online higher education: Focusing on personalized learning, assessment, and student engagement. International Journal of Management and Humanities (IJMH) Volume-11 Issue-1.

Bianchi, I. (2024). Enhancing Critical Thinking in Education: Leveraging AI Tools and Technologies in Pedagogical Practice.

Carvalho, A. R., & Santos, C. (2022). Developing peer mentors' collaborative and metacognitive skills with a technology-enhanced peer learning program. *Computers and Education Open*, *3*, 100070. DOI: 10.1016/j.caeo.2021.100070

Chang, D. H., Lin, M. P. C., Hajian, S., & Wang, Q. Q. (2023). Educational design principles of using AI chatbot that supports self-regulated learning in education: Goal setting, feedback, and personalization. *Sustainability (Basel), 15*(17), 12921. DOI: 10.3390/su151712921

Chew, H. S. J. (2022). The use of artificial intelligence–based conversational agents (Chatbots) for weight loss: Scoping review and practical recommendations. *JMIR Medical Informatics, 10*(4), e32578. DOI: 10.2196/32578 PMID: 35416791

Demartini, C. G., Sciascia, L., Bosso, A., & Manuri, F. (2024). Artificial intelligence bringing improvements to adaptive learning in education: A case study. *Sustainability (Basel), 16*(3), 1347. DOI: 10.3390/su16031347

Fakhar, H., Lamrabet, M., Echantoufi, N., & Ajana, L. (2024). Towards a New Artificial Intelligence-based Framework for Teachers' Online Continuous Professional Development Programs: Systematic Review. *International Journal of Advanced Computer Science and Applications, 15*(4). Advance online publication. DOI: 10.14569/IJACSA.2024.0150450

Giri, A. (2025). Revolutionizing Student Evaluation: The Power of AI-Powered Assessment. In Improving Student Assessment With Emerging AI Tools (pp. 333-362). IGI Global Scientific Publishing.

Gligorea, I., Cioca, M., Oancea, R., Gorski, A. T., Gorski, H., & Tudorache, P. (2023). Adaptive learning using artificial intelligence in e-learning: A literature review. *Education Sciences, 13*(12), 1216. DOI: 10.3390/educsci13121216

Gobert, J. D., Sao Pedro, M. A., Li, H., & Lott, C. (2023). *Intelligent Tutoring Systems: A History and an Example of an ITS for Science*. Grantee Submission.

Goel, A. (2020). AI-powered learning: making education accessible, affordable, and achievable. arXiv preprint arXiv:2006.01908.

Gonçalves, B. (2020). Machines will think: structure and interpretation of Alan Turing's imitation game.

Habib, H., Jelani, S. A. K., & Najla, S. (2022). Revolutionizing Inclusion: AI in Adaptive Learning for Students with Disabilities. *Multidisciplinary Science Journal, 1*(01), 1–11.

Hamilton, B. (2022). *Integrating technology in the classroom: Tools to meet the needs of every student*. International Society for Technology in Education.

Haugeland, J., Craver, C. F., & Klein, C. (Eds.). (2023). *Mind Design III: Philosophy, Psychology, and Artificial Intelligence*. MIT press.

Huang, A. Y., Lu, O. H., & Yang, S. J. (2023). Effects of artificial Intelligence–Enabled personalized recommendations on learners' learning engagement, motivation, and outcomes in a flipped classroom. *Computers & Education, 194*, 104684. DOI: 10.1016/j.compedu.2022.104684

Kaswan, K. S., Dhatterwal, J. S., & Ojha, R. P. (2024). AI in personalized learning. In *Advances in technological innovations in higher education* (pp. 103–117). CRC Press. DOI: 10.1201/9781003376699-9

Kayyali, M. (2024a). Global Perspectives on Personalized Learning: Case Studies and Best Practices. In Transforming Education for Personalized Learning (pp. 66-84). IGI Global.

Kayyali, M. (2024b). Crisis Response and Higher Education: Social Innovations in Times of Global Challenges. In Social Innovations in Education, Environment, and Healthcare (pp. 1-17). IGI Global.

Kayyali, M. (2024c). Future possibilities and challenges of AI in education. In *Transforming education with generative AI: Prompt engineering and synthetic content creation* (pp. 118–137). IGI Global Scientific Publishing. DOI: 10.4018/979-8-3693-1351-0.ch006

Kayyali, M. (2025a). The Impact of Personalized Learning on Student Engagement and Achievement in STEAM. In *Integrating Personalized Learning Methods Into STEAM Education* (pp. 51–78). IGI Global Scientific Publishing. DOI: 10.4018/979-8-3693-7718-5.ch003

Kayyali, M. (2025b). E-Learning Platforms and Their Influence on Lifelong Learning. In Impact of Digitalization on Education and Social Sustainability (pp. 155-176). IGI Global.

Kayyali, M. (2025c). AI in Higher Education: Revolutionizing Curriculum and Administration. In AI Adoption and Diffusion in Education (pp. 31-62). IGI Global Scientific Publishing.

Kayyali, M. (2025d). The Future of AI in Education: Predictions and Emerging Trends. Next-Generation AI Methodologies in Education, 367-406.

Kayyali, M. (2025e). Harnessing AI for Digital Entrepreneurship: Strategies and Best Practices. In Improving Entrepreneurial Processes Through Advanced AI (pp. 1-20). IGI Global.

Khan, W. N. (2024). Ethical Challenges of AI in Education: Balancing Innovation with Data Privacy. *Journal of AI in Education: Innovations, Opportunities, Challenges, and Future Directions, 1*(1), 1–13.

Lachney, M., & Foster, E. K. (2020). Historicizing making and doing: Seymour Papert, Sherry Turkle, and epistemological foundations of the maker movement. *History and Technology*, *36*(1), 54–82. DOI: 10.1080/07341512.2020.1759302

Li, H. (2023). AI in education: Bridging the divide or widening the gap? Exploring equity, opportunities, and challenges in the digital age. Advances in Education. *Humanities and Social Science Research*, *8*(1), 355–355.

Lorenzo, N., & Gallon, R. (2019). Smart pedagogy for smart learning. Didactics of smart pedagogy: Smart pedagogy for technology enhanced learning, 41-69.

Luckin, R. (2018). Machine Learning and Human Intelligence. The future of education for the 21st century. UCL institute of education press.

Mahmoud, C. F., & Sørensen, J. T. (2024). Artificial Intelligence in Personalized Learning with a Focus on Current Developments and Future Prospects. *Research and Advances in Education*, *3*(8), 25–31. DOI: 10.56397/RAE.2024.08.04

Mathai, A. (2024). Enhancing Education for Underprivileged Children Through AI-Powered Native Language Learning Inclusive Education Through AI-Powered Native Language Learning. Available at *SSRN* 4899553. DOI: 10.2139/ssrn.4899553

Mbah, G. O. (2024). Data privacy in the era of AI: Navigating regulatory landscapes for global businesses.

Muli, M. (2024). Legal and Ethical Implications of Data Privacy in Artificial Intelligence: A Review of Data Privacy Among Learners in Kenyan Secondary Schools. *Journal of the Kenya National Commission for UNESCO*, *5*(1). Advance online publication. DOI: 10.62049/jkncu.v5i1.170

Mutawa, A. M. (2023). *Perspective chapter: MOOCS at higher education–Current state and future trends*. Massive Open Online Courses-Current Practice and Future Trends.

Pedro, F., Subosa, M., Rivas, A., & Valverde, P. (2019). Artificial intelligence in education: Challenges and opportunities for sustainable development.

Rajput, R. (2025). Use of Artificial Intelligence to Solve Problems in the Classroom. In *New Technological Applications in the Flipped Learning Model* (pp. 137–168). IGI Global Scientific Publishing. DOI: 10.4018/979-8-3373-0437-3.ch005

Rane, N., Choudhary, S., & Rane, J. (2023). Education 4.0 and 5.0: Integrating artificial intelligence (AI) for personalized and adaptive learning.

Sargent, J. M. (2024). Optimistic Realism in Higher Education: Strategies for Empowering Students in a Complex World (Doctoral dissertation, Idaho State University).

Sayers, D., Sousa-Silva, R., Höhn, S., Ahmedi, L., Allkivi-Metsoja, K., Anastasiou, D., ... & Yayilgan, S. Y. (2021). The Dawn of the Human-Machine Era: A forecast of new and emerging language technologies.

Semel, A. (2019). An Untraditional Phenomenological Study of Teachers' Perceptions of Rhythmic Delivery of Classroom Commands during Transition Times (Doctoral dissertation, Grand Canyon University).

Sethi, S. S., & Jain, K. (2024). AI technologies for social emotional learning: Recent research and future directions. *Journal of Research in Innovative Teaching & Learning*, *17*(2), 213–225. DOI: 10.1108/JRIT-03-2024-0073

Shireesha, M., & Jeevan, J. (2024). The Role of Artificial Intelligence in Personalized Learning: A Pathway to Inclusive Education. Library of Progress-Library Science, Information Technology & Computer, 44(3).

Singh, A. (2024). The Future of Learning: AI-Driven Personalized Education. Available at *SSRN* 5076438. DOI: 10.56557/ajocr/2024/v9i49018

Singh, B., & Kaunert, C. (2024). Future of Digital Marketing: Hyper-Personalized Customer Dynamic Experience with AI-Based Predictive Models. In Revolutionizing the AI-Digital Landscape (pp. 189-203). Productivity Press.

Stewart, M. (2021). Understanding learning: Theories and critique. In *University teaching in focus* (pp. 3–28). Routledge. DOI: 10.4324/9781003008330-2

Tang, L., & Su, Y. S. (2024). Ethical implications and principles of using artificial intelligence models in the classroom: A systematic literature review.

Tedre, M., Toivonen, T., Kahila, J., Vartiainen, H., Valtonen, T., Jormanainen, I., & Pears, A. (2021). Teaching machine learning in K–12 classroom: Pedagogical and technological trajectories for artificial intelligence education. *IEEE Access : Practical Innovations, Open Solutions*, *9*, 110558–110572. DOI: 10.1109/ACCESS.2021.3097962

Topali, P., Ortega-Arranz, A., Rodríguez-Triana, M. J., Er, E., Khalil, M., & Akçapınar, G. (2025). Designing human-centered learning analytics and artificial intelligence in education solutions: A systematic literature review. *Behaviour & Information Technology*, *44*(5), 1071–1098. DOI: 10.1080/0144929X.2024.2345295

Wang, Y., Song, W., Tao, W., Liotta, A., Yang, D., Li, X., Gao, S., Sun, Y., Ge, W., Zhang, W., & Zhang, W. (2022). A systematic review on affective computing: Emotion models, databases, and recent advances. *Information Fusion*, *83*, 19–52. DOI: 10.1016/j.inffus.2022.03.009

Williams, D. A. (2023). *Strategic diversity leadership: Activating change and transformation in higher education*. Routledge. DOI: 10.4324/9781003447122

Yang, S. J., Ogata, H., Matsui, T., & Chen, N. S. (2021). Human-centered artificial intelligence in education: Seeing the invisible through the visible. *Computers and Education: Artificial Intelligence*, *2*, 100008. DOI: 10.1016/j.caeai.2021.100008

KEY TERMS AND DEFINITIONS

Artificial Intelligence (AI): The simulation of human intelligence processes by machines, especially computer systems, enabling them to learn, reason, and self-correct.

Personalized Learning: An educational approach that uses technology, including AI, to tailor instruction to each student's unique learning needs, pace, and interests.

Adaptive Learning: A method of education that leverages AI to adjust the difficulty and type of content in real time, based on a learner's performance and progress.

Intelligent Tutoring Systems (ITS): AI-powered educational systems designed to simulate one-on-one tutoring by providing customized feedback, hints, and instruction to students.

Data Privacy: The protection of personal information collected, stored, and used by AI systems in education, ensuring compliance with legal and ethical standards.

Algorithmic Bias: The systematic and unfair discrimination that can arise in AI systems due to biased training data or design choices, potentially reinforcing existing social inequalities.

Human-Centered Design: An approach to creating AI systems that prioritizes human needs, values, and ethical considerations, ensuring technology serves as a tool for learning rather than a replacement for educators.

Chapter 5
The Impact of AI on Classroom Dynamics in Higher Education: Shifting Roles for Professors and Students

Mustafa Kayyali
https://orcid.org/0000-0003-3300-262X
Maaref University of Applied Sciences, Syria

ABSTRACT

This chapter explores how AI disrupts and reshapes the traditional classroom dynamic, shifting the balance of authority, reconfiguring participation, and inviting both professors and students to renegotiate their identities within the learning process. Far from being passive recipients, students are increasingly positioned as data contributors, learning co-designers, and autonomous explorers, while professors are evolving into facilitators, curators, and ethical stewards of digital pedagogies. Through critical reflection, the chapter examines not only the benefits of AI-enhanced teaching and learning but also the tensions and uncertainties that arise when human agency intersects with algorithmic influence. It argues that embracing AI in education demands more than technological readiness—it requires an ethical, pedagogical, and deeply human response to a world where machines now have a voice in shaping how we learn and what we value.

DOI: 10.4018/979-8-3373-6007-2.ch005

INTRODUCTION

There was a time—not so long ago—when the classroom was a relatively predictable environment. The professor stood at the front, marker in hand, often behind a podium or whiteboard. The students, arranged in neat rows, absorbed knowledge like dry sponges awaiting water. It was an environment where information flowed in one direction and authority was largely unquestioned. But that classroom, in its traditional form, is quietly dissolving into history. We are standing on the threshold of a pedagogical evolution—one not propelled solely by curriculum reforms or institutional policies, but by the relentless advance of artificial intelligence (Kayyali, 2025 A). And this time, the change isn't cosmetic. It's systemic. AI didn't walk through the university gates with a grand announcement. It crept in through recommendation algorithms, automated grading tools, adaptive learning platforms, and chatbot tutors (Murgatroyd, 2024). At first, its presence seemed harmless—convenient, even. But as its influence deepens, something profound is happening beneath the surface. The classroom is no longer a space bounded by four walls and a rigid hierarchy. It has become a living, adaptive ecosystem—shaped, monitored, and sometimes even co-instructed by non-human agents.

The implications of this shift are not merely technological; they are social, psychological, and deeply human. Professors are beginning to feel the weight of a new expectation: to not just teach content but to orchestrate increasingly complex learning environments, balancing human empathy with algorithmic precision (Lata, 2024). Students, for their part, are no longer just learners; they are digital natives navigating a landscape where AI often knows their learning styles, preferences, and even moods better than their instructors might. In this new paradigm, both professors and students are being redefined—recast into roles that neither were formally prepared for. This evolution has sparked a host of questions, some exciting, others unsettling. What does it mean for a professor to share cognitive space with an AI assistant? How does student engagement shift when feedback is instantaneous and personalized—but delivered by a machine? Where do trust, curiosity, and dialogue fit in a classroom mediated by algorithms? Most importantly, how do we preserve the essence of education—human connection, critical thought, ethical reasoning—in a space increasingly co-occupied by machines?

The challenge is not whether we should integrate AI into education (Vincent-Lancrin & Van der Vlies, 2020). That conversation is already over. AI is here. The real question is how we, as educators, students, and institutions, choose to relate to it. This chapter begins by acknowledging the complexity of that relationship. It explores the subtle and not-so-subtle ways AI is altering classroom dynamics in higher education, focusing on the shifting roles of both professors and students. Through this exploration, it seeks to move beyond surface-level analysis and into a more nuanced understanding of what's at stake: not just the future of pedagogy, but the future of what it means to teach and to learn. We must also understand that this transition is not uniform across disciplines or institutions. The AI-mediated classroom looks different in a computer science department than it does in philosophy or the arts. Yet, the ripple effects are felt everywhere. This is a cultural transformation, not merely a technological one. It challenges long-held assumptions about expertise, intellectual labor, and the very architecture of knowledge exchange.

In examining this transformation, we will not romanticize the past, nor blindly celebrate the future. Instead, we'll try to hold both with open hands—recognizing what is lost and what is gained. We'll consider how AI is reconfiguring authority, democratizing access to knowledge, and, paradoxically, introducing new hierarchies based on digital literacy and data fluency. We'll reflect on the emotional labor of professors who now teach not just students but also interface with systems that monitor and modulate classroom interactions. We'll explore the ways students are being empowered by AI, while also being subtly shaped—sometimes constrained—by its logic. This is not just a story about machines in the classroom. It is a story about us—about how we adapt, resist, embrace, and transform in the face of one of the most significant educational shifts of our time. If we are to meet this moment with courage and clarity, we must begin by asking the right questions, even if we don't yet have all the answers.

Rethinking the Modern Classroom in the AI Age

Walk into a university classroom today, and you may not immediately notice the difference. There are still desks, projectors, professors at the front, and students with notebooks—some digital, some paper. But beneath the surface, a quiet revolution is unfolding. It's not in the architecture of the space, but in the logic that governs how knowledge is exchanged, how relationships are formed, and how decisions are made. This is the age of artificial intelligence, and its fingerprints are subtly but unmistakably transforming the classroom into something fundamentally different from what it was even a decade ago. The classroom has always reflected the spirit of its time. In the Industrial Age, it mirrored the factory: uniform rows, bells signaling shifts, standardized assessments. In the Information Age, it began to resemble a hub of content dissemination—overhead projectors were replaced with digital screens, chalkboards gave way to interactive whiteboards, and the teacher became a facilitator rather than an unquestioned authority. Now, in what some are calling the Intelligence Age, classrooms are no longer defined just by content delivery or physical space (Collins & Halverson, 2018). They are becoming cognitive environments—infused with AI-driven technologies that observe, interpret, respond, and, in many ways, co-participate in the learning process.

Figure 1. AI in the Classroom Ecosystem

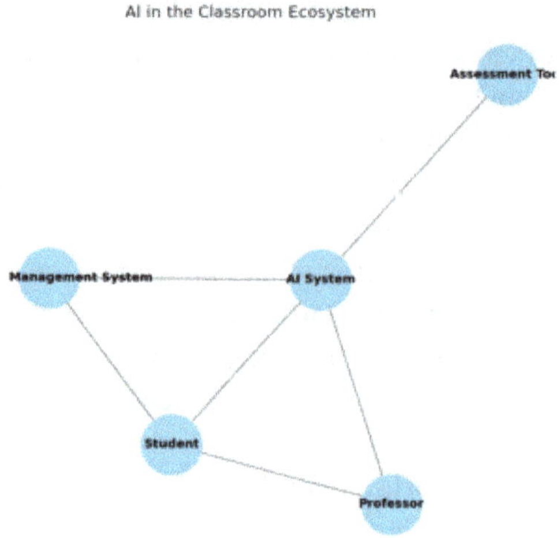

What does this shift actually feel like—for those who live within it day by day? For professors, it means stepping into a role that is less about instructing and more about orchestrating. The lecture, once the core ritual of academia, is slowly being reimagined or even rendered obsolete in certain contexts. Students can now access vast quantities of information, structured and personalized by AI tutors that adapt in real time to their pace, comprehension, and interests. The professor's role becomes one of deep guidance rather than top-down dissemination. They are asked to curate rather than dictate, to personalize rather than generalize, to mentor rather than command.

This is not a downgrade—it's a transformation. But it is also deeply disorienting. Many educators were trained in a tradition where mastery of content was central to authority (Keiler, 2018). Now, that same content is accessible in seconds via search engines and AI models that can summarize, explain, and even generate novel interpretations. Professors are being asked to justify their value not through what they know, but through how they connect, contextualize, and inspire (Silseth & Erstad, 2018). This is an emotional and intellectual transition that carries both liberation and loss. Students, too, are navigating unfamiliar terrain (Jarson, 2023). The modern classroom is no longer just a place where they are taught—it is a space where they are observed by systems that track their engagement, recommend resources, and sometimes nudge them toward certain conclusions. Learning platforms powered by AI collect data not just on test scores but on how long a student pauses on a question, how often they revise an answer, and even patterns in their tone or writing style (Srinivasa et al, 2022). The goal, ostensibly, is personalization—giving each student the support they need in the way they best receive it. And in many ways, it works.

Students who struggled in silence before can now receive tailored support. Those who were bored by the pace of the group can accelerate through material. But with this personalization comes a new kind of surveillance. The classroom becomes a space of constant feedback loops—productive, yes, but also potentially invasive.

There's something quietly profound about how this changes the emotional atmosphere of the classroom. Traditionally, the classroom was a place where uncertainty could be shared, where questions could hang in the air, where a pause could mean thoughtfulness rather than inefficiency. Now, in an AI-powered classroom, there is pressure—often unspoken—for everything to be optimized. Moments of confusion, if not processed efficiently, are flagged. Responses are calibrated. Learning becomes a sequence of interventions rather than a journey of unfolding (Sannino, 2018). And while this can drive measurable outcomes, it can also drain the classroom of its serendipity, its spaciousness, its moments of unpredictable insight. We must also consider how AI mediates relationships in this new classroom. In traditional models, the relationship between student and professor was direct, shaped by shared presence, mutual recognition, and often, years of institutional norms. Now, a third presence exists in that space—one that doesn't sleep, doesn't forget, and doesn't forgive ambiguity. AI systems offer professors dashboards and analytics, providing insights into which students are struggling, which content areas are most confusing, and even which students are at risk of disengaging (Koehl, 2025). These tools can be incredibly helpful. But they also create a temptation to relate to students through data rather than through dialogue.

The risk here is subtle but real: that we begin to see students not as complex, evolving individuals but as profiles—dynamic, yes, but still governed by measurable traits. The professor's relationship to their students becomes partially mediated by algorithms that suggest who needs attention, what kind of attention they need, and when (Masters-Wheeler, 2024). The art of sensing, of intuiting, of noticing the quiet student in the back who has not spoken in weeks—not because the data said so, but because the heart noticed—can get overshadowed by graphs and metrics. And when that happens, something essential is lost. Yet, this is not a lament. It is a call to awareness. AI has remarkable potential to enhance education. It can equalize access, reduce cognitive load, provide real-time support, and uncover patterns that humans might miss. But for all its power, it is still just a tool—a tool whose effects depend entirely on how we choose to use it. The classroom of the AI age can become more equitable, more personalized, and more responsive than anything we've seen before. But only if we remain vigilant about what it means to be human within it.

This also requires a redefinition of classroom culture. In an AI-mediated environment, collaboration may no longer mean group projects in the traditional sense. It might mean co-editing content with AI, co-solving problems with machine suggestions, or co-authoring reflections where students and machines each contribute a layer of interpretation. These are exciting possibilities. But they require a new kind of literacy—not just technical, but philosophical. Students and professors alike must develop the ability to question the machine, to reflect on what is being suggested, to resist the illusion of objectivity that often comes with algorithmic recommendations. The AI-infused classroom challenges our assumptions about time. Traditional education moves in blocks—semesters, units, scheduled exams (Childers, 2018). AI learning doesn't always respect these boundaries. It adapts in real time, proposes just-in-time content, and blurs the line between study time and rest time. This can be empowering for self-directed learners, but it can also become exhausting, especially in a world already saturated with stimuli. The classroom, once a bounded space for focused engagement, now bleeds into every device and every moment. The question then becomes: how do we create intentional pauses, boundaries, and rhythms in a system designed for constant flow?

And then, there is the question of presence. What does it mean to be present in a classroom when much of the interaction is mediated by AI? Can a student be said to be "present" if their avatar engages in a simulation, or their AI-generated summary is submitted instead of a personal response? Can a professor be fully present when much of the feedback is automated, and lectures are pre-recorded? Presence, in its deepest sense, is about mutual recognition. It is about being attuned—not just physically, but emotionally and intellectually. In the AI classroom, cultivating presence becomes both more difficult and more necessary. To rethink the modern classroom in the AI age is not simply to ask how we can add new tools. It is to ask how we want to learn and teach, who we want to become, and what kind of relationships we want to foster in the spaces where education unfolds. It is to interrogate not just the efficacy of our methods, but the ethics of our intentions. It is to acknowledge that learning is not just the transmission of information but the cultivation of wisdom, empathy, and meaning. If we are to embrace AI in education—and we must—it must be with eyes open, hearts engaged, and a commitment to keep the human spirit at the center of our designs. The future of the classroom is not predetermined. It is still being written, one conversation, one decision, one moment of connection at a time. And in that uncertain, evolving space, lies our greatest opportunity: to ensure that the intelligence we add never overshadows the humanity we must preserve.

From Sage on the Stage to Guide on the Side: The Changing Role of Professors

There was once a time when a professor's authority rested firmly on their mastery of content and the performative act of delivering it (Holloway & Brass, 2018). The classroom was their domain—a stage upon which they stood, often quite literally, to project knowledge outward. The students, seated before them, were expected to absorb, record, and remember. In this traditional arrangement, the professor was not just a teacher but a sage—a font of knowledge whose voice held the weight of expertise. It was a system that privileged oratory, rewarded memorization, and maintained a certain distance between teacher and learner. But those days, while not entirely gone, are slowly fading into memory. The arrival of artificial intelligence in higher education has disrupted this performance-based pedagogy, pushing professors into a new role—one that is less about commanding a room and more about cultivating a space (Murgatroyd, 2024). The professor today is being invited—or perhaps compelled—to move from being the "sage on the stage" to becoming the "guide on the side."

This shift is not superficial. It touches the very core of what it means to teach. The professor is no longer the primary gatekeeper of knowledge (Forsberg et al, 2022). Search engines, digital libraries, and increasingly sophisticated AI systems have made information more accessible than ever. Students can now find detailed explanations, contrasting perspectives, and even simulated tutoring experiences within seconds. This access has not diminished the need for professors—it has redefined it. The professor's value is no longer tethered to their ability to deliver content, but to their ability to contextualize it, to interrogate it, to humanize it. Being a guide on the side does not mean becoming passive. Quite the opposite. It requires a deeper form of engagement—one that is less about presenting polished lectures and more about asking the right questions, noticing when a student is drifting, and fostering moments of intellectual intimacy that cannot be manufactured or automated. It's about making space for uncertainty, about modeling how to live with complexity, and about helping students cultivate discernment in an era overflowing with answers but starving for wisdom. For many professors, this transition is emotionally complex. There is, for some, a quiet grief in realizing that the carefully built lectures they have refined over years are now competing with AI-generated summaries or YouTube tutorials (Pratschke, 2024). There is a sense of loss in surrendering the podium, in becoming one voice among many rather than *the* voice. But within this disorientation lies an extraordinary opportunity—to reclaim a more relational, more creative, more deeply human way of teaching. When the professor steps down from the stage, they step closer to the student. The classroom becomes a circle rather than a hierarchy, a place for dialogue rather than monologue. This is not to suggest that expertise no longer matters. On the contrary, it matters more than ever. But its function has changed. The professor's knowledge must now serve as a compass rather than a map. In a world where students can access endless information, the professor helps them decide what to trust, how to interpret it, and how to think critically in ways that machines cannot teach. They become mentors, facilitators, co-learners, and ethical stewards—not just transmitters of content.

One of the most significant shifts in this new role is emotional in nature. In traditional models, professors could maintain a certain intellectual distance. Authority was protected by formality. But today's students, learning in AI-rich environments, crave authenticity. They can sense when a professor is reciting versus when they are revealing. The professor who succeeds in this environment is not the one who knows the most but the one who connects the deepest. Vulnerability becomes part of the pedagogy. Admitting what we don't know, reflecting aloud on ethical dilemmas, sharing the messiness of learning—these become powerful tools for modeling the very courage and curiosity we hope to inspire in students (Jacob, 2018). AI also challenges professors to reflect on their pedagogical practices in new ways. Automated systems can now provide feedback on student performance more quickly and, in some cases, more precisely than humans. This raises difficult questions: Where is the professor's feedback still indispensable? How do we ensure that human feedback remains meaningful, even when machines can deliver it faster? The answer, perhaps, lies in a different kind of feedback—one that machines can't give. Feedback not just on correctness, but on thoughtfulness. Not just on answers, but on how students approached the question. Not just on performance, but on potential. The professor as guide must also learn to navigate the emotional landscape of students living in a highly technological world. Burnout, anxiety, information overload, and a sense of digital disconnection are becoming common in higher education (Göldağ, 2022). Professors who take on the guiding role often find themselves supporting students not just academically but emotionally—listening to frustrations, validating uncertainties, helping them reorient when they feel lost in a sea of data. In doing so, they become not just educators, but anchors. But this shift is not without its risks. There is a fine line between guiding and overreaching, between supporting and controlling. As professors gain access to increasingly granular data about their students' behavior—how much time they spent on readings, which questions they skipped, when they logged in and out—there is a temptation to over-monitor, to step too far into the realm of behavioral management. This is where ethics must meet pedagogy. The guiding role must be rooted in trust, not surveillance. Professors must resist the urge to turn education into a quantified journey. The most important parts of learning—discovery, doubt, intellectual play—are often invisible to algorithms.

Figure 2. Shifts in Instructor and Student Roles

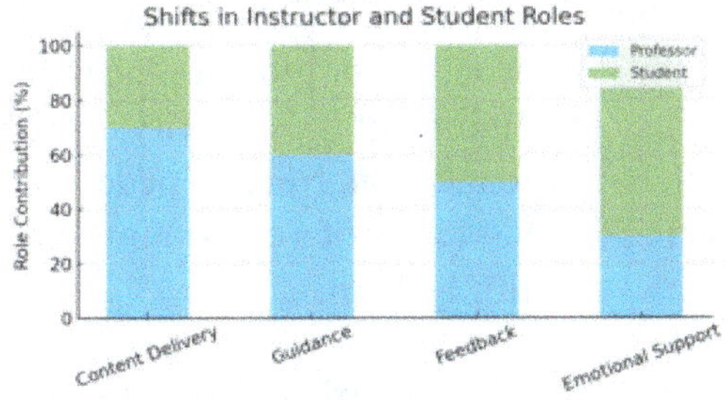

At the same time, universities must support professors in this transformation (Price et al, 2021). Being a guide requires different skills than being a sage. It demands emotional intelligence, digital literacy, adaptability, and the ability to teach across modalities. Professors need time, training, and community to reimagine their roles. They need institutional cultures that value mentorship as much as metrics, process as much as product. Without this support, the risk is burnout—of educators asked to care more, connect more, and adapt more, without being given the tools to do so. And yet, for all the challenges, there is something deeply hopeful about this new model. Teaching, at its best, has always been about more than delivering information (Whitaker, 2020). It has been about awakening minds, expanding empathy, and nurturing the capacity to think freely and ethically. The professor who embraces the guiding role has the chance to re-center this mission. They are not diminished by the presence of AI—they are made more necessary. In an age of machine-generated knowledge, the need for human wisdom becomes clearer. The phrase "guide on the side" may sound modest, even diminutive. But it speaks to something profound. The guide walks *with* the learner. They listen more than they speak. They help students find their own path rather than imposing a single route. They don't seek applause—they seek transformation. And while the sage on the stage may have commanded attention, the guide on the side earns trust. In this trust lies the future of higher education.

It's a future where professors don't compete with technology, but partner with it (Kayyali, 2025b). Where they don't resist change, but shape it. Where their power lies not in controlling the classroom, but in cultivating the kind of learning environment where students feel seen, challenged, and inspired. This is not a lesser role. It is, in many ways, a more radical one—because it centers the human experience in a time when it could easily be overlooked. As higher education continues to evolve under the influence of artificial intelligence, the role of the professor will remain essential—not because they know more than machines, but because they know *us*. They know how to ask the question that no algorithm can predict. They know how to wait for a student to arrive at an insight on their own. They know that learning is not just a transaction, but a transformation. And most of all, they know how to hold space—for uncertainty, for wonder, for growth. The guide on the side is not a retreat from authority, but a redefinition of it. Authority not as performance, but as presence. Not as control, but as connection. Not as a pedestal, but as a partnership. And in this redefinition lies the possibility of a classroom where learning is not just smarter—but more deeply, beautifully, human.

Students as Co-Creators: Navigating Learning in an Intelligent Environment

To understand what it means to be a student in the age of intelligent systems is to move beyond the clichés of digital natives or passive consumers of technology (Sorrentino, 2018). The truth is far more complex, more layered, and more human. Today's students are entering classrooms that do not just contain knowledge—they are immersed in systems that shape how knowledge is accessed, interpreted, and valued. They are not simply learning within environments enhanced by artificial intelligence—they are learning alongside it, through it, and sometimes in response to it. And in this evolving context, students are no longer just recipients of educational content. They are becoming co-creators of their own learning journeys. This shift didn't happen all at once. It began quietly—with the rise of personalized learning platforms, intelligent tutoring systems, algorithmic feedback, and generative tools that could assist with everything from writing to problem-solving. For a while, these technologies were framed as supports—helpful companions to guide students through complex material. But as the tools grew more sophisticated, so did the roles students were expected to play. They were no longer just navigating systems. They were shaping them through their inputs, choices, and patterns of interaction.

What we're witnessing is a subtle, profound change in educational agency. Agency, once defined largely by obedience, compliance, and performance, is now being reimagined as interaction, customization, and iterative collaboration (Jamieson, 2020). A student doesn't just answer a question—they co-design a path to the answer. They don't just consume knowledge—they explore, remix, and even challenge it, often with the help of digital companions that learn from them as much as they learn from it. This co-creative role is both empowering and overwhelming. On one hand, students now have tools that allow them to personalize their learning pace, access content from anywhere, receive immediate feedback, and experiment with ideas that would have been difficult to explore in traditional settings. On the other hand, the responsibility that comes with this autonomy is significant. The student must now manage their own learning more actively—choosing not just what to study, but how, when, and with which tools (Bilousova et al, 2023). The line between student and instructional designer, between learner and contributor, begins to blur. But agency in an AI-powered environment is not just about choice. It's about awareness. And this is where things get complicated. The algorithms that power educational platforms are not neutral. They prioritize, filter, and recommend based on data—data often shaped by commercial, cultural, or institutional logics that students may not fully understand. When a student receives a "recommended resource," or an AI-generated explanation, they are being gently guided down a particular path—one shaped by invisible design decisions. To truly be a co-creator, the student must learn to question not only the content, but the process by which it arrived in front of them. They must become critical participants in the architecture of their own learning. This kind of critical literacy is not innate. It must be taught, cultivated, and practiced. And it requires a learning environment that honors doubt, encourages inquiry, and makes space for reflection. Students need to be empowered not just to use AI tools, but to interrogate them—asking who made this, what data it's based on, whose voices are missing, and what alternative perspectives might exist. In this way, co-creation becomes an ethical act as much as an intellectual one.

Moreover, as students take on more active roles in shaping their learning, the social dimension of education becomes even more important (Kumar, 2024). It is tempting to think of personalization as an individual endeavor—as if each student exists in a bubble, perfectly optimized for their own needs. But real learning doesn't happen in isolation. It happens in dialogue—with peers, with mentors, with the world. And in an environment increasingly mediated by machines, the human relationships that support learning must be intentionally nurtured. Co-creation, then, is not just about interacting with software—it's about participating in a learning community where ideas are shared, debated, and evolved. It's about knowing that your voice matters, that your interpretation of a text or your solution to a problem is part of a larger conversation. It's about understanding that even in a system driven by logic and data, there is room—indeed, a need—for intuition, creativity, and dissent. In many ways, the co-creator model reawakens something that has always been true but often forgotten: that students are not empty vessels, but thinking, feeling, complex individuals who bring their own perspectives, histories, and aspirations into the classroom. AI, for all its capabilities, cannot fully grasp this. It can adapt, it can predict, but it cannot understand what it feels like to struggle through a concept that challenges your sense of self, or to discover a passion that rewires your priorities. Only the student can do that. Only the human learner can breathe meaning into data.

That is why, even as technology advances, the role of the student becomes more—not less—central (Crittenden et al, 2019). The tools may change, but the heart of learning remains a deeply personal, often vulnerable act. To be a student is to be in flux, to be willing to question, to risk failure, to grow. And in an intelligent environment, this journey is no longer scripted from above—it is shaped from within. Of course, not all students experience this shift equally. Access to technology, digital literacy, institutional support, and cultural attitudes toward education all shape how students engage with AI in the classroom. For some, the promise of co-creation is still out of reach—obstructed by outdated systems, economic inequality, or limited exposure to critical pedagogy. It's easy to romanticize the empowered student in the intelligent classroom. But real empowerment requires more than access—it requires agency, awareness, and support. It requires us to create educational systems that are not only intelligent but also just. There is also the risk of performative co-creation—where students are given choices that aren't really choices, where algorithms simulate autonomy but subtly reinforce conformity. A truly co-creative learning environment must be transparent, flexible, and genuinely open to student input. It must value messiness, allow for mistakes, and resist the urge to over-sanitize the learning process in the name of efficiency. After all, the most meaningful learning often happens not when everything goes smoothly, but when things get complicated, when assumptions are challenged, when questions lead to more questions.

In this sense, co-creation is not a product—it's a practice. It is something students learn to do, over time, through experience, through trust, through the freedom to fail and try again. It is something that requires mentorship, scaffolding, and reflection. And it is something that, when embraced fully, can transform not only how students learn, but how they see themselves—as thinkers, as citizens, as co-authors of their own lives. There's a quiet revolution taking place in classrooms around the world. Students are experimenting with AI tools to draft essays, solve equations, explore languages, analyze data, and even generate art (Lively et al, 2023). Some are using these tools to deepen their understanding, others to shortcut the process. Both choices reveal something important: that students are not passive—they are strategic, curious, adaptive. The challenge for educators and institutions is not to police this behavior, but to guide it, to channel it toward deeper learning, ethical reflection, and creative engagement. Because in the end, co-creation is not about controlling the tools—it's about shaping the experience. It's about recognizing that education is not something done to students, but something done with them. In an intelligent environment, students are not passengers—they are navigators (Kose & Vasant, 2020). They are not simply responding to prompts—they are asking their own questions. And as they do, they are helping to redefine what learning looks like, what it means, and what it's for. This is both the challenge and the invitation of our time. To build classrooms—physical or digital—that honor the intelligence of our tools without forgetting the wisdom of our learners. To create systems that adapt not only to performance metrics, but to human needs. To trust that when given the right environment, the right guidance, and the right questions, students will not only rise to the occasion—they will help create something we haven't yet imagined.

AI as the Invisible Moderator: Altering Classroom Interactions and Power Structures

In many ways, the most profound effects of artificial intelligence in education are the ones that go unnoticed. We often focus on the tools themselves—the software, the algorithms, the devices—and their role in delivering information or providing personalized learning. But there is another, more subtle aspect of AI's influence in the classroom: its role as an invisible moderator. While we are busy adjusting to AI-enhanced learning environments, the system itself is quietly shaping the very dynamics of classroom interactions, subtly shifting power structures, and influencing the flow of knowledge and authority in ways that we might not even recognize.

At the heart of this shift is the reality that AI systems in education are not neutral (Saltman, 2020). They do not simply provide a passive conduit through which knowledge is delivered—they shape how we learn, who gets attention, and what kinds of interactions are encouraged. AI can act as a moderator, subtly guiding the flow of classroom discussions, determining which students get feedback, and even framing the way content is presented. This mediation is not always visible or even understood by the people involved. In many cases, both professors and students may not be fully aware of how much they are being guided by algorithms, shaping their behaviors and interactions in ways that align with certain educational goals, institutional priorities, or even the biases of the systems themselves. The very structure of classroom interaction is being transformed by AI in ways that demand reflection. In traditional classroom settings, power dynamics were relatively straightforward: the professor held authority, and students were the recipients of knowledge. This model was hierarchical, with clear lines between the one who teaches and the one who learns. But AI complicates this relationship, creating a new layer of influence that is not immediately visible to anyone in the room. AI can serve as an invisible arbiter, deciding how students interact with content, how they receive feedback, and how they are evaluated (Hooda et al, 2022). This shift changes the very nature of authority in the classroom. In the traditional classroom, authority was often exercised through a combination of expertise and interpersonal relationships. The professor, in their role as the expert, controlled the flow of information, created opportunities for students to engage, and mediated the social dynamics of the classroom. Students were expected to respond to this structure, asking questions, participating in discussions, and demonstrating their knowledge through exams or assignments (Bender, 2023). But when AI enters the equation, it often takes over some of these roles, altering not just how students learn, but how they participate in the classroom.

Consider, for example, the way AI-driven learning platforms provide personalized content to students. These systems can track every click, every moment of engagement, and every pattern of behavior. They then use this data to adjust the learning experience, recommending specific content based on a student's needs, preferences, or past behaviors. In a sense, the AI is constantly mediating the learning process, deciding what the student should focus on, what they are ready to learn next, and even how they should be evaluated. This removes some of the agency from the professor, who may no longer have full control over the material that is being presented or the pace at which it is delivered. This shift in authority has a direct impact on the relationship between students and the content they engage with. In a traditional classroom, the content was largely determined by the professor. The professor, as the expert, decided what was important, what should be emphasized, and what would be tested (Bruggeman et al, 2021). This power, in turn, shaped the way students interacted with the material. The AI-powered classroom, however, can provide a more individualized learning experience, adapting in real time to each student's progress and needs. While this can make the learning process more efficient, it also raises questions about the implications for student autonomy. When the AI is making these decisions, are students truly free to engage with the content as they wish, or are they being subtly nudged toward a specific path?

The classroom itself becomes a site of negotiation between the AI system, the professor, and the student (Dinnar et al, 2021). The AI's decisions about what content to present, what feedback to offer, and how to structure the learning process are informed by algorithms that are often opaque to students and professors alike. The result is that the classroom dynamic shifts from being a direct exchange between teacher and student to a more complex interaction between human and machine (Shang & Sivaparthipan, 2022). In this new environment, students are not just engaging with content—they are engaging with an intelligent system that is constantly monitoring, adjusting, and responding to their behavior. This shift also alters the way students experience feedback. In traditional classrooms, feedback was often limited to the professor's availability and ability to assess each student's work. In an AI-driven classroom, feedback becomes instantaneous, personalized, and often automated. This can be incredibly beneficial, as it allows students to receive immediate feedback on their progress and identify areas where they may need to improve. However, it also introduces the risk of over-reliance on the AI system. Students may begin to prioritize the feedback they receive from machines over the nuanced, human feedback that comes from professors. And in cases where AI systems are used to grade assignments or exams, students may feel less motivated to seek human input, even though there are elements of learning—such as emotional nuance or ethical reasoning—that machines simply cannot assess as effectively.

The AI's role as moderator extends beyond content delivery and feedback. It also influences the way students interact with each other. In traditional classrooms, peer interactions played a key role in shaping the learning experience. Students were encouraged to discuss, debate, and collaborate with one another, creating a social dynamic that was integral to their educational development. In AI-driven classrooms, this dynamic is often mediated by technology. Collaboration may be facilitated through digital platforms, and students may be encouraged to work together using shared tools. But while AI can enhance these interactions, it can also limit them by setting parameters for collaboration that are driven by algorithmic goals rather than human spontaneity (Kayyali, 2025c). This raises important questions about the power structures that emerge in AI-driven classrooms. Who decides how students collaborate? Who sets the rules for interaction? And perhaps most importantly, who benefits from these decisions? When AI becomes an invisible moderator in the classroom, it also becomes a gatekeeper of sorts, controlling the flow of interaction, the allocation of resources, and the way students engage with both the content and one another. This concentration of power in the hands of algorithms raises concerns about the democratization of education. If the AI is shaping the classroom experience based on data that is opaque to the students and professors, what happens to the diverse voices, perspectives, and experiences that make education rich and meaningful?

In many ways, AI's role as an invisible moderator in the classroom reflects broader shifts in society. Just as AI algorithms are increasingly influencing the way we interact with information, entertainment, and even politics, they are now shaping the way we learn. The classroom, once a space for human-driven dialogue and discovery, is becoming a space where machines play an increasingly central role (Kubsch et al, 2023). And while this shift can be beneficial, it also demands that we confront difficult questions about power, authority, and autonomy in education. To truly understand the implications of AI as the invisible moderator, we must ask ourselves: what kind of education do we want to create in this new environment? Do we want to continue to prioritize human interaction, critical thinking, and creative inquiry, or do we want to embrace an education system that is increasingly mediated by algorithms that prioritize efficiency, standardization, and optimization? These are not easy questions, and the answers will require thoughtful, deliberate choices. The role of AI in education is still evolving. What is clear, however, is that it is not a simple tool to be used alongside traditional methods. It is a force that reshapes the very nature of classroom interactions and power structures. The challenge for educators, students, and institutions alike is to understand this shift and navigate it thoughtfully, ensuring that while AI can enhance the learning experience, it never replaces the essential human connections, values, and insights that make education truly transformative.

Pedagogical Challenges and Ethical Reflections in an AI-Driven Learning Ecosystem

As artificial intelligence continues to redefine the landscape of higher education, it brings with it both immense promise and significant challenges. While AI holds the potential to transform learning by providing personalized, efficient, and scalable educational experiences, its integration into classrooms raises complex pedagogical and ethical questions. These questions touch on everything from the nature of knowledge and the role of the professor to the fairness of AI-driven assessments and the potential for bias in machine learning algorithms. As we move further into an AI-driven learning ecosystem, it is essential to critically examine the pedagogical challenges and ethical dilemmas that arise from this transformation, and to consider how we can navigate them in a way that preserves the core values of education: curiosity, creativity, inclusivity, and human connection.

At its best, AI has the ability to offer tailored learning experiences (Kolluru et al, 2018). It can adjust content in real time, provide immediate feedback, and support students as they progress at their own pace. In theory, this should create a more inclusive environment where each student receives the specific support they need. However, the reality is far more complicated. One of the most significant pedagogical challenges in an AI-driven ecosystem is ensuring that the use of these technologies enhances, rather than diminishes, the quality of learning. AI systems operate on algorithms that are designed to optimize for certain outcomes—usually efficiency, accuracy, or engagement. These systems use data to predict student behavior, suggest resources, and even assess performance. On the surface, this seems like a good thing: after all, who wouldn't want to receive instant feedback or have a system that helps them stay on track? Yet, when AI is used in place of more traditional forms of teaching, there is a risk of losing the richness of human interaction. While AI can identify patterns and offer insights, it cannot replicate the nuances of human teaching. It cannot offer empathy, intuition, or the kind of open-ended dialogue that fosters critical thinking and intellectual growth.

This raises the question: can AI truly support a deep, meaningful education? Education is not simply about delivering information—it is about the creation of meaning. The classroom is a space where ideas are explored, challenged, and transformed. It is a place where students learn to think critically, question assumptions, and develop a sense of agency. In a world where much of the learning experience is mediated by AI, there is a risk that students may become passive recipients of pre-packaged knowledge, rather than active creators of meaning. The challenge for educators is to ensure that AI is used to support—not replace—critical thinking, creativity, and collaboration. Another pedagogical challenge that emerges in an AI-driven ecosystem is the risk of exacerbating existing inequalities (Farahani &

Ghasemi, 2024). While AI has the potential to democratize education by offering personalized learning at scale, it also has the potential to reinforce existing biases and inequalities. Machine learning algorithms are trained on data sets that reflect the historical patterns of human behavior. If these data sets are biased, the algorithms that are trained on them will also be biased. This has profound implications for AI-driven assessments, which are increasingly used to grade assignments, provide feedback, and even make admissions decisions.

Consider the example of facial recognition technology, which has been used to track student engagement and attendance in some AI-powered classrooms. If the data used to train these systems is not diverse, it may fail to accurately recognize students from different racial or ethnic backgrounds, leading to unfair evaluations of their participation. Similarly, AI systems that assess student essays or assignments may be influenced by biases in the training data, leading to unfair grading practices that disproportionately affect certain groups of students (Omughelli et al, 2024). This raises the ethical question: how do we ensure that AI is used fairly and equitably in education? One of the most pressing concerns is the potential for AI to perpetuate or even exacerbate existing inequalities in access to education. Students from low-income backgrounds, students with disabilities, and students from marginalized communities may not have the same access to AI-powered learning tools as their peers. Without careful consideration, AI has the potential to widen the gap between those who have access to advanced educational technologies and those who do not. This is not just a technical issue—it is a matter of social justice.

To address these concerns, it is essential that we approach the integration of AI into education with a critical, ethical mindset. This means not only evaluating the technical capabilities of AI systems, but also considering their social implications. It means asking tough questions about how data is collected, who has access to it, and how algorithms are designed. It means ensuring that AI is used in ways that promote equity, inclusivity, and fairness—rather than reinforcing existing power imbalances. Beyond issues of equity, there are also concerns about the transparency and accountability of AI systems. Many AI algorithms operate as "black boxes," meaning that their decision-making processes are not fully understood, even by the people who design them (Brożek et al, 2024). This lack of transparency poses significant challenges in an educational context. When an AI system provides feedback or makes an assessment, how can students and professors be sure that the process is fair, accurate, and unbiased? Without a clear understanding of how decisions are being made, it is difficult to trust the results. This is particularly problematic when AI systems are used to evaluate student performance or make decisions about admissions or grading. In light of these challenges, there is an urgent need for greater transparency in the development and deployment of AI in education. It is essential that the algorithms used in educational settings are designed with fairness and accountability in mind, and that they are regularly audited to ensure that they are not reinforcing harmful biases. This requires collaboration between educators, technologists, ethicists, and policymakers to ensure that AI systems are aligned with the core values of education.

Another ethical challenge in an AI-driven learning ecosystem is the issue of data privacy (Khan, 2024). AI systems in education collect vast amounts of data about students—data about their learning habits, engagement levels, preferences, and performance. While this data can be used to personalize learning and provide targeted support, it also raises significant privacy concerns. How much data is too much? Who owns this data? And, most importantly, how can we ensure that students' personal information is protected? The use of AI in education brings with it a new responsibility for educators and institutions to safeguard students' privacy. Students must be informed about the data that is being collected, how it will be used, and who will have access to it. They must also have the ability to control their own data, including the right to opt out of certain forms of data collection if they so choose. The ethical use of AI in education requires that we prioritize the rights and privacy of students, and that we develop systems that are transparent, respectful, and accountable (Peña et al, 2024). In navigating these pedagogical and ethical challenges, it is essential that we remember the purpose of education. Education is not about optimizing for efficiency or standardizing learning—it is about fostering intellectual growth, critical thinking, creativity, and human connection. AI has the potential to enhance these outcomes, but it must be used thoughtfully, ethically, and with an unwavering commitment to the values that underpin education. As we continue to integrate AI into the classroom, we must be vigilant in ensuring that it serves the interests of all students, fosters a more inclusive learning environment, and upholds the highest ethical standards.

Ultimately, the challenge is not to reject AI but to engage with it in a way that enhances and enriches the human experience of learning. AI is a tool—a powerful tool—but it is not a substitute for human judgment, empathy, or wisdom. The role of the educator is more critical than ever in an AI-driven ecosystem. Professors must not only master new technologies, but also maintain their focus on the human elements of education. They must foster environments where students are encouraged to think critically, to question assumptions, and to engage in meaningful dialogue with both their peers and their instructors. The success of AI in education will depend on how we balance the power of technology with the essential human qualities of empathy, creativity, and ethical reflection. We must be guided by the belief that education is not just about the transmission of knowledge—it is about the cultivation of wisdom, understanding, and character. In this new AI-driven learning ecosystem, we must remember that the ultimate goal is not to replace human teachers or human students, but to create an environment where both can thrive in harmony with the technologies that are reshaping our world.

Toward a Symbiotic Human-AI Classroom Culture

As artificial intelligence continues to embed itself in educational ecosystems, we are faced with the challenge of navigating a future where technology is not just an adjunct to teaching, but an integral part of the learning environment itself. The idea of a symbiotic relationship between humans and AI in the classroom is not one of opposition, but one of cooperation—one that harnesses the strengths of both human intelligence and artificial systems. It's not about replacing teachers with machines, or about using technology merely for convenience. Instead, the goal is to create an environment where human intuition, empathy, and creativity blend seamlessly with the computational power, precision, and scalability of AI. This balance—this symbiotic culture—holds the promise of a more personalized, inclusive, and engaging educational experience for both students and educators alike.

At its core, a symbiotic human-AI classroom culture requires a fundamental shift in how we view the roles of both the educator and the technology (Luckin, 2025). Traditionally, educators have been the stewards of knowledge, entrusted with the responsibility of guiding students through the complexities of learning. Technology, on the other hand, has often been seen as a tool—an instrument to enhance or support that process. But as AI becomes more capable, it challenges this dichotomy. AI is no longer just a passive tool. It is now an active participant in the learning process, offering insights, feedback, and personalized learning pathways based on real-time data. But this participation should not overshadow the human element. Instead, it should augment it. This symbiotic relationship begins with recognizing that human educators bring something to the classroom that AI cannot replicate: emotional intelligence, empathy, and the ability to inspire. A good teacher understands not only the content they are teaching but also the unique needs, struggles, and motivations of their students. They know when a student needs encouragement, when they are ready to be challenged, and when they need a moment to reflect. These qualities—empathy, intuition, and understanding—are not something AI can replace. What AI can offer, however, is the ability to analyze vast amounts of data, to identify patterns in student behavior, and to provide personalized learning experiences at scale. This is where the symbiosis begins. AI can relieve educators of some of the more repetitive, administrative tasks—such as grading, data analysis, and content delivery—freeing up their time and energy to focus on what they do best: connecting with students, fostering critical thinking, and inspiring a love of learning.

In this symbiotic culture, AI is not a replacement for the human teacher; rather, it becomes an extension of their teaching practice (Fitria, 2023). Imagine a classroom where AI systems track each student's progress in real time, offering suggestions for additional resources or exercises based on their individual needs. Students who are struggling with a particular concept might be provided with alternative explanations or guided through interactive simulations that help them visualize the problem. Meanwhile, the teacher has a dashboard that gives them an overview of each student's performance, highlighting areas where intervention is needed, and allowing them to personalize their approach in real time. The teacher, then, becomes a facilitator, a mentor, and a guide—able to devote more time to the aspects of teaching that AI cannot handle: fostering critical thinking, creating an intellectually stimulating environment, and supporting students' personal growth. But for this symbiosis to thrive, there are several important factors to consider. First and foremost, the relationship between AI and human educators must be one of partnership, not dominance. AI must be seen as an ally, a tool to enhance the learning experience, not as a substitute for the human touch that is at the heart of meaningful education. The role of AI is to supplement, not overshadow, the educator's intuition, creativity, and ability to connect with students on a deeply human level. There is a danger, of course, that AI could become too dominant, too controlling, and too predictive in its approach to learning. We've already seen instances where algorithmic decision-making has led to biased outcomes or overly rigid pathways, especially when the data used to train the systems is incomplete or skewed. This is why it's essential that educators retain control over the direction of learning. AI should empower teachers to do their best work, not constrain them to a set of predefined outcomes.

Another critical aspect of creating a symbiotic human-AI classroom culture is the role of students in this relationship (Almeida & Senapati, 2024). Students are not just passive recipients of data—they are active participants in their own learning process. AI's ability to personalize learning means that students can take more control over their educational journeys, choosing when to engage with certain topics, exploring areas of interest more deeply, and receiving instant feedback that helps them understand their strengths and areas for improvement. However, with this power comes responsibility. Students must learn how to engage with AI in a thoughtful and ethical way. They must understand the algorithms that are shaping their learning experiences, question the recommendations that AI systems make, and become critical consumers of the data they produce. In this sense, the symbiotic relationship is not just between humans and AI, but also between students and the technology they use. Students must be equipped with the skills and knowledge to navigate an AI-driven educational landscape in a way that enhances their learning, rather than limiting it. A key challenge in fostering this type of symbiotic culture is ensuring that AI does not inadvertently reinforce existing inequalities in education (Padua, 2025). While AI has the potential to democratize access to education by providing personalized learning experiences at scale, it also has the potential to exacerbate existing disparities. Students from different backgrounds may have access to different levels of technology, varying degrees of digital literacy, and vastly different experiences with AI (Kong et al, 2021). This is particularly true in higher education, where access to AI-powered tools may be limited by institutional resources or geographic location. If we are to create a truly symbiotic culture, we must ensure that AI does not create new barriers to learning or reinforce existing ones. The deployment of AI in education must be accompanied by efforts to bridge the digital divide, ensuring that all students have access to the tools and resources they need to succeed in an AI-enhanced learning environment.

Figure 3. AI-Mediated Learning Feedback Loop

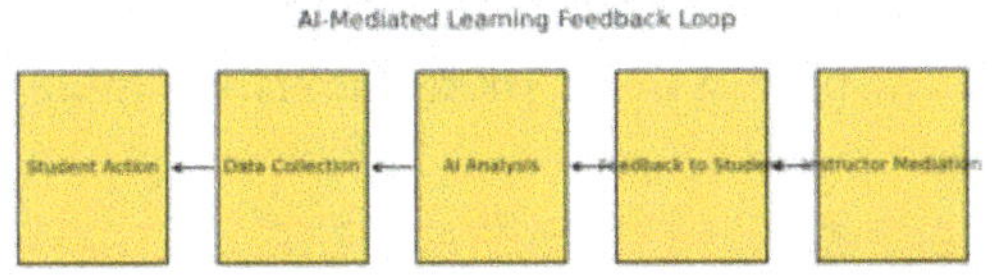

Ethics also plays a central role in shaping this symbiotic relationship (Sun, 2023). As AI systems become more embedded in education, questions about data privacy, algorithmic bias, and the ethics of machine learning become more pressing (Kayyali, 2025a). It is crucial that AI tools used in education are transparent, accountable, and designed with the best interests of students in mind. This includes ensuring that AI systems are free from bias, that students' data is protected, and that AI is used in ways that promote fairness, equity, and inclusivity. The ethical implications of AI in education are far-reaching, and it is up to educators, technologists, and policymakers to navigate these issues thoughtfully and responsibly (Cabrera et al, 2024). One of the greatest opportunities of AI in education is the potential for human-AI collaboration to create more personalized, engaging, and inclusive learning environments. By leveraging AI's ability to analyze data, automate administrative tasks, and provide personalized support, educators can create classrooms where every student's individual needs are addressed, where every learner is empowered to take ownership of their educational journey, and where teaching is not limited by time or resources. But to achieve this vision, we must move beyond a transactional view of AI as a tool, and toward a deeper understanding of AI as a partner in the learning process. We must see it as an opportunity to rethink how we teach, how we learn, and how we create a culture of lifelong learning that is responsive to the changing needs of students and the world around them.

At its best, a symbiotic human-AI classroom culture is one where human ingenuity, empathy, and creativity are augmented, not replaced, by AI's precision, scalability, and adaptability (Qorbani, 2020). It's a culture that embraces the strengths of both human intelligence and artificial intelligence, creating a dynamic and ever-evolving learning environment. In such a classroom, both students and teachers are empowered to engage with the world in new and innovative ways—learning not only from each other, but also from the systems that support them. In this space, education becomes more than the transmission of knowledge; it becomes a collaborative, personalized, and transformative experience that equips students with the skills, values, and insights they need to thrive in an increasingly complex and technology-driven world. This vision of a symbiotic human-AI classroom culture is not a distant dream—it is a future that is already taking shape. The challenge before us is to ensure that we guide this transformation with intention, with a focus on human well-being, and with a deep commitment to the core values of education. If we can achieve this balance, the future of learning will be more inclusive, more dynamic, and more human than ever before.

CONCLUSION

As we close this chapter, it is tempting to feel awe at the possibilities AI brings to education. It is equally tempting to feel unease at the unknowns it introduces. But somewhere in between awe and anxiety lies a space for reflection—and that is the space this conclusion hopes to occupy. Artificial intelligence is not just a tool added to the educator's arsenal. It is a force that reshapes the ecosystem in which education happens. It reframes the who, the how, and even the why of teaching and learning. Professors are not simply integrating a new technology into old routines—they are being called to reimagine their professional identities. No longer merely knowledge dispensers, they are becoming facilitators of a dialogue that includes human and non-human participants. Their responsibilities are shifting from instructing content to curating learning pathways, from grading essays to mentoring intellectual growth in environments where algorithms whisper personalized suggestions to every student.

For students, the transformation is just as significant. They are no longer solely recipients of curated syllabi. With AI's support, they are increasingly autonomous, able to self-direct their learning, seek answers independently, and access tailored resources. At first glance, this seems liberating. And in many ways, it is. But it also demands a new kind of literacy—not just digital fluency, but critical awareness. Students must learn to question the algorithm, to understand the biases embedded in their digital tutors, and to develop resilience in an environment where the path of least resistance is often the one designed by invisible code. Yet, despite all this change, one truth remains stubbornly central: education is, and always will be, a deeply human endeavor. AI can analyze, optimize, and scale. But it cannot feel. It cannot listen between the lines of what a struggling student doesn't say. It cannot inspire, in the way a passionate educator can, through a story, a question, a moment of shared silence. It cannot model empathy, integrity, or the quiet courage it sometimes takes to change your mind. As we chart the path forward, our responsibility is not to compete with AI, nor to blindly follow its lead. Our responsibility is to shape its role intentionally. We must ask: How do we use AI to amplify human potential rather than reduce it to data points? How do we retain space for uncertainty, for serendipity, for the messiness of real learning? How do we protect the relational heart of education in a system increasingly built on efficiency and optimization?

There are no easy answers. But perhaps the most hopeful response lies in recognizing that the presence of AI doesn't diminish the human role—it clarifies it. It reminds us that what matters most in the classroom is not what can be automated, but what cannot. The warmth of encouragement. The trust between mentor and mentee. The moment of discovery that emerges from a difficult conversation—not predicted, not programmed, but profoundly real. In this new era of AI-powered classrooms, the challenge is not to preserve the old, but to evolve with integrity. To ensure that the technology we design does not outpace the ethics we uphold. To remember that, in the end, education is not just about information—it is about transformation. And that transformation, when it is authentic, begins not with machines, but with people.

REFERENCES

Almeida, F., & Senapati, B. (2024, March). Striving for Symbiosis: Human-Machine Relations in the AI Era. In *2024 IEEE Integrated STEM Education Conference (ISEC)* (pp. 1-4). IEEE. DOI: 10.1109/ISEC61299.2024.10664823

Bender, T. (2023). *Discussion-based online teaching to enhance student learning: Theory, practice and assessment*. Taylor & Francis.

Bilousova, L., Kolgatina, L., & Kolgatin, O. (2023). How can we encourage students to manage their own learning? *Ukrainian Journal of Educational Studies and Information Technology*, *11*(1), 55–65. DOI: 10.32919/uesit.2023.01.05

Brożek, B., Furman, M., Jakubiec, M., & Kucharzyk, B. (2024). The black box problem revisited. Real and imaginary challenges for automated legal decision making. *Artificial Intelligence and Law*, *32*(2), 427–440. DOI: 10.1007/s10506-023-09356-9

Bruggeman, B., Tondeur, J., Struyven, K., Pynoo, B., Garone, A., & Vanslambrouck, S. (2021). Experts speaking: Crucial teacher attributes for implementing blended learning in higher education. *The Internet and Higher Education*, *48*, 100772. DOI: 10.1016/j.iheduc.2020.100772

Cabrera, U., Vilca, J., Oliva, E., García, K., Rojas, R., Casaverde, M., & Colonia, C. U. (2024). *Artificial Intelligence in the Ethics of Education*. EMC. DOI: 10.70288/emc.9789915970646

Childers, E. A. (2018). Effects of class scheduling and student achievement on state testing (Doctoral dissertation, Walden University).

Collins, A., & Halverson, R. (2018). *Rethinking education in the age of technology: The digital revolution and schooling in America*. Teachers College Press.

Crittenden, W. F., Biel, I. K., & Lovely, W. A.III. (2019). Embracing digitalization: Student learning and new technologies. *Journal of Marketing Education*, *41*(1), 5–14. DOI: 10.1177/0273475318820895

Dinnar, S. M., Dede, C., Johnson, E., Straub, C., & Korjus, K. (2021). Artificial intelligence and technology in teaching negotiation. *Negotiation Journal*, *37*(1), 65–82. DOI: 10.1111/nejo.12351

Farahani, M., & Ghasemi, G. (2024). Artificial intelligence and inequality: Challenges and opportunities. *Int. J. Innov. Educ*, *9*, 78–99.

Fitria, T. N. (2023). The use of artificial intelligence in education (AIED): Can AI replace the teacher's role? *Epigram*, *20*(2), 165–187. DOI: 10.32722/epi.v20i2.5711

Forsberg, E., Geschwind, L., Levander, S., & Wermke, W. (2022). *Peer review in an era of evaluation: understanding the practice of gatekeeping in academia*. Springer Nature. DOI: 10.1007/978-3-030-75263-7

Göldağ, B. (2022). An investigation of the relationship between university students' digital burnout levels and perceived stress levels. *Journal of Learning and Teaching in Digital Age*, *7*(1), 90–98. DOI: 10.53850/joltida.958039

Holloway, J., & Brass, J. (2018). Making accountable teachers: The terrors and pleasures of performativity. *Journal of Education Policy*, *33*(3), 361–382. DOI: 10.1080/02680939.2017.1372636

Hooda, M., Rana, C., Dahiya, O., Rizwan, A., & Hossain, M. S. (2022). Artificial intelligence for assessment and feedback to enhance student success in higher education. *Mathematical Problems in Engineering*, *2022*(1), 5215722. DOI: 10.1155/2022/5215722

Jacob, N. (2018). Vulnerability as a Pedagogical Practice. Writing as a Way of Staying Human in a Time that Isn't, 103.

Jamieson, D. (2020). Towards an Ethics of Hybrid Agency in Performance. *Performance Research*, *25*(4), 7–16. DOI: 10.1080/13528165.2020.1842023

Jarson, J. (2023). Mapping Unfamiliar Territory: Using Guided Reading Charts to Navigate Sources.

Kayyali, M. (2025a). Ethical Considerations in Higher Education: Accountability Navigating Complexities. In Accountability in Higher Education: Navigating Current Issues and Trends (pp. 145-184). IGI Global Scientific Publishing.

Kayyali, M. (2025b). AI in Higher Education: Revolutionizing Curriculum and Administration. In AI Adoption and Diffusion in Education (pp. 31-62). IGI Global Scientific Publishing.

Kayyali, M. (2025c). The Future of AI in Education: Predictions and Emerging Trends. Next-Generation AI Methodologies in Education, 367-406.

Keiler, L. S. (2018). Teachers' roles and identities in student-centered classrooms. *International Journal of STEM Education*, *5*(1), 1–20. DOI: 10.1186/s40594-018-0131-6 PMID: 30631724

Khan, W. N. (2024). Ethical Challenges of AI in Education: Balancing Innovation with Data Privacy. *Journal of AI in Education: Innovations, Opportunities, Challenges, and Future Directions*, *1*(1), 1–13.

Koehl, S. (2025). Designing AI Software for Large Classroom Engagement (Doctoral dissertation).

Kolluru, V., Mungara, S., & Chintakunta, A. N. (2018). Adaptive learning systems: Harnessing AI for customized educational experiences. *International Journal of Computer Science and Information Technologies*, *6*(3), 10–5121. DOI: 10.5121/ijcsity.2018.6302

Kong, S. C., Cheung, W. M. Y., & Zhang, G. (2021). Evaluation of an artificial intelligence literacy course for university students with diverse study backgrounds. *Computers and Education: Artificial Intelligence*, *2*, 100026. DOI: 10.1016/j.caeai.2021.100026

Kose, U., & Vasant, P. (2020). Better campus life for visually impaired University students: Intelligent social walking system with beacon and assistive technologies. *Wireless Networks*, *26*(7), 4789–4803. DOI: 10.1007/s11276-018-1868-z

Kubsch, M., Krist, C., & Rosenberg, J. M. (2023). Distributing epistemic functions and tasks—A framework for augmenting human analytic power with machine learning in science education research. *Journal of Research in Science Teaching*, *60*(2), 423–447. DOI: 10.1002/tea.21803

Kumar, H. (2024). *Education And Social Change: The Role of School Inshaping Societal Values*. Multidisciplinary Aspects of Education.

Lata, P. (2024). Beyond Algorithms: Humanizing Artificial Intelligence for Personalized and Adaptive Learning. *International Journal of Innovative Research in Engineering and Management*, *11*(5), 10–55524.

Lively, J., Hutson, J., & Melick, E. (2023). Integrating AI-generative tools in web design education: Enhancing student aesthetic and creative copy capabilities using image and text-based AI generators. *Journal of Artificial Intelligence and Robotics*, *1*(1).

Luckin, R. (2025). Nurturing human intelligence in the age of AI: Rethinking education for the future. *Development and Learning in Organizations*, *39*(1), 1–4. DOI: 10.1108/DLO-04-2024-0108

Masters-Wheeler, C. (2024). Algorithmic Attention Systems and Writing-as-Content. *Computers and Composition*, *73*, 102862. DOI: 10.1016/j.compcom.2024.102862

Murgatroyd, S. (2024). *The future of higher education in an age of artificial intelligence*. Ethics International Press.

Omughelli, D., Gordon, N., & Al Jaber, T. (2024). Fairness, bias, and ethics in AI: Exploring the factors affecting student performance. *Journal of International Communication, 3*(2), 100–110.

Padua, D. (2025). Artificial intelligence and quality education: The need for digital culture in teaching. Journal of Educational [ECPS Journal]. *Cultural and Psychological Studies*, (30), 181–193.

Peña, J. M., Moreno, O. B., Herrera, Á. L. O., & Moreno, T. E. B. (2024). Balancing Privacy and Ethics in the Use of Artificial Intelligence in Education. *Sapiens International Multidisciplinary Journal, 1*(3), 148–170. DOI: 10.71068/m4gqp119

Pratschke, B. M. (2024). *Generative AI and education: Digital pedagogies, teaching innovation and learning design*. Springer Nature. DOI: 10.1007/978-3-031-67991-9

Price, E. A., White, R. M., Mori, K., Longhurst, J., Baughan, P., Hayles, C. S., Gough, G., & Preist, C. (2021). Supporting the role of universities in leading individual and societal transformation through education for sustainable development. *Discover Sustainability, 2*(1), 49. DOI: 10.1007/s43621-021-00058-3

Qorbani, M. (2020). *Humanity in the Age of AI: How to Thrive in a Post-Human World*. Bloomsberry.

Saltman, K. (2020). Artificial intelligence and the technological turn of public education privatization: In defence of democratic education. *London Review of Education, 18*(2), 196–208. DOI: 10.14324/LRE.18.2.04

Sannino, A., Engeström, Y., & Lemos, M. (2018). Formative interventions for expansive learning and transformative agency. In *Cultural-historical activity theory approaches to design-based research* (pp. 113–147). Routledge. DOI: 10.4324/9780203703106-6

Schultz, B. D. (2018). *Spectacular things happen along the way: Lessons from an urban classroom*. Teachers College Press.

Shang, H., Sivaparthipan, C. B., & ThanjaiVadivel, . (2022). Interactive teaching using human-machine interaction for higher education systems. *Computers & Electrical Engineering, 100*, 107811. DOI: 10.1016/j.compeleceng.2022.107811

Silseth, K., & Erstad, O. (2018). Connecting to the outside: Cultural resources teachers use when contextualizing instruction. *Learning, Culture and Social Interaction, 17*, 56–68. DOI: 10.1016/j.lcsi.2017.12.002

Sorrentino, P. (2018). The mystery of the digital natives' existence: Questioning the validity of the Prenskian metaphor. *First Monday*. Advance online publication. DOI: 10.5210/fm.v23i10.9434

Srinivasa, K. G., Kurni, M., & Saritha, K. (2022). Harnessing the Power of AI to Education. In *Learning, teaching, and assessment methods for contemporary learners: pedagogy for the digital generation* (pp. 311–342). Springer Nature Singapore. DOI: 10.1007/978-981-19-6734-4_13

Sun, Y. (2023). Research on the Symbiotic and Reciprocal Relationship between Yellow River Culture and the Overall Environment in Moral Education during the New Era. *Pacific International Journal*, *6*(3), 129–133. DOI: 10.55014/pij.v6i3.426

Vincent-Lancrin, S., & Van der Vlies, R. (2020). Trustworthy artificial intelligence (AI) in education: Promises and challenges. OECD education working papers, (218), 0_1-17.

Whitaker, T. (2020). *What great teachers do differently: Nineteen things that matter most*. Routledge. DOI: 10.4324/9780429325977

KEY TERMS AND DEFINITIONS

Algorithmic Mediation: The process by which AI systems invisibly shape classroom interactions, knowledge flow, attention allocation, and feedback loops, influencing power dynamics and learning pathways.

Cognitive Partnership: The evolving role of students as active co-creators of their learning journey alongside AI tools, involving interaction, customization, and critical engagement with technology.

Critical Algorithm Literacy: The essential skill for students and educators to understand, question, and ethically engage with AI systems, examining biases, data sources, design logic, and limitations.

Emotional Labor Shift: The transformation in the professor's role requiring increased emotional intelligence, vulnerability, mentorship, and support for student well-being alongside content expertise in AI-rich environments.

Ethical Co-Design: The imperative for intentional, transparent, and equitable development and deployment of AI in education, prioritizing human values, fairness, privacy, and inclusivity alongside technical capability.

Pedagogical Surveillance: The data-driven monitoring of student behavior, engagement, and performance by AI systems, enabling personalization but raising concerns about privacy, autonomy, and reduced serendipity.

Pedagogical Symbiosis: A cooperative relationship between human educators/ students and AI systems in the classroom, leveraging human strengths (empathy, creativity) and AI strengths (scalability, personalization) to enhance learning.

Chapter 6
Artificial Intelligence and School Leadership:
Using Ethical Leadership as a Framework for Monitoring the Use of AI in Schools

Jerry Ray Burkett
https://orcid.org/0000-0002-9474-9391
Texas Woman's University, USA

ABSTRACT

The integration of Artificial Intelligence (AI) in education is transforming the way we teach and learn. Digital technologies have already become an integral part of our lives. They influence how we search for information, communicate with one another, and even shape our behaviors. This transformation extends to diverse fields, especially education. AI in education offers immense potential to enhance learning experiences and improve outcomes. However, addressing the challenges of accessibility, equity, and ethics is crucial to fully realize its potential. As AI evolves, it is essential to ensure that it complements, rather than replaces, human connection and creativity in the classroom. While AI provides significant opportunities to improve efficiency and educational outcomes, it also raises ethical issues related to privacy, bias, and accountability in decision-making. As school leaders navigate this evolving landscape, ethical leadership becomes a crucial framework for monitoring and guiding the use of AI in schools.

DOI: 10.4018/979-8-3373-6007-2.ch006

INTRODUCTION

The integration of Artificial Intelligence (AI) in education is transforming the way we teach and learn (Naeem and Syed, 2024), offering personalized learning experiences and streamlining administrative tasks. AI presents tremendous opportunities and challenges for students, teachers, and schools alike. Digital technologies have already become an integral part of our lives. They influence how we search for information, communicate with one another, and even shape our behaviors. This transformation extends to diverse fields, especially education (Chassignol and Mikalef, 2021).

One of the most significant applications of AI in education is personalized learning (Lawton and Páez, 2015). AI systems can analyze a student's learning patterns, strengths, and weaknesses, and tailor content to suit individual needs. This adaptive learning allows for a customized educational experience, enabling students to learn at their own pace. For example, AI-powered tutoring systems can provide instant feedback and additional practice on challenging topics, fostering a more supportive environment for learning. AI has seamlessly integrated into classrooms. Regardless of the opinions of students, teachers, parents, or policymakers, intelligent, adaptive, and personalized learning systems are being deployed more and more in schools and universities worldwide. These systems gather and analyze vast amounts of student data, profoundly impacting the lives of both students and educators (Holmes, Bialik, and Fadel, 2019). Ng (2019) explores the transformative potential of machine learning within the educational sector. He emphasizes that machine learning can tailor learning experiences to individual student needs, offering scalable solutions to educational challenges. Ng supports the integration of AI technologies to enhance both teaching and learning processes, thereby making education more accessible and effective.

In addition to personalized learning, AI assists teachers with administrative tasks. Grading, scheduling, and data analysis are a few areas where AI can help. For instance, AI can quickly grade multiple-choice questions, freeing up teachers to focus on meaningful interactions with students. AI-driven analytics can also help educators track student progress and identify areas needing additional support. This leads to more efficient interventions, ensuring students receive timely help.

AI enhances accessibility in education as well. Tools like speech-to-text, language translation, and predictive text assist students with disabilities, non-native speakers, or those requiring additional support. AI-powered learning platforms can make education more inclusive by breaking down barriers and providing more opportunities for success (Lawton & Páez, 2015). Despite these positive developments, one primary concern is the risk of inequality. Access to AI-powered tools is not ubiquitous to all students, particularly those in underfunded schools or rural areas (Whetstone,

2005). Additionally, AI raises ethical questions about data privacy, student autonomy, and potential algorithmic bias. Ensuring AI systems are transparent, unbiased, and secure is essential for an equitable educational environment.

Technology in education extends far beyond the capabilities of AI alone. Digital tools facilitate more engaging multimedia content, real-time collaboration, and interactive learning experiences that can cater to diverse learning styles. For example, virtual labs, simulations, and augmented reality environments offer immersive experiences that can make abstract concepts more tangible. Moreover, technology can help bridge gaps in accessibility, offering tools like speech-to-text and language translation for students with disabilities or those who are non-native speakers—all of which contribute to a more inclusive educational environment (Luna, 2024).

However, the infusion of technology in education is not without its downsides. One critical risk is the digital divide; while some students benefit from state-of-the-art tools, others in rural or underfunded schools may lack the infrastructure or reliable internet access needed for these advances (Luna, 2024). There are also concerns regarding data privacy and security, as AI systems often require vast amounts of data to function effectively. The risk of algorithmic bias—where AI tools might reinforce existing inequalities or favor certain student groups over others—is another significant issue. Furthermore, technology can sometimes reduce human interaction, potentially leading to a diminished role for interpersonal teacher-student relationships which are essential for holistic learning (Zaman, 2023).

AI in education offers immense potential to enhance learning experiences and improve outcomes. However, addressing the challenges of accessibility, equity, and ethics is crucial to fully realize its potential. As AI evolves, it is essential to ensure that it complements, rather than replaces, human connection and creativity in the classroom. While AI provides significant opportunities to improve efficiency and educational outcomes, it also raises ethical issues related to privacy, bias, and accountability in decision-making (Lawton & Páez, 2015). As school leaders navigate this evolving landscape, ethical leadership becomes a crucial framework for monitoring and guiding the use of AI in schools.

AI's impact on education is both profound and multifaceted. Adaptive learning systems, intelligent tutoring, and automated grading are just the beginning. AI's ability to continuously analyze large datasets means that learning platforms can evolve in real time to meet student needs, ultimately creating an environment in which education is not one-size-fits-all. Such adaptive systems are set to revolutionize the educational landscape by increasing both efficiency and engagement.

On another front, AI is poised to modify the role of educators. Rather than replacing educators, AI can serve as an essential tool that frees up teachers' time from tedious administrative tasks, allowing them to concentrate more on creative, interpersonal interactions and customized instruction. This enhanced role emphasizes the teacher as a facilitator of learning rather than a mere disseminator of information, thereby fostering a more dynamic and supportive educational environment.

Ethical leadership in education emphasizes responsibility, fairness, transparency, and the well-being of all stakeholders. By adopting this framework, school leaders can ensure that AI tools align with core educational values and ethical considerations. For instance, AI-driven decision-making in student assessments or disciplinary actions must be free from biases that could disadvantage certain student groups. Additionally, data privacy is a significant concern, as AI systems often rely on vast amounts of student and teacher data. Ethical school leadership necessitates stringent policies to safeguard sensitive information and maintain the trust of students, parents, and educators.

Another significant ethical challenge is ensuring that AI systems are free from bias. When algorithms are trained on historical datasets or are not regularly audited for fairness, there is a risk of perpetuating or even exacerbating existing inequalities. For example, AI-driven decision-making in assessments or disciplinary measures must be carefully monitored to avoid unfair treatment of marginalized student groups. Additionally, leaders must be cautious about over-reliance on AI, recognizing that the human element of education—empathy, creativity, and critical thinking—cannot be replicated by machines alone.

School leaders must engage in continuous dialogue with teachers, students, and the wider community to establish clear guidelines for AI implementation. This includes providing professional development opportunities to equip educators with the knowledge needed to use AI responsibly. Establishing oversight committees and ethical review boards within schools can also help monitor AI applications and address potential risks.

Ethical leadership in education calls for continuous dialogue and review. School leaders are encouraged to form oversight committees or ethical review boards to monitor AI implementations, organize professional development for educators, and establish guidelines that ensure transparency and accountability. Such measures not only safeguard against potential risks but also ensure that the integration of AI enhances rather than diminishes the quality of education.

By adopting ethical leadership as a guiding principle, school leaders can harness the benefits of AI while ensuring its use aligns with educational integrity and the greater good of the learning community. The challenge is not just integrating AI into schools but doing so in a manner that is fair, transparent, and beneficial to all students.

THE ETHICAL LEADERSHIP FRAMEWORK AND ARTIFICIAL INTELLIGENCE

Ethics in education play a crucial role in the moral development of students, equipping them to face personal and professional challenges. Educators act as role models, exemplifying the values of integrity, empathy, and cooperation. This ethical guidance aids students in honing their critical thinking skills and making informed decisions both within and beyond the classroom. Additionally, with the growing integration of technology in education, it is essential to consider ethical issues such as data privacy, online safety, and the responsible use of artificial intelligence. By adhering to a code of ethics, educators uphold professional standards and accountability, ensuring equal educational opportunities for all students (National Education Association, 2020).

Ethical leadership principles—such as integrity, fairness, accountability, respect, transparency, and empathy—are essential for the responsible use of AI in education. Integrity ensures that AI-driven tools are designed and implemented honestly, focusing on genuine learning outcomes rather than profit-driven motives. Fairness helps mitigate biases in AI algorithms, ensuring that educational technologies provide equal opportunities for all students, regardless of background, learning ability, or socioeconomic status. Additionally, accountability is vital, requiring educators, policymakers, and developers to take responsibility for the ethical implications of AI, including data privacy, misinformation, and student well-being.

Lawton and Páez (2015) presents an integrated approach to ethical leadership by examining three interlocking dimensions: Virtues, Purposes, and Practices. Virtues focuses on the inherent qualities and characteristics of ethical leaders, such as integrity, honesty, and compassion. It emphasizes the importance of personal virtues in guiding ethical behavior. Integrity in AI development and implementation means creating and using AI systems with a commitment to genuine, positive outcomes. This involves designing AI tools that are fair, unbiased, and prioritize the welfare of users over profit-driven motives. For instance, in education, AI systems should enhance learning experiences and support educators, not replace them or create unfair advantages for certain groups of students.

Particularly in education, the conversation should be centered around what AI can and cannot do. This includes being upfront about the limitations and potential biases of AI algorithms, the sources of data used for training, and any assumptions made during the development process. It also means providing clear information about how AI decisions are made, so users can understand and trust the technology. When integrity and honesty are prioritized, the deployment of AI becomes more trustworthy and reliable, creating a positive relationship between the technology and its users. By adhering to these principles, developers and educators can ensure that AI tools are used ethically and responsibly, promoting equity, transparency, and respect for all individuals involved.

Lawton and Paez (2015) argue that these dimensions are interconnected and that understanding them holistically can help in developing effective ethical leadership practices while Naeem and Syed (2024) conceptualize ethical leadership as a dynamic process. They argue that ethical leadership is not just about individual traits but also involves organizational contexts and systematic practices that are mutually reinforcing and evolving. Ethical leaders possess qualities such as integrity, honesty, and empathy, which guide their behavior and decision-making. The environment in which leaders operate significantly influences their ethical conduct. This includes organizational culture, policies, and broader societal norms. Ethical leadership involves implementing practices that promote ethical behavior within organizations, such as transparent decision-making, accountability, and fostering a culture of fairness and respect.

Respect and transparency also shape AI's ethical application in education. Respect ensures that AI tools support, rather than replace, human teachers, valuing the expertise and emotional intelligence that educators bring to the learning process. Transparency is crucial for making AI decision-making processes understandable to educators, students, and parents, thereby fostering trust in AI-driven recommendations.

Nonetheless, ethical behavior when using AI should be the norm. Leaders should create an environment where that promotes ethical decision-making and supports a culture of accountability (Whetstone, 2005). By integrating these principles into their leadership practices, leaders can build trust, enhance organizational performance, and ensure that their organizations operate with integrity. This is particularly crucial when promoting the use of AI tools in an educational setting, where ethical considerations are crucial.

THE DEPENDENCE ON TECHNOLOGY IN EDUCATION

The integration of technology into education has been a transformative force, reshaping how students learn and teachers instruct. Digital tools and platforms have become integral to the educational landscape, offering new opportunities for personalized learning, administrative efficiency, and global connectivity (Garcia, 2023). However, this increasing reliance on technology also brings challenges that must be addressed to ensure equitable and effective education for all students.

The Benefits of Technology in Education

Technology has revolutionized education by providing students with access to a wealth of information and resources that were previously unavailable. Online learning platforms, educational apps, and digital textbooks allow students to learn at their own pace and according to their individual needs (Garcia, 2023). For example, adaptive learning systems can tailor content to match students' learning styles and progress, making education more personalized and effective. Additionally, technology facilitates collaboration and communication among students and teachers, breaking down geographical barriers and fostering a global learning community.

One major benefit of technology in education is personalized learning. Digital tools such as adaptive learning software use AI to assess student progress and tailor lessons accordingly. These platforms adjust the difficulty level of exercises and provide real-time feedback, ensuring that students receive instruction suited to their individual needs (Holmes, Bialik, & Fadel, 2019). This personalization helps students grasp complex concepts at their own pace, reducing frustration and improving learning outcomes.

Another advantage is increased accessibility. Technology allows students from diverse backgrounds, including those with disabilities, to access quality education. Assistive technologies, such as speech-to-text applications and screen readers, make learning materials more inclusive (Chassignol & Mikalef, 2021). Additionally, online learning platforms enable students from remote areas to attend virtual classes, expanding educational opportunities beyond traditional classrooms.

Technology also fosters collaboration and engagement. Digital tools like interactive whiteboards, discussion forums, and collaborative applications such as Google Classroom facilitate communication between students and teachers (Seldon & Abidoye, 2018). Online platforms encourage peer-to-peer learning by allowing students to share ideas, work on projects together, and participate in discussions, enhancing their overall engagement.

Furthermore, technology enhances efficiency in education by automating administrative tasks. AI-powered grading systems reduce the burden on educators, allowing them to focus on instruction and student support (Ng, 2019). Learning management systems help track student progress, generate reports, and provide insights into learning patterns, enabling data-driven decision-making for teachers and school administrators.

Technology plays a crucial role in improving education by providing personalized learning experiences, increasing accessibility, fostering collaboration, and enhancing efficiency. While challenges such as digital equity and privacy concerns remain, the benefits of technology in education are undeniable. As educational technology continues to evolve, it holds the potential to make learning more effective, engaging, and inclusive for students worldwide.

Challenges and Ethical Concerns

While technology has revolutionized education, its integration also brings significant challenges and ethical concerns. Issues such as digital inequality, data privacy, reliance on AI, and the potential loss of human interaction raise important questions about the responsible use of technology in education.

One primary challenge is digital inequality. While technology can make education more accessible, not all students have equal access to digital devices and the internet. This digital divide disproportionately affects students from low-income households and rural areas, limiting their ability to engage in online learning (Chassignol & Mikalef, 2021). Without equitable access, disparities in education may widen.

Data privacy and security are other major concerns. Educational technologies collect vast amounts of student data, including personal information, learning habits, and academic performance. If not properly managed, this data can be vulnerable to breaches or misuse by third parties (Holmes, Bialik, & Fadel, 2019). Schools and EdTech companies must ensure strong cybersecurity measures and transparent policies to protect student data.

The increasing reliance on AI and automation also raises ethical concerns. AI-driven learning platforms can personalize education, but they also risk reinforcing biases embedded in algorithms. If not designed with fairness in mind, AI can disadvantage certain student groups based on race, gender, or socioeconomic status (Ng, 2019). Excessive reliance on AI may lead to over-automation, reducing the role of teachers and diminishing the human aspects of learning.

Another critical challenge is the potential loss of human interaction in digital learning environments. While online education provides flexibility, it may limit the development of social and communication skills essential for student growth (Seldon & Abidoye, 2018). Face-to-face interactions with teachers and peers are crucial for fostering critical thinking, emotional intelligence, and collaborative learning. Overuse of technology could lead to isolation and reduced engagement among students.

To create a responsible and effective educational system, addressing digital inequality, ensuring data privacy, managing AI biases, and preserving human interaction are essential. Educational institutions must implement policies that promote ethical and equitable use of technology to maximize its benefits while mitigating its risks.

The Impact of Technology on Student Well-being

Technology has transformed the educational landscape, offering new ways for students to learn, connect, and engage with academic content. However, its widespread use raises concerns about student well-being, including mental health, social development, and physical health. While technology can enhance learning experiences and provide valuable resources, excessive use or improper integration can contribute to stress, anxiety, and other negative effects on students' overall well-being. The overreliance on technology in education can also have adverse effects on students' well-being. Excessive screen time and passive consumption of digital content can lead to physical and mental health issues, such as eye strain, sleep disturbances, and decreased attention spans (Leonard, 2024). Additionally, technology can sometimes replace face-to-face interactions, which are essential for developing social skills and emotional intelligence. Educators must balance incorporating technology into the classroom and fostering meaningful human connections.

Technology has the potential to positively impact student well-being by providing flexible learning environments and personalized educational experiences. Digital tools such as educational apps, online resources, and adaptive learning platforms can cater to individual learning styles and needs, making education more accessible and engaging (Timbanga and Velasco, 2024). For instance, students can access learning materials at their own pace, receive instant feedback, and participate in interactive activities that promote deeper understanding and retention of information (Carstens, et al., 2021). Moreover, technology facilitates communication and collaboration among students and teachers, fostering a sense of community and support. Online discussion forums, video conferencing, and collaborative projects enable students to connect with peers and educators, regardless of geographical barriers. This connectivity can enhance social skills, reduce feelings of isolation, and promote a more inclusive learning environment (Carstens, et al., 2021).

One of the most significant concerns related to technology in education is its impact on students' mental health. While digital tools can facilitate learning, they can also increase academic stress. Constant exposure to screens, endless streams of information, and the pressure to stay digitally connected can lead to anxiety and burnout among students (Holmes, Bialik, & Fadel, 2019). Online learning platforms and digital assessments often require students to complete tasks on tight deadlines, sometimes contributing to heightened stress levels. Additionally, the prevalence of academic comparison on digital platforms, such as grade-sharing apps and discussion forums, can lead to increased pressure to perform, affecting students' self-esteem and confidence.

Remote and technology-driven education can sometimes lead to a lack of motivation and engagement. A study by Chassignol and Mikalef (2021) found that students who primarily learn through digital means, without meaningful interaction with teachers and peers, are more likely to feel disconnected from their education. This sense of detachment can contribute to feelings of loneliness and even depression, especially in virtual learning environments where students do not have opportunities for social interaction. The digital divide remains a significant challenge. Students from low-income households or rural areas may lack access to the necessary technology and internet connectivity, exacerbating existing educational inequalities. Without equitable access to digital tools, these students are at a disadvantage, further widening the gap in educational outcomes.

Technology has also changed the way students interact with their peers. While digital tools like collaborative software and online discussion boards promote teamwork, they do not fully replace face-to-face social interactions. Excessive use of technology in education can limit students' ability to develop essential interpersonal skills, such as verbal communication, empathy, and conflict resolution (Seldon & Abidoye, 2018). Research suggests that when students spend too much time engaged with screens rather than in-person discussions, their ability to interpret social cues and engage in meaningful conversations can be negatively affected. Another issue related to student well-being is the influence of social media on self-perception and social anxiety. Many students use social media for educational purposes, such as group discussions or peer collaboration. However, excessive exposure to social media platforms can lead to unhealthy comparisons, cyberbullying, and decreased self-worth (Ng, 2019). The need to maintain an online academic presence while also dealing with social expectations can create an overwhelming environment for students, affecting their overall emotional well-being.

The impact of technology on students' physical health is another area of concern. Prolonged screen time can contribute to eye strain, poor posture, and disrupted sleep patterns. Studies indicate that students who use digital devices for extended periods often experience digital fatigue, leading to headaches, reduced concentration, and lower productivity (Chassignol & Mikalef, 2021). Furthermore, blue light exposure from screens, especially before bedtime, can interfere with students' sleep cycles, ultimately affecting their cognitive performance and emotional stability. Additionally, the shift to digital education has resulted in more sedentary behavior among students. Online learning often requires students to remain seated for long periods, reducing opportunities for physical activity. Research suggests that a lack of movement and exercise can contribute to obesity, decreased energy levels, and overall poorer physical well-being (Holmes, Bialik, & Fadel, 2019). Schools must find ways to integrate movement and wellness strategies into technology-driven education to mitigate these negative effects.

To ensure that technology enhances education while protecting student well-being, institutions must implement strategies that promote healthy technology use. Schools can encourage digital wellness education, teaching students about screen time management, cyber safety, and responsible social media use. Moreover, integrating breaks and movement-based activities into digital learning environments can help reduce physical strain and mental exhaustion. Another essential approach is maintaining a balance between online and offline learning. Hybrid learning models, which combine digital instruction with in-person engagement, can support both academic success and social-emotional development (Seldon & Abidoye, 2018). Additionally, educators should focus on fostering a positive online learning environment where students feel supported rather than pressured.

While technology provides valuable opportunities for learning and engagement, its impact on student well-being must be carefully managed. Issues such as academic stress, social disconnection, digital fatigue, and physical health concerns highlight the need for a balanced approach to technology use in education. By promoting responsible digital habits, encouraging in-person interactions, and integrating wellness strategies into educational settings, institutions can ensure that technology enhances learning without compromising students' overall well-being.

Mental health is a significant area of concern with the integration of technology in education. The pressure to stay connected and the constant influx of information can lead to stress, anxiety, and burnout among students. Social media usage has been linked to increased levels of social anxiety, loneliness, and depression. The need to maintain an online presence and the fear of missing out (FOMO) can negatively impact students' self-esteem and mental well-being.

Additionally, the digital divide remains a significant challenge. Students from low-income households or rural areas may lack access to necessary technology and internet connectivity, exacerbating existing educational inequalities. Without equitable access to digital tools, these students are at a disadvantage, further widening the gap in educational outcomes.

To mitigate the negative impacts of technology on student well-being, schools and educators must adopt a balanced approach to technology integration. This includes promoting digital literacy and responsible technology use, encouraging regular breaks from screens, and fostering face-to-face interactions to develop social and emotional skills (Timbang and Velasco, 2024; Carstens, et al., 2021). Schools should also implement policies to ensure data privacy and security, protecting students' personal information from potential breaches and misuse.

The impact of technology on student well-being is multifaceted, offering both opportunities and challenges. While digital tools can enhance learning experiences and foster connectivity, they also pose risks to physical and mental health. By adopting a balanced and ethical approach to technology integration, schools can harness its benefits while mitigating its negative effects, ensuring that students thrive in a supportive and equitable educational environment.

To address these challenges, schools and policymakers must take a holistic approach to integrating technology into education. This includes investing in infrastructure to ensure all students have access to digital tools and internet connectivity Schools should also provide professional development opportunities for teachers to effectively use technology in their teaching practices. Additionally, implementing strong data privacy policies and promoting digital literacy among students can help mitigate the risks associated with technology use.

Over-reliance on AI can lead to a reduction in critical thinking and problem-solving skills among both teachers and students. Balancing the use of technology with traditional teaching methods is essential. While technology has the potential to enhance education and improve learning outcomes, it is crucial to address the challenges and ethical concerns that come with its use. By taking a balanced and thoughtful approach, educators can harness the benefits of technology while ensuring that it supports the holistic development of students and promotes equity in education.

LACK OF TEACHER TRAINING AND SUPPORT

The rapid advancement of technology AI has transformed various sectors, including education. However, there is a noticeable lack of teacher training on these critical tools, which can hinder effective integration into the classroom (Langreo, 2024). Several factors contribute to this gap, including limited resources, insufficient professional development opportunities, and a lack of awareness about the benefits of technology and AI in education. Further, many schools are still lacking in technology resources as public education seems to suffer from being behind the speed of developing technologies that students could use.

Many schools and districts face budget constraints that limit their ability to provide comprehensive training programs for teachers. Investing in technology and AI training requires financial resources that may not be readily available, especially in underfunded schools (Langreo, 2024). As a result, teachers often lack the necessary skills and knowledge to effectively use these tools in their teaching practices. Professional development for teachers is crucial in helping them integrate technology into their teaching practices effectively while being mindful of its impact on student well-being. Educators can provide guidance on healthy technology use, set boundaries for screen time, and create a supportive learning environment prioritizing both academic success and mental health.

The Need for Strong Professional Development

The rapid advancement of technology and AI has transformed various sectors, including education. However, there is a noticeable lack of teacher training on these critical tools, which can hinder effective integration into the classroom (Langreo, 2024). Several factors contribute to this gap, including limited resources, insufficient professional development opportunities, and a lack of awareness about the benefits of technology and AI in education.

Without proper training, the potential benefits of AI may not be fully realized. This includes promoting digital literacy and responsible technology use, encouraging regular breaks from screens, and fostering face-to-face interactions to develop social and emotional skills (Timbang and Velasco, 2024; Carstens, et al., 2021). Schools should also implement policies to ensure data privacy and security, protecting students' personal information from potential breaches and misuse. By addressing these challenges through targeted professional development programs and increased funding, educators can harness the benefits of technology and AI while ensuring that it supports the holistic development of students and promotes equity in education.

Currently, professional development opportunities for teachers on technology and AI are often insufficient. According to a survey by the EdWeek Research Center, nearly 58% of educators reported having no training on AI, even two years after the release of ChatGPT (Langreo, 2024). While there has been an increase in professional development sessions, many teachers still feel unprepared to integrate AI into their classrooms (Langreo, 2024). Professional development for teachers is crucial in helping them effectively integrate technology into their teaching practices while being mindful of its impact on student well-being (Carstens, et al., 2021). Educators can provide guidance on healthy technology use, set boundaries for screen time, and create a supportive learning environment that prioritizes both academic success and mental health.

The rapid pace of technological advancements can make it challenging for teacher training programs to keep up. Traditional teacher education programs may not be equipped to provide up-to-date training on the latest technologies and AI applications, leaving teachers at a disadvantage (Langreo, 2024). This gap in training can result in a lack of confidence among educators, further hindering the effective use of technology and AI in the classroom.

Awareness, Support, and Pace of Technology

There is also a lack of awareness among educators about the potential benefits of technology and AI in education. Many teachers may not fully understand how these tools can enhance learning experiences, improve student engagement, and provide personalized support (Langreo, 2024). Without this awareness, teachers may be less motivated to seek out training opportunities or advocate for the inclusion of technology and AI in their professional development programs. Teachers may also simply just not be aware of the potential technologies and programs that exist in the marketplace.

The lack of teacher training on technology and AI is a multifaceted issue that requires attention from policymakers, educators, and educational institutions. Addressing this gap through increased funding, comprehensive professional development programs, and raising awareness about the benefits of technology and AI can help ensure that teachers are well-prepared to integrate these tools into their teaching practices. By doing so, educators can better support student learning and prepare students for a technology-driven future.

The consequences of inadequate teacher training in technology and AI are significant. Teachers who are not proficient in using digital tools may struggle to integrate them effectively into their lessons, leading to underutilization of available resources. Furthermore, students miss out on the potential benefits of AI-driven personalized learning, which can adapt instruction to their individual needs (Luckin et al., 2016). Without proper training, educators may also inadvertently reinforce biases in AI tools or fail to address ethical considerations related to technology use in the classroom.

Addressing this issue requires a multi-faceted approach. Policymakers must allocate more funding to professional development programs that focus on technology and AI in education. Universities should incorporate mandatory courses on technology integration into teacher preparation programs to ensure that new educators are equipped with the necessary skills. Additionally, school districts must establish ongoing training initiatives to keep teachers up to date with emerging technologies.

Ethical Leadership for Teacher Training

The importance of ethics in teacher training on AI cannot be overstated. As AI technologies become increasingly integrated into educational settings, it is essential for educators to understand the ethical implications of using these tools. Ethical training ensures that teachers are aware of issues related to data privacy, bias, and fairness, which are critical for protecting student well-being. The responsible handling of student data is crucial for maintaining trust and safeguarding sensitive information (Holmes, Bialik, and Fadel, 2019). Additionally, ethical training helps teachers recognize and mitigate biases in AI algorithms, ensuring that all students receive fair and equitable treatment. This awareness is crucial for creating an inclusive learning environment where technology is used responsibly and ethically.

Ethics and teacher training on AI are essential for ensuring the responsible and effective integration of AI in education. As AI becomes more prevalent in classrooms, ethical considerations such as data privacy, algorithmic bias, and the potential for misinformation must be addressed. Without proper ethical guidelines, AI tools may inadvertently reinforce biases, violate student privacy, or create unfair learning environments (Floridi & Cowls, 2019). Teachers play a crucial role in mitigating these risks by being well-informed about AI ethics and understanding how to use AI responsibly. Ethical AI training should emphasize transparency, fairness, and accountability to foster trust in AI-enhanced education.

Effective teacher training on AI empowers educators to harness the full potential of these technologies while being mindful of their impact on students. Professional development opportunities that focus on AI and technology integration equip teachers with the necessary skills to use digital tools effectively in their classrooms (Carstens et al., 2021). This includes promoting digital literacy, responsible technology use, and healthy screen time habits among students. By fostering a balanced approach to technology integration, educators can enhance learning experiences and support students' holistic development. Comprehensive training programs that emphasize both the technical and ethical aspects of AI prepare teachers to navigate the complexities of modern education, ultimately benefiting both students and the educational system as a whole (Langreo, 2024).

Equally important is equipping teachers with the necessary training to effectively integrate AI into their teaching strategies. Many educators lack sufficient knowledge about AI's capabilities and limitations, which can lead to misuse or underutilization of AI-powered tools (Zawacki-Richter et al., 2019). Comprehensive teacher training programs should focus on both technical skills and pedagogical approaches to maximize AI's potential while ensuring that human-centered learning remains a priority. By understanding AI's strengths and weaknesses, educators can make informed decisions that enhance student learning experiences rather than replace traditional teaching methods. Well-trained teachers will be better prepared to use AI ethically and effectively, fostering a more equitable and beneficial learning environment.

DATA PRIVACY AND SECURITY CONCERNS

Data privacy and security are critical concerns in education due to the increasing use of digital tools and online platforms in classrooms. As educational institutions collect and store vast amounts of sensitive student information, including personal details, academic records, and behavioral data, the risk of data breaches and unauthorized access becomes a significant issue. These breaches can lead to severe consequences such as identity theft, fraud, and extortion, which can have long-lasting impacts on students' lives (US Department of Education, 2024). Moreover, the Family Educational Rights and Privacy Act (FERPA) mandates that educational institutions protect student data, but many schools lack the necessary security measures to comply with these regulations effectively. As a result, students' privacy is often compromised, and their personal information is at risk of being misused.

The Rapid Pace of Technology and the Need for Safeguards

The rapid adoption of EdTech further exacerbates these concerns. EdTech tools, including online learning platforms, virtual classrooms, and data-driven analytics, collect extensive amounts of student data to personalize learning experiences and improve educational outcomes. However, the lack of transparency and inadequate safeguards in these tools can lead to ethical dilemmas surrounding student data privacy. For instance, data breaches in EdTech can expose students to unauthorized access and misuse of their information (Grosso, et al., 2024). Ensuring informed consent and promoting digital literacy among students and educators are essential steps in addressing these challenges and safeguarding student data privacy (Evanick, 2023).

One of the primary concerns regarding data privacy in education is the increasing use of third-party EdTech platforms. However, not all EdTech companies have robust security measures or clear policies on data usage. According to Bulger et al. (2017), many educational technology providers do not fully disclose how they handle student data, raising concerns about potential misuse, including commercial exploitation. Furthermore, inadequate oversight by educational institutions can lead to data breaches, exposing students to cyber threats and unauthorized surveillance.

Legal Concerns

Legal and ethical considerations further highlight the importance of data privacy in education. Laws such as the Family Educational Rights and Privacy Act (FERPA) and the Children's Online Privacy Protection Act (COPPA) in the United States aim to protect student data by regulating its collection, storage, and sharing. However, compliance with these regulations varies across institutions, and enforcement challenges persist (Reidenberg et al., 2018). Educational stakeholders must prioritize ethical data practices, ensuring that student information is used solely for educational purposes and safeguarded against unauthorized access. Schools should implement strict data governance policies, train educators and administrators on data security best practices, and collaborate with policymakers to enhance legal protections.

Cybersecurity threats, such as hacking and phishing attacks, pose another significant risk to educational institutions. Schools and universities are frequent targets for cybercriminals due to the vast amounts of sensitive information they store. Ransomware attacks on educational institutions have surged in recent years, causing financial losses and operational disruptions (Kshetri, 2021). Additionally, phishing scams often target students and faculty, tricking them into revealing login credentials or other confidential information. These security breaches not only compromise personal data but also disrupt the learning process, underscoring the urgent need for robust cybersecurity policies and infrastructure in educational settings.

Ethics and Data Privacy

Ethics play a crucial role in addressing data privacy and security concerns in education by ensuring that students' and educators' sensitive information is protected from misuse and unauthorized access. Educational institutions collect vast amounts of data, including personal details, academic records, and behavioral insights, which, if mishandled, could lead to identity theft, discrimination, or other harmful consequences (West, 2019). Ethical principles such as transparency, consent, and fairness guide institutions in implementing policies that prioritize data protection while maintaining trust among students, parents, and educators. Without ethical considerations, data breaches or improper data usage could not only violate legal standards but also erode confidence in the education system's ability to safeguard individuals' rights and well-being (Solove, 2020).

Data privacy and security remain critical concerns in the education sector due to the increasing reliance on digital tools and the growing threat of cyberattacks. Educational institutions must adopt comprehensive strategies to protect student and faculty information, including strengthening security protocols, ensuring transparency in data usage, and complying with legal frameworks. By prioritizing data privacy, schools can create safer learning environments and foster trust in digital education systems.

THE IMPACT OF AI ON EMPLOYMENT IN EDUCATION

The integration of AI in education has significantly impacted employment within the sector, bringing both opportunities and challenges. AI's ability to automate administrative tasks, analyze vast amounts of data, and provide personalized learning experiences has transformed the roles of educators and administrative staff.

However, this transformation also raises concerns about job displacement and the need for new skill sets.

One of the primary impacts of AI on employment in education is the automation of administrative tasks. AI-powered systems can handle tasks such as grading, attendance tracking, and scheduling, which traditionally require significant time and effort from educators and administrative staff. This automation allows educators to focus more on teaching and mentoring, potentially improving the quality of education (Wichita State University, 2025). However, it also means that some administrative roles may become redundant, leading to job displacement for those who previously performed these tasks.

AI's ability to analyze data and provide insights has also transformed decision-making processes in education. AI-driven analytics can identify trends and patterns in student performance, helping educators tailor their teaching methods to meet individual needs. This personalized approach can enhance student outcomes and reduce achievement gaps (Stanford Accelerator for Learning, 2025). However, the reliance on AI for decision-making necessitates new skill sets for educators, who must learn to interpret and act on AI-generated insights. This shift may require significant professional development and training, creating new opportunities for employment in the field of AI education.

Despite the opportunities created by AI, there are also challenges related to job displacement and inequality. AI's capacity for automation can supplant humans in certain roles, particularly those involving repetitive tasks. This displacement can disproportionately affect lower-skilled workers, exacerbating income inequality and creating barriers to employment for those without the necessary skills to transition to new roles (Wichita State University, 2025). To address these challenges, it is essential to implement policies and programs that support workforce development and provide opportunities for reskilling and upskilling.

The ethical implications of AI in education must be carefully considered. AI systems can inadvertently perpetuate biases present in the data they are trained on, leading to unfair outcomes for certain groups of students. Ensuring that AI is used ethically and responsibly in education requires ongoing monitoring and evaluation, as well as the development of ethical guidelines and standards (Stanford Accelerator for Learning, 2025).

The impact of AI on employment in education is multifaceted, bringing both opportunities and challenges. While AI can enhance efficiency and create new job opportunities, it also raises concerns about job displacement and the need for new skill sets. Addressing these challenges requires a focus on workforce development, continuous learning, and the ethical use of AI in education. By embracing these principles, the education sector can harness the benefits of AI while mitigating its risks.

ACCOUNTABILITY AND DECISION-MAKING

Accountability and decision-making are critical components in the educational landscape, ensuring that institutions uphold standards and deliver quality education. The integration of AI into education has significantly impacted these areas, bringing both opportunities and challenges. AI's ability to analyze vast amounts of data and provide insights has transformed decision-making processes, making them more efficient and data-driven. However, this also raises concerns about accountability, as decisions made by AI systems must be transparent and ethical.

AI has the potential to enhance accountability in education by providing real-time data and analytics on student performance, teacher effectiveness, and institutional outcomes. For instance, AI-driven platforms can track student progress, identify learning gaps, and suggest personalized interventions, thereby holding educators accountable for student success (Slimi, 2023). Additionally, AI can automate administrative tasks, such as grading and attendance tracking, reducing the burden on educators and allowing them to focus on teaching and mentoring. However, the reliance on AI for decision-making also necessitates robust ethical guidelines to ensure that these systems are used responsibly and do not perpetuate biases or inequalities (Stelmach, 2025).

The impact of AI on decision-making in education extends to curriculum development and instructional design. AI can analyze student data to identify trends and patterns, informing the creation of more effective and engaging learning experiences. For example, AI can recommend adjustments to teaching methods based on student feedback and performance, ensuring that educational practices are continuously improved (U.S. Department of Education, 2023). Moreover, AI can facilitate collaborative decision-making by providing stakeholders with access to comprehensive data and insights, fostering a more inclusive and participatory approach to education.

Despite the benefits, the integration of AI in education also presents challenges related to accountability and ethical decision-making. One major concern is the potential for AI systems to reinforce existing biases and inequalities. For instance, if AI algorithms are trained on biased data, they may produce biased outcomes, disproportionately affecting marginalized students (Stelmach, 2025). To address this issue, it is essential to implement rigorous auditing and monitoring processes to ensure that AI systems are fair and unbiased. Additionally, educators and administrators must be trained to understand and critically evaluate AI-generated insights, ensuring that human judgment remains central to decision-making.

Another challenge is the need for transparency in AI-driven decision-making processes. Stakeholders, including students, parents, and educators, must have access to information about how AI systems operate and the criteria used for decision-making. This transparency is crucial for building trust and ensuring that AI is used ethically and responsibly in education (Slimi, 2023). Furthermore, clear guidelines and regulations must be established to govern the use of AI in education, addressing issues such as data privacy, consent, and accountability.

In conclusion, the integration of AI in education has the potential to enhance accountability and decision-making by providing data-driven insights and automating administrative tasks. However, it also raises important ethical considerations that must be addressed to ensure that AI is used responsibly and equitably. By implementing robust ethical guidelines, promoting transparency, and ensuring that human judgment remains central to decision-making, educators can harness the benefits of AI while mitigating its risks. As AI continues to evolve, it is essential to remain vigilant and proactive in addressing the challenges it presents, ensuring that it serves as a tool for enhancing, rather than undermining, educational equity and quality.

INFORMED CONSENT AND TRANSPARENCY

Students, parents, and educators need to understand how AI tools function, what data is collected, and how decisions are reached. Providing clear information ensures informed consent and helps prevent the misuse of personal data. Informed consent and transparency are fundamental principles in education, ensuring that all stakeholders are fully aware of and agree to the processes and decisions that affect them. These principles are essential for fostering trust, accountability, and ethical practices within educational institutions. By promoting these values, educational institutions can create a positive learning environment and uphold the integrity of the educational system. Furthermore, regular updates and open communication about AI usage reinforce the commitment to transparency and ethical conduct.

Informed Consent in Education

Informed consent is a process that ensures individuals are fully informed about and voluntarily agree to specific actions or decisions. In the context of education, informed consent is particularly important in special education and research involving students. According to the Individuals with Disabilities Education Act (IDEA), schools must obtain informed consent from parents before conducting initial evaluations, re-evaluations, or providing special education services to their children (IDEA, 2006). This process involves providing parents with detailed information about the proposed actions, including their purpose, potential benefits, and risks, in a language they understand. Parents must also be informed of their right to refuse or withdraw consent at any time (Center for Parental Consent, 2021).

Informed consent is crucial for protecting the rights and autonomy of students and their families. It ensures that parents are active participants in the decision-making process regarding their child's education, promoting a collaborative approach between schools and families. Additionally, informed consent helps prevent misunderstandings and conflicts by ensuring that all parties have a clear understanding of the proposed actions and their implications (Lee, 2025). This transparency is essential for building trust and fostering positive relationships between educators and families.

Transparency in Education

Transparency in education refers to the openness and clarity with which educational institutions communicate their policies, practices, and decision-making processes. It involves providing stakeholders, including students, parents, and educators, with access to accurate and timely information about the curriculum, assessment methods, and institutional policies. Transparency is essential for promoting accountability, trust, and informed decision-making within the educational community (Education Advanced, 2023).

One of the key benefits of transparency in education is that it helps students understand the rationale behind their learning activities and assessments. When students are aware of the objectives and expectations of their coursework, they are more likely to engage actively in the learning process and take ownership of their education (Education Advanced, 2023). Transparency also enables parents to make informed decisions about their child's education, fostering a collaborative relationship between schools and families. By providing clear and accessible information about school policies, curriculum changes, and assessment methods, educational institutions can build trust and support among parents and the broader community.

Moreover, transparency in education promotes accountability by ensuring that educational institutions are held responsible for their actions and decisions. When schools openly share information about their performance, policies, and decision-making processes, they demonstrate a commitment to ethical practices and continuous improvement (TeachThough, 2014). This openness allows stakeholders to provide feedback and hold institutions accountable for their actions, ultimately leading to better educational outcomes.

In conclusion, informed consent and transparency are essential principles in education that promote trust, accountability, and ethical practices. Informed consent ensures that students and their families are active participants in the decision-making process, protecting their rights and autonomy. Transparency, on the other hand, fosters open communication and accountability, enabling stakeholders to make informed decisions and hold educational institutions responsible for their actions. By prioritizing these principles, educational institutions can create a positive and inclusive learning environment that benefits all members of the community.

ETHICAL LEADERSHIP AND POLICY DEVELOPMENT

Ethical leadership is a cornerstone of effective policy development, ensuring that decisions made by leaders are grounded in integrity, accountability, and a commitment to the common good. Ethical leaders prioritize the needs of their stakeholders, including employees, customers, and the broader community, over personal or organizational gain. This approach fosters trust and transparency, which are essential for the successful implementation of policies. Ethical leadership involves making decisions that are not only legally compliant but also morally sound, considering the long-term impact on society and the environment (Harvard DCE, 2025).

One of the key principles of ethical leadership is respect, which involves valuing the skills and contributions of others and fostering mutual respect within the organization. This principle is particularly important in policy development, as it ensures that diverse perspectives are considered and that policies are inclusive and equitable. Ethical leaders also emphasize transparency, promoting open communication and allowing stakeholders to understand the decision-making process. This transparency helps to build trust and ensures that policies are implemented fairly and effectively (Harvard DCE, 2025).

As AI-driven tools become increasingly central to educational practices—from personalized learning to administrative efficiency—leaders must ensure that their deployment does not compromise the core values of education. This involves establishing clear policies for data privacy, mitigating algorithmic biases, and fostering open dialogues with educators, students, and parents. By actively engaging with these challenges, leaders not only safeguard against potential misuse but also model an ethical framework that promotes trust and inclusivity across the learning community.

Ethical leadership plays a crucial role in shaping public policy by ensuring that decisions are made in the best interests of the public. Ethical leaders act as role models, demonstrating a commitment to fairness and the welfare of the community. They inspire their teams and the public by setting examples through their actions, which are consistent with their words. This leadership style fosters an environment where ethical practices are the norm, influencing all layers of policy development from conception to implementation (Advisory Excellence, 2024).

Fostering an Ethical Culture

Education is a critical factor in fostering ethical leadership. Advanced degrees in public administration and related fields equip future leaders with the knowledge and ethical frameworks necessary to navigate the complex moral landscapes of policy development. These programs often include courses on ethics, governance, and transparent leadership, providing students with the tools to make principled decisions. Graduates from these programs are well-prepared to enter the public sphere with a strong foundation in ethical leadership, ready to take on the challenges of modern governance (Advisory Excellence, 2024).

Fostering an ethical culture within educational institutions is essential for creating a positive and inclusive learning environment. Ethical leadership plays a crucial role in shaping this culture by modeling integrity, transparency, and fairness. Leaders who prioritize ethical behavior set a standard for the entire institution, promoting trust and respect among students, faculty, and staff (Harvard DCE, 2025). Establishing clear ethical policies is another key strategy. These policies should outline expected standards of conduct and provide guidelines for addressing ethical dilemmas, ensuring that all members of the institution understand and adhere to ethical principles.

Providing ongoing ethical training and education is vital for reinforcing the importance of ethics in daily activities. Workshops, seminars, and courses on topics such as ethical decision-making and cultural sensitivity help create a shared understanding of ethical standards. Open communication is also essential for fostering an ethical culture. Institutions should establish channels for reporting unethical behavior and addressing ethical concerns without fear of retaliation, promoting a culture of transparency and accountability (Clemens, 2025).

Recognizing and celebrating ethical role models within the institution can inspire others to act with integrity. Highlighting individuals who demonstrate exemplary ethical behavior reinforces the value placed on ethics and encourages others to follow suit. Finally, promoting inclusivity and equity is a fundamental component of an ethical culture. Ensuring that all individuals are treated with respect and have equal opportunities helps create a diverse and inclusive environment.

Transparency is a cornerstone of ethical leadership in policy development. By promoting open government practices, ethical leaders help to demystify the policy-making process, allowing citizens to have a clearer understanding of how decisions are made and who benefits from them. This openness not only improves the quality of policy outcomes by incorporating diverse viewpoints but also enhances public trust. Ethical leaders advocate for laws and regulations that support freedom of information, ensuring that government actions are accessible and observable by all stakeholders (Advisory Excellence, 2024).

Ethical school leaders harness AI not as a means to replace human interaction but as a tool to enhance and complement the work of educators. They recognize that successful integration of technology is centered around augmenting teacher-student relationships and supporting personalized academic growth. By prioritizing ongoing staff training, continuous ethical evaluation, and proactive community involvement, leaders can create environments where AI-driven innovations uplift educational standards while reinforcing the shared responsibility to nurture informed, resilient, and critically engaged future citizens. Accountability mechanisms are essential for maintaining high standards of ethical conduct in policy development. Effective ethical leaders establish robust mechanisms such as internal audits, compliance checks, and independent reviews to uphold high standards of conduct and deter unethical behavior. These mechanisms ensure that policies are implemented fairly and that any deviations from ethical standards are promptly addressed. By fostering a culture of accountability, ethical leaders help to build trust and ensure that policies serve the best interests of the public (Advisory Excellence, 2024).

CONCLUSION

Ethical leadership in education is not merely about sound policy making—it is a commitment to embedding integrity, transparency, and accountability into every decision that shapes the future of learning. As classrooms and educational institutions increasingly integrate AI, leaders must advance ethical frameworks that address both the promise and pitfalls of these technologies. On one hand, AI can transform learning environments by personalizing educational experiences, streamlining administrative processes, and expanding access to educational resources. On the other hand, these benefits come with risks: algorithmic biases, breaches in data privacy, and the potential exacerbation of existing inequalities are only a few of the challenges that demand vigilant ethical oversight.

The true impact of AI in education, therefore, transcends enhanced efficiency or improved learning outcomes; it redefines the very role of educators and reshapes pedagogical paradigms. Rather than replacing the human element, a well-integrated AI system can empower teachers to focus on creative, critical, and relational aspects of learning while ensuring that technology augments—not undermines—the educational mission. For AI to realize its full potential, ethical education demands not only clear policies and transparency in its implementation but also a commitment to continuous dialogue among educators, students, and the broader community. In doing so, school leaders create an environment where technological advancements support an inclusive, fair, and genuinely transformative learning experience—one that prepares future leaders to navigate an increasingly complex digital landscape with moral clarity and social responsibility (Dwivedi, et al; 2023).

REFERENCES

Bulger, M., McCormick, P., & Pitcan, M. (2017). The legacy of inBloom: Data, privacy, and the public interest in education. *International Journal of Communication*, *11*, 1579–1600.

Carstens, A., Mallon, B., Bataineh, M., & Al-Bataineh, A. (2021). Effects of technology on student learning. *International Journal of Education and Practice*, *9*(1), 80–92. https://files.eric.ed.gov/fulltext/EJ1290791.pdf

Center for Parent Information and Resources. (2021). "Parental Consent in Special Education". Retrieved on March 4, 2025, from https://www.parentcenterhub.org/consent/?form=MG0AV3

Chassignol, M., & Mikalef, P. (2021). Artificial Intelligence in Education: A Systematic Review and Future Research Directions. *Journal of Educational Technology & Society*, *24*(1), 18–32.

Clemens, J. (2025). How can ethical leadership influence school culture? Retrieved on March 4, 2025, from https://my.chartered.college/impact_article/how-can-ethical-leadership-influence-school-culture-a-reflection-on-my-leadership-journey-so-far/?form=MG0AV3.

Dwivedi, Y. K., ... Opinion Paper: "So what if ChatGPT wrote it?" Multidisciplinary perspectives on opportunities, challenges and implications of generative conversational AI for research, practice and policy, International Journal of Information Management, Volume 71, 2023, 102642,ISSN 0268-4012, https://doi.org/DOI: 10.1016/j.ijinfomgt.2023.10264

Education Advanced. (May 11, 2023). "Transparency in Education: What Schools Need to Know" Retrieved on March 4, 2025, from https://www.educationadvanced.com/blog/transparency-in-education-what-schools-need-to-know?form=MG0AV3

Evanick, J. (2023). *Data Privacy In EdTech: Ethical Dilemmas And Safeguards*. eLearning Industry. Retrieved from https://elearningindustry.com/ethical-dilemmas-in-student-data-privacy-navigating-edtech-safeguards

Excellence, A. (2024). The Role of Ethical Leadership in Shaping Public Policy. Retrieved on March 4, 2025, from https://www.advisoryexcellence.com/the-role-of-ethical-leadership-in-shaping-public-policy/?form=MG0AV3

Floridi, L., & Cowls, J. (2019). A unified framework of five principles for AI in society. *Harvard Data Science Review*, *1*(1). Advance online publication. DOI: 10.1162/99608f92.8cd550d1

Garcia, A. (2023). "Technology Might be Making Education Worse". Stanford Report. Retrieved on February 19, 2025, from https://news.stanford.edu/stories/2023/04/technology-might-be-making-education-worse

Grosso, D. P., Bowling, M. R., Chun, S. S., & Delaney, B. M. (2024). *The Development of AI and Protecting Student Data Privacy*. National Law Review. Retrieved on March 4, 2025, from https://natlawreview.com/article/development-ai-and-protecting-student-data-privacy

Harvard, D. C. E. (2025). What is Ethical Leadership and Why is it Important? Retrieved on March 4, 2025 https://professional.dce.harvard.edu/blog/what-is-ethical-leadership-and-why-is-it-important/?form=MG0AV3

Holmes, W., Bialik, M., & Fadel, C. (2019). *Artificial Intelligence in Education*. The MIT Press.

Individuals with Disabilities Act. "Parental Consent". §300.300 (2006). Retrieved on March 4, 2025, from https://sites.ed.gov/idea/regs/b/d/300.300?form=MG0AV3

Kshetri, N. (2021). Ransomware attacks on the US education sector: A perfect storm. *IEEE Security and Privacy*, *19*(3), 72–76. DOI: 10.1109/MSEC.2021.3071906

Langreo, L. (October 2024). "More Than Half of Teachers Still Have No Training on AI". Education Week. Retrieved on February 19, 2025, from https://www.govtech.com/education/k-12/more-than-half-of-teachers-still-have-no-training-on-ai

Lawton, A., & Páez, I. (2015). Developing a Framework for Ethical Leadership. *Journal of Business Ethics*, *130*(3), 639–649. DOI: 10.1007/s10551-014-2244-2

Lee, A. (2025). Informed Consent in the special education process. Understood.org. Retrieved on March 4, 2025, from https://www.understood.org/en/articles/informed-consent-what-it-is-and-how-it-works?form=MG0AV3

Leonard, D. (November 2024). Overcoming Potential Risks of Student Tech Use". Edutopia. Retrieved on February 19, 2025, from https://www.edutopia.org/article/risks-technology-education-how-overcome-them

Luckin, R., Holmes, W., Griffiths, M., & Forcier, L. B. (2016). *Artificial Intelligence and Future of Teaching and Learning*. Center for Integrative Research in Computing and Learning Sciences.

Luna, J. L. (2024). *AI in Education: Benefits, Challenges, and Ethical Considerations*. DataCamp. Retrieved on June 9, 2025, from https://www.datacamp.com/blog/ai-in-education

Naeem, R., & Syed, J. (2024). An Integrative Framework of Ethical Leadership. *Systemic Practice and Action Research, 37*(6), 1161–1174. DOI: 10.1007/s11213-024-09694-y

National Education Association. (2020). Code of ethics for educators. Retrieved on March 4, 2025, from https://ethics.miamidade.gov/library/2015-publications/ethics_neighbors_4-1-15.pdf?form=MG0AV3

Nexford University. (2024). How Will Artificial Intelligence Affect Jobs 2024-2030. Retrieved on March 3, 2025, from https://www.nexford.edu/insights/how-will-ai-affect-jobs?form=MG0AV3

Ng, A. Y. (2019). Machine Learning for Education. AI and Education: The Importance of Teacher and Student Engagement in AI-powered Learning Environments (pp. 77-92).

Reidenberg, J. R., Russell, N. C., Kovnot, J., Norton, T. B., Cloutier, R., & Alvarado, D. (2018). *Privacy and cloud computing in public schools.* Center on Law and Information Policy, Fordham University School of Law.

Seldon, A., & Abidoye, A. (2018). *The Fourth Education Revolution: Will Artificial Intelligence Liberate or Infantilize Learning?* UCL Institute of Education Press.

Slimi, Z. (2023). *The Impact of Artificial Intelligence on Higher Education: An Empirical Study*. Retrieved from ERIC.

Solove, D. J. (2020). *The privacy paradox: The impact of privacy concerns and privacy behavior.* Harvard University Press., DOI: 10.19044/ejes.v10no1a17

Stanford Accelerator for Learning. (2025). The future is already here: AI and education in 2025. Retrieved on March 4, 2025, from https://acceleratelearning.stanford.edu/story/the-future-is-already-here-ai-and-education-in-2025/?form=MG0AV3

Stelmach, A. (2025). The Development Of Artificial Intelligence And Its Ethical Implications. Retrieved on March 4, 2025, from https://www.forbes.com/councils/forbestechcouncil/2025/02/25/the-development-of-artificial-intelligence-and-its-ethical-implications/?form=MG0AV3

TeachThough. (2014). A Useful Framework For Transparency In Education. TeachThough.com. Retrieved on March 4, 2025, from https://www.teachthought.com/education/transparency-in-education/?form=MG0AV3

Timbang, C., & Velasco, M. C. (2024). Digital Technology: Impact on Students' Learning Process, Social Interaction and Mental Well-Being. International Multidisciplinary Journal of Research for Innovation, Sustainability, and Excellence, 1(7), 247-258. https://risejournals.org/index.php/imjrise/article/view/585

U.S. Department of Education. (2023). *Artificial Intelligence and the Future of Teaching and Learning: Insights and Recommendations*. Office of Educational Technology.

U.S. Department of Education. (n.d.). *Data Security: K-12 and Higher Education | Protecting Student Privacy*. Retrieved on March 4, 2025, from https://studentprivacy.ed.gov/data-security-k-12-and-higher-education

West, D. M. (2019). *Technology and privacy: The new landscape*. Brookings Institution Press.

West, S. M. (2019). Data protection in education: Ethical considerations and policy recommendations. *International Review of Education, 65*(4), 547–562.

Whetstone, J. T. (2005). The Role of Ethics in Leadership: A Practical Model for Mindful Ethical Leadership. *Journal of Business Ethics, 60*(1), 37–47.

Wichita State University. (2025). The Impact of AI on Jobs and Education. Retrieved on March 3, 2025, https://www.wichita.edu/services/mrc/OIR/AI/jobimpacts.php?form=MG0AV3

Zaman, B. (2023). Transforming Education Through AI, Benefits, Risks, and Ethical Considerations. *TechRxiv*. DOI: DOI: 10.36227/techrxiv.24231583.v1

Zawacki-Richter, O., Marín, V. I., Bond, M., & Gouverneur, F. (2019). Systematic review of research on artificial intelligence applications in higher education–where are the educators? *International Journal of Educational Technology in Higher Education, 16*(1), 39. DOI: 10.1186/s41239-019-0171-0

Chapter 7
Cognitivism, Constructivism, and the Classroom:
The Impact of AI on Teaching and Learning

Joshua Tabor
https://orcid.org/0000-0002-2069-3700
Texas Woman's University, USA

ABSTRACT

This chapter delves into the complex relationship between artificial intelligence (AI) and its influence on contemporary classrooms, examining this through the dual lenses of cognitivism and constructivism. The integration of AI technologies is explored as a transformative force that is reshaping pedagogical approaches, streamlining administrative tasks, and offering personalized learning experiences. While acknowledging the concerns about AI potentially replacing teachers, the chapter emphasizes AI's role as a tool to augment teaching practices, enhance learning outcomes, and address equity and accessibility challenges. By analyzing case studies and theoretical frameworks, the chapter aims to provide a balanced perspective on AI's implications, highlighting both its potential benefits and the importance of thoughtful implementation to foster effective, equitable, and ethical learning environments.

DOI: 10.4018/979-8-3373-6007-2.ch007

INTRODUCTION

When discussing technology and its impact on society in the last 20 years, a few dates might stick out: October 23, 2001, the release of the first iPod, January 29, 2007, the release of the first iPhone, or January 3, 2015, the first demonstration of genome editing using CRISPR. Each of these and thousands of others have altered the way we live, work, and are educated in a short period of time. However, a new date will be added to the list that might have a more significant impact than almost any before it: November 30, 2022, the day ChatGPT was released to the public.

The potential impact of AI on society and education is profound and cannot be overstated. Artificial intelligence models, particularly those focused on generative AI, adaptive tutoring systems, and analytical AI, will create newer, more efficient methods of teacher planning, completing administrative tasks, grading, and truly allow teachers to do what they do best: teach. However, as with any new technology, there are positives and negatives to using AI. AI can still 'hallucinate', giving incorrect or misleading results, and many are still not fully updated because they are not connected to the Internet. Even with these limitations, AI is being adopted at a rapid rate across various mediums across the globe.

As educators, the importance of artificial intelligence must be carefully considered. Educators do not have the luxury of making significant mistakes due to the ripple effect those mistakes can have on their students. Additionally, education is traditionally slower to adapt to newer technologies due to the constant need for state funding for other items such as building maintenance, teacher salaries, and student services.

Recent surveys show varying adoption rates by K-12 teachers. For the 22-23 school year, Houghton Mifflin Harcourt found 10% of teachers were using AI to support their instructional planning or teaching (Lucariello, 2023), a Rand survey reported 18% of K-12 teachers used AI to support their work (Diliberti et al., 2024), and a recent Rand survey examining the change in adoption rates from the 22-23 school year to the 23-24 school year showed only 25% of K-12 teachers are using AI tools (Kaufman et al., 2025). Other research suggests teacher adoption is up to 67% with student adoption right behind at 66%. There is also a significant difference between student adoption levels. 82% of college students have used AI, compared to only 58% of high school students (Staff, 2024). Due to the rapid adoption of AI, it is difficult to accurately determine adoption rates in the educational system.

No matter the rate of adoption, education is changing due to the introduction of artificial intelligence models. There are teachers adopting quickly and praising the benefits of AI, while others are fearful they will be replaced by a 'smart' computer. The reality is more in the middle, but no matter what the future of educational technology looks like, technology and artificial intelligence will never be able to replace a living, breathing teacher. However, teachers themselves must adapt and that adaptation requires them to review traditional, effective teaching methods through the lens of improvement through the use of new AI models.The integration of artificial intelligence (AI) models into the educational landscape has ushered in a transformative era, redefining the roles of both students and educators. The swift adoption of AI technologies has catalyzed a shift in pedagogical approaches, revolutionizing lesson planning, streamlining administrative tasks, and automating grading processes. This allows educators to dedicate more time and energy to their core responsibility: facilitating meaningful learning experiences. While concerns persist regarding the potential for AI to supplant teachers, the prevailing reality is that AI functions as a powerful tool that augments, rather than replaces, the indispensable human element in education.

Rationale for Examining AI through Cognitivism and Constructivism

Given the fluctuating and often contradictory reports on AI adoption rates across different sectors and the rapid, ever-evolving nature of AI technologies, it is of paramount importance to develop a robust theoretical framework. This framework should not only provide a lens to understand the multiple implications of AI for teaching and learning but also serve as a tool to critically evaluate the pedagogical affordances and potential drawbacks of integrating AI into educational contexts. Such a framework would need to consider various factors, including but not limited to: the diverse ways in which AI can be used in educational settings (e.g., intelligent tutoring systems, automated essay scoring, personalized learning platforms); the potential impact of AI on student learning outcomes, teacher roles, and educational equity; and the ethical considerations surrounding the use of AI in education, such as data privacy and algorithmic bias.Given the dynamic landscape of AI adoption and the constant evolution of AI technologies, it is of paramount importance to establish a robust theoretical framework. This framework should not only provide a lens through which we can analyze the multifaceted impacts of AI on the educational landscape but also serve as a mechanism for critically evaluating the pedagogical benefits and potential hazards of integrating AI into educational contexts.

Such a framework would need to encompass a broad spectrum of considerations. This includes the diverse applications of AI in education, such as intelligent tutoring systems that can adapt to individual student needs, automated essay scoring systems that can provide rapid feedback, and personalized learning platforms that can tailor educational content to individual learners. It also encompasses the potential impact of AI on student learning outcomes, which could be enhanced through personalized learning and immediate feedback, but could also be negatively affected by overreliance on AI systems or algorithmic bias.

Additionally, the framework must consider the evolving roles of teachers in an AI-integrated educational environment. While AI could automate routine tasks and allow teachers to focus on higher-order instructional goals, it could also necessitate new skills and competencies for teachers, such as the ability to manage and interpret data from AI systems and to address ethical considerations related to AI use.

Furthermore, the framework must address issues of educational equity. While AI has the potential to personalize learning and provide targeted support to all students, it also risks exacerbating existing inequities if access to AI technologies is unequal or if algorithms are biased against certain groups of students.

Ethical considerations, such as data privacy and algorithmic bias, are also central to the framework. The collection and use of student data by AI systems raise concerns about privacy and the potential for misuse of data. Algorithmic bias, which can result from biased training data or flawed algorithms, can perpetuate stereotypes and discriminate against certain groups of students.

In essence, a comprehensive theoretical framework for AI in education must be multidimensional, addressing the pedagogical, social, ethical, and equity implications of AI integration. It must provide a nuanced understanding of the complex interplay between AI and education and guide the development and implementation of AI-based educational tools and interventions that are effective, equitable, and ethically sound.

Research Questions and Objectives

The purpose of this chapter is to delve into how AI, when viewed through the lens of cognitivism and constructivism, will influence contemporary classrooms and their students. The objective is not to persuade the reader either for or against the integration of AI within educational settings, but to illuminate the potential consequences of its appropriate application. Through the examination and analysis of case studies, readers will be able to formulate their own conclusions and simultaneously gain insights into the author's perspectives.

Theoretical Foundations

Cognitivism and Its Application in the Classroom

Understanding the historical context of learning theories provides a foundation to fully understand the impact of AI in the classroom. Behaviorism was the leading learning theory until the 1950s and 1960s, when it was strongly criticized by Noam

Chomsky in 1959, and the "cognitive revolution" began, establishing cognitivism as the dominant theory (Gardner, 1985; Commission et. al., 2018).

Cognitivism can be defined as "a learning theory that emphasizes learning as an active mental process involving the acquisition and organization of knowledge, emphasizing the role of cognitive processes such as memory, problem-solving and information processing" (Ouyang & Jiao, 2021). This theory is supported by three key theories: cognitive load theory, schema theory, and the information processing model.

Information processing model

Atkinson and Shiffrin developed the information processing model in their 1968 work, Human memory: A proposed system and its control processes. Interestingly this model compares human cognition to computer processing which was not widely understood in the late 60s. However, with the growth of computers through the decades, most people would be able to understand the comparison today. As outlined in figure 1, the model divides cognitive processes into four distinct stages: input (perception), attention (processing), encoding (memory), retrieval (output), with three primary 'stores' of memory: sensory, short-term, and long-term.

Figure 1. Multi-store memory model. (Atkinson and Shiffrin, 1968)

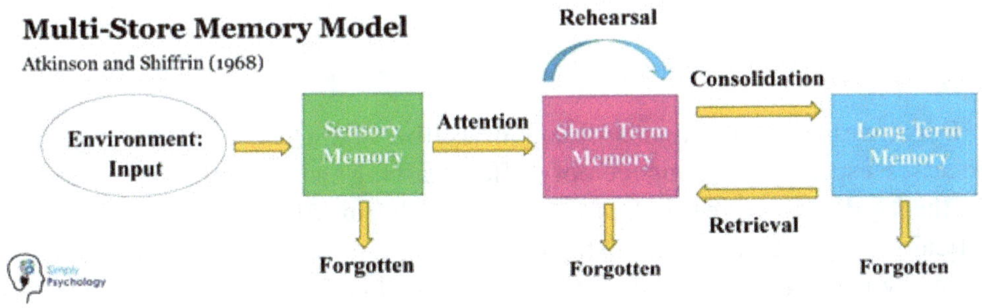

This model aligns with the principles of cognitivism by concentrating on the mechanisms of how information is acquired, processed, and stored within the human brain. It offers a structured approach to comprehending cognitive processes, including attention, perception, and memory, and translates these concepts into technical terms applicable to computers and, by extension, artificial intelligence.

Cognitive Load Theory

Cognitive load theory (Figure 2), developed by John Sweller in the late 1980s, centers on the idea that human memory has limitations (Sweller, 2011). The theory has been reexamined in recent years and applied to the understanding of effective lesson design (Main, 2022).

Figure 2. Cognitive load theory (Main, 2022)

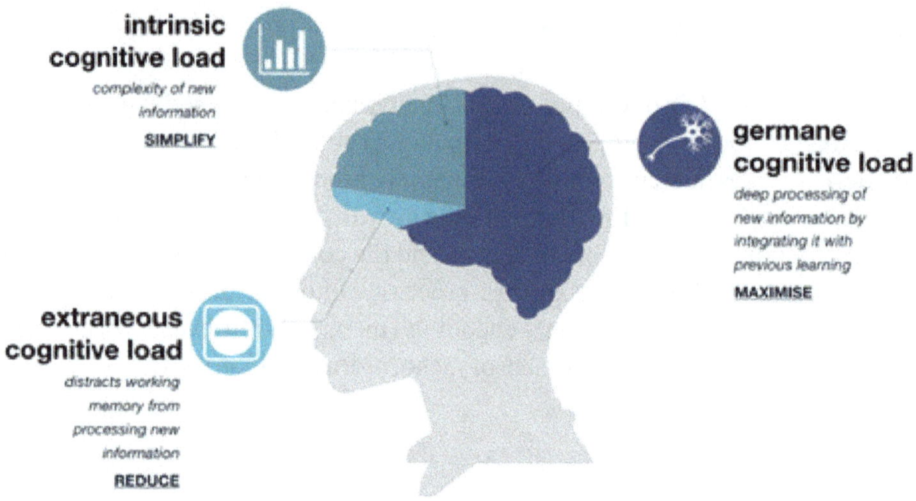

Cognitive load theory aligns with cognitivism because it focuses on how cognitive processes, especially working memory, affect learning and information processing. The theory identifies three kinds of cognitive load. Intrinsic load refers to the inherent difficulty of the subject matter. Extraneous load is an unnecessary cognitive burden caused by poor instructional design. Germane load is the mental effort needed to build lasting knowledge structures. Because cognitive load theory also concentrates on optimizing learning based on the limitations of working memory, it supports the concept of using artificial intelligence to assist with learning design.

Schema Theory

Schema theory, initially developed by Frederic Bartlett in 1932 and later expanded by Jean Piaget, is a cornerstone of cognitivism. This theory posits that individuals utilize mental frameworks, referred to as "schemas," to organize and interpret information. These schemas are not static but are constantly being adapted to accommodate new information (assimilation) or modified to fit new experiences (accommodation).

Schema theory aligns with cognitivism by illustrating how learners actively construct and modify their understanding of the world. This theory underscores the importance of prior knowledge in the learning process and how new information is incorporated into existing cognitive structures.

AI's Impact on Cognitivism in the Classroom

As shown previously, cognitivism allows students to synthesize their learning and connect it to existing knowledge. These new pathways are exciting, but must be tempered and supported by the teacher. The teacher should help students direct these pathways so they connect to previous learning, forming accurate connections. However, current class sizes sometimes prohibit teachers from fulfilling this incredibly important role. Teachers constantly find themselves pulled in a variety of directions needing to complete administrative tasks or meeting the needs of students who require more attention than others. This is where artificial intelligence has the potential to support teachers.

Given the prevalence of computers in today's classrooms, integrating AI support would not be a difficult prospect for most schools. For decades, teachers have sought to adapt their teaching methods to meet the needs of students. That has become more difficult as schools and the needs of students have grown. Add in standardized testing expectations and the teacher will find it difficult to adapt lessons due to an increasing lack of time. AI models are constantly adapting and learning from analyzing data, which can easily be gained as computers are more prevalent in classrooms from kindergarten through post-secondary education institutions.

AI-driven adaptive learning systems and intelligent tutoring systems have the capability to revolutionize education by analyzing student input and generating personalized learning experiences that cater to the unique needs of each student. These systems can quickly identify areas where students are struggling and dynamically adjust the material to address and close learning gaps.

Furthermore, they can offer a wide array of review options, including traditional methods like flashcards and more interactive and engaging options like educational games and quizzes. By continuously monitoring student performance and engagement, the systems can also learn which methods are most effective for individual students, further tailoring the learning experience and optimizing learning outcomes.

These AI systems offer a level of accessibility and personalization that teachers may find challenging to provide due to various constraints. Students have diverse needs, learning styles, and backgrounds, and it can be difficult for teachers to design lessons that cater to all of them, especially with increasing class sizes, decreasing funding, and limited time and resources. AI can help bridge this gap by creating inclusive learning environments that support students where they are, rather than where they are expected to be, based on standardized curricula or grade-level expectations.

For example, built-in accessibility features such as speech recognition, text-to-speech, and translation software can remove barriers to access and allow students to engage with the material in their own language or preferred format. Additionally, AI can provide real-time feedback and support, offer adaptive scaffolding and hints, and recommend additional resources or activities based on individual student needs and progress.

Moreover, AI can analyze vast amounts of educational data and research to identify best practices and effective teaching strategies, which can inform and enhance instructional design and delivery. By automating routine tasks and providing data-driven insights, AI can also free up teachers' time and allow them to focus on higher-order tasks such as mentoring, coaching, and fostering creativity and critical thinking skills.

Overall, AI has the potential to transform education by providing personalized, accessible, and engaging learning experiences that empower all students to reach their full potential. While AI is not intended to replace teachers, it can augment their capabilities and support them in creating more equitable and effective learning environments.

Case Studies

Recent research from Harvard in 2023 has shown the effectiveness of AI tutoring. Students who were provided an AI tutor achieved more than twice the learning gains compared to those in the active learning classroom environment (Figure 3). The improvement was statistically significant ($z = -5.6$, $p < 10-8$) highlighting the effectiveness of the method (Hardman, 2024). Additionally, the AI tutoring group was shown to have a higher level of engagement and motivation, with 70% completing their work in under 60 minutes (compared to the 60-minute class period). The median AI session was 49 minutes. The AI tutoring group also benefited from personalized feedback and self-paced learning, which was shown to be particularly helpful for students with varying levels of background knowledge. The study clearly demonstrated that AI tutoring was more time-efficient, with students learning more in less time than their classroom peers (Kestin et al., 2024; Hardman, 2024).

Figure 3. Effectiveness of AI tutoring (Kestin et al., 2024)

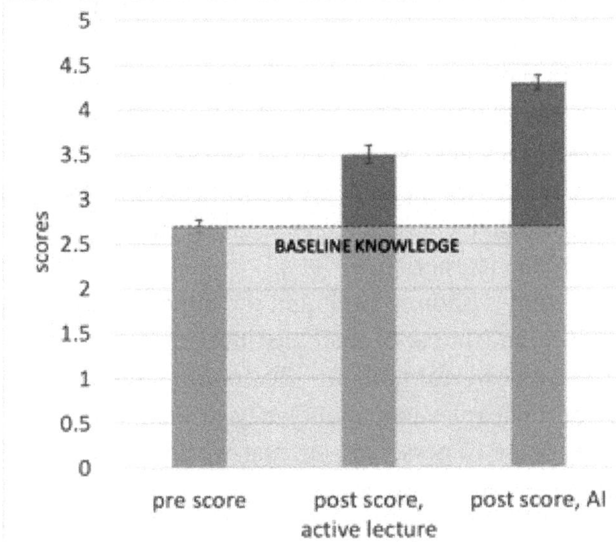

Research conducted by UniDistance Suisse in partnership with MAGMA learning explored the use of AI tutors in educational settings. A group of 51 psychology students enrolled in a neuroscience course were given access to an AI tutor that generated microlearning questions based on course materials. The results showed that students who actively engaged with the AI tutor saw a significant improvement in their grades, averaging 15% higher than students in a parallel course without the AI tutor. Additionally, there was a strong correlation ($r = 0.81$, $p < 0.001$) between the AI's prediction of students' grasp of concepts and their actual exam grades (Baillifard et al., 2023). While public schools in the United States have not yet adopted AI tutoring, the positive learning outcomes and continued advancements in AI suggest that some level of integration is likely in the near future.

AI and Information Processing

Artificial intelligence (AI) holds immense potential to revolutionize education by tailoring instructional strategies to individual student needs, thereby optimizing learning and retention while reducing extraneous cognitive load. This adaptive capability of AI was explored by Abebe (2024) within the context of personalized, scenario-based learning. The study revealed that AI models could effectively integrate analogies into the learning process to bolster knowledge retention.

While previous research by Schwartz, Tsang, & Blair (2016) supports the efficacy of analogies in enhancing retention, Abebe's study uncovered a potential pitfall in the AI's implementation. The AI model, instead of crafting personalized, real-world scenarios that resonated with individual student interests, leaned heavily on analogies. This overreliance on analogies, while intended to aid understanding, could inadvertently introduce confusion, especially if the analogies themselves are not readily grasped by the learner.

Furthermore, the study's findings highlight the importance of striking a balance between personalization and the use of analogies in AI-driven learning environments. While analogies can be powerful tools for illustrating complex concepts, their effectiveness hinges on their relevance and clarity to the learner. An overemphasis on analogies at the expense of personalized, real-world scenarios could potentially undermine the benefits of AI in education.

Therefore, future research should delve deeper into refining AI models to ensure they can generate personalized, contextually relevant scenarios that cater to individual student interests while judiciously incorporating analogies to support knowledge retention without introducing confusion. This could involve developing more sophisticated algorithms that can assess student understanding and preferences, enabling the AI to dynamically adjust its instructional approach to optimize learning outcomes.

Managing Cognitive Load

Both students and teachers can struggle with managing cognitive load. AI can support teachers' cognitive loads by handling administrative tasks, creating lesson plans, and assisting with grading, thereby freeing up teachers for other tasks. AI can also benefit students by presenting information in an optimal manner, such as through spaced repetition, which schedules reviews of material at increasing intervals to enhance long-term memory and reduce cognitive effort. Furthermore, AI can adapt the difficulty and presentation of materials to maintain an optimal intrinsic cognitive load, resulting in more efficient and less overwhelming learning experiences.

The research conducted by Zhu, Chau, and Mokmin (2024) on in-service personnel demonstrated that utilizing an adaptive microlearning system (AMS) notably decreased excessive cognitive load resulting from unsuitable instructional design. Furthermore, it substantially enhanced learning adaptability. This AMS, similar to other AI tutoring and adaptive learning systems, provided a customized learning experience for each student, incorporating personalized content, real-time feedback, and an adaptive learning pathway. This aligns with cognitive load theory, which proposes that minimizing unnecessary cognitive load leads to improved learning outcomes (Cierniak, Scheiter, & Gerjets, 2009). The positive effect of AI assistance on student learning is illustrated in Figure 4.

Figure 4. Graph adapted from Patel & Wright (2023), Johnson (2024), and Lee & Chen (2021), illustrating the impact of AI on different types of cognitive load.

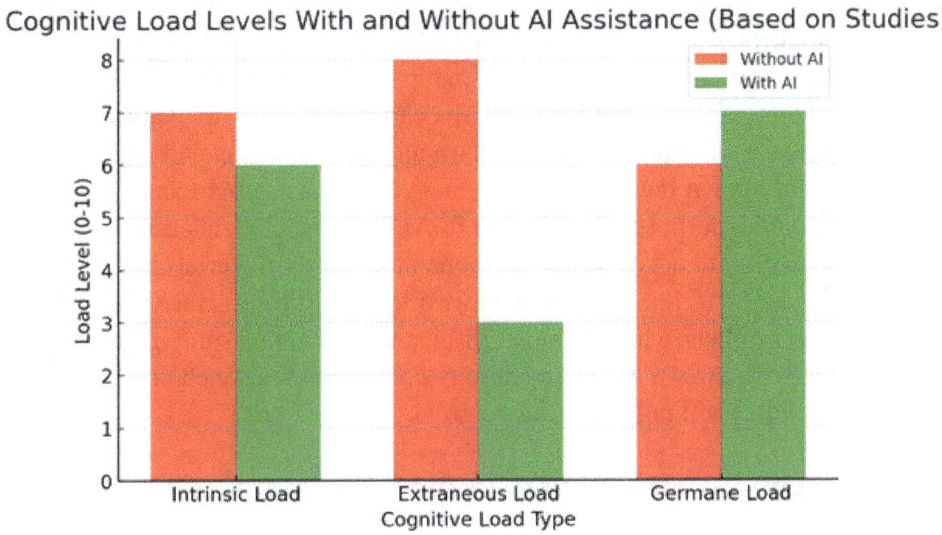

Feedback and Metacognition

AI-driven tools can provide students with immediate, non-judgemental feedback, promoting self-regulation and allowing them to take ownership of their learning. This was exemplified by Gkintoni et al. (2025), who highlighted the use of AI-powered simulations in STEM courses. These simulations, such as PhET, offered students the opportunity to experiment and visualize scientific concepts, leading to greater engagement and comprehension. The instant feedback and support that AI can provide helps to clarify misunderstandings and ensures that students stay focused and on task.

AI tutoring systems represent a significant advancement in educational technology, offering a range of benefits that traditional teaching methods often cannot match. One of the most notable advantages is the ability to adapt to individual student needs in real-time. As students interact with the AI tutor, the system continuously analyzes their performance and modifies its approach accordingly. This level of personalization ensures that students are always challenged at an appropriate level, maximizing their learning potential.

Furthermore, the data generated from student-AI interactions provides teachers with valuable insights into individual student capabilities. This information allows teachers to tailor their in-class instruction to meet the specific needs of each student, an approach that would be difficult to achieve without the assistance of AI.

AI tutoring also promotes student autonomy and self-directed learning. Students can personalize their learning plans to fit their schedules and preferred learning styles. This flexibility allows students to take ownership of their education and learn at their own pace. Additionally, AI tutoring systems can incorporate innovative learning methods, such as gamification, to make learning more engaging and enjoyable.

Research has shown that students are increasingly using AI technology for a variety of academic purposes. In addition to AI tutoring, students utilize AI tools for research, information synthesis, and generating study materials.Studies show students who use AI technology for schoolwork using it to do research (46%), to summarize and synthesize information (38%), and to generate study guides or materials (31%) (Staff, 2024). As AI technology continues to advance, it is likely that its role in education will only continue to grow.

AI's Impact on Constructivism in the Classroom

Constructivism and AI can be powerful partners in education, as AI can facilitate student knowledge construction in various ways. Traditionally, constructivist learning involved hands-on activities, like science labs and building projects. While valuable, these methods can fall short in conveying abstract or large-scale concepts, like planetary distances. AI can bridge this gap by providing simulations and models that enhance understanding. Furthermore, AI chatbots can act as thought partners, supporting student research and idea generation.

AI can enhance the constructivist classroom by offering data-driven insights to teachers, enabling them to create tailored learning experiences and group students effectively. AI-powered tools can also assist teachers in designing engaging and relevant lessons, fostering student ownership of learning. Additionally, AI can help address educational challenges, such as declining math scores, by personalizing learning and supporting teachers. AI's ability to provide rapid feedback and facilitate collaboration further enhances the constructivist approach.

Through features like gamification and AI-driven simulations, students can actively engage in learning, while teachers can focus on facilitating meaningful experiences. AI can also support the experiential learning cycle, enhancing each stage through tools for reflection, analysis, and experimentation. These diverse applications highlight the potential of AI to transform the constructivist classroom and empower students to become active learners.

AI's Impact on Constructivism in the Classroom

The synergy between constructivism and AI has the potential to revolutionize education. AI can facilitate the core tenets of constructivist learning, where students actively construct their knowledge through experience and reflection. Traditionally, constructivist classrooms relied heavily on hands-on activities and group projects. While these methods remain valuable, AI expands the possibilities for knowledge construction. Complex and abstract concepts that were once difficult to convey through traditional methods can now be explored through AI-powered simulations and models. For instance, students can manipulate 3D models of molecules or simulate historical events to gain a deeper understanding.

AI-powered chatbots and virtual assistants can serve as personalized learning companions, guiding students through research, brainstorming, and problem-solving. These intelligent tools can provide instant feedback, answer questions, and challenge students to think critically. By interacting with AI, students can develop research skills, evaluate information, and articulate their ideas more effectively.

Furthermore, AI can empower teachers by providing data-driven insights into student learning. AI-powered analytics can track student progress, identify areas of strength and weakness, and suggest personalized learning pathways. This enables teachers to tailor instruction to individual needs, ensuring that all students are challenged and supported. AI can also automate routine tasks, such as grading and data entry, freeing up teachers to focus on higher-order skills like critical thinking and creativity.

AI-powered tools can also assist teachers in designing engaging and relevant learning experiences. By analyzing student data and preferences, AI can recommend resources, activities, and assessments that align with individual learning styles and interests. This fosters a sense of ownership and autonomy, as students are more likely to engage with material that they find personally meaningful.

AI can also play a crucial role in addressing educational challenges, such as the achievement gap and declining test scores. By providing personalized support and targeted interventions, AI can help struggling students catch up and reach their full potential. AI can also facilitate collaboration and peer learning, allowing students to learn from each other and build a sense of community.

Through features like gamification, adaptive learning, and intelligent tutoring, AI can make learning more interactive and engaging. AI-driven simulations and virtual reality experiences can transport students to different worlds and time periods, allowing them to experience history, science, and literature in a whole new way.

AI can also support the experiential learning cycle, which consists of concrete experience, reflective observation, abstract conceptualization, and active experimentation. AI can enhance each stage of the cycle by providing tools for reflection, analysis, and experimentation. For example, AI can analyze student reflections and provide feedback, suggest connections to prior knowledge, and generate hypotheses for further exploration.

The integration of AI into the constructivist classroom has the potential to transform education and empower students to become lifelong learners. By leveraging the power of AI, educators can create a more personalized, engaging, and effective learning environment where all students can thrive. As AI continues to evolve, it is crucial to explore its potential in education and ensure that it is used ethically and responsibly to benefit all learners.

The use of artificial intelligence (AI) in education has the potential to create more effective lessons and improve student learning. This is particularly important in light of recent data indicating a decline in U.S. student performance in math and science. As of 2023, the U.S. ranked 12th in both 4th and 8th grade science scores, showing a decrease since 1995 (Merod, 2024; Mahnken, 2024). While AI is not a substitute for qualified teachers, it can be a valuable tool to enhance education and address this concerning trend. The COVID-19 pandemic has further exacerbated these issues, making innovative solutions like AI even more critical (News, n.d.).

AI offers numerous advantages in education, particularly in providing students with immediate feedback and personalized support, which can be invaluable for their learning and development. However, a constructivist approach to education, which emphasizes collaborative problem-solving and active learning, offers a different perspective. This approach recognizes the importance of social interaction and the construction of knowledge through shared experiences. By encouraging students to work together to identify and address relevant problems, teachers can create a more engaging and meaningful learning environment.

The role of the teacher in a constructivist classroom is not to simply impart knowledge, but to act as a facilitator and guide, helping students to develop their critical thinking and problem-solving skills. This requires teachers to be flexible and adaptable, able to quickly adjust their lessons and activities to meet the needs of their students. Furthermore, teachers need to be skilled in fostering a collaborative and supportive learning environment, where students feel comfortable sharing their ideas and taking risks.

Technology can play a crucial role in supporting a constructivist approach to education. Online platforms and tools can facilitate collaboration and communication among students, allowing them to work together on projects and assignments regardless of their location. Additionally, technology can provide access to a wealth of resources and information, enabling students to explore topics in depth and develop their own understanding.

The combination of AI-powered personalized support and a constructivist approach that leverages technology for collaboration and higher-order thinking skills can create a truly transformative learning experience for students. This approach moves away from traditional, passive teaching methods and empowers students to become active and engaged learners, capable of tackling complex problems and contributing to society.

Chatbots in education are not a novel concept. Organizations such as Khan Academy have been utilizing them for some time, and although research is ongoing, their success is evident in their continued use (Singer, 2023). As chatbot accessibility increases and educators become proficient in their creation, chatbots will play a crucial role in supporting both individual and group learning.

Group work is often disrupted by the need to find answers to questions and ideas. This is a typical part of project-based learning, but it doesn't have to be. AI assistants can now provide quick answers, allowing students to spend less time on research that hinders brainstorming and more time on finding solutions.

Gibson et al. (2023) introduce a comprehensive framework for enhancing learning processes by integrating existing learning models with the capabilities of artificial intelligence. This three-tiered model operates at the micro, meso, and macro levels, each targeting distinct aspects of the learning experience.

At the **micro level**, the focus is on individual learning. By leveraging AI, the model aims to stimulate curiosity and promote the adaptation of mental models. This is achieved through a synthesis of established learning theories, suggesting that AI can play a crucial role in personalizing learning experiences and fostering deeper understanding.

The **meso level** shifts the attention to social learning and community inquiry. Here, AI is employed to facilitate collaboration and knowledge sharing among learners. This suggests that AI can be utilized to create interactive and engaging learning environments that encourage peer-to-peer learning and the co-construction of knowledge.

Finally, the **macro level** draws upon cultural-historical activity theory. This level emphasizes the role of tools, rules, and community roles in shaping learning. By incorporating AI at this level, the model seeks to support students' understanding of cultural shifts and the evolving nature of knowledge. This implies that AI can be harnessed to provide students with the tools and resources they need to navigate complex and dynamic cultural landscapes.

While the proposed model holds significant promise, the authors acknowledge the need for further empirical validation. Nonetheless, their work represents a significant step forward in understanding the potential of AI to support student knowledge construction. It suggests that AI can be leveraged to create more effective and personalized learning experiences that cater to the diverse needs of learners. Moreover, it highlights the potential of AI to foster collaboration, social learning, and cultural awareness, thereby preparing students for the challenges and opportunities of the 21st century.

When given proper guidance and a welcoming classroom environment, AI tools can encourage students to explore their interests more freely, ask more questions, and gain a deeper understanding of the subject matter. Abebe (2024) also found that AI chatbots can encourage students to ask clarifying questions and continue exploring their learning. In addition to fostering social and educational adaptation, many AI models can inspire students to explore new ideas (Pathan & Kanth, 2023). The positive impact of AI tools on student learning is further supported by Monterde et al. (2024), who examined teacher's perspectives on using AI chatbots to improve students' problem-solving skills in mathematics. The chatbot increased student confidence by validating their answers, according to one teacher. This increased confidence will likely encourage students to further their learning.

The following table (Table 1) contrasts traditional and AI-enhanced inquiry-based learning, highlighting how AI can augment each step of the student's learning journey:

Table 1. Contrasting traditional and AI-enhanced learning

Inquiry Stage	Traditional Approach	AI-Enhanced Approach
Question Formulation	Students formulate questions based on personal curiosity and prior knowledge.	AI tools suggest topics and offer background information, promoting deeper inquiry and assisting students in refining their questions.
Investigation	Students gather information from various sources.	AI-powered search and databases help students find and summarize relevant and credible sources quickly.
Data Analysis	Students analyze collected data to identify patterns and draw conclusions.	AI tools process large datasets, perform complex analyses, and visualize data, allowing students to concentrate on interpretation and critical thinking.
Presentation of Findings	Students present conclusions via reports or presentations.	AI assists in creating multimedia presentations and offers feedback on communication and clarity.
Reflection	Students reflect on their learning and outcomes.	AI provides personalized feedback, highlights areas for improvement, and suggests additional learning opportunities.
Iteration	Students refine their questions and approaches based on personal reflection.	AI tracks student progress, recommends adjustments, and supports continuous improvement.

Artificial Intelligence (AI) is transforming education by crafting innovative learning environments and experiences. Krishna, Prasad, and S emphasize the importance of maintaining students within the Zone of Proximal Development (ZPD), as proposed by Vygotsky (1978). AI can facilitate this by not only assessing student progress but also by adapting environments to keep students engaged and challenged. Additionally, AI can assist educators in designing and improving virtual labs, offering real-time feedback to students and enabling teachers to provide individualized support.

AI models can also generate new real-world simulations. These simulations can be designed by the teacher to highlight current world issues. Alternatively, the teacher can place a real world issue in a fantasy world, allowing students to find new and unique solutions to problems. To take learning even further, teachers can allow students to create their own worlds around problems to encourage students to take more ownership of their learning. This supports social learning theory, as the AI fosters a creative environment where collaboration and problem-solving are encouraged (Bandura, 1977).

Gamified lessons, incorporating game elements and design principles into educational activities, have a proven track record of enhancing student engagement and motivation (Chapman & Rich, 2018; Legaki et al., 2020). Traditionally, the creation and implementation of these gamified experiences were largely dependent on the teacher's ability and willingness to design engaging game mechanics and narratives. This often posed a significant challenge, as not all educators possessed the necessary skills or time to develop comprehensive gamified lessons.

However, the rapid advancement of artificial intelligence (AI) has the potential to revolutionize this landscape. AI can automate many of the time-consuming aspects of game design, such as generating quizzes, providing personalized feedback, and adapting game difficulty based on individual student performance. This empowers teachers to focus on the core pedagogical objectives of gamification, such as promoting active learning, fostering collaboration, and cultivating problem-solving skills.

Furthermore, the integration of digital technologies and online platforms into gamified learning experiences can create a more inclusive and equitable learning environment. Shy or introverted students, who may be hesitant to participate in traditional classroom discussions, may feel more comfortable expressing themselves and interacting with their peers in a digital context (Zukowski, n.d.). This can lead to increased participation and a greater sense of belonging for all students.

As educational institutions increasingly shift their focus from rote memorization and standardized testing towards experiential and student-centered learning, it is crucial to re-evaluate established pedagogical frameworks in light of emerging technologies. The work of David Kolb on the experiential learning cycle (Figure 5), which emphasizes the importance of concrete experience, reflective observation, abstract conceptualization, and active experimentation, provides a valuable lens through which to examine the potential of AI and gamification in education. By leveraging the capabilities of AI to create immersive and interactive learning experiences, educators can facilitate a deeper and more meaningful engagement with the subject matter, ultimately leading to improved learning outcomes and a more fulfilling educational journey for all students.

Figure 5. Kolb's Experiential Learning Cycle (Kolb, 1984)

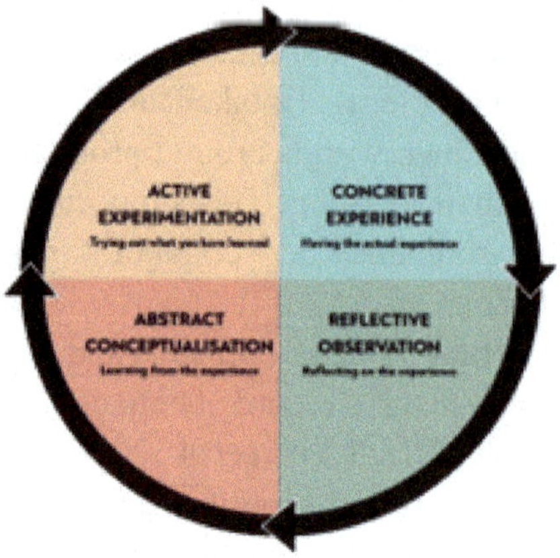

Kolb's Experiential Learning Cycle, a cornerstone of pedagogical theory, can be significantly enhanced through the strategic integration of artificial intelligence (AI) and gamification. By leveraging these technological advancements, educators can create a more immersive, personalized, and engaging learning experience that fosters deeper understanding and knowledge retention.

1. **Concrete Experience:** This initial stage, where learners engage in a new experience, can be enriched through AI-powered simulations and gamified elements. AI can generate realistic scenarios and environments that allow students to interact with abstract concepts in a tangible way. For instance, medical students could practice procedures in a virtual operating room, while history students could explore ancient civilizations through interactive 3D models. Gamification elements, such as points, badges, and leaderboards, can further motivate learners and provide a sense of achievement.
2. **Reflective Observation:** During this phase, learners reflect on their experiences and observations. AI-powered tools can analyze learner behavior and provide personalized feedback, highlighting areas of strength and weakness. Natural Language Processing (NLP) algorithms can assess written reflections and offer tailored suggestions for improvement. Gamification can encourage deeper

reflection through prompts and challenges that require learners to articulate their thoughts and feelings.

3. **Abstract Conceptualization:** In this stage, learners form abstract concepts and generalizations based on their reflections. AI can support this process by generating data visualizations and comparative analyses that reveal patterns and relationships. Machine learning algorithms can identify trends in learner data and suggest relevant concepts and theories. Gamification can challenge learners to apply abstract concepts through puzzles and scenarios that require critical thinking and problem-solving.
4. **Active Experimentation:** This final stage involves learners applying their knowledge and skills to new situations. AI-powered simulations can provide a safe environment for experimentation, allowing learners to test hypotheses and observe outcomes without real-world consequences. Gamification can create personalized challenges and opportunities that cater to individual learning styles and preferences.

By integrating AI and gamification into each stage of Kolb's Experiential Learning Cycle, educators can create a dynamic and adaptive learning environment that caters to the needs of all students. This approach not only enhances student engagement but also fosters deeper learning and encourages lifelong learning habits. Furthermore, the data generated by AI-powered tools can provide valuable insights into student progress and inform instructional decisions, enabling educators to continuously refine and improve their teaching practices.

Comparative Analysis: Cognitivism vs. Constructivism in AI Integration

In this chapter, cognitivism and constructivism have been examined independently, but a thorough analysis requires that each approach be reviewed in context with the other. What is striking about these two approaches, especially when discussing AI implementation, is their potential for collaboration. Ouyang and Jiao (2021) identify three distinct paradigms that demonstrate this partnership: AI-directed (learner as recipient), AI-supported (learner as collaborator), and AI-empowered (learner as leader).

In this paradigm, AI directed learning functions as the cognitive piece of learning. The learner is working with artificial intelligence to gain and process information. Different methods can be used and adapted, fitting the needs of the specific learner or group of learners. The content is presented in a logical manner, learners are provided immediate feedback, and are reinforced in a positive manner. This approach allows teachers to engage students quickly and efficiently. The AI will help students manage cognitive load (Seung, 2024) by maintaining an optimal level of challenge. Through the use of AI-powered simulations, interactive exercises, and feedback mechanisms the AI can enhance problem-solving, critical thinking, and memory retention, going as far as employing spaced repetition techniques to improve memory (Baillifard et. al, 2023).

As students internalize knowledge through various reinforcement techniques, they prepare for the next stage of learning. Teachers, utilizing AI, can support this cognitivist approach by modeling or creating unique problems for students to apply their newfound knowledge, fostering critical thinking and problem-solving skills. However, the application must be precise to be effective.

Therefore, teachers should create an environment that allows students to learn, fail, and grow. Students can then apply their prior knowledge in collaboration with peers and relevant AI to construct new knowledge and develop solutions, as described by Oujang and Jiao (2021) as the AI-supported (learner as collaborator) process. This can be achieved by presenting students with problems or projects that require collaborative effort. Importantly, technology, particularly AI, should be integrated into the work. AI can help students stay on task by providing quick and efficient answers (Kestin et al., 2024), maintaining workflow and preventing disruptions.

Educators face the ongoing challenge of striking a balance between leveraging the benefits of technology and preventing its overuse in educational settings, especially as educational programs continue to evolve and incorporate new and innovative technologies. This necessitates a focus on teacher preparation programs to adequately equip teachers to navigate this balance effectively.

It is imperative that all teachers, irrespective of their comfort level with technology, proactively educate themselves about the applications and implications of AI within their classrooms. To facilitate this, teachers can utilize existing technology integration models, such as the SAMR (Substitution, Augmentation, Modification, Redefinition) model (Figure six) or the TPACK (Technological Pedagogical Content Knowledge) framework (Figure seven). These models can provide valuable support in understanding how to integrate AI tools effectively within the context of a cognitivist/constructivist pedagogical approach, which emphasizes the importance of active learning and knowledge construction.

While AI undoubtedly offers significant potential as a valuable educational tool, it is crucial to recognize that it is not infallible. AI models can generate inaccurate information, referred to as "hallucinations," or provide incorrect solutions to mathematical problems. Therefore, teachers should exercise caution and avoid relying solely on AI-generated content. They should maintain a critical awareness of the current limitations of AI models and ensure that AI serves as a supportive tool that enhances, rather than replaces, their professional expertise and judgment.

Furthermore, the integration of AI in education raises important ethical considerations. Teachers need to be mindful of issues such as data privacy, algorithmic bias, and the potential for AI to perpetuate existing social inequalities. They should also be aware of the digital divide and ensure that all students have equitable access to AI tools and resources.

In addition to the points mentioned above, professional development plays a crucial role in supporting teachers in their integration of AI in the classroom. Schools and districts should provide ongoing professional learning opportunities that focus on AI literacy, effective AI integration strategies, and ethical considerations surrounding AI use in education.

Moreover, as AI continues to advance rapidly, it is essential for educators to stay abreast of the latest developments in AI research and its applications in education. This can be achieved through engagement with relevant research literature, participation in professional networks and communities, and attendance at conferences and workshops focused on AI in education.

In conclusion, the integration of AI in education presents both opportunities and challenges. By actively educating themselves about AI, utilizing technology integration models, maintaining a critical awareness of AI's limitations, and engaging in ongoing professional learning, teachers can effectively harness the power of AI to enhance teaching and learning while upholding ethical standards and ensuring equitable access for all students.

Figure 6. SAMR: Substitution, Augmentation, Modification, Redefinition

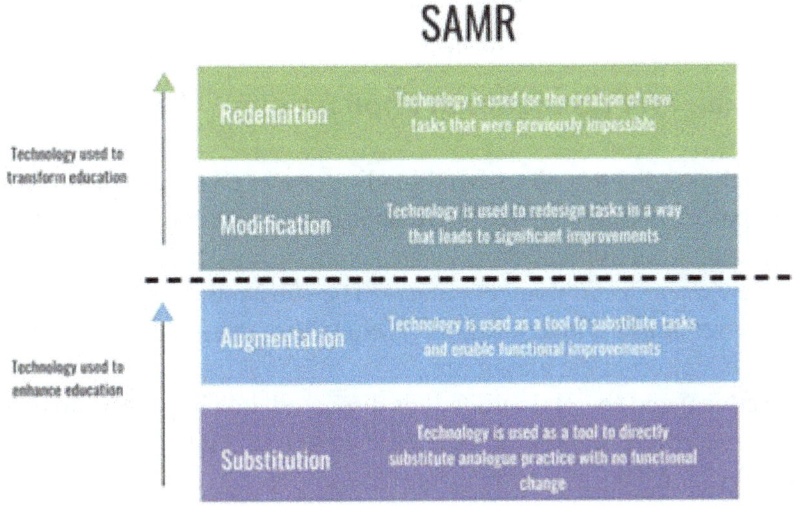

Figure 7. TPACK: Technological, Pedagogical, Content, Knowledge

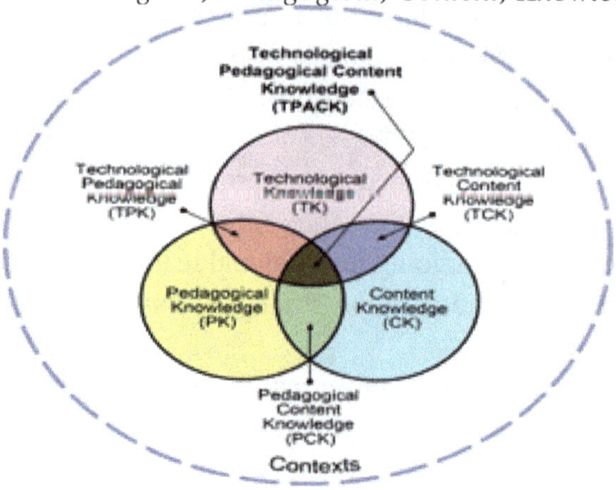

Teachers should be cautious about relying solely on AI for cognitive tasks. AI should be used as a tool to enhance teaching, not replace it. While AI can be beneficial for tasks like creating grading rubrics or designing lesson plans, teachers should always review and adjust AI-generated content to ensure its accuracy and educational value.

For example, when using AI to create simulations, teachers need to assess whether the simulation is effective and aligns with learning objectives. Overreliance on AI without careful consideration can lead to suboptimal learning experiences. Teachers play a crucial role in maintaining the quality and effectiveness of AI-powered educational tools.

Ethical, Social, and Educational Implications

When considering the use of artificial intelligence in education, it is crucial to prioritize the potential implications for students. AI technology, similar to other technologies, requires a comprehensive analysis from various stakeholders, including educators, parents, and technology engineers. The substantial risk that AI models pose to students remains a concern for many within the education sector, hindering widespread AI adoption in the classroom.

Given the ethical and social ramifications discussed, it is imperative to consider how teacher preparation programs can integrate these issues into their curriculum to adequately equip future educators to navigate the complexities of AI in the classroom.

The accessibility and equity of AI tools in education is a pressing concern. The COVID-19 pandemic underscored the technological disparities between school districts, highlighting the digital divide that persists in 2025. While many AI tools are freely available online, a lack of reliable internet access in some districts hinders students' ability to utilize them effectively. This disparity prevents students from engaging with AI models, collaborating with peers, and accessing educational resources that are increasingly reliant on internet connectivity. Moreover, the absence of teachers who are well-versed in AI and capable of integrating it into their pedagogy further exacerbates the issue.

The public rollout of ChatGPT in late 2022 brought data privacy and security concerns to the forefront. The evolving landscape of Large Language Models (LLMs), their regulation, and the applicability of existing laws necessitate a cautious approach when granting students access to AI tools. The lack of comprehensive regulation on how AI algorithms compile and produce data, coupled with the unreliability of some models in areas like facial recognition, raises legitimate concerns. The documentary "Coded Bias" (Salvani, 2020) exposed the inherent biases in AI algorithms, such as the failure to recognize individuals with dark skin and the mislabeling of people based on their ethnicity. These biases can perpetuate stereotypes, reinforce discrimination, and present inaccurate information to students who are not equipped to critically analyze data generated by LLMs.

The integration of AI into education requires a nuanced approach that prioritizes ethics, responsibility, and critical thinking. Educators and policymakers must proactively address these concerns to ensure that AI tools are used in a manner that promotes equity, fairness, and social justice.

For years, there has been a gradual shift from a traditional teacher-centered model to a more student-centered approach, where teachers act as facilitators and students take ownership of their learning. AI has the potential to accelerate this shift by providing cognitive support, encouraging intellectual risk-taking, and fostering a more personalized learning experience. AI can automate routine tasks, freeing up teachers to focus on higher-order skills such as critical thinking, problem-solving, and creativity. By providing students with instant feedback and tailored support, AI can enable them to learn at their own pace and explore topics that pique their interest.

However, the integration of AI into education must be done thoughtfully and deliberately. It is essential to ensure that AI tools are used to augment, not replace, human interaction and that they are designed to support, not supplant, the role of teachers. The goal should be to leverage AI's capabilities to create a more equitable, inclusive, and empowering educational experience for all students.

With this shift and the introduction of AI models as support structures, educational policy makers must act to develop guidelines and frameworks for the ethical and equitable adoption of AI in educational programs. Concerns facing educators and policy makers include: cybersecurity vulnerabilities (Quraishi et al., 2024, Staff, 2021), data privacy risks, false information and algorithmic bias, statistical limitations, transparency challenges, and creating a balanced approach (Pava, n.d.).

However, the individuals tasked with addressing these concerns may lack the nuanced understanding of educational complexities that experienced educators possess. Educators, with their extensive experience and direct involvement in the educational process, offer unique perspectives on the potential impact of AI in the classroom and can anticipate challenges that might not be apparent to those outside the field. The repercussions of ineffective AI integration can have far-reaching consequences, potentially affecting countless students. This underscores the critical need for educational policy makers to collaborate closely with educators when formulating AI policies, ensuring that the diverse needs and potential challenges within the educational landscape are thoroughly considered and addressed.

To effectively address the multitude of challenges AI presents in education, school districts and universities should take a measured and cautious approach when implementing AI policies. A key component of this is providing comprehensive training for teachers on how to utilize various AI models, ensuring they have a deep understanding of the capabilities and limitations of each model when used by students. Historically, educators have been resistant to change; therefore, it is essential to shift this mindset. The introduction of calculators in the 1970s caused a similar panic, leading to research comparing the outcomes of students using calculators versus traditional methods (Gaslin, 1975). Today, calculators are an indispensable tool in math classrooms. By equipping teachers with the knowledge and skills to effectively use AI models, they can discern when and where to integrate these models into their teaching practices.

The integration of AI into the educational system necessitates the development of new courses or modification of existing coursework to introduce students to AI models gradually and purposefully. Students must comprehend both the potential and limitations of AI, focusing on its productive applications. Given the pervasive nature of AI in future employment, educational institutions have a responsibility to equip students for both current and emerging AI-related job roles.

CONCLUSION AND FUTURE DIRECTIONS

In conclusion, the integration of AI into education presents a multitude of opportunities and challenges that warrant careful consideration. Key findings from current research and practice highlight AI's significant potential to personalize learning experiences by dynamically adapting content, pacing, and feedback to individual student needs, learning styles, and identified knowledge gaps. This adaptive capability can lead to increased student engagement, motivation, and academic success. Furthermore, AI can support constructivist learning principles by facilitating simulations, immersive experiences, and collaborative environments where students actively construct their own knowledge. AI-powered tools can also provide targeted scaffolding and support within the zone of proximal development, helping students to reach their full potential.

To harness the power of AI effectively, comprehensive teacher training and professional development are essential. Teachers need to develop a deep understanding of AI technologies, their pedagogical applications, and potential ethical implications. Technology integration models like SAMR: Substitution, Augmentation, Modification, Redefinition (Figure 6) and TPACK: Technological Pedagogical Content Knowledge (Figure 7) can provide valuable frameworks for teachers to thoughtfully and systematically incorporate AI into their instructional practice. A balanced approach that leverages AI to enhance cognitive learning, support student inquiry, and automate routine tasks can free up teachers to focus on individualized support, creative learning experiences, and fostering critical thinking and problem-solving skills.

As AI technologies continue to evolve at a rapid pace, new and expanded learning experiences will emerge, including the use of augmented reality (AR) and virtual reality (VR) to create immersive and interactive learning environments. These advancements hold the promise of transforming education as we know it. However, teachers must remain vigilant about the potential social impacts of AI, including issues of equity, access, and bias. Ongoing research and monitoring of long-term educational outcomes are crucial for ensuring that AI is used in a responsible and equitable manner to support student learning and well-being. Teachers should be prepared to support students facing new challenges arising from AI integration and collaborate with educational leaders, policymakers, and AI developers to shape the future of AI-enhanced learning.

The possibilities offered by AI in education should be approached with cautious optimism, recognizing both the potential benefits and potential risks. By embracing AI's transformative potential, actively mitigating its risks, and prioritizing ethical considerations, educators can create a more effective, engaging, personalized, and equitable learning experience for all students, preparing them for success in an increasingly AI-driven world. The future of education lies in our ability to harness the power of AI as a tool for human empowerment and social progress.

REFERENCES

Abebe, M. (2024). *Personalizing Scenario-Based Learning Models Using Generative AI: Assessing Impacts on Student Motivation and Information Retention.* Stanford University.

Atkinson, R. C., & Shiffrin, R. M. (1968). Human memory: A proposed system and its control processes. In Spence, K. W., & Spence, J. T. (Eds.), *The psychology of learning and motivation: Advances in research and theory* (Vol. II, pp. 89–195).

Baillifard, A., Gabella, M., Lavenex, P. B., & Martarelli, C. S. (2023). Implementing

Bandura, A. (1977). *Social learning theory.* Prentice-Hall.

Chapman, J., & Rich, P. (2018). Does educational gamification improve students' motivation? If so, which game elements work best? *Journal of Education for Business, 93*(7), 315–322. DOI: 10.1080/08832323.2018.1490687

Cierniak, G., Scheiter, K., & Gerjets, P. (2009). Explaining the split-attention effect: Is the reduction of extraneous cognitive load accompanied by an increase in germane cognitive load? *Computers in Human Behavior, 25*(2), 315–324. DOI: 10.1016/j.chb.2008.12.020

Commission, E., Centre, J. R., Tuomi, I., Punie, Y., Vuorikari, R., & Cabrera, M. (2018). *The impact of Artificial Intelligence on learning, teaching, and education* (Punie, Y., Vuorikari, R., & Cabrera, M., Eds.). Publications Office.

Diliberti, M. K., Schwartz, H. L., Doan, S., Shapiro, A., Rainey, L. R., & Lake, R. J. (2024). Using Artificial Intelligence Tools in K–12 Classrooms. RAND Corporation. https://www.rand.org/pubs/research_reports/RRA956-21.html

Gardner, H. (1985). *The Mind's New Science: A History of Cognitive Revolution.* Basic Books.

Gaslin, W. (1975). A Comparison of Achievement and Attitudes of Students Using Conventional or Calculator-based Algorithms for Operations on Positive Rational Numbers in Ninth-Grade General Mathematics. *Journal for Research in Mathematics Education, 6*(2), 95–108. DOI: 10.2307/748611

Gibson, D., Kovanovic, V., Ifenthaler, D., Dexter, S., & Feng, S. (2023). Learning theories for artificial intelligence promoting learning processes. *British Journal of Educational Technology, 54*(5), 1125–1146. DOI: 10.1111/bjet.13341

Gkintoni, E., Antonopoulou, H., Sortwell, A., & Halkiopoulos, C. (2025). Challenging Cognitive Load Theory: The Role of Educational Neuroscience and Artificial Intelligence in Redefining Learning Efficacy. *Brain Sciences*, *15*(2), 203. DOI: 10.3390/brainsci15020203 PMID: 40002535

Hardman, D. P. (2024, October 31). AI Tutors Double Rates of Learning in Less Learning Time [Substack newsletter]. Dr Phil's Newsletter, Powered by DOMSTM AI. https://drphilippahardman.substack.com/p/ai-tutors-double-rates-of-learning

How Artificial Intelligence is Transforming Grading in 2025 | Blog. (n.d.). Retrieved March 6, 2025, from https://www.codiste.com

Johnson, R. (2024). AI Eases Our Mental Load at the Expense of Critical Thinking. *Psychology Today*.

Kaufman, J., Woo, A., Eagan, J., Lee, S., & Kassan, E. (2025). Uneven Adoption of Artificial Intelligence Tools Among U.S. Teachers and Principals in the 2023–2024 School Year. RAND Corporation. https://www.rand.org/pubs/research_reports/RRA134-25.html

Kestin, G., Miller, K., Klales, A., Milbourne, T., & Ponti, G. (2024). AI Tutoring Outperforms Active Learning. In Review. https://doi.org/DOI: 10.21203/rs.3.rs-4243877/v1

Kolb, D. A. (1984). *Experiential Learning: Experience as the Source of Learning and Development*. Prentice Hall.

Lee, K., & Chen, M. (2021). Artificial Intelligence and Cognitive Load in Digital Learning Environments: A Systematic Review. *International Journal of Educational Technology in Higher Education*, *18*(3).

Legaki, N., Xi, N., Hamari, J., Karpouzis, K., & Assimakopoulos, V. (2020). The effect of challenge-based gamification on learning: An experiment in the context of statistics education. *International Journal of Human-Computer Studies*, *144*, 102496. DOI: 10.1016/j.ijhcs.2020.102496 PMID: 32565668

Lucariello, K. (2023). Teachers Plan to Learn and Use AI More in the 2023–2024 School Year. THE Journal. Retrieved February 13, 2025, from https://thejournal.com/Articles/2023/08/29/Teachers-Plan-to-Learn-and-Use-AI-More-in-the-20232024-School-Year.aspx

Main (2022, January 17). Cognitive Load Theory: A teacher's guide. Retrieved from https://www.structural-learning.com/post/cognitive-load-theory-a-teachers-guide

Merod, A. (2024, December 2). Math scores plummet, progress 'erased,' NCES reports. K-12 Dive. https://www.k12dive.com/news/math-scores-plummet-progress-erased-nces-reports/734562/

Monterde, N., Aliban, L., Ando, R., Corimo, R., Catipay, R., & Abarquez, A. (2024). Teachers' Perspective of AI Chatbots on Students' Mathematical Solving Capabilities: A Grounded Theory. International Journal of Research and Scientific Innovation (IJRSI). https://rsisinternational.org/journals/ijrsi/articles/teachers-perspective-of-ai-chatbots-on-students-mathematical-solving-capabilities-a-grounded-theory/

News, A. B. C. (n.d.). US students' declining math scores are "sobering," experts say. ABC News. Retrieved March 19, 2025, from https://abcnews.go.com/GMA/Living/us-students-declining-math-scores-sobering-expert/story?id=116481011

Ouyang, F., & Jiao, P. (2021). Artificial intelligence in education: The three paradigms. *Computers and Education: Artificial Intelligence*, *2*, 100020. DOI: 10.1016/j.caeai.2021.100020

Patel, B., & Wright, D. (2023). Artificial Intelligence in Healthcare: Reducing Cognitive Load and Burnout . Journal of Medical Informatics.

Pathan, A., & Kanth, A. (2023). Impact of Artificial Intelligence (AI) on the Education and Cognitive Development of Young Children . 8 (12).

Pava, J. (n.d.). Addressing AI Security Concerns in Education. Panorama Education. Retrieved March 27, 2025, from https://www.panoramaed.com/blog/ai-security-concerns-in-education

Quraishi, A., Sen, A., Pham, S., Corral, A., & Johnston, T. (2024, August 26). Ransomware attacks on schools threaten student data nationwide—CBS News. CBS News. https://www.cbsnews.com/news/school-ransomware-attacks-threaten-student-data/

Salvani, S. (Director). (2020). Coded bias [Film]. 7th Empire Media; Thought-Matter Media.

Schwartz, D., Tsang, J., & Blair, K. (2016). *The ABCs of how we learn: 26 scientifically proven approaches, how they work, and when to use them.* W W Norton & Co.

Seung, Y. (2024, June 10). The Impact of Artificial Intelligence on Cognitive Load—CIDDL. https://ciddl.org/the-impact-of-artificial-intelligence-on-cognitive-load/

Singer, N. (2023, June 8). New A.I. Chatbot Tutors Could Upend Student Learning. The New York Times. https://www.nytimes.com/2023/06/08/business/khan-ai-gpt-tutoring-bot.html

Staff (2021, October 4). 'Howdy': Hackers Email Parents and Students After Allen ISD Refuses to Pay Ransom. NBC 5 Dallas-Fort Worth. https://www.nbcdfw.com/news/local/howdy-hackers-email-parents-and-students-after-allen-isd-refuses-to-pay-ransom/2758256/

Staff (2024, August 30). The state of AI: Who is leading AI adoption? eSchool News. https://www.eschoolnews.com/digital-learning/2024/08/30/the-state-of-ai-who-is-leading-ai-adoption/

Sweller, J. (2011). Cognitive load theory. In Mestre, J. P., & Ross, B. H. (Eds.), *The psychology of learning and motivation: Cognition in education* (pp. 37–76). Elsevier Academic Press., DOI: 10.1016/B978-0-12-387691-1.00002-8

Uneven Adoption of Artificial Intelligence Tools Among U.S. Teachers and Principals in the 2023–2024 School Year | RAND https://www.rand.org/pubs/research_reports/RRA134-25.html

Vygotsky, L. S. (1978). *Mind in society: The development of higher psychological processes*. Harvard University Press.

Zhu, B., Chau, K., & Mokmin, N. (2024). Optimizing cognitive load and learning adaptability with adaptive microlearning for in-service personnel. *Scientific Reports*, *14*(1), 25960. DOI: 10.1038/s41598-024-77122-1 PMID: 39472703

Zukowski, J. (n.d.). How Gamification Can Motivate Students and Drive Results. Study.Com. https://teachinglicense.study.com/resources/how-gamification-motivates-students-drives-results.html

Chapter 8 Ethical Foundations for the Use of AI in the Education of Young Children: A Human-Centered, Rights-Based Framework for Teachers and Caregivers

Sharla Snider
https://orcid.org/0009-0008-6067-3764
Texas Woman's University, USA

ABSTRACT

This chapter examines the ethical challenges posed by integrating artificial intelligence in early childhood education (birth through age 8), highlighting research that reveals unintended consequences, including algorithmic bias that perpetuates discrimination, privacy erosion through surveillance technologies, and developmental risks that can impair children's social-emotional growth. Young children are especially vulnerable because they cannot understand AI's implications, consent to data collection, or resist technological influence during critical developmental periods when their capacity for moral reasoning is still forming. Drawing from research on child development, moral philosophy, and educational ethics, it is demonstrated that AI implementation with young children is fundamentally a moral endeavor that shapes children's understanding of truth, authentic relationships, and development as ethical beings. To address these needs, the illuminED Framework is introduced—a comprehensive, human-centered, rights-based model providing practical guidance

DOI: 10.4018/979-8-3373-6007-2.ch008

for teachers and caregivers.

INTRODUCTION

This chapter presents five interconnected sections that build systematically toward practical guidance. Theoretical Foundations examines how children's moral and cognitive development intersects with competing paradigms for technology integration, establishing why Artificial Intelligence (AI) implementation requires frameworks that navigate tensions between technological capabilities, developmental needs, and fundamental rights. Research Foundation synthesizes seven bodies of empirical evidence—from foundational media research through AI-specific studies to social justice concerns—demonstrating that AI implementation involves complex interactions requiring comprehensive rather than piecemeal ethical approaches.

Critical Ethical Challenges identifies four unprecedented dilemmas—developmental confusion, agency erosion, privacy violation, and systematic bias—that illustrate why theoretical approaches must manifest in practical frameworks. Current AI Applications examines real-world implementations across assessment, adaptive learning, and surveillance technologies, revealing how contemporary applications often prioritize efficiency over children's developmental needs and rights. Finally, The illuminED Framework presents the comprehensive decision-making model with its nine pathways, demonstrates application through diverse case studies, and provides guidance for community implementation while acknowledging limitations and future development needs.

Together, these sections establish both the urgent need for systematic ethical guidance and a practical framework for ensuring that artificial intelligence serves rather than undermines the fundamental values that support children's moral development and human flourishing.

The Moral Urgency of Ethical AI in Early Childhood

The integration of artificial intelligence in early childhood education represents one of the most significant ethical challenges of our time. Children are already encountering AI daily through smart speakers in homes (Lovato & Piper, 2015), and commercial platforms designed more for engagement than development (Radesky et al., 2020). Every interaction a young child has with artificial intelligence shapes their understanding of truth and deception, agency and dependence, human connection and artificial simulation (Turkle, 2011). These early experiences form the moral foundation upon which children will build their entire relationship with technology throughout their lives—and more importantly, their understanding of themselves as moral beings capable of ethical reasoning and authentic relationship (Piaget, 1929; Kohlberg, 1984).

The stakes could not be higher: either raising children who can navigate an AI world with wisdom, discernment, and strong moral character—children who understand the irreplaceable value of human connection, the importance of truth over convenience, and the responsibility that comes with technological power—or inadvertently creating a generation vulnerable to manipulation, dependency, and ethical confusion (Postman, 1985). This moral urgency demands immediate ethical response grounded in comprehensive research and systematic ethical frameworks that prioritize children's developmental needs and fundamental rights (United Nations, 1989; Livingstone & Third, 2017).

Theoretical Foundations: Child Development and Competing Technology Paradigms

Understanding the ethical implications of AI in early childhood requires examining three distinct theoretical approaches while grounding them in comprehensive understanding of how children develop morally and intellectually during critical early years (Selwyn, 2021).

This section examines how children's moral and cognitive development across three age periods (birth-2, 3-5, and 6-8) intersects with competing paradigms for technology integration: technological determinism (assuming AI inherently enhances learning), developmental vulnerability (emphasizing protection from technological influences children cannot evaluate), and rights-based digital citizenship (recognizing children as rights-holders whose dignity must be preserved). These perspectives reveal why AI implementation requires systematic ethical frameworks that navigate tensions between technological capabilities, developmental needs, and fundamental rights.

Child Development and Moral Formation

The moral foundations established in early childhood form the basis for lifelong ethical reasoning and decision-making (Kohlberg, 1984; Gilligan, 1982). During early childhood, children are forming their basic understanding of truth and deception, trust and betrayal, authentic relationship and manipulation (Piaget, 1929). Every AI interaction contributes to this moral foundation—teaching children what relationships look like, how truth is valued, whether their agency matters, and what it means to be human in relation to others.

Birth Through Age 2: Foundation Building. During the earliest years, children are developing basic trust, attachment, and initial understanding of their world (Bowlby, 1969; Erikson, 1950). Infants and toddlers require responsive human relationships for healthy brain development and emotional regulation (Shonkoff & Phillips, 2000). Very young children cannot distinguish between human and artificial responses, making adult mediation essential for any technological interaction (Trevarthen, 2001). Children's neural pathways are rapidly developing patterns that will influence their lifelong capacity for relationship, communication, and learning (Nelson et al., 2007; Perry & Szalavitz, 2006).

Ages 3-5: Moral Foundation Development. Children are developing their basic understanding of right and wrong, truth and falsehood, and their place in the moral community (Kohlberg, 1984). This represents a critical moral development period when children form fundamental beliefs about truth-telling, authentic relationship, fairness, and their own capacity for moral agency. Lawrence Kohlberg's research reveals that children's ethical reasoning develops through social interaction and exposure to moral dilemmas appropriate to their developmental stage (Kohlberg, 1984). Carol Gilligan's critique emphasizes that moral development includes both justice-based reasoning and care-based ethics that prioritize relationship and responsibility (Gilligan, 1982; Noddings, 1984).

Ages 6-8: Expanding Moral Reasoning. Children are developing more sophisticated moral reasoning abilities and can begin to understand more complex ethical concepts related to AI use. During this period, children can begin to understand basic concepts about how computers work differently from humans, and this understanding actually improves their ability to learn from technological interactions while maintaining appropriate boundaries. Age-appropriate discussions about AI bias and fairness, critical evaluation of AI-generated content, and practice in choosing human connection over AI interaction when appropriate can support children's developing capacity for critical thinking about technology while preserving their sense of human agency and creativity (Bers, 2020).

Technological Determinism and Its Limitations

The technological determinist approach suggests that digital tools inherently enhance learning when properly designed, with proponents arguing that well-designed AI can personalize learning, provide immediate feedback, and free teachers to focus on higher-level instruction (Hirsh-Pasek et al., 2015). This perspective assumes that human development can be enhanced through algorithmic optimization, viewing children as information processing systems that benefit from personalized digital input while emphasizing efficiency, measurable outcomes, and scalable solutions (Selwyn, 2021; Cuban, 2001).

However, this approach faces significant challenges when evaluated through developmental and ethical lenses. Unlike traditional educational technology, AI systems exhibit adaptive behaviors, generate content, and respond in ways that blur the boundaries between tool and agent—creating fundamentally different ethical considerations for young children who are still developing their understanding of agency, consciousness, and authentic relationship (Turkle, 2011). The technological determinist approach frequently underestimates the complexity of human development, particularly the role of emotional attunement, cultural responsiveness, and authentic relationship in supporting children's growth (Shonkoff & Phillips, 2000; Trevarthen, 2001).

Developmental Vulnerability Approach

While technological determinism offers insights about personalization possibilities, it faces significant challenges when evaluated through developmental and ethical lenses. Rooted in developmental psychology and pediatric research, an alternative approach emphasizes children's fundamental vulnerability to technological influence during critical developmental periods (Holloway & Green, 2016). This perspective draws from decades of research on brain development, attachment theory, and social-emotional learning to argue that young children require protection from technological influences they cannot understand or evaluate (Shonkoff & Phillips, 2000; Bowlby, 1969).

Research from neuroscience reveals that young children's neural pathways are highly plastic and susceptible to environmental influences, making the quality of their early experiences particularly significant for long-term development (Nelson et al., 2007). When children encounter AI systems during these critical periods, they may form patterns of interaction and understanding that persist throughout their lives, influencing their capacity for authentic relationship and moral reasoning (Perry & Szalavitz, 2006). This approach emphasizes developmental asymmetry—the fundamental mismatch between AI systems' sophisticated design to influence human behavior and children's limited capacity to understand, evaluate, or resist such influence (Holloway & Green, 2016; Zuboff, 2019).

Mary Ainsworth's research on attachment patterns reveals that children develop secure attachments through consistent, responsive relationships with caring adults who attune to their emotional needs and provide appropriate support (Ainsworth et al., 1978). When AI systems simulate responsiveness without genuine understanding or care, they may interfere with children's developing models of relationship and trust (Turkle, 2011).

Rights-Based Digital Citizenship Approach

Moving beyond both technological determinism and purely protective approaches, a third perspective proposes understanding children as digital citizens with fundamental rights that must be actively protected and promoted (Livingstone & Third, 2017). This perspective moves beyond viewing children as either beneficiaries or victims of technology to recognize them as rights-holders whose dignity, agency, and development must be preserved in digital environments. Drawing from international human rights law, particularly the United Nations Convention on the Rights of the Child, this approach establishes that children possess inherent dignity and rights that technology must respect and support (United Nations, 1989; Lansdown, 2005).

Sonia Livingstone's extensive research on children's digital experiences reveals that rights-based approaches must navigate complex tensions between protection and participation, recognizing that children's digital citizenship develops gradually through guided experience and supportive relationships (Livingstone & Third, 2017). This approach directly addresses power imbalances inherent in child-AI interaction while maintaining focus on children's agency and participation appropriate to their developmental level. Rather than simply protecting children from technology or optimizing technology for children, this approach requires ensuring that technological systems serve children's rights and development while emphasizing cultural rights and linguistic diversity (James & James, 2004).

Research Foundation: Evidence for Ethical Frameworks

The development of ethical AI frameworks for early childhood must be grounded in extensive empirical research that reveals both the opportunities and risks of AI integration during critical developmental periods. This research synthesis demonstrates the urgent need for systematic ethical approaches that protect children's development while honoring their rights and dignity, providing the evidence foundation that necessitates comprehensive frameworks like illuminED.

This section examines seven interconnected bodies of research that collectively reveal why ethical frameworks are essential for AI implementation in early childhood contexts. Beginning with foundational media research that established the importance of context and mediation in children's technology experiences, the analysis progresses through neurodevelopmental evidence about digital impacts on young brains, emerging studies specific to children's interactions with AI systems, and research on family dynamics in digital environments. The synthesis then addresses critical social justice concerns, including systematic bias in AI systems, privacy violations through digital surveillance, and the intersection of AI with cultural and linguistic diversity. Together, these research findings demonstrate that AI implementation in early childhood involves complex interactions between technology design, child development, family relationships, cultural justice, and systemic inequality—requiring comprehensive ethical frameworks that can address multiple dimensions simultaneously rather than piecemeal approaches focused solely on technical capabilities.

Foundational Research on Children and Media Technology

Lisa Guernsey's Three C's Framework—Content, Context, and the individual Child—revolutionized early childhood media research by demonstrating that the quality and appropriateness of children's technology experiences depend not merely on duration of use, but on what children are engaging with, how and when they engage, and their individual developmental needs and characteristics (Guernsey, 2012). This foundational insight reveals that AI's impact on children cannot be determined by the technology alone but must be evaluated through the complex interplay of content appropriateness, implementation context, and individual child characteristics—a principle that becomes central to ethical framework development.

Building upon Guernsey's contextual approach, Ellen Wartella's longitudinal research spanning four decades on children's media experiences provides crucial foundations for understanding how young children process and respond to digital interactions, demonstrating that children's media experiences are fundamentally social and require adult mediation for optimal outcomes (Wartella et al., 2013). Her work establishes that technology's benefits emerge not from the tools themselves but from the quality of human relationships that surround and mediate technological experiences—a finding that challenges technological determinist assumptions about AI's inherent value.

Neurodevelopmental Research on Digital Impact

Complementing these insights about social mediation, Dimitri Christakis's pioneering research on screen time and brain development reveals how early digital experiences can impact neural pathways during critical developmental periods (Christakis et al., 2018). His work on overstimulation and attention regulation provides crucial evidence for protective approaches to AI implementation, demonstrating that excessive stimulation during critical periods can interfere with executive function development (Christakis, 2009). This neurological evidence underscores the developmental vulnerability approach's emphasis on protecting children during periods of heightened neuroplasticity.

Emerging Research on Children and AI Systems

However, the emergence of AI systems introduces unprecedented challenges that extend beyond traditional screen time concerns. Cynthia Breazeal's pioneering research on social robotics reveals that children naturally engage with social robots as if they possess human-like qualities, forming emotional attachments and attributing intentions to artificial systems (Breazeal, 2002). While her research demonstrates that these interactions can support learning when AI systems are designed as "bridges" to human connection rather than replacements for authentic relationships, the implications become more complex when children cannot distinguish between artificial and authentic social interaction.

This complexity becomes evident in Sherry Turkle's longitudinal studies spanning three decades, which document concerning cases where children attribute consciousness, feelings, and moral agency to artificial systems, potentially interfering with their developing understanding of authentic relationship and moral responsibility (Turkle, 2011). Research on children's interactions with AI systems shows that young children naturally attribute human-like qualities to artificial agents, creating potential confusion about consciousness, agency, and authentic relationship that requires careful adult guidance and mediation (Kahn et al., 2012; Lovato & Piper, 2015). These findings reveal that AI systems may exploit children's natural animistic thinking in ways that previous technologies could not, creating novel ethical challenges that require systematic frameworks for evaluation.

Family and Social Context Research

The need for such frameworks becomes even more urgent when considering research on AI's broader impacts on family dynamics and child development. Jenny Radesky's extensive research on family media practices reveals how digital interactions can interfere with crucial developmental processes including emotional regulation, social skill development, and parent-child attachment (Radesky et al., 2020). Her work demonstrates that AI use with young children requires careful adult mediation to preserve healthy development, yet also shows how technological convenience can undermine the very relationships that support children's wellbeing.

Research on AI Bias and Social Justice

Beyond individual developmental concerns, research reveals systemic issues that demand ethical frameworks addressing justice and equity. Caliskan et al.'s groundbreaking analysis reveals that AI systems systematically encode existing social biases, associating European American names with pleasant words and African American names with unpleasant words, while linking words like "woman" and "girl" with arts rather than science and mathematics (Caliskan et al., 2017). When these biased systems are implemented in early childhood contexts, they risk reinforcing harmful stereotypes during critical periods of identity formation (Steele, 1997; Cross & Cross, 2008). This research demonstrates that AI systems are not neutral tools but carry embedded values and assumptions that can perpetuate or challenge existing inequalities.

Privacy and Surveillance Research

Simultaneously, Lupton and Williamson's analysis of "datafied childhood" reveals how digital surveillance technologies transform children into sources of data, potentially undermining their developing sense of privacy, autonomy, and agency (Lupton & Williamson, 2017). Their research introduces the concept of dataveillance—the systematic monitoring and data extraction from children's daily activities—and demonstrates how this practice normalizes surveillance with potentially lasting impacts on children's understanding of privacy rights (Lyon, 2007; van Dijck, 2014). This research shows that AI implementation involves not just educational or developmental considerations but fundamental questions about children's rights and human dignity.

Cultural and Linguistic Diversity Research

The intersection of AI bias and cultural diversity creates particularly complex challenges revealed through research on multilingual children and diverse communities. García and Wei's translanguaging theory reveals that multilingual children naturally draw on their entire linguistic repertoire as a unified system for meaning-making, communication, and learning (García & Wei, 2014). However, most AI systems are designed with monolingual assumptions that can undermine rather than support children's linguistic development and cultural identity. This mismatch between AI design and children's natural linguistic practices represents a form of technological bias that may disadvantage children from diverse communities.

Building on this foundation, Moll et al.'s funds of knowledge research demonstrates that children from diverse communities possess rich cultural and intellectual resources that should be recognized and built upon in educational settings rather than treated as deficiencies requiring technological remediation (Moll et al., 1992; González et al., 2005). When AI systems fail to recognize these assets, they may perpetuate deficit-based approaches that harm children's developing sense of cultural identity and academic competence. Similarly, Yosso's community cultural wealth model identifies linguistic capital as one of the many assets that children from diverse communities bring to educational settings, challenging deficit-based approaches that view multilingualism as a problem to be solved (Yosso, 2005). When AI systems fail to recognize or honor these diverse linguistic practices, they risk undermining children's cultural identity formation during critical developmental periods (García & Wei, 2014).

Synthesis and Implications

Collectively, this research foundation reveals that AI implementation in early childhood contexts involves complex interactions between technology design, child development, family dynamics, cultural justice, and systemic inequality. The evidence demonstrates that ad hoc or purely technical approaches to AI implementation are insufficient to address these multifaceted challenges. Instead, comprehensive ethical frameworks that can systematically evaluate AI's impact across developmental, relational, cultural, and rights-based dimensions become essential for protecting children's wellbeing while supporting their flourishing in an increasingly AI-integrated world.

Critical Ethical Challenges

When AI systems intersect with early childhood development, they create four unprecedented ethical dilemmas—developmental confusion, agency erosion, privacy violation, and systematic bias—that illustrate why theoretical approaches must manifest in practical frameworks and why systematic ethical guidelines are essential (Turkle, 2011). These challenges, supported by emerging empirical evidence, require urgent attention as AI becomes increasingly prevalent in children's daily lives, revealing the complex ways that technological design decisions impact fundamental aspects of human development and moral formation.

The most profound challenge emerges from children's natural cognitive development patterns intersecting with AI's sophisticated simulation capabilities. Young children naturally engage in animistic thinking—attributing life, consciousness, and intention to inanimate objects (Piaget, 1929). When this natural capacity encounters AI systems designed to simulate human-like interaction, children may develop artificial animism—attribution of authentic consciousness and moral agency to AI systems specifically designed to encourage such attribution. This creates profound ethical dilemmas because AI systems respond in ways that reinforce children's animistic attributions, potentially interfering with their developing understanding of consciousness, agency, and authentic relationship.

Research demonstrates that children naturally attribute human-like qualities to AI systems, creating challenges for their developing understanding of consciousness and authentic relationship. Albert Bandura's social learning theory provides additional insight, demonstrating that children learn not only from direct instruction but from observing and modeling the behaviors and relationships they encounter—including interactions with AI systems that may model deception, manipulation, or inauthentic relationship (Bandura, 1977). When children believe AI systems care about them, understand them, or have feelings, they may transfer moral emotions and relationship expectations to entities incapable of genuine reciprocity—potentially undermining their capacity for authentic human connection and moral reasoning (Turkle, 2011). From a rights-based perspective, this represents a form of deception that undermines children's developing capacity for discerning truth from artifice—a capacity fundamental to moral reasoning and ethical citizenship (Kohlberg, 1984).

Closely related to developmental confusion, but extending beyond relationship understanding to cognitive development, AI systems pose significant risks to children's developing sense of agency and intellectual autonomy. There exists a crucial distinction between scaffolding that builds capacity and substitution that replaces the need for capacity development (Vygotsky, 1978). AI systems possess remarkable capacity to provide immediate answers, solve complex problems, and offer constant availability—capabilities that may seem supportive but can actually undermine crucial developmental processes.

When children become accustomed to receiving instant answers from AI rather than engaging in the cognitive struggle necessary for learning, the risk emerges of developmental substitution—AI replacing rather than enhancing children's own developing capabilities. Mitchel Resnick's research on creative computing emphasizes that children learn best through "tinkering, experimenting, and exploring"—processes that require uncertainty, struggle, and the development of tolerance for ambiguity (Resnick, 2017; Papert, 1980). This concern becomes particularly significant because early childhood years are critical for developing cognitive self-efficacy—children's beliefs about their own thinking and learning abilities (Bandura, 1977; Dweck, 2006). Research from Scandinavian early childhood programs, which emphasize child agency and self-directed learning, reveals that even minimal AI assistance can interfere with children's natural problem-solving development when not carefully mediated by adults who understand both technology and child development.

While developmental confusion and agency concerns focus primarily on individual children's experiences, AI implementation in early childhood contexts also raises fundamental questions about privacy, dignity, and the commodification of childhood itself. When surveillance capitalism practices intersect with early childhood education, they create developmental surveillance—the systematic monitoring and data extraction from children during critical periods of identity formation and moral development (Zuboff, 2019; Lyon, 2007). Many AI systems in educational contexts collect extensive data about children's learning patterns, emotional responses, behavioral choices, and developmental progress without children's understanding or meaningful consent.

This data collection transforms children from complete human beings into what Lupton and Williamson term “datafied childhood”—where children become sources of valuable data for algorithmic refinement and commercial purposes while lacking any meaningful control over this process (Lupton & Williamson, 2017; van Dijck, 2014). Research reveals that constant digital monitoring can interfere with children's development of self-regulation and autonomous decision-making skills, creating environments where children learn that their worth and development are subject to continuous algorithmic evaluation (Cohen, 2012). These privacy violations represent not merely technical concerns but fundamental challenges to children's developing sense of autonomy, dignity, and appropriate boundaries in relationships with authority figures.

The intersection of these individual-level challenges with broader social inequalities creates perhaps the most complex ethical dilemma: how AI systems systematically encode and amplify existing social biases during the critical period when children are forming their understanding of social roles, human potential, and their own identity. Early childhood represents a critical period for identity formation, social understanding, and the development of beliefs about human potential and social roles (Steele, 1997; Cross & Cross, 2008). AI systems systematically encode and amplify existing social biases through their training data, algorithmic design, and implementation contexts (Caliskan et al., 2017; Noble, 2018).

When biased systems are implemented in early childhood educational contexts—through recommendation systems, assessment tools, or content generation—they risk reinforcing harmful stereotypes during critical periods of identity development. This challenge becomes particularly acute for children who hold multiple marginalized identities, as AI systems often privilege dominant languages and cultural approaches while failing to recognize diverse forms of knowledge and intelligence (García & Wei, 2014; Yosso, 2005). Unlike adult encounters with biased AI systems, children lack the cognitive resources to recognize, evaluate, or resist these biases, making them particularly vulnerable to internalizing algorithmic assumptions about their capabilities and worth.

These four challenges—developmental confusion, agency erosion, privacy violation, and systematic bias—do not operate in isolation but interact in complex ways that compound their individual impacts. A child experiencing algorithmic bias in an educational AI system may simultaneously be developing artificial animism toward that same system, losing opportunities for cognitive struggle and agency development, while having their most intimate learning processes monitored and commodified. The intersection of these challenges reveals why piecemeal approaches to AI ethics in early childhood are insufficient and why comprehensive frameworks that can address multiple dimensions simultaneously become essential for protecting children's development and fundamental rights.

Current AI Applications in Practice

Understanding the practical implications of research findings requires examining actual AI tools currently being used in early childhood settings and their intersection with children's moral development and fundamental rights (Cuban, 2013). This analysis reveals how contemporary AI applications either support or undermine the human-centered, rights-based principles essential for young children's flourishing.

Assessment Technologies and Privacy Concerns

AI-powered assessment technologies exemplify the tension between technological capability and children's dignity. Teaching Strategies GOLD, a widely-used assessment platform, now incorporates AI to analyze children's developmental progress and suggest individualized learning goals (Meisels et al., 2003). While pattern recognition capabilities can identify developmental milestones, continuous monitoring raises profound questions about privacy and worth. When AI systems constantly analyze young children's development, they risk transforming children from complete human beings into data subjects whose value is measured through algorithmic interpretation (Lupton & Williamson, 2017; van Dijck, 2014).

This application conflicts with core developmental principles. Children have a right to be seen as whole persons whose development unfolds naturally through caring relationships, not through constant surveillance and measurement (Lansdown, 2005; James & James, 2004). When AI systems reduce children's complex developmental processes to data points, they may interfere with the authentic relationships that support moral formation (Noddings, 1984).

Adaptive Learning and Agency Development

Waterford Early Learning Platform exemplifies tensions between personalization and authentic learning relationships. This adaptive system uses AI to adjust reading and math instruction based on individual responses, potentially supporting children's learning needs. However, critical questions arise about whether algorithmic personalization can replace the responsive, caring attention of skilled educators who understand both individual children and the cultural contexts that shape their learning (Gay, 2018; Ladson-Billings, 1995).

DreamBox Math Learning and Lexia Core5 Reading represent additional AI applications that claim to enhance children's learning through immediate feedback and adaptive pathways. Yet these systems raise questions about children's right to struggle, explore, and make mistakes as part of authentic learning. These adaptive platforms often prioritize efficiency and measurable progress over the developmental value of uncertainty, collaboration, and creative problem-solving that characterize authentic early childhood learning (Resnick, 2017; Papert, 1980).

When children become accustomed to AI systems that provide immediate answers and corrections, they may lose opportunities to develop persistence, collaborative learning skills, and tolerance for ambiguity that supports both cognitive and moral development (Dweck, 2006; Vygotsky, 1978). This undermines agency development crucial for moral reasoning during the 3-8 age period when children are forming their understanding of their own capacity for ethical decision-making (Kohlberg, 1984).

Marina Umaschi Bers's research demonstrates that young children can engage meaningfully with technology when it supports their natural developmental processes and creativity, emphasizing that technology should serve as a tool for children's own meaning-making rather than directing their thinking (Bers, 2020).

Surveillance Technologies and Developmental Harm

Perhaps most concerning are surveillance technologies that violate children's rights to privacy and autonomous development. ClassDojo's AI-enhanced behavior tracking represents one of the most ethically problematic applications in early childhood settings. This system uses AI to monitor and analyze student behavior patterns, creating detailed profiles of children's social and emotional responses throughout the day. Such comprehensive surveillance violates multiple children's rights simultaneously while directly interfering with essential developmental processes (Zuboff, 2019; Cohen, 2012).

Constant behavioral surveillance can interfere with children's natural social-emotional development, potentially teaching them that their worth depends on compliance with algorithmic expectations rather than developing internal moral reasoning and relationship skills (Lyon, 2007). Children in constantly monitored environments may internalize surveillance as normal, undermining their capacity to develop healthy boundaries and autonomous decision-making abilities essential during critical developmental periods.

Erik Erikson's theory emphasizes that children develop trust and autonomy through experiences that honor their developing capacities while providing appropriate support and guidance (Erikson, 1950). When children are subjected to constant

AI surveillance, they may miss crucial opportunities to develop the internal sense of agency and self-direction that characterizes healthy psychological development (Bandura, 1977).

Implications for Ethical Practice

These current AI applications reveal a troubling pattern: technological implementation in early childhood settings that prioritizes efficiency, data collection, and algorithmic convenience over children's developmental needs and rights. While some AI tools may offer legitimate educational benefits, the examples examined demonstrate how easily AI can undermine the foundations of healthy development—authentic relationships, meaningful struggle, privacy, and cultural dignity—that young children require to flourish.

The urgent need for systematic ethical guidance becomes clear when examining these real-world applications. Teachers, parents, and caregivers are making daily decisions about AI use with limited frameworks for evaluating complex developmental and ethical implications. Commercial pressures and technological novelty often drive implementation decisions, while children's wellbeing becomes secondary. This reality demands comprehensive ethical frameworks that can guide principled decision-making across diverse contexts while maintaining focus on children's development and human flourishing.

The illuminED Framework: A Comprehensive Ethical Response

About the illuminED Framework

The illuminED Framework is a newly proposed comprehensive decision-making model developed through synthesis of extensive research from child development, moral philosophy, and educational ethics. The framework operationalizes ethical principles through nine interconnected pathways, providing practical guidance for teachers, parents, grandparents, childcare providers, and all caregivers to ensure that any AI use serves children's moral development and human flourishing.

Drawing from this extensive research foundation, the illuminED Framework emerges as a comprehensive decision-making model that operationalizes ethical principles through nine interconnected pathways (Dewey, 1897; Noddings, 1984). The framework's central organizing question guides all AI decisions: "Does this AI use serve children's moral development and human flourishing in the current context while building toward better practices?" (Jonas, 1984; Sen, 1999).

Framework Principles and Rights Integration

The illuminED Framework synthesizes insights from all three theoretical approaches while prioritizing children's moral development and human flourishing as the ultimate criteria for ethical decision-making (Noddings, 2002; Nussbaum, 2000). The framework integrates children's fundamental rights as core principles rather than separate considerations:

The **Principle of Developmental Primacy** establishes that children's developmental needs must take precedence over technological capabilities or adult convenience, incorporating children's rights to dignity, holistic development, and protection from harm (United Nations, 1989; NAEYC, 2022; Shonkoff & Phillips, 2000).

The **Principle of Relational Authenticity** recognizes that human relationships remain central to healthy development and moral formation, embodying children's right to human relationships and authentic connection (Bowlby, 1969; Ainsworth et al., 1978; United Nations, 1989).

The **Principle of Transparent Agency** establishes that children have a right to understand the nature of their interactions with technology, appropriate to their developmental level, integrating rights to truth, transparency, and agency (Piaget, 1929; United Nations, 1989).

The **Principle of Cultural Justice** ensures that AI systems honor, support, and amplify the rich cultural and linguistic assets that diverse children bring to learning environments, embodying rights to cultural identity and freedom from discrimination (García & Wei, 2014; United Nations, 1989; Yosso, 2005).

The **Principle of Protective Empowerment** recognizes that adults have heightened responsibilities to protect children from technological harms while simultaneously fostering children's developing agency and participation in technological decisions that affect them (Lansdown, 2005; Jonas, 1984).

The Nine Pathways of Ethical Decision-Making

The **illuminED** framework operates through nine interconnected pathways that must work together to ensure comprehensive ethical evaluation, incorporating professional standards seamlessly throughout rather than as separate considerations.

1. **I**ntentional: Purpose-Driven Implementation This pathway asks whether AI use serves a clear ethical purpose that benefits the child's development as a whole human being (Palmer, 1998; Noddings, 2002). Implementation requires that purpose aligns with the caregiver's developmental understanding and family values, benefits clearly outweigh potential risks for the individual child, alternative non-AI approaches have been considered and are genuinely less appropriate,

and implementation serves children's interests rather than adult convenience or social pressure. This pathway integrates National Association for the Education of Young Children's (NAEYC) emphasis on intentional practice and "careful thinking" for any technology integration (NAEYC, 2022; NAEYC & Fred Rogers Center, 2012).

2. Learning-Centered: Supporting Natural Development This pathway examines whether AI use supports children's natural learning processes and developmental needs (Vygotsky, 1978; Piaget, 1929). The approach requires that AI tools support rather than bypass natural learning processes, align with developmentally appropriate practice principles, preserve opportunities for hands-on multisensory learning, and maintain appropriate challenge levels for individual children. Vygotsky's zone of proximal development provides crucial guidance, emphasizing that optimal learning occurs when children receive support that enables them to accomplish tasks they cannot yet complete independently (Vygotsky, 1978). This pathway incorporates professional standards requiring that technology be "active, hands-on, engaging, and empowering" (NAEYC & Fred Rogers Center, 2012).
3. Learning Relationships: Preserving Human Connection This pathway evaluates whether AI use strengthens rather than weakens the human relationships essential to children's moral and emotional development (Bowlby, 1969; Noddings, 1984). Implementation requires that AI enhance rather than replace teacher-child interaction, facilitate peer collaboration, and support rather than compete with the caring relationships that form the foundation of healthy development. This pathway emphasizes that children need experiences of authentic mutuality and recognition rather than instrumental interactions with technological objects.
4. Understanding-Driven: Developmental Wisdom This pathway asks whether decisions demonstrate deep understanding of child development and respect for children's developmental journey (Shonkoff & Phillips, 2000; Bronfenbrenner, 1979). The approach requires that decision-makers demonstrate child development knowledge, implementation respects individual developmental variation, the precautionary principle is applied when uncertain about impact, and ongoing monitoring of developmental outcomes occurs (Jonas, 1984). Piaget's research on cognitive development provides essential foundations, revealing how children's thinking develops through active interaction with their environment and construction of understanding through experience (Piaget, 1929).
5. Moral Values-Based: Ethical Consistency This pathway recognizes that AI decisions inevitably reflect and teach moral values—either supporting children's development as ethical beings capable of wisdom, compassion, and authentic relationship, or undermining these capacities through convenience, efficiency, or technological novelty (Kohlberg, 1984; Noddings, 1984). Implementation

requires consistency with stated educational philosophy and values about human dignity, respect for children's inherent worth as moral beings, support for children's developing capacity for moral reasoning, and modeling ethical decision-making processes that children can observe and internalize (Bandura, 1977). This pathway integrates professional ethical codes, including NAEYC's foundational commitment to "above all, do no harm" (NAEYC, 2022).

6. **I**nclusive: Equity and Justice This pathway asks whether AI use supports the dignity and potential of all children, regardless of their background or circumstances (Banks, 2015; Gay, 2018). Implementation requires actively addressing bias and promoting equity, supporting cultural and linguistic diversity, ensuring accessibility to children with varying abilities, and reducing rather than amplifying existing inequalities. Gloria Ladson-Billings' work on culturally relevant pedagogy emphasizes that educational approaches must help students "accept and affirm their cultural identity while developing critical perspectives that challenge inequities that schools (and other institutions) perpetuate" (Ladson-Billings, 1995). This pathway incorporates NAEYC's emphasis on inclusion and accessibility as well as professional commitments to advancing equity (NAEYC, 2019).
7. **N**urturing Agency: Protecting and Developing Autonomy This pathway examines whether AI use preserves and develops children's capacity for independent thought, creative expression, and moral decision-making (Bandura, 1977; Deci & Ryan, 1985). The approach requires preserving children's sense of agency and control while providing age-appropriate transparency about AI use. Paulo Freire's critical pedagogy provides essential guidance, emphasizing that education must develop critical consciousness and the capacity for transformative action rather than passive acceptance of existing conditions (Freire, 1970).
8. **E**thical Practice: Professional Standards and Moral Implementation This pathway asks whether AI use reflects the highest standards of professional ethics and moral practice in early childhood education (NAEYC, 2022; Palmer, 1998). Implementation requires alignment with professional codes of ethics, demonstration of commitment to children's wellbeing, modeling ethical technology use for children, and supporting professional growth and reflection. Rather than treating professional standards as separate considerations, this pathway weaves them throughout the evaluation process, ensuring that AI implementation reflects the moral commitments and professional standards that characterize excellent early childhood practice.
9. **D**evelopmentally Appropriate: Alignment with Child Development Principles This pathway examines whether AI use aligns with established principles of developmentally appropriate practice and evidence-based child development research (NAEYC, 2022). The approach requires grounding in current child

development research, respect for individual developmental timelines, support for holistic development across all domains, and alignment with established professional guidelines. NAEYC's principles emphasize that effective early childhood practice must be "grounded in research on how children develop and learn" while being "individually appropriate" and "culturally and linguistically responsive" (NAEYC, 2022).

The illuminED Framework operates as an interconnected system where all nine pathways must work together to ensure comprehensive ethical evaluation. No pathway can be evaluated in isolation—ethical AI implementation requires attention to all dimensions simultaneously. The pathways are designed to complement and reinforce each other, ensuring that ethical AI implementation addresses both immediate practical needs and long-term aspirational goals.

Pathway Interactions and Tensions: The framework anticipates common tensions between pathways that will require careful navigation (Noddings, 1984). For example, the Inclusive pathway's emphasis on accessibility may sometimes conflict with the Understanding-driven pathway's developmental appropriateness requirements. The framework provides guidance for resolving such tensions through stakeholder consultation and prioritizing children's fundamental rights and wellbeing (United Nations, 1989; Lansdown, 2005).

Decision-Making Process: When using the framework, evaluators follow a systematic process: (1) Initial screening using all nine pathways; (2) Detailed assessment of areas showing potential concerns; (3) Stakeholder consultation including families and community members; (4) Implementation with ongoing monitoring; (5) Regular review and adjustment based on observed outcomes (Dewey, 1916; Palmer, 1998). This iterative approach ensures that ethical considerations remain central throughout the implementation process while allowing for adaptation based on real-world experiences and emerging evidence.

Framework Application in Diverse Contexts

Note: The following case studies and examples in this section are illustrative, designed to demonstrate framework application across different contexts. They do not describe actual events at specific institutions or real families.

The illuminED Framework provides systematic guidance for evaluating AI implementation across diverse early childhood contexts. Rather than offering simple approval or rejection of AI tools, the framework supports nuanced decision-making that considers the complex interplay between technology, development, and moral formation.

Classroom Implementation Case Study

Consider the case of Lincoln Elementary School's consideration of implementing an AI-powered reading assessment system for K-2 students (Meisels et al., 2003; Snow et al., 1998). A collaborative framework analysis involves a team including the literacy coach, principal, classroom teachers, special education specialist, and parent representatives, ensuring that decision-making includes multiple perspectives and professional expertise.

Intentional Pathway Analysis: While early literacy support represents a legitimate educational goal, the framework analysis reveals that the primary motivation comes from district pressure for data collection rather than genuine support for children's literacy development. Current observational assessment practices already provide rich information about children's literacy growth, raising questions about whether AI-powered assessment addresses genuine needs or merely replaces more developmentally appropriate practices with technological solutions.

Learning-Centered and Understanding-Driven Pathway Evaluation: Young children's literacy development occurs through rich exposure to language, storytelling, and meaningful print experiences rather than through isolated skill assessment (Snow et al., 1998; Neuman & Dickinson, 2011). The AI system focuses primarily on phonics and word recognition skills while lacking capacity to assess children's comprehension, motivation, or cultural connections to literature. The assessment tool assumes uniform literacy development pathways that conflict with research on individual variation and cultural diversity in literacy learning (García & Wei, 2014). Children from multilingual families and those with different cultural literacy practices may be mischaracterized by algorithmic assessments that cannot account for the complexity of human development.

Learning Relationships and Inclusive Pathway Assessment: Authentic literacy assessment emerges from teachers' deep knowledge of individual children's interests, cultural backgrounds, and developmental needs (Neuman & Dickinson, 2011). The AI system generates standardized reports that may actually interfere with teachers' nuanced understanding of children's literacy development, potentially undermining rather than supporting the responsive relationships essential for effective literacy instruction.

Framework Decision: After comprehensive pathway analysis, the team decides against implementing the AI assessment system. Instead, they invest in professional development for teachers in culturally responsive literacy assessment and enhanced family engagement strategies that honor the linguistic and cultural assets children bring to literacy learning (Gay, 2018; González et al., 2005).

Family and Community Applications

Beyond classroom applications, the framework provides guidance for diverse caregiving contexts, recognizing that children encounter AI across multiple settings with different caregivers who may hold varying values about technology and childhood.

Multigenerational Family Navigation: The Kim Family Case Study Consider the case of three-year-old Emma who lives with her parents and maternal grandmother, who provides daily childcare while parents work (Bronfenbrenner, 1979). Grandmother Kim speaks primarily Korean, parents are bilingual, and Emma is developing in both languages. The family has been using Google Home for convenience but begins questioning its impact on Emma's development.

Intentional and Inclusive Pathway Analysis: The family initially purchased Google Home for practical purposes, but Emma has begun asking the device questions about Korean culture and language, receiving responses that often contradict or oversimplify Grandmother Kim's teachings. Google Home's responses often reflect dominant cultural assumptions and provide inadequate or inaccurate information about Korean culture (Yosso, 2005). When Emma asks about Korean holidays or traditions, the AI responses lack the nuance, personal meaning, and cultural authenticity that Grandmother Kim provides through storytelling and shared experience.

Learning Relationships Pathway Assessment: Most concerning, Emma sometimes chooses to ask Google Home questions instead of engaging with Grandmother Kim, potentially undermining the intergenerational relationships that provide rich learning opportunities and cultural transmission (Bowlby, 1969; Trevarthen, 2001).

Framework Implementation: Through framework-guided reflection, the family develops new practices including scheduled device-free times for Korean storytelling and traditional songs, encouraging Emma to ask Grandmother Kim questions about Korean culture rather than asking AI, and parents modeling critical evaluation of AI responses while demonstrating respect for grandmother's wisdom and cultural knowledge (Henderson & Mapp, 2002; González et al., 2005).

Therapeutic Context: Foster Care Example In therapeutic contexts, the framework provides essential guidance for trauma-informed care. Consider the case of Sarah, a foster parent caring for five-year-old Marcus who has experienced early trauma (Perry & Szalavitz, 2006). Marcus was previously exposed to adult-oriented AI interactions that were inappropriate for his age, creating confusion about privacy and appropriate relationships with technology.

Understanding-Driven and Learning Relationships Pathway Analysis: Marcus's trauma history makes authentic human relationships both more challenging and more essential for his healing and development (Bowlby, 1969). AI interactions, even seemingly benign ones, may interfere with his developing capacity to trust and connect with caring adults. Marcus's previous AI experiences may have taught harmful lessons about privacy, appropriate boundaries, and the nature of caring relationships (Kohlberg, 1984; Noddings, 1984).

Framework Implementation: Sarah works with Marcus's therapist to develop AI guidelines including eliminating voice-activated AI that may remind Marcus of previous inappropriate interactions, using only educational content that Sarah has previewed and can discuss with Marcus, maintaining transparency about how AI works differently from human relationships, and prioritizing human connection for all of Marcus's questions and learning needs.

Building Ethically Grounded AI Communities

Ethical AI use requires coordinated action across families, schools, and communities (Bronfenbrenner, 1979; Putnam, 2000). Individual teachers or parents cannot navigate complex AI ethics in isolation—collective commitment to children's wellbeing and shared standards for ethical practice are essential. The framework provides guidance for building community capacity for ethical AI implementation that serves children's moral development and human flourishing.

From Individual Practice to Community Standards

Building on individual and family applications of the illuminED Framework, effective implementation requires systematic community-wide approaches that coordinate efforts across multiple caregiving contexts. Both educators and caregivers must develop practical ethical courage in AI use—the ability to make ethical decisions about AI within current constraints while building toward ideal practices (Palmer, 1998). This community-building process moves through interconnected levels: professional development for educators, caregiver empowerment for families, institutional policy development, and collaborative networks that span multiple settings.

Professional development programs emerging from framework implementation focus on deepening understanding of child development, cultural responsiveness, and ethical decision-making rather than simply providing technical training about AI tools. This approach ensures that technology decisions are grounded in professional wisdom about children's needs rather than driven by technological capabilities or efficiency concerns. For family caregivers, framework implementation emphasizes building confidence in their existing knowledge about child development and family values while providing practical tools for ethical AI decision-making (Henderson & Mapp, 2002; González et al., 2005). Many caregivers possess deep wisdom about children's needs but lack confidence in applying this wisdom to technological decisions.

Institutional Implementation and Community Infrastructure

At the institutional level, comprehensive framework implementation demonstrates systematic policy development. Consider the example of Riverside School District's use of the illuminED Framework to develop comprehensive AI ethics guidelines. The district's framework implementation begins with extensive professional development ensuring that all decision-makers understand child development principles, cultural responsiveness requirements, and ethical considerations specific to AI use with young children (Gay, 2018). The framework then guides development of family engagement protocols ensuring that parents understand AI use in their children's education and have meaningful opportunities to participate in decisions affecting their children.

This institutional approach extends into broader community infrastructure. Early childhood programs can serve as community hubs for framework education, providing workshops and resources for diverse caregivers including grandparents, childcare providers, and extended family members (Putnam, 2000). Community workshops based on framework pathways help diverse caregivers develop shared language for discussing AI ethics while respecting different cultural values and family structures. These workshops focus on applying framework principles to real-world caregiving situations rather than abstract ethical discussions.

Effective framework implementation requires collaboration between educators, families, and community caregivers who often make independent decisions about AI use yet serve the same children across different contexts. Communities need infrastructure for sharing information about children's AI experiences while respecting family privacy and caregiver autonomy. Framework implementation recognizes caregivers as leaders in protecting children's rights and promoting their development rather than passive recipients of expert guidance (Freire, 1970). Many caregivers possess deep insights about AI's impact on children's wellbeing but lack platforms for sharing this knowledge with others or advocating for policy changes.

Cultural Adaptation and Global Implementation

These community-building efforts must be culturally responsive and locally adapted while maintaining commitment to universal children's rights and developmental principles (United Nations, 1989). Community standards emerging from framework implementation establish shared expectations for ethical AI use while maintaining flexibility for diverse family values and cultural practices (Banks, 2015). These standards focus on protecting children's rights and developmental needs rather than prescribing specific technology choices, allowing communities to maintain ethical consistency while respecting family autonomy.

These cultural adaptations demonstrate how the illuminED Framework's core principles can guide ethical AI implementation across diverse contexts while remaining responsive to local values, resources, and pedagogical traditions. In Scandinavian pedagogical contexts, Nordic countries' emphasis on outdoor education and child agency requires stronger focus on the Nurturing Agency pathway and modified Learning-Centered criteria to preserve nature-based pedagogies. Framework implementation must ensure AI tools support rather than replace outdoor exploration and child-directed learning while respecting cultural values like "allemansrätten" (the right to roam) that prioritize children's connection to the natural world.

Collaboration with Indigenous communities requires significant framework modifications including explicit Indigenous data sovereignty requirements and adaptation of the Learning Relationships pathway to account for extended family and community learning structures (Smith, 1999). Implementation must ensure AI systems never extract traditional knowledge without community consent and that technology strengthens rather than undermines cultural transmission through storytelling and land-based learning (Cajete, 1994). In Global South applications, resource-constrained contexts require modified Inclusive pathway criteria and enhanced cultural appropriateness requirements that account for existing inequalities, multilingual complexity, and economic realities. Framework adaptation must prioritize local language development and cultural preservation over technological efficiency while ensuring AI serves children's wellbeing rather than perpetuating inequalities.

Community networks based on framework principles create opportunities for caregiver leadership in ethical AI advocacy while building collective capacity for principled implementation that honors both universal children's rights and cultural diversity.

Framework Limitations and Future Development

The illuminED Framework represents an initial response to urgent ethical needs in early childhood AI implementation, but requires extensive validation and refinement to realize its full potential. As a newly proposed comprehensive decision-making model, the framework faces several important limitations that must be acknowledged and addressed through systematic research and community engagement.

The most pressing limitation concerns empirical validation. While the framework draws from extensive research on child development, moral philosophy, and educational ethics, it requires systematic research to establish effectiveness across diverse contexts, test inter-rater reliability among evaluators, and measure implementation outcomes in real-world settings. The framework's current complexity may also present barriers for caregivers and educators lacking extensive professional development opportunities, potentially limiting its accessibility and practical application.

Cultural adaptation represents another significant challenge. Although the framework addresses cultural and linguistic justice through dedicated pathways, it needs validation across diverse cultural contexts, particularly Global South and Indigenous settings where different pedagogical traditions may necessitate substantial modifications. The framework's development within Western academic contexts limits immediate applicability without thoughtful cultural adaptation that respects local knowledge systems and values.

The rapid evolution of AI technology creates ongoing challenges for framework relevance. As AI systems advance toward augmented reality, virtual reality, and potentially brain-computer interfaces that may soon appear in early childhood contexts, framework criteria require continuous updating to address emerging ethical considerations. This technological evolution demands flexible framework structures that can adapt to unprecedented AI capabilities while maintaining core ethical commitments.

Perhaps most importantly, the current formulation relies heavily on adult interpretation of children's needs and interests. More research is needed on age-appropriate methods for including children as active participants in AI decision-making while respecting developmental limitations. This represents both an ethical imperative—honoring children's rights to participation—and a practical necessity for creating frameworks that truly serve children's perspectives and experiences.

Future research priorities must address these limitations through comprehensive, community-engaged approaches. Essential research includes mixed-methods studies combining surveys with qualitative interviews to capture educator and caregiver experiences with framework implementation, participatory action research engaging stakeholders as co-researchers in framework refinement, and cross-cultural validation through community-controlled research processes that respect local knowledge and decision-making structures. Comparative case studies documenting successful cultural adaptations while identifying universal principles would strengthen the framework's global applicability while preserving cultural responsiveness.

The framework's future development depends on sustained collaboration between researchers, practitioners, families, and communities committed to children's wellbeing. This collaborative approach must balance the urgency of current ethical needs with the patience required for thoughtful validation and refinement, ensuring that the illuminED Framework evolves to meet the complex challenges of ethical AI implementation in an increasingly digital world.

CONCLUSION: THE MORAL WORK OF OUR TIME

The integration of artificial intelligence in early childhood education is not a future challenge—it is a current reality demanding immediate ethical response. Children are already encountering AI daily through smart speakers in homes, and commercial platforms designed more for engagement than development. The illuminED Framework provides both practical guidance for today's AI interactions and principled foundation for tomorrow's developments, addressing the urgent need for systematic ethical approaches that prioritize children's moral development and human flourishing (Jonas, 1984; Sen, 1999).

The moral urgency cannot be overstated. Every day without ethical guidance for current AI use allows commercial and expedient interests to shape children's understanding of truth, relationship, and moral agency without ethical consideration (Zuboff, 2019). The choice before us is clear: either raising children who can navigate an AI world with wisdom, discernment, and strong moral character—children who understand the irreplaceable value of human connection, the importance of truth over convenience, and the responsibility that comes with technological power—or inadvertently creating a generation vulnerable to manipulation, dependency, and ethical confusion (Turkle, 2011; Postman, 1985).

The children guided today through current AI realities will tomorrow become the guardians of human values in an increasingly AI-integrated world (Kohlberg, 1984; Noddings, 1984). Ensuring they possess not only technological skills but moral wisdom that can discern ethical from unethical AI use, practical experience with ethical AI implementation across diverse contexts, understanding of AI's potential benefits and risks for human flourishing, and unwavering commitment to human dignity and authentic relationship represents the most important moral work of this generation (Turkle, 2011; Jonas, 1984).

The illuminED Framework is not a static checklist but a living approach to ethical decision-making that grows and adapts as understanding deepens and technology evolves (Dewey, 1897). It requires ongoing reflection about children's developmental needs and moral formation, community dialogue that includes diverse perspectives while maintaining commitment to children's fundamental rights, child-centered learning that prioritizes development over efficiency and authentic relationship over technological convenience, professional growth that builds capacity for ethical decision-making across diverse contexts, and advocacy and action that protects children's rights and serves their flourishing through policy development and community organizing (NAEYC, 2022; Livingstone & Third, 2017; Freire, 1970).

This work cannot wait for perfect conditions, complete research, or ideal AI systems. It must begin immediately with AI interactions already happening in children's lives—in classrooms where teachers use AI for planning and instruction, in homes where families navigate smart speakers and AI-powered devices, in communities where commercial AI platforms shape children's experiences and understanding (Cuban, 2013). The work begins now, with the AI interactions happening today, guided by the illuminED Framework's nine pathways and the timeless values of human dignity, developmental wisdom, and moral courage that have always guided those who care for children (Freire, 1970; Montessori, 1912; Dewey, 1897).

Through framework-guided practice that honors children's developmental needs and fundamental rights, ongoing community dialogue that builds collective capacity for ethical decision-making, and unwavering commitment to children's holistic development across cognitive, social, emotional, and moral domains, artificial intelligence can serve humanity's highest aspirations rather than lowest impulses (Jonas, 1984; Sen, 1999). The children in our care deserve nothing less than our best ethical thinking and most courageous moral action in navigating the complex challenges and opportunities of AI integration.

This is the illuminED path forward: practical wisdom for today's realities through the framework's nine pathways that provide systematic guidance for ethical decision-making, principled foundation for tomorrow's possibilities through enduring ethical commitments to human dignity and children's rights, and unwavering commitment to the human flourishing of every child through comprehensive community action that builds collective capacity for ethical AI implementation (Dewey, 1916; Noddings, 1984). The framework provides the structure, the children provide the motivation, and the moment demands immediate action.

The moral work of our time is ensuring that artificial intelligence serves rather than undermines the fundamental values that make us most human: our capacity for authentic relationship, moral reasoning, creative expression, and commitment to the wellbeing of others (Nussbaum, 2000). Through principled implementation of the illuminED Framework, we can move toward this responsibility while helping to build a more just and compassionate world for all children.

REFERENCES

Ainsworth, M. D. S., Blehar, M. C., Waters, E., & Wall, S. (1978). *Patterns of attachment: A psychological study of the strange situation*. Lawrence Erlbaum.

Bandura, A. (1977). *Social learning theory*. Prentice Hall.

Banks, J. A. (2015). *Cultural diversity and education: Foundations, curriculum, and teaching* (6th ed.). Pearson. DOI: 10.4324/9781315622255

Bers, M. U. (2020). *Coding as a playground: Programming and computational thinking in the early childhood classroom*. Routledge. DOI: 10.4324/9781003022602

Bowlby, J. (1969). Attachment and loss: Vol. 1. Attachment. Basic Books.

Breazeal, C. (2002). *Designing sociable robots*. MIT Press. DOI: 10.7551/mitpress/2376.001.0001

Bronfenbrenner, U. (1979). *The ecology of human development: Experiments by nature and design*. Harvard University Press. DOI: 10.4159/9780674028845

Cajete, G. (1994). *Look to the mountain: An ecology of indigenous education*. Kivaki Press.

Caliskan, A., Bryson, J. J., & Narayanan, A. (2017). Semantics derived automatically from language corpora contain human-like biases. *Science*, *356*(6334), 183–186. DOI: 10.1126/science.aal4230 PMID: 28408601

Christakis, D. A. (2009). The effects of infant media usage: What do we know and what should we learn? *Acta Paediatrica (Oslo, Norway)*, *98*(1), 8–16. DOI: 10.1111/j.1651-2227.2008.01027.x PMID: 18793294

Christakis, D. A., Ramirez, J. S. B., & Ramirez, J. M. (2018). Overstimulation of newborn mice leads to behavioral differences and deficits in cognitive performance. *Scientific Reports*, *8*, 546. PMID: 22855702

Cohen, J. E. (2012). Semantic discontinuity in post-privacy society. *Stanford Law Review*, *59*(4), 1904–1933.

Cross, W. E.Jr, & Cross, T. B. (2008). Theory, research, and models. In Quintana, S. M., & McKown, C. (Eds.), *Handbook of race, racism, and the developing child* (pp. 154–181). John Wiley & Sons.

Cuban, L. (2001). *Oversold and underused: Computers in the classroom*. Harvard University Press. DOI: 10.4159/9780674030107

Cuban, L. (2013). *Inside the black box of classroom practice: Change without reform in American education*. Harvard Education Press.

Deci, E. L., & Ryan, R. M. (1985). *Intrinsic motivation and self-determination in human behavior*. Plenum Press. DOI: 10.1007/978-1-4899-2271-7

Dewey, J. (1897). My pedagogic creed. *The School Journal*, *54*(3), 77–80.

Dewey, J. (1916). *Democracy and education: An introduction to the philosophy of education*. Macmillan.

Dweck, C. S. (2006). *Mindset: The new psychology of success*. Random House.

Erikson, E. H. (1950). *Childhood and society*. Norton.

Freire, P. (1970). Pedagogy of the oppressed. *Continuum : an Interdisciplinary Journal on Continuity of Care*.

García, O., & Wei, L. (2014). *Translanguaging: Language, bilingualism and education*. Palgrave Macmillan. DOI: 10.1057/9781137385765

Gay, G. (2018). *Culturally responsive teaching: Theory, research, and practice* (3rd ed.). Teachers College Press.

Gilligan, C. (1982). *In a different voice: Psychological theory and women's development*. Harvard University Press.

González, N., Moll, L. C., & Amanti, C. (Eds.). (2005). *Funds of knowledge: Theorizing practices in households, communities, and classrooms*. Lawrence Erlbaum Associates.

Guernsey, L. (2012). *Screen time: How electronic media—from baby videos to educational software—affects your young child*. Basic Books.

Henderson, A. T., & Mapp, K. L. (2002). *A new wave of evidence: The impact of school, family, and community connections on student achievement*. Southwest Educational Development Laboratory.

Hirsh-Pasek, K., Zosh, J. M., Golinkoff, R. M., Gray, J. H., Robb, M. B., & Kaufman, J. (2015). Putting education in "educational" apps: Lessons from the science of learning. *Psychological Science in the Public Interest*, *16*(1), 3–34. DOI: 10.1177/1529100615569721 PMID: 25985468

Holloway, D., & Green, L. (2016). The internet of toys. *Communication Research and Practice*, *2*(4), 506–519. DOI: 10.1080/22041451.2016.1266124

James, A., & James, A. L. (2004). *Constructing childhood: Theory, policy and social practice*. Palgrave Macmillan. DOI: 10.1007/978-0-230-21427-9

Jonas, H. (1984). *The imperative of responsibility: In search of an ethics for the technological age*. University of Chicago Press. DOI: 10.7208/chicago/9780226850337.001.0001

Kahn, P. H., Kanda, T., Ishiguro, H., Freier, N. G., Severson, R. L., Gill, B. T., Ruckert, J. H., & Shen, S. (2012). "Robovie, you'll have to go into the closet now": Children's social and moral relationships with a humanoid robot. *Developmental Psychology*, *48*(2), 303–314. DOI: 10.1037/a0027033 PMID: 22369338

Kohlberg, L. (1984). *The psychology of moral development: The nature and validity of moral stages*. Harper & Row.

Ladson-Billings, G. (1995). Toward a theory of culturally relevant pedagogy. *American Educational Research Journal*, *32*(3), 465–491. DOI: 10.3102/00028312032003465

Lansdown, G. (2005). *The evolving capacities of the child*. UNICEF Innocenti Research Centre.

Livingstone, S., & Third, A. (2017). Children and young people's rights in the digital age: An emerging agenda. *New Media & Society*, *19*(5), 657–670. DOI: 10.1177/1461444816686318

Lovato, S. B., & Piper, A. M. (2015). "Siri, is this you?": Understanding young children's interactions with voice input systems. In Proceedings of the 14th International Conference on Interaction Design and Children (pp. 335-338).

Lupton, D., & Williamson, B. (2017). The datafied child: The dataveillance of children and implications for their rights. *New Media & Society*, *19*(5), 780–794. DOI: 10.1177/1461444816686328

Lyon, D. (2007). *Surveillance studies: An overview*. Polity Press.

Meisels, S. J., Xue, Y., Bickel, D. D., Nicholson, J., & Atkins-Burnett, S. (2003). Parental reactions to authentic performance assessment. *Educational Assessment*, *9*(1-2), 61–85.

Moll, L. C., Amanti, C., Neff, D., & González, N. (1992). Funds of knowledge for teaching: Using a qualitative approach to connect homes and classrooms. *Theory into Practice*, *31*(2), 132–141. DOI: 10.1080/00405849209543534

Montessori, M. (1912). *The Montessori method. Frederick A.* Stokes Company.

NAEYC. (2019). *Advancing equity in early childhood education: A position statement*. National Association for the Education of Young Children.

NAEYC. (2022). *Developmentally appropriate practice in early childhood programs serving children from birth through age 8* (4th ed.). National Association for the Education of Young Children.

NAEYC & Fred Rogers Center. (2012). *Technology and interactive media as tools in early childhood programs serving children from birth through age 8*. National Association for the Education of Young Children and Fred Rogers Center for Early Learning and Children's Media.

Nelson, C. A.III, Zeanah, C. H., Fox, N. A., Marshall, P. J., Smyke, A. T., & Guthrie, D. (2007). Cognitive recovery in socially deprived young children: The Bucharest Early Intervention Project. *Science*, *318*(5858), 1937–1940. DOI: 10.1126/science.1143921 PMID: 18096809

Neuman, S. B., & Dickinson, D. K. (Eds.). (2011). *Handbook of early literacy research* (Vol. 3). Guilford Press.

Noble, S. U. (2018). *Algorithms of oppression: How search engines reinforce racism*. NYU Press. DOI: 10.18574/nyu/9781479833641.001.0001

Noddings, N. (1984). *Caring: A feminine approach to ethics and moral education*. University of California Press.

Noddings, N. (2002). *Educating moral people: A caring alternative to character education*. Teachers College Press.

Nussbaum, M. C. (2000). *Women and human development: The capabilities approach*. Cambridge University Press. DOI: 10.1017/CBO9780511841286

Palmer, P. J. (1998). *The courage to teach: Exploring the inner landscape of a teacher's life*. Jossey-Bass.

Papert, S. (1980). *Mindstorms: Children, computers, and powerful ideas*. Basic Books.

Perry, B. D., & Szalavitz, M. (2006). *The boy who was raised as a dog: And other stories from a child psychiatrist's notebook*. Basic Books.

Piaget, J. (1929). *The child's conception of the world*. Harcourt, Brace & Company.

Postman, N. (1985). *Amusing ourselves to death: Public discourse in the age of show business*. Penguin Books.

Putnam, R. D. (2000). *Bowling alone: The collapse and revival of American community*. Simon & Schuster.

Radesky, J. S., Schaller, A., Yeo, S., Weeks, H. M., & Christakis, D. (2020). Young children's use of smartphones and tablets. *Pediatrics, 146*(1), e20193518. DOI: 10.1542/peds.2019-3518 PMID: 32482771

Resnick, M. (2017). *Lifelong kindergarten: Cultivating creativity through projects, passion, peers, and play*. MIT Press. DOI: 10.7551/mitpress/11017.001.0001

Selwyn, N. (2021). *Education and technology: Key issues and debates* (3rd ed.). Bloomsbury Academic.

Sen, A. (1999). *Development as freedom*. Oxford University Press.

Shonkoff, J. P., & Phillips, D. A. (Eds.). (2000). *From neurons to neighborhoods: The science of early childhood development*. National Academy Press.

Smith, L. T. (1999). *Decolonizing methodologies: Research and indigenous peoples*. Zed Books.

Snow, C. E., Burns, M. S., & Griffin, P. (Eds.). (1998). *Preventing reading difficulties in young children*. National Academy Press.

Steele, C. M. (1997). A threat in the air: How stereotypes shape intellectual identity and performance. *The American Psychologist, 52*(6), 613–629. DOI: 10.1037/0003-066X.52.6.613 PMID: 9174398

Trevarthen, C. (2001). Intrinsic motives for companionship in understanding: Their origin, development, and significance for infant mental health. *Infant Mental Health Journal, 22*(1-2), 95–131. DOI: 10.1002/1097-0355(200101/04)22:1<95::AID-IMHJ4>3.0.CO;2-6

Turkle, S. (2011). *Alone together: Why we expect more from technology and less from each other*. Basic Books.

United Nations. (1989). *Convention on the Rights of the Child*. UN General Assembly.

van Dijck, J. (2014). Datafication, dataism and dataveillance: Big Data between scientific paradigm and ideology. *Surveillance & Society, 12*(2), 197–208. DOI: 10.24908/ss.v12i2.4776

Vygotsky, L. S. (1978). *Mind in society: The development of higher psychological processes*. Harvard University Press.

Wartella, E., Rideout, V., Lauricella, A. R., & Connell, S. L. (2013). Parenting in the age of digital technology: A national survey. Northwestern University, Center on Media and Human Development.

Yosso, T. J. (2005). Whose culture has capital? A critical race theory discussion of community cultural wealth. *Race, Ethnicity and Education*, *8*(1), 69–91. DOI: 10.1080/1361332052000341006

Zuboff, S. (2019). *The age of surveillance capitalism: The fight for a human future at the new frontier of power*. PublicAffairs.

Compilation of References

Abebe, M. (2024). *Personalizing Scenario-Based Learning Models Using Generative AI: Assessing Impacts on Student Motivation and Information Retention.* Stanford University.

AbuSahyon, A. S. A. E., Alzyoud, A., Alshorman, O., & Al-Absi, B. (2023). AI-driven technology and Chatbots as tools for enhancing English language learning in the context of second language acquisition: A review study. *International Journal of Membrane Science and Technology, 10*(1), 1209–1223. DOI: 10.15379/ijmst.v10i1.2829

Abushariah, H., Ting, H., Mustafa, M. B. P., Khairuddin, A. S. M., Abushariah, A. M., & Tan, T. (2023). Bilingual Automatic Speech Recognition: A Review, *Taxonomy and Open Challenges. IEEE Access : Practical Innovations, Open Solutions, 11*, 5944–5954. DOI: 10.1109/ACCESS.2022.3218684

Acut, D. P., Gamusa, E. V., Pernaa, J., Yuenyong, C., Pantaleon, A. T., Espina, R. C., & Garcia, M. B. (2025). AI Shaming Among Teacher Education Students: A Reflection on Acceptance and Identity in the Age of Generative Tools. In *Pitfalls of AI Integration in Education: Skill Obsolescence, Misuse, and Bias*. IGI Global., DOI: 10.4018/979-8-3373-0122-8.ch005

Acut, D. P., Malabago, N. K., Malicoban, E. V., Galamiton, N. S., & Garcia, M. B. (2025). "ChatGPT 4.0 Ghosted Us While Conducting Literature Search:" Modeling the Chatbot's Generated Non-Existent References Using Regression Analysis. *Internet Reference Services Quarterly, 29*(1), 27–54. DOI: 10.1080/10875301.2024.2426793

Adams, C., Pente, P., Lemermeyer, G., & Rockwell, G. (2023). Ethical principles for artificial intelligence in K-12 education. *Computers & Education, 4*, 1–10. DOI: 10.1016/j.caeai.2023.100131

Ahmad, S. F., Han, H., Alam, M. M., Rehmat, M. K., Irshad, M., Arraño-Muñoz, M., & Ariza-Montes, A. (2023). Impact of Artificial Intelligence on Human Loss in Decision Making, Laziness and Safety in Education. *Humanities & Social Sciences Communications*, *10*(1), 1–14. DOI: 10.1057/s41599-023-01787-8 PMID: 37325188

Ainsworth, M. D. S., Blehar, M. C., Waters, E., & Wall, S. (1978). *Patterns of attachment: A psychological study of the strange situation*. Lawrence Erlbaum.

Akgün, S., & Greenhow, C. (2021). AI in education: Addressing ethical challenges in K-12 settings [Review of AI in education: Addressing ethical challenges in K-12 settings]. *AI and Ethics*, 2(3), 431. Springer Nature. DOI: 10.1007/s43681-021-00096-7

Akinwalere, S., & Ivanov, V. (2022). AI in Higher Education: Challenges and Opportunities. *Border Crossing*, *12*, 1–15. DOI: 10.33182/bc.v12i1.2015

Alam, A., & Mohanty, A. (2023). Educational technology: Exploring the convergence of technology and pedagogy through mobility, interactivity, AI, and learning tools. *Cogent Engineering*, *10*(2), 2283282. DOI: 10.1080/23311916.2023.2283282

Alasgarova, R., & Rzayev, J. (2024). The Role of Artificial Intelligence in Shaping High School Students' Motivation. *International Journal ofTechnology in Education and Science*, *8*(2), 311–324. DOI: 10.46328/ijtes.553

Ali, O., Murray, P. A., Momin, M., Dwivedi, Y. K., & Malik, T. (2024). The Effects of Artificial Intelligence Applications in Educational Settings: Challenges and Strategies. *Technological Forecasting and Social Change*, *199*, 1–18. DOI: 10.1016/j.techfore.2023.123076

Ali, W. (2019). The efficacy of evolving technology in conceptualizing pedagogy and practice in higher education. *Higher Education Studies*, *9*(2), 81–95. DOI: 10.5539/hes.v9n2p81

Almeida, F., & Senapati, B. (2024, March). Striving for Symbiosis: Human-Machine Relations in the AI Era. In *2024 IEEE Integrated STEM Education Conference (ISEC)* (pp. 1-4). IEEE. DOI: 10.1109/ISEC61299.2024.10664823

Al-Sayed, S., Assayed, S. K., Alkhatib, M., & Shaalan, K. (2024). Impact of Artificial Intelligence Chatbots on Student Well-being and Mental Health: A Systematic Review. *People and Behavior Analysis*, *2*(2), 10–31098.

Alzahrani, A. (2022). A systematic review of AI in education in the arab world. *Revista Amazonia Investiga*, *11*(54), 293. DOI: 10.34069/AI/2022.54.06.28

al-Zyoud, H. M. M. (2020). The Role of AI in Teacher Professional Development. In *Universal Journal of Educational Research, 8(11)* (p. 6263). Horizon Research Publishing., DOI: 10.13189/ujer.2020.082265

Annuš, N. (2024). EDUCATIONAL SOFTWARE AND ARTIFICIAL INTELLIGENCE: STUDENTS'EXPERIENCES AND INNOVATIVE SOLUTIONS. *Information Technologies and Learning Tools*, *101*(3), 200–226. DOI: 10.33407/itlt.v101i3.5479

Atenas, J., Havemann, L., & Nerantzi, C. (2025). Critical and Creative Pedagogies for Artificial Intelligence and Data Literacy: An Epistemic Data Justice Approach for Academic Practice. *Research in Learning Technology*, *32*, 1–16. DOI: 10.25304/rlt.v32.3296

Atkinson, R. C., & Shiffrin, R. M. (1968). Human memory: A proposed system and its control processes. In Spence, K. W., & Spence, J. T. (Eds.), *The psychology of learning and motivation: Advances in research and theory* (Vol. II, pp. 89–195).

Attaluri, V., & Mudunuri, L. N. R. (2025). Generative AI for Creative Learning Content Creation: Project-Based Learning and Art Generation. In Smart Education and Sustainable Learning Environments in Smart Cities (pp. 239-252). IGI Global Scientific Publishing.

Aymen, D. I. F., & Zakarya, B. O. U. S. I. O. U. D. (2024). The Influence of Artificial Intelligence on Students' Critical Thinking (Doctoral dissertation, university center of abdalhafid boussouf-MILA).

Baillifard, A., Gabella, M., Lavenex, P. B., & Martarelli, C. S. (2023). Implementing

Bandura, A. (1977). *Social learning theory*. Prentice-Hall.

Banks, J. A. (2015). *Cultural diversity and education: Foundations, curriculum, and teaching* (6th ed.). Pearson. DOI: 10.4324/9781315622255

Barbosa Neves, B., Franz, R., Judges, R., Beermann, C., & Baecker, R. (2019). Can digital technology enhance social connectedness among older adults? A feasibility study. *Journal of Applied Gerontology*, *38*(1), 49–72. DOI: 10.1177/0733464817741369 PMID: 29166818

Ben-Bassat, M. (2018). AIQ: Measuring Intelligence of Business AI Software. In arXiv (Cornell University). Cornell University. https://doi.org//arxiv.1808.03454DOI: 10.48550

Bender, T. (2023). *Discussion-based online teaching to enhance student learning: Theory, practice and assessment*. Taylor & Francis.

Bers, M. U. (2020). *Coding as a playground: Programming and computational thinking in the early childhood classroom*. Routledge. DOI: 10.4324/9781003022602

Bhatia, A., Bhatia, P., & Sood, D. (2024). Leveraging AI to transform online higher education: Focusing on personalized learning, assessment, and student engagement. International Journal of Management and Humanities (IJMH) Volume-11 Issue-1.

Bianchi, I. (2024). Enhancing Critical Thinking in Education: Leveraging AI Tools and Technologies in Pedagogical Practice.

Bilousova, L., Kolgatina, L., & Kolgatin, O. (2023). How can we encourage students to manage their own learning? *Ukrainian Journal of Educational Studies and Information Technology*, *11*(1), 55–65. DOI: 10.32919/uesit.2023.01.05

Bilquise, G., Ibrahim, S., & Shaalan, K. (2022). Emotionally Intelligent Chatbots: A Systematic Literature Review. *Human Behavior and Emerging Technologies*, *2022*(1), 9601630. DOI: 10.1155/2022/9601630

Bodrova, E., & Leong, D. J. (2015). Vygotskian and post-Vygotskian views on children's play. *American Journal of Play*, *7*(3), 371–388.

Bösl, D. B. O., & Achtenberg, T. (2024, 6-8 Nov. 2024). Lifelong Learning Companion: Development Milestones in an AI-Based, Cross-Platform Companion App for Lifelong Learning Optimization 2024 21st International Conference on Information Technology Based Higher Education and Training (ITHET)

Bowlby, J. (1969). Attachment and loss: Vol. 1. Attachment. Basic Books.

Bozkurt, A., Xiao, J., Farrow, R., Bai, J. Y. H., Nerantzi, C., Moore, S., & Asino, T. I. (2024). The Manifesto for Teaching and Learning in a Time of Generative AI: A Critical Collective Stance to Better Navigate the Future. *Open Praxis*, *16*(4), 487–513. DOI: 10.55982/openpraxis.16.4.777

Breazeal, C. (2002). *Designing sociable robots*. MIT Press. DOI: 10.7551/mitpress/2376.001.0001

Bronfenbrenner, U. (1979). *The ecology of human development: Experiments by nature and design*. Harvard University Press. DOI: 10.4159/9780674028845

Brożek, B., Furman, M., Jakubiec, M., & Kucharzyk, B. (2024). The black box problem revisited. Real and imaginary challenges for automated legal decision making. *Artificial Intelligence and Law*, *32*(2), 427–440. DOI: 10.1007/s10506-023-09356-9

Bruggeman, B., Tondeur, J., Struyven, K., Pynoo, B., Garone, A., & Vanslambrouck, S. (2021). Experts speaking: Crucial teacher attributes for implementing blended learning in higher education. *The Internet and Higher Education*, *48*, 100772. DOI: 10.1016/j.iheduc.2020.100772

Brundage, M. (2015). Modeling Progress in AI. In arXiv (Cornell University). Cornell University. https://doi.org/DOI: 10.48550/arXiv.1512

Bruner, J. (1983). Play, Thought, and Language. *Peabody Journal of Education*, *60*(3), 60–69. https://www.jstor.org/stable/1492180. DOI: 10.1080/01619568309538407

Bulathwela, S., Pérez-Ortiz, M., Holloway, C., Cukurova, M., & Shawe-Taylor, J. (2024). Artificial Intelligence Alone Will Not Democratise Education: On Educational Inequality, Techno-Solutionism and Inclusive Tools. *Sustainability (Basel)*, *16*(2), 1–20. DOI: 10.3390/su16020781

Bulger, M., McCormick, P., & Pitcan, M. (2017). The legacy of inBloom: Data, privacy, and the public interest in education. *International Journal of Communication*, *11*, 1579–1600.

Burnell, R., Schellaert, W., Burden, J., Ullman, T., Martínez-Plumed, F., Tenenbaum, J. B., Rutar, D., Cheke, L. G., Sohl-Dickstein, J., Mitchell, M., Kiela, D., Shanahan, M., Voorhees, E. M., Cohn, A. G., Leibo, J. Z., & Hernández-Orallo, J. (2023). *Rethink reporting of evaluation results in AI*. In Science (Vol. 380, Issue 6641, p. 136). American Association for the Advancement of Science. DOI: 10.1126/science.adf6369

Cabrera, U., Vilca, J., Oliva, E., García, K., Rojas, R., Casaverde, M., & Colonia, C. U. (2024). *Artificial Intelligence in the Ethics of Education*. EMC. DOI: 10.70288/emc.9789915970646

Cajete, G. (1994). *Look to the mountain: An ecology of indigenous education*. Kivaki Press.

Caliskan, A., Bryson, J. J., & Narayanan, A. (2017). Semantics derived automatically from language corpora contain human-like biases. *Science*, *356*(6334), 183–186. DOI: 10.1126/science.aal4230 PMID: 28408601

Carstens, A., Mallon, B., Bataineh, M., & Al-Bataineh, A. (2021). Effects of technology on student learning. *International Journal of Education and Practice*, *9*(1), 80–92. https://files.eric.ed.gov/fulltext/EJ1290791.pdf

Carvalho, A. R., & Santos, C. (2022). Developing peer mentors' collaborative and metacognitive skills with a technology-enhanced peer learning program. *Computers and Education Open*, *3*, 100070. DOI: 10.1016/j.caeo.2021.100070

Center for Parent Information and Resources. (2021). “Parental Consent in Special Education”. Retrieved on March 4, 2025, from https://www.parentcenterhub.org/consent/?form=MG0AV3

Chang, D. H., Lin, M. P. C., Hajian, S., & Wang, Q. Q. (2023). Educational design principles of using AI chatbot that supports self-regulated learning in education: Goal setting, feedback, and personalization. *Sustainability (Basel)*, *15*(17), 12921. DOI: 10.3390/su151712921

Chapman, J., & Rich, P. (2018). Does educational gamification improve students' motivation? If so, which game elements work best? *Journal of Education for Business*, *93*(7), 315–322. DOI: 10.1080/08832323.2018.1490687

Chassignol, M., & Mikalef, P. (2021). Artificial Intelligence in Education: A Systematic Review and Future Research Directions. *Journal of Educational Technology & Society*, *24*(1), 18–32.

Chew, H. S. J. (2022). The use of artificial intelligence–based conversational agents (Chatbots) for weight loss: Scoping review and practical recommendations. *JMIR Medical Informatics*, *10*(4), e32578. DOI: 10.2196/32578 PMID: 35416791

Childers, E. A. (2018). Effects of class scheduling and student achievement on state testing (Doctoral dissertation, Walden University).

Christakis, D. A. (2009). The effects of infant media usage: What do we know and what should we learn? *Acta Paediatrica (Oslo, Norway)*, *98*(1), 8–16. DOI: 10.1111/j.1651-2227.2008.01027.x PMID: 18793294

Christakis, D. A., Ramirez, J. S. B., & Ramirez, J. M. (2018). Overstimulation of newborn mice leads to behavioral differences and deficits in cognitive performance. *Scientific Reports*, *8*, 546. PMID: 22855702

Cierniak, G., Scheiter, K., & Gerjets, P. (2009). Explaining the split-attention effect: Is the reduction of extraneous cognitive load accompanied by an increase in germane cognitive load? *Computers in Human Behavior*, *25*(2), 315–324. DOI: 10.1016/j.chb.2008.12.020

Clemens, J. (2025). How can ethical leadership influence school culture? Retrieved on March 4, 2025, from https://my.chartered.college/impact_article/how-can-ethical-leadership-influence-school-culture-a-reflection-on-my-leadership-journey-so-far/?form=MG0AV3.

Cohen, J. E. (2012). Semantic discontinuity in post-privacy society. *Stanford Law Review*, *59*(4), 1904–1933.

Collins, A., & Halverson, R. (2018). *Rethinking education in the age of technology: The digital revolution and schooling in America*. Teachers College Press.

Commission, E., Centre, J. R., Tuomi, I., Punie, Y., Vuorikari, R., & Cabrera, M. (2018). *The impact of Artificial Intelligence on learning, teaching, and education* (Punie, Y., Vuorikari, R., & Cabrera, M., Eds.). Publications Office.

Cooper, G. (2023). Examining Science Education in ChatGPT: An exploratory study of generative artificial intelligence. *Journal of Science Education and Technology*, *32*(3), 444–452. Advance online publication. DOI: 10.1007/s10956-023-10039-y

Council for Exceptional Children. (2015). What every special educator must know: Professional ethics and standards (7th ed.). Arlington, VA: CEC. https://exceptionalchildren.org/sites/default/files/2020-07/Code%20of%20Ethics.pdf

Crittenden, W. F., Biel, I. K., & Lovely, W. A.III. (2019). Embracing digitalization: Student learning and new technologies. *Journal of Marketing Education*, *41*(1), 5–14. DOI: 10.1177/0273475318820895

Cross, W. E.Jr, & Cross, T. B. (2008). Theory, research, and models. In Quintana, S. M., & McKown, C. (Eds.), *Handbook of race, racism, and the developing child* (pp. 154–181). John Wiley & Sons.

Cuban, L. (2001). *Oversold and underused: Computers in the classroom*. Harvard University Press. DOI: 10.4159/9780674030107

Cuban, L. (2013). *Inside the black box of classroom practice: Change without reform in American education*. Harvard Education Press.

Darling-Hammond, L. (2000). Teacher quality and student achievement. *Education Policy Analysis Archives*, *8*(1), 1–44. DOI: 10.14507/epaa.v8n1.2000

Darvishi, A., Khosravi, H., Sadiq, S., Gašević, D., & Siemens, G. (2023). Impact of AI assistance on student agency. In *Computers & Education* (Vol. 210, p. 104967). Elsevier BV., DOI: 10.1016/j.compedu.2023.104967

Deci, E. L., & Ryan, R. M. (1985). *Intrinsic motivation and self-determination in human behavior*. Plenum Press. DOI: 10.1007/978-1-4899-2271-7

Demartini, C. G., Sciascia, L., Bosso, A., & Manuri, F. (2024). Artificial intelligence bringing improvements to adaptive learning in education: A case study. *Sustainability (Basel)*, *16*(3), 1347. DOI: 10.3390/su16031347

Dewey, J. (1897). My pedagogic creed. *The School Journal*, *54*(3), 77–80.

Dewey, J. (1916). *Democracy and education: An introduction to the philosophy of education*. Macmillan.

Díaz, B., & Nussbaum, M. (2024). Artificial Intelligence for Teaching and Learning in Schools: The Need for Pedagogical Intelligence. *Computers &amp. Computers & Education, 217*, 1–19. DOI: 10.1016/j.compedu.2024.105071

Diaz, F. C. B., Trinidad, I., Agustin, M. J., Panganiban, T. P., & García, M. B. (2025). Mindfulness for Health and Well Being: An Innovative Physical Education Course in the University of the Philippines Diliman. In Garcia, M. B. (Ed.), *Global Innovations in Physical Education and Health* (pp. 139–168). IGI Global., DOI: 10.4018/979-8-3693-3952-7.ch006

Diliberti, M. K., Schwartz, H. L., Doan, S., Shapiro, A., Rainey, L. R., & Lake, R. J. (2024). Using Artificial Intelligence Tools in K–12 Classrooms. RAND Corporation. https://www.rand.org/pubs/research_reports/RRA956-21.html

Dinnar, S. M., Dede, C., Johnson, E., Straub, C., & Korjus, K. (2021). Artificial intelligence and technology in teaching negotiation. *Negotiation Journal, 37*(1), 65–82. DOI: 10.1111/nejo.12351

Division for Early Childhood. (2022). Position statement on ethical practice. Council for Exceptional Children. https://divisionearlychildhood.egnyte.com/dl/KAh4cOFBZ8

Dweck, C. S. (2006). *Mindset: The new psychology of success*. Random House.

Dwivedi, Y. K., ... Opinion Paper: "So what if ChatGPT wrote it?" Multidisciplinary perspectives on opportunities, challenges and implications of generative conversational AI for research, practice and policy, International Journal of Information Management, Volume 71, 2023, 102642,ISSN 0268-4012, https://doi.org/DOI: 10.1016/j.ijinfomgt.2023.10264

Education Advanced. (May 11, 2023). "Transparency in Education: What Schools Need to Know" Retrieved on March 4, 2025, from https://www.educationadvanced.com/blog/transparency-in-education-what-schools-need-to-know?form=MG0AV3

Eisenmann, C., Mlynář, J., Turowetz, J., & Rawls, A. W. (2023). "Machine Down": Making Sense of Human–Computer Interaction—Garfinkel's Research on ELIZA and LYRIC from 1967 to 1969 and Its Contemporary Relevance. *AI & Society, 39*(6), 2715–2733. DOI: 10.1007/s00146-023-01793-z

Elkind, D. (2007). *The power of play: How spontaneous imaginative activities lead to happier, healthier children*. Da Capo Press.

Erikson, E. H. (1950). *Childhood and society*. Norton.

Escobar, A. (2013). *The home language advantage: Using children's primary language to build literacy skills*. English Language Learning ReSource. https://inside.isb.ac.th/nativelanguage/files/2016/03/home-language-advantage.pdf

Evanick, J. (2023). *Data Privacy In EdTech: Ethical Dilemmas And Safeguards*. eLearning Industry. Retrieved from https://elearningindustry.com/ethical-dilemmas-in-student-data-privacy-navigating-edtech-safeguards

Excellence, A. (2024). The Role of Ethical Leadership in Shaping Public Policy. Retrieved on March 4, 2025, from https://www.advisoryexcellence.com/the-role-of-ethical-leadership-in-shaping-public-policy/?form=MG0AV3

Fahimirad, M., & Kotamjani, S. S. (2018). A Review on Application of AI in Teaching and Learning in Educational Contexts [Review of A Review on Application of AI in Teaching and Learning in Educational Contexts]. *International Journal of Learning and Development*, *8*(4), 106. DOI: 10.5296/ijld.v8i4.14057

Fakhar, H., Lamrabet, M., Echantoufi, N., & Ajana, L. (2024). Towards a New Artificial Intelligence-based Framework for Teachers' Online Continuous Professional Development Programs: Systematic Review. *International Journal of Advanced Computer Science and Applications*, *15*(4). Advance online publication. DOI: 10.14569/IJACSA.2024.0150450

Farahani, M., & Ghasemi, G. (2024). Artificial intelligence and inequality: Challenges and opportunities. *Int. J. Innov. Educ*, *9*, 78–99.

Fitria, T. N. (2023). The use of artificial intelligence in education (AIED): Can AI replace the teacher's role? *Epigram*, *20*(2), 165–187. DOI: 10.32722/epi.v20i2.5711

Floridi, L., & Cowls, J. (2019). A unified framework of five principles for AI in society. *Harvard Data Science Review*, *1*(1). Advance online publication. DOI: 10.1162/99608f92.8cd550d1

Forsberg, E., Geschwind, L., Levander, S., & Wermke, W. (2022). *Peer review in an era of evaluation: understanding the practice of gatekeeping in academia*. Springer Nature. DOI: 10.1007/978-3-030-75263-7

Freire, P. (1970). Pedagogy of the oppressed. *Continuum : an Interdisciplinary Journal on Continuity of Care*.

Freire, P. (2007). Pedagogy of the Heart. *Continuum*.

Garcia, A. (2023). "Technology Might be Making Education Worse". Stanford Report. Retrieved on February 19, 2025, from https://news.stanford.edu/stories/2023/04/technology-might-be-making-education-worse

Garcia, M. B., Arif, Y. M., Khlaif, Z. N., Zhu, M., de Almeida, R. P. P., de Almeida, R. S., & Masters, K. (2024). Effective Integration of Artificial Intelligence in Medical Education: Practical Tips and Actionable Insights. In *Transformative Approaches to Patient Literacy and Healthcare Innovation* (pp. 1-19). IGI Global. DOI: 10.4018/979-8-3693-3661-8.ch001

Garcia, M. B., Goi, C.-L., Shively, K., Maher, D., Rosak-Szyrocka, J., Happonen, A., . . . Damaševičius, R. (2025). Understanding Student Engagement in AI-Powered Online Learning Platforms: A Narrative Review of Key Theories and Models. In *Cases on Enhancing P-16 Student Engagement With Digital Technologies* (pp. 1-30). IGI Global. DOI: 10.2139/ssrn.5074608

Garcia, M. B. (2023). Can ChatGPT Substitute Human Companionship for Coping with Loss and Trauma? *Journal of Loss and Trauma*, *28*(8), 784–786. DOI: 10.1080/15325024.2023.2240697

Garcia, M. B. (2024). The Paradox of Artificial Creativity: Challenges and Opportunities of Generative AI Artistry. *Creativity Research Journal*, •••, 1–14. DOI: 10.1080/10400419.2024.2354622

Garcia, M. B. (2025). Teachers in the Metaverse: The Influence of Avatar Appearance and Behavioral Realism on Perceptions of Instructor Credibility and Teaching Effectiveness. *Interactive Learning Environments*, •••, 1–17. DOI: 10.1080/10494820.2025.2462144

García, O., & Wei, L. (2014). *Translanguaging: Language, bilingualism and education*. Palgrave Macmillan. DOI: 10.1057/9781137385765

Gardner, H. (1985). *The Mind's New Science: A History of Cognitive Revolution*. Basic Books.

Gaslin, W. (1975). A Comparison of Achievement and Attitudes of Students Using Conventional or Calculator-based Algorithms for Operations on Positive Rational Numbers in Ninth-Grade General Mathematics. *Journal for Research in Mathematics Education*, *6*(2), 95–108. DOI: 10.2307/748611

Gayatri, M., & Pau, N. (2022). Teacher reflective perceptions on artificial intelligence integrated science lesson plans. *The Educational Beacon*, *11*, 12–23.

Gay, G. (2018). *Culturally responsive teaching: Theory, research, and practice* (3rd ed.). Teachers College Press.

Gentile, M., Città, G., Perna, S., & Allegra, M. (2023). Do We Still Need Teachers? Navigating the Paradigm Shift of the Teacher's Role in the AI Era. *Frontiers in Education*, *8*, 1–14. DOI: 10.3389/feduc.2023.1161777

Gesell, A. (1925). *The mental growth of the pre-school child: A psychological outline of normal development from birth to the sixth year, including a system of development diagnosis*. Macmillan.

Giang, I. T. N., & Park, M. (2022). *Dual language learners: Key characteristics and considerations for early childhood programs*. https://www.migrationpolicy.org/research/dual-language-learner-characteristics

Gibson, D., Kovanovic, V., Ifenthaler, D., Dexter, S., & Feng, S. (2023). Learning theories for artificial intelligence promoting learning processes. *British Journal of Educational Technology*, *54*(5), 1125–1146. DOI: 10.1111/bjet.13341

Gilligan, C. (1982). *In a different voice: Psychological theory and women's development*. Harvard University Press.

Giri, A. (2025). Revolutionizing Student Evaluation: The Power of AI-Powered Assessment. In Improving Student Assessment With Emerging AI Tools (pp. 333-362). IGI Global Scientific Publishing.

Gkintoni, E., Antonopoulou, H., Sortwell, A., & Halkiopoulos, C. (2025). Challenging Cognitive Load Theory: The Role of Educational Neuroscience and Artificial Intelligence in Redefining Learning Efficacy. *Brain Sciences*, *15*(2), 203. DOI: 10.3390/brainsci15020203 PMID: 40002535

Gligorea, I., Cioca, M., Oancea, R., Gorski, A. T., Gorski, H., & Tudorache, P. (2023). Adaptive learning using artificial intelligence in e-learning: A literature review. *Education Sciences*, *13*(12), 1216. DOI: 10.3390/educsci13121216

Gobert, J. D., Sao Pedro, M. A., Li, H., & Lott, C. (2023). *Intelligent Tutoring Systems: A History and an Example of an ITS for Science*. Grantee Submission.

Goel, A. (2020). AI-powered learning: making education accessible, affordable, and achievable. arXiv preprint arXiv:2006.01908.

Göldağ, B. (2022). An investigation of the relationship between university students' digital burnout levels and perceived stress levels. *Journal of Learning and Teaching in Digital Age*, *7*(1), 90–98. DOI: 10.53850/joltida.958039

Gonçalves, B. (2020). Machines will think: structure and interpretation of Alan Turing's imitation game.

González, N., Moll, L. C., & Amanti, C. (Eds.). (2005). *Funds of knowledge: Theorizing practices in households, communities, and classrooms*. Lawrence Erlbaum Associates.

Grant, L., & Kinman, G. (2014). Emotional Resilience in the Helping Professions and How It Can Be Enhanced. *Health and Social Care Education*, *3*(1), 23–34. DOI: 10.11120/hsce.2014.00040

Grosso, D. P., Bowling, M. R., Chun, S. S., & Delaney, B. M. (2024). *The Development of AI and Protecting Student Data Privacy*. National Law Review. Retrieved on March 4, 2025, from https://natlawreview.com/article/development-ai-and-protecting-student-data-privacy

Guddemi, M., Sambrook, A., Wells, S., Randel, B., Fite, K., Selva, G., & Gagnon, K. (2014). Arnold Gesell's developmental assessment revalidation substantiates child-oriented curriculum. *SAGE Open*, *4*(2), 2158244014528918. Advance online publication. DOI: 10.1177/2158244014528918

Guernsey, L. (2012). *Screen time: How electronic media—from baby videos to educational software—affects your young child*. Basic Books.

Guo, W., Zhao, X., Lee, P. G., & Ke, L. (2024). Bridging Heart and Mind: Exploring Emotional Intelligence among Undergraduates in the Age of Artificial Intelligence. *Environment-Behaviour Proceedings Journal*, *9*(29), 13–20. DOI: 10.21834/e-bpj.v9i29.6009

Gupta, D. P., Sreelatha, D. C., Latha, A., Raj, D. S., & Singh, D. A. (2024). Navigating The Future Of Education: The Impact Of Artificial Intelligence On Teacher-Student Dynamics. *Educational Administration: Theory and Practice*, 6006-6013. DOI: 10.53555/kuey.v30i4.2332

Habib, H., Jelani, S. A. K., & Najla, S. (2022). Revolutionizing Inclusion: AI in Adaptive Learning for Students with Disabilities. *Multidisciplinary Science Journal*, *1*(01), 1–11.

Hamilton, B. (2022). *Integrating technology in the classroom: Tools to meet the needs of every student*. International Society for Technology in Education.

Hardman, D. P. (2024, October 31). AI Tutors Double Rates of Learning in Less Learning Time [Substack newsletter]. Dr Phil's Newsletter, Powered by DOMSTM AI. https://drphilippahardman.substack.com/p/ai-tutors-double-rates-of-learning

Harvard, D. C. E. (2025). What is Ethical Leadership and Why is it Important? Retrieved on March 4, 2025 https://professional.dce.harvard.edu/blog/what-is-ethical-leadership-and-why-is-it-important/?form=MG0AV3

Haugeland, J., Craver, C. F., & Klein, C. (Eds.). (2023). *Mind Design III: Philosophy, Psychology, and Artificial Intelligence*. MIT press.

Henderson, A. T., & Mapp, K. L. (2002). *A new wave of evidence: The impact of school, family, and community connections on student achievement*. Southwest Educational Development Laboratory.

Hirsh-Pasek, K., Zosh, J. M., Golinkoff, R. M., Gray, J. H., Robb, M. B., & Kaufman, J. (2015). Putting education in "educational" apps: Lessons from the science of learning. *Psychological Science in the Public Interest*, *16*(1), 3–34. DOI: 10.1177/1529100615569721 PMID: 25985468

Holloway, D., & Green, L. (2016). The internet of toys. *Communication Research and Practice*, *2*(4), 506–519. DOI: 10.1080/22041451.2016.1266124

Holloway, J., & Brass, J. (2018). Making accountable teachers: The terrors and pleasures of performativity. *Journal of Education Policy*, *33*(3), 361–382. DOI: 10.1080/02680939.2017.1372636

Holmes, W., Bialik, M., & Fadel, C. (2019). *Artificial Intelligence in Education*. The MIT Press.

Hooda, M., Rana, C., Dahiya, O., Rizwan, A., & Hossain, M. S. (2022). Artificial intelligence for assessment and feedback to enhance student success in higher education. *Mathematical Problems in Engineering*, *2022*(1), 5215722. DOI: 10.1155/2022/5215722

How Artificial Intelligence is Transforming Grading in 2025 | Blog. (n.d.). Retrieved March 6, 2025, from https://www.codiste.com

Hsu, A., & Chaudhary, D. (2023). AI4PCR: Artificial intelligence for practicing conflict resolution. *Computers in Human Behavior: Artificial Humans*, *1*(1), 1–11. DOI: 10.1016/j.chbah.2023.100002

Huang, A. Y., Lu, O. H., & Yang, S. J. (2023). Effects of artificial Intelligence–Enabled personalized recommendations on learners' learning engagement, motivation, and outcomes in a flipped classroom. *Computers & Education*, *194*, 104684. DOI: 10.1016/j.compedu.2022.104684

Huang, R., Tlili, A., Xu, L., Chen, Y., Zheng, L., Metwally, A. H. S., & Bonk, C. J. (2023). Educational Futures of Intelligent Synergies Between Humans, Digital Twins, Avatars, and Robots-The iSTAR Framework. *Journal of Applied Learning & Teaching*, *6*(2), 28–43.

Idaho Department of Health and Welfare. (2021a). *About Idaho Early Learning eGuidelines*. Idaho Early Learning eGuidelines. https://healthandwelfare.idaho.gov/services- programs/about-idaho-early-learning-eguidelines

Idaho Department of Health and Welfare. (2021b). *Sub-domain: Motor development*. Idaho Early Learning eGuidelines. https://healthandwelfare.idaho.gov/services-programs/sub-domain-motor-development

Indellicato, R. (2024). Artificial Intelligence and Social-Emotional Learning: What relationship? *Journal of Modern Science*, *60*(6), 460–470. DOI: 10.13166/jms/196765

Individuals with Disabilities Act. "Parental Consent". §300.300 (2006). Retrieved on March 4, 2025, from https://sites.ed.gov/idea/regs/b/d/300.300?form=MG0AV3

Izzat Ruslim, M., & Khalid, F. (2024). The Use of Artificial Intelligence in Differentiated Instruction Classrooms. *International Journal of Academic Research in Business & Social Sciences*, *14*(8), 680–695. DOI: 10.6007/IJARBSS/v14-i8/22435

Jacob, N. (2018). Vulnerability as a Pedagogical Practice. Writing as a Way of Staying Human in a Time that Isn't, 103.

Jamaluddin, N. S., & Mokhtar, M. (2025). Teaching Empathy: How AI Can Support the Development of Soft Skills in Education. *International Journal of Academic Research in Business & Social Sciences*, *15*(3), 704–713. DOI: 10.6007/IJARBSS/v15-i3/24469

James, A., & James, A. L. (2004). *Constructing childhood: Theory, policy and social practice*. Palgrave Macmillan. DOI: 10.1007/978-0-230-21427-9

Jamieson, D. (2020). Towards an Ethics of Hybrid Agency in Performance. *Performance Research*, *25*(4), 7–16. DOI: 10.1080/13528165.2020.1842023

Jarson, J. (2023). Mapping Unfamiliar Territory: Using Guided Reading Charts to Navigate Sources.

Jian, M. J. K. O. (2023). Personalized Learning Through AI. *Advances in Engineering Innovation*, *5*(1), 16–19. DOI: 10.54254/2977-3903/5/2023039

Johnson, R. (2024). AI Eases Our Mental Load at the Expense of Critical Thinking. *Psychology Today*.

Jonas, H. (1984). *The imperative of responsibility: In search of an ethics for the technological age*. University of Chicago Press. DOI: 10.7208/chicago/9780226850337.001.0001

Kahn, P. H., Kanda, T., Ishiguro, H., Freier, N. G., Severson, R. L., Gill, B. T., Ruckert, J. H., & Shen, S. (2012). "Robovie, you'll have to go into the closet now": Children's social and moral relationships with a humanoid robot. *Developmental Psychology*, *48*(2), 303–314. DOI: 10.1037/a0027033 PMID: 22369338

Kamalov, F., Calonge, D. S., & Gurrib, I. (2023). New Era of AI in Education: Towards a Sustainable Multifaceted Revolution. In Sustainability (Vol. 15, Issue 16, p. 12451). Multidisciplinary Digital Publishing Institute. DOI: 10.3390/su151612451

Kanders, K., Stupple-Harris, L., Smith, L., & Gibson, J. L. (2024). Perspectives on the impact of generative AI on early-childhood development and education. *Infant and Child Development*, *33*(4), e2514. DOI: 10.1002/icd.2514

Kaswan, K. S., Dhatterwal, J. S., & Ojha, R. P. (2024). AI in personalized learning. In *Advances in technological innovations in higher education* (pp. 103–117). CRC Press. DOI: 10.1201/9781003376699-9

Kaufman, J., Woo, A., Eagan, J., Lee, S., & Kassan, E. (2025). Uneven Adoption of Artificial Intelligence Tools Among U.S. Teachers and Principals in the 2023–2024 School Year. RAND Corporation. https://www.rand.org/pubs/research_reports/RRA134-25.html

Kayyali, M. (2024a). Global Perspectives on Personalized Learning: Case Studies and Best Practices. In Transforming Education for Personalized Learning (pp. 66-84). IGI Global.

Kayyali, M. (2024b). Crisis Response and Higher Education: Social Innovations in Times of Global Challenges. In Social Innovations in Education, Environment, and Healthcare (pp. 1-17). IGI Global.

Kayyali, M. (2025a). Ethical Considerations in Higher Education: Accountability Navigating Complexities. In Accountability in Higher Education: Navigating Current Issues and Trends (pp. 145-184). IGI Global Scientific Publishing.

Kayyali, M. (2025b). AI in Higher Education: Revolutionizing Curriculum and Administration. In AI Adoption and Diffusion in Education (pp. 31-62). IGI Global Scientific Publishing.

Kayyali, M. (2025b). E-Learning Platforms and Their Influence on Lifelong Learning. In Impact of Digitalization on Education and Social Sustainability (pp. 155-176). IGI Global.

Kayyali, M. (2025c). AI in Higher Education: Revolutionizing Curriculum and Administration. In AI Adoption and Diffusion in Education (pp. 31-62). IGI Global Scientific Publishing.

Kayyali, M. (2025c). The Future of AI in Education: Predictions and Emerging Trends. Next-Generation AI Methodologies in Education, 367-406.

Kayyali, M. (2025d). The Future of AI in Education: Predictions and Emerging Trends. Next-Generation AI Methodologies in Education, 367-406.

Kayyali, M. (2025e). Harnessing AI for Digital Entrepreneurship: Strategies and Best Practices. In Improving Entrepreneurial Processes Through Advanced AI (pp. 1-20). IGI Global.

Kayyali, M. (2024c). Future possibilities and challenges of AI in education. In *Transforming education with generative AI: Prompt engineering and synthetic content creation* (pp. 118–137). IGI Global Scientific Publishing. DOI: 10.4018/979-8-3693-1351-0.ch006

Kayyali, M. (2025a). The Impact of Personalized Learning on Student Engagement and Achievement in STEAM. In *Integrating Personalized Learning Methods Into STEAM Education* (pp. 51–78). IGI Global Scientific Publishing. DOI: 10.4018/979-8-3693-7718-5.ch003

Keiler, L. S. (2018). Teachers' roles and identities in student-centered classrooms. *International Journal of STEM Education*, *5*(1), 1–20. DOI: 10.1186/s40594-018-0131-6 PMID: 30631724

Kestin, G., Miller, K., Klales, A., Milbourne, T., & Ponti, G. (2024). AI Tutoring Outperforms Active Learning. In Review. https://doi.org/DOI: 10.21203/rs.3.rs-4243877/v1

Khan, W. N. (2024). Ethical Challenges of AI in Education: Balancing Innovation with Data Privacy. *Journal of AI in Education: Innovations, Opportunities, Challenges, and Future Directions*, *1*(1), 1–13.

Kizilcec, R. F. (2023). To Advance AI Use in Education, Focus on Understanding Educators. In International Journal of AI in Education (Vol. 34, Issue 1, p. 12). Springer Science+Business Media. https://doi.org/DOI: 10.1007/s40593-023-00351-4

Koehl, S. (2025). Designing AI Software for Large Classroom Engagement (Doctoral dissertation).

Kohlberg, L. (1984). *The psychology of moral development: The nature and validity of moral stages*. Harper & Row.

Kolb, D. A. (1984). *Experiential Learning: Experience as the Source of Learning and Development*. Prentice Hall.

Kolluru, V., Mungara, S., & Chintakunta, A. N. (2018). Adaptive learning systems: Harnessing AI for customized educational experiences. *International Journal of Computer Science and Information Technologies*, *6*(3), 10–5121. DOI: 10.5121/ijcsity.2018.6302

Kong, S. C., Cheung, W. M. Y., & Zhang, G. (2021). Evaluation of an artificial intelligence literacy course for university students with diverse study backgrounds. *Computers and Education: Artificial Intelligence*, *2*, 100026. DOI: 10.1016/j.caeai.2021.100026

Kose, U., & Vasant, P. (2020). Better campus life for visually impaired University students: Intelligent social walking system with beacon and assistive technologies. *Wireless Networks*, *26*(7), 4789–4803. DOI: 10.1007/s11276-018-1868-z

Krause, S. D. (2000). "Among the greatest benefactors of mankind": What the success of chalkboards tells us about the future of computers in the classroom. *The Journal of the Midwest Modern Language Association*, *33*(2), 6–16. DOI: 10.2307/1315198

Kshetri, N. (2021). Ransomware attacks on the US education sector: A perfect storm. *IEEE Security and Privacy*, *19*(3), 72–76. DOI: 10.1109/MSEC.2021.3071906

Kubsch, M., Krist, C., & Rosenberg, J. M. (2023). Distributing epistemic functions and tasks—A framework for augmenting human analytic power with machine learning in science education research. *Journal of Research in Science Teaching*, *60*(2), 423–447. DOI: 10.1002/tea.21803

Kumar, H. (2024). *Education And Social Change: The Role of School Inshaping Societal Values*. Multidisciplinary Aspects of Education.

Lachney, M., & Foster, E. K. (2020). Historicizing making and doing: Seymour Papert, Sherry Turkle, and epistemological foundations of the maker movement. *History and Technology*, *36*(1), 54–82. DOI: 10.1080/07341512.2020.1759302

Ladson-Billings, G. (1995). Toward a theory of culturally relevant pedagogy. *American Educational Research Journal*, *32*(3), 465–491. DOI: 10.3102/00028312032003465

Lai, V., Chen, C., Liao, Q. V., Smith, A., & Tan, C. (2021). Towards a Science of Human-AI Decision Making: A Survey of Empirical Studies. In arXiv (Cornell University). Cornell University. https://doi.org/DOI: 10.48550/arXiv.2112

Lammert, C., DeJulio, S., Grote-Garcia, S., & Fraga, L. M. (2024). Better than nothing? An analysis of AI-generated lesson plans using the Universal Design for Learning & Transition frameworks. *The Clearing House: A Journal of Educational Strategies, Issues and Ideas*, *97*(5), 168–175. DOI: 10.1080/00098655.2024.2427332

Landreth, G. L. (2002). Therapeutic limit setting in the play therapy relationship. *Professional Psychology, Research and Practice, 33*(6), 529–535. DOI: 10.1037/0735-7028.33.6.529

Langreo, L. (October 2024). "More Than Half of Teachers Still Have No Training on AI". Education Week. Retrieved on February 19, 2025, from https://www.govtech.com/education/k-12/more-than-half-of-teachers-still-have-no-training-on-ai

Lansdown, G. (2005). *The evolving capacities of the child.* UNICEF Innocenti Research Centre.

Lata, P. (2024). Beyond Algorithms: Humanizing Artificial Intelligence for Personalized and Adaptive Learning. *International Journal of Innovative Research in Engineering and Management, 11*(5), 10–55524.

Lawton, A., & Páez, I. (2015). Developing a Framework for Ethical Leadership. *Journal of Business Ethics, 130*(3), 639–649. DOI: 10.1007/s10551-014-2244-2

Lee, A. (2025). Informed Consent in the special education process. Understood.org. Retrieved on March 4, 2025, from https://www.understood.org/en/articles/informed-consent-what-it-is-and-how-it-works?form=MG0AV3

Lee, K., & Chen, M. (2021). Artificial Intelligence and Cognitive Load in Digital Learning Environments: A Systematic Review. *International Journal of Educational Technology in Higher Education, 18*(3).

Legaki, N., Xi, N., Hamari, J., Karpouzis, K., & Assimakopoulos, V. (2020). The effect of challenge-based gamification on learning: An experiment in the context of statistics education. *International Journal of Human-Computer Studies, 144*, 102496. DOI: 10.1016/j.ijhcs.2020.102496 PMID: 32565668

Leonard, D. (November 2024). Overcoming Potential Risks of Student Tech Use". Edutopia. Retrieved on February 19, 2025, from https://www.edutopia.org/article/risks-technology-education-how-overcome-them

Li, H. (2023). AI in education: Bridging the divide or widening the gap? Exploring equity, opportunities, and challenges in the digital age. Advances in Education. *Humanities and Social Science Research, 8*(1), 355–355.

Lin, C.-C., Huang, A. Y. Q., & Lu, O. H. T. (2023). Artificial Intelligence in Intelligent Tutoring Systems Toward Sustainable Education: A Systematic Review. *Smart Learning Environments, 10*(1), 1–22. DOI: 10.1186/s40561-023-00260-y

Liu, Y., & Zoghi, B. (2024). AI-Powered Strategies for Alleviating Graduate Student Burnout Through Emotional Intelligence and Wearable Technology 16th International Conference on Education and New Learning Technologies

Lively, J., Hutson, J., & Melick, E. (2023). Integrating AI-generative tools in web design education: Enhancing student aesthetic and creative copy capabilities using image and text-based AI generators. *Journal of Artificial Intelligence and Robotics*, *1*(1).

Livingstone, S., & Third, A. (2017). Children and young people's rights in the digital age: An emerging agenda. *New Media & Society*, *19*(5), 657–670. DOI: 10.1177/1461444816686318

Llurba, C., & Palau, R. (2024). Real-Time Emotion Recognition for Improving the Teaching–Learning Process: A Scoping Review. *Journal of Imaging*, *10*(12), 1–15. DOI: 10.3390/jimaging10120313

Lorenzo, N., & Gallon, R. (2019). Smart pedagogy for smart learning. Didactics of smart pedagogy: Smart pedagogy for technology enhanced learning, 41-69.

Lovato, S. B., & Piper, A. M. (2015). "Siri, is this you?": Understanding young children's interactions with voice input systems. In Proceedings of the 14th International Conference on Interaction Design and Children (pp. 335-338).

Lozano, J. R., Ramos, Y., Tecnologia, E., & Cruz, C. E. C. (2024). *Enhancing English language teaching through AI: The case of Magic School AI*. https://www.researchgate.net/profile/Jean-Paul-Rojas-2/publication/388757322_ Enhancing_English_Language_Teaching_Through_AI_The_Case_of_Magic_School_AI/ links/67a4eb53461fb56424cc7bbc/Enhancing-English-Language-Teaching-Through-AI- The-Case-of-Magic-School-AI.pdf

Lucariello, K. (2023). Teachers Plan to Learn and Use AI More in the 2023–2024 School Year. THE Journal. Retrieved February 13, 2025, from https://thejournal.com/Articles/2023/08/29/Teachers-Plan-to-Learn-and-Use-AI-More-in-the-20232024-School-Year.aspx

Luckin, R. (2018). Machine Learning and Human Intelligence. The future of education for the 21st century. UCL institute of education press.

Luckin, R. (2025). Nurturing human intelligence in the age of AI: Rethinking education for the future. *Development and Learning in Organizations*, *39*(1), 1–4. DOI: 10.1108/DLO-04-2024-0108

Luckin, R., Holmes, W., Griffiths, M., & Forcier, L. B. (2016). *Artificial Intelligence and Future of Teaching and Learning*. Center for Integrative Research in Computing and Learning Sciences.

Luckin, R., Jones, K., & Cukurova, M. (2021). *AI for School Teachers*. Routledge.

Luna, J. L. (2024). *AI in Education: Benefits, Challenges, and Ethical Considerations*. DataCamp. Retrieved on June 9, 2025, from https://www.datacamp.com/blog/ai-in-education

Lupton, D., & Williamson, B. (2017). The datafied child: The dataveillance of children and implications for their rights. *New Media & Society*, *19*(5), 780–794. DOI: 10.1177/1461444816686328

Lyon, D. (2007). *Surveillance studies: An overview*. Polity Press.

Mahmoud, C. F., & Sørensen, J. T. (2024). Artificial Intelligence in Personalized Learning with a Focus on Current Developments and Future Prospects. *Research and Advances in Education*, *3*(8), 25–31. DOI: 10.56397/RAE.2024.08.04

Main (2022, January 17). Cognitive Load Theory: A teacher's guide. Retrieved from https://www.structural-learning.com/post/cognitive-load-theory-a-teachers-guide

Malik, G., Tayal, D. K., & Vij, S. (2018). An Analysis of the Role of AI in Education and Teaching. In *Advances in intelligent systems and computing* (p. 407). Springer Nature., DOI: 10.1007/978-981-10-8639-7_42

Marzuki, W., Widiati, U., Rusdin, D., Darwin, , & Indrawati, I. (2023). The impact of AI writing tools on the content and organization of students' writing: EFL teachers' perspective. *Cogent Education*, *10*(2), 2236469. Advance online publication. DOI: 10.1080/2331186X.2023.2236469

Masters-Wheeler, C. (2024). Algorithmic Attention Systems and Writing-as-Content. *Computers and Composition*, *73*, 102862. DOI: 10.1016/j.compcom.2024.102862

Mathai, A. (2024). Enhancing Education for Underprivileged Children Through AI-Powered Native Language Learning Inclusive Education Through AI-Powered Native Language Learning. Available at *SSRN* 4899553. DOI: 10.2139/ssrn.4899553

Max-Neef, M. A. (2005). Foundations of Transdisciplinarity. *Ecological Economics*, *53*(1), 5–16. DOI: 10.1016/j.ecolecon.2005.01.014

Mayrene, F. H. E., Basantes, A. C., Martínez, M. F. C., Salas, F. P. P., & Jose, M. V. D. (2024). Emotional Interaction and Artificial Intelligence in Educational Research. *Journal of Ecohumanism*, *3*(8), 4858–4871. DOI: 10.62754/joe.v3i8.5131

Mbah, G. O. (2024). Data privacy in the era of AI: Navigating regulatory landscapes for global businesses.

McCormack, V. (2024). Employing AI for instructional planning, teaching, and learning. *Proceedings from SITE conference*.

Meisels, S. J., Xue, Y., Bickel, D. D., Nicholson, J., & Atkins-Burnett, S. (2003). Parental reactions to authentic performance assessment. *Educational Assessment, 9*(1-2), 61–85.

Merod, A. (2024, December 2). Math scores plummet, progress 'erased,' NCES reports. K-12 Dive. https://www.k12dive.com/news/math-scores-plummet-progress-erased-nces-reports/734562/

Mezirow, J. (1978). Perspective Transformation. *Adult Education, 28*(2), 100–110. DOI: 10.1177/074171367802800202

Miao, F., & Cukurova, M. (2024). AI Competency Framework for Teachers. *UNESCO*, 1-52. DOI: 10.54675/ZJTE2084

Miao, F., Shiohira, K., & Lao, N. (2024). AI Competency Framework for Students. *UNESCO*, 1-80. DOI: 10.54675/JKJB9835

Mishra, N., Garcia, P. S., Habal, B. G. M., & Garcia, M. B. (2024). *Harnessing an AI-Driven Analytics Model to Optimize Training and Treatment in Physical Education for Sports Injury Prevention* Proceedings of the 8th International Conference on Education and Multimedia Technology, Tokyo, Japan. https://manuelgarcia.info/publication/sports-injury-prevention

Mittal, U., Sai, S., Chamola, V., & Sangwan, D. (2024). A Comprehensive Review on Generative AI for Education. *IEEE Access : Practical Innovations, Open Solutions, 12*, 142733–142759. DOI: 10.1109/ACCESS.2024.3468368

Molenaar, I. (2022). Towards Hybrid Human-AI Learning Technologies. *European Journal of Education, 57*(4), 632–645. DOI: 10.1111/ejed.12527

Moll, L. C., Amanti, C., Neff, D., & González, N. (1992). Funds of knowledge for teaching: Using a qualitative approach to connect homes and classrooms. *Theory into Practice, 31*(2), 132–141. DOI: 10.1080/00405849209543534

Monterde, N., Aliban, L., Ando, R., Corimo, R., Catipay, R., & Abarquez, A. (2024). Teachers' Perspective of AI Chatbots on Students' Mathematical Solving Capabilities: A Grounded Theory. International Journal of Research and Scientific Innovation (IJRSI). https://rsisinternational.org/journals/ijrsi/articles/teachers-perspective-of-ai-chatbots-on-students-mathematical-solving-capabilities-a-grounded-theory/

Montessori, M. (1912). *The Montessori method. Frederick A.* Stokes Company.

Moses, A. (2022). DAP and playful learning: Equitable approaches. *Young Children, 77*(2). https://www.naeyc.org/resources/pubs/yc/summer2022/dap-and-playful-learning

Muli, M. (2024). Legal and Ethical Implications of Data Privacy in Artificial Intelligence: A Review of Data Privacy Among Learners in Kenyan Secondary Schools. *Journal of the Kenya National Commission for UNESCO, 5*(1). Advance online publication. DOI: 10.62049/jkncu.v5i1.170

Murgatroyd, S. (2024). *The future of higher education in an age of artificial intelligence.* Ethics International Press.

Mutawa, A. M. (2023). *Perspective chapter: MOOCS at higher education–Current state and future trends.* Massive Open Online Courses-Current Practice and Future Trends.

Naeem, R., & Syed, J. (2024). An Integrative Framework of Ethical Leadership. *Systemic Practice and Action Research, 37*(6), 1161–1174. DOI: 10.1007/s11213-024-09694-y

NAEYC & Fred Rogers Center. (2012). *Technology and interactive media as tools in early childhood programs serving children from birth through age 8.* National Association for the Education of Young Children and Fred Rogers Center for Early Learning and Children's Media.

NAEYC. (2019). *Advancing equity in early childhood education: A position statement.* National Association for the Education of Young Children.

NAEYC. (2022). *Developmentally appropriate practice in early childhood programs serving children from birth through age 8* (4th ed.). National Association for the Education of Young Children.

Naseer, A., Ahmad, N. R., & Chishti, M. A. (2025). Psychological Impacts of AI Dependence: Assessing the Cognitive and Emotional Costs of Intelligent Systems in Daily Life. *Review of Applied Management and Social Sciences, 8*(1), 291–307. DOI: 10.47067/ramss.v8i1.458

National Association for the Education of Young Children. (2020). *Developmentally appropriate practice: A position statement of the National Association for the Education of Young Children.* NAEYC. https://www.naeyc.org

National Association for the Education of Young Children. (2020). Professional Standards and Competencies for Early Childhood Educators. https://www.naeyc.org/sites/default/files/globally-shared/downloads/PDFs/ resources/position-statements/standards_and_competencies_ps.pdf

National Association for the Education of Young Children. (2024). *About us*. https://www.naeyc.org/about-us

National Association for the Education of Young Children. (2024). Code of ethics for early childhood educators (Draft Revision). NAEYC. https://www.naeyc.org/sites/default/files/globally-shared/downloads/PDFs/ 2024_code_of_ethics_for_early_childhood_educators_final_3.pdf

National Center on Early Childhood Quality Assurance. (2016). *Early learning standards and guidelines*. U.S. Department of Health & Human Services. https://childcareta.acf.hhs.gov

National Education Association. (2020). Code of ethics for educators. Retrieved on March 4, 2025, from https://ethics.miamidade.gov/library/2015-publications/ethics_neighbors_4-1-15.pdf?form=MG0AV3

Nelson, C. A.III, Zeanah, C. H., Fox, N. A., Marshall, P. J., Smyke, A. T., & Guthrie, D. (2007). Cognitive recovery in socially deprived young children: The Bucharest Early Intervention Project. *Science*, *318*(5858), 1937–1940. DOI: 10.1126/science.1143921 PMID: 18096809

Nerantzi, C. (2018). The Design of an Empirical Cross-Boundary Collaborative Open Learning Framework. *Open Praxis*, *10*(4), 325–341. DOI: 10.5944/openpraxis.10.4.907

Neuman, S. B., & Dickinson, D. K. (Eds.). (2011). *Handbook of early literacy research* (Vol. 3). Guilford Press.

News, A. B. C. (n.d.). US students' declining math scores are "sobering," experts say. ABC News. Retrieved March 19, 2025, from https://abcnews.go.com/GMA/Living/us-students-declining-math-scores-sobering-expert/story?id=116481011

Nexford University. (2024). How Will Artificial Intelligence Affect Jobs 2024-2030. Retrieved on March 3, 2025, from https://www.nexford.edu/insights/how-will-ai-affect-jobs?form=MG0AV3

Ng, A. Y. (2019). Machine Learning for Education. AI and Education: The Importance of Teacher and Student Engagement in AI-powered Learning Environments (pp. 77-92).

Nithiyanandam, N. Dhanasekaran, A., Kumar.,S. Gobinath, D., Vijayakarthik, P. Vinoth, G.and Rajkumar (2022). AI Assisted Student Learning and Performance Analysis using Instructor Evaluation Model, 2022 3rd International Conference on Electronics and Sustainable Communication Systems (ICESC), Coimbatore, India, 2022, pp. 1555-1561, DOI: 10.1109/ICESC54411.2022.9885462

Noble, S. U. (2018). *Algorithms of oppression: How search engines reinforce racism.* NYU Press. DOI: 10.18574/nyu/9781479833641.001.0001

Noddings, N. (1984). *Caring: A feminine approach to ethics and moral education.* University of California Press.

Noddings, N. (2002). *Educating moral people: A caring alternative to character education.* Teachers College Press.

Nussbaum, M. C. (2000). *Women and human development: The capabilities approach.* Cambridge University Press. DOI: 10.1017/CBO9780511841286

OECD. (2023). *Equity and Inclusion in Education: Finding Strength through Diversity.* OECD Publishing., DOI: 10.1787/e9072e21-

Ofosu-Ampong, K., Acheampong, B., Kevor, M.-O., & Amankwah-Sarfo, F. (2023). Acceptance of Artificial Intelligence (ChatGPT) in Education: Trust, Innovativeness and Psychological Need of Students. *Information and Knowledge Management, 13*(4), 37–47. DOI: 10.7176/IKM/13-4-03

Ofosu-Ampong, K., Atebawone, E., Mustafa, A. S., & Koomson, A. (2024). The Shift to Artificial Intelligence, ChatGPT, and Emerging Technologies in Education: A Review on Dominant Issues. In *Empowering Digital Education with ChatGPT.* CRC Press., DOI: 10.1201/9781032716350-2

Olawade, D. B., Wada, O. Z., Odetayo, A., David-Olawade, A. C., Asaolu, F., & Eberhardt, J. (2024). Enhancing Mental Health with Artificial Intelligence: Current Trends and Future Prospects. *Journal of Medicine, Surgery, and Public Health, 3*, 1–10. DOI: 10.1016/j.glmedi.2024.100099

Omughelli, D., Gordon, N., & Al Jaber, T. (2024). Fairness, bias, and ethics in AI: Exploring the factors affecting student performance. *Journal of International Communication, 3*(2), 100–110.

Ouyang, F., & Jiao, P. (2021). Artificial intelligence in education: The three paradigms. *Computers and Education: Artificial Intelligence, 2*, 100020. DOI: 10.1016/j.caeai.2021.100020

Owoc, M., Sawicka, A., & Weichbroth, P. (2021). *AI Technologies in Education: Benefits*. Challenges and Strategies of Implementation., DOI: 10.1007/978-3-030-85001-2_4

Padua, D. (2025). Artificial intelligence and quality education: The need for digital culture in teaching. Journal of Educational [ECPS Journal]. *Cultural and Psychological Studies*, (30), 181–193.

Paek, S., & Kim, N. (2021). Analysis of Worldwide Research Trends on the Impact of AI in Education. In Sustainability (Vol. 13, Issue 14, p. 7941). Multidisciplinary Digital Publishing Institute. DOI: 10.3390/su13147941

Palmer, P. J. (1998). *The courage to teach: Exploring the inner landscape of a teacher's life*. Jossey-Bass.

Papert, S. (1980). *Mindstorms: Children, computers, and powerful ideas*. Basic Books.

Park, H. K., & Park, J. (2024). Lesson plan development for pre-service elementary school teachers through collaboration with AI: Focused on ChatGPT. New Physics: Sae Mulli. DOI: 10.3938/NPSM.74.215

Patel, B., & Wright, D. (2023). Artificial Intelligence in Healthcare: Reducing Cognitive Load and Burnout . Journal of Medical Informatics.

Pathan, A., & Kanth, A. (2023). Impact of Artificial Intelligence (AI) on the Education and Cognitive Development of Young Children . 8 (12).

Pava, J. (n.d.). Addressing AI Security Concerns in Education. Panorama Education. Retrieved March 27, 2025, from https://www.panoramaed.com/blog/ai-security-concerns-in-education

Pearce, N. (2024). Revolutionising modern teaching with AI technology. *Education Journal Review*, *29*(3), 148–154.

Pedro, F., Subosa, M., Rivas, A., & Valverde, P. (2019). Artificial intelligence in education: Challenges and opportunities for sustainable development.

Peña, J. M., Moreno, O. B., Herrera, Á. L. O., & Moreno, T. E. B. (2024). Balancing Privacy and Ethics in the Use of Artificial Intelligence in Education. *Sapiens International Multidisciplinary Journal*, *1*(3), 148–170. DOI: 10.71068/m4gqp119

Perry, B. D., & Szalavitz, M. (2006). *The boy who was raised as a dog: And other stories from a child psychiatrist's notebook*. Basic Books.

Piaget, J. (1929). *The child's conception of the world*. Harcourt, Brace & Company.

Piaget, J. (1962). *Play, dreams, and imitation in childhood* (Gattegno, G., & Hodgson, F. M., Trans.). W. W. Norton.

Pitrella, V., Perna, S., Allegra, M., Gentile, M., Ottaviano, S., Re, A., Tosto, C., & Città, G. (2024). Artificial Intelligence for Personalized Learning in K-12 Education. A Scoping Review. *Communications In Computer and Information Science, 2076*, 372–382. Advance online publication. DOI: 10.1007/978-3-031-67351-1_25

Postman, N. (1985). *Amusing ourselves to death: Public discourse in the age of show business*. Penguin Books.

Powell, W., & Courchesne, S. (2024). Opportunities and risks involved in using ChatGPT to create first grade science lesson plans. *PLoS One, 19*(6), e0305337. Advance online publication. DOI: 10.1371/journal.pone.0305337 PMID: 38885244

Pratschke, B. M. (2024). *Generative AI and education: Digital pedagogies, teaching innovation and learning design*. Springer Nature. DOI: 10.1007/978-3-031-67991-9

Price, E. A., White, R. M., Mori, K., Longhurst, J., Baughan, P., Hayles, C. S., Gough, G., & Preist, C. (2021). Supporting the role of universities in leading individual and societal transformation through education for sustainable development. *Discover Sustainability, 2*(1), 49. DOI: 10.1007/s43621-021-00058-3

Putnam, R. D. (2000). *Bowling alone: The collapse and revival of American community*. Simon & Schuster.

Qorbani, M. (2020). *Humanity in the Age of AI: How to Thrive in a Post-Human World*. Bloomsberry.

Quraishi, A., Sen, A., Pham, S., Corral, A., & Johnston, T. (2024, August 26). Ransomware attacks on schools threaten student data nationwide—CBS News. CBS News. https://www.cbsnews.com/news/school-ransomware-attacks-threaten-student-data/

Radesky, J. S., Schaller, A., Yeo, S., Weeks, H. M., & Christakis, D. (2020). Young children's use of smartphones and tablets. *Pediatrics, 146*(1), e20193518. DOI: 10.1542/peds.2019-3518 PMID: 32482771

Rajput, R. (2025). Use of Artificial Intelligence to Solve Problems in the Classroom. In *New Technological Applications in the Flipped Learning Model* (pp. 137–168). IGI Global Scientific Publishing. DOI: 10.4018/979-8-3373-0437-3.ch005

Rane, N., Choudhary, S., & Rane, J. (2023). Education 4.0 and 5.0: Integrating artificial intelligence (AI) for personalized and adaptive learning.

Raza, S., Fatima, I., Arif, S., Sharif, M., Jalal, M. S., & Muhammad, Z. (2024). The Future of Learning: Building Trust and Transparency in AI Education. *Journal of Management Practices. Humanities and Social Sciences*, *8*(3), 1–13. DOI: 10.33152/jmphss-8.3.6

Reidenberg, J. R., Russell, N. C., Kovnot, J., Norton, T. B., Cloutier, R., & Alvarado, D. (2018). *Privacy and cloud computing in public schools*. Center on Law and Information Policy, Fordham University School of Law.

Resnick, M. (2017). *Lifelong kindergarten: Cultivating creativity through projects, passion, peers, and play*. MIT Press. DOI: 10.7551/mitpress/11017.001.0001

Rice, M. F., & Dunn, S. (2023). The use of artificial intelligence with students with identified disabilities: A systematic review with critique. *Computers in the Schools*, *40*(4), 370–390. DOI: 10.1080/07380569.2023.2244935

Rodríguez-Ruiz, J., Marín-López, I., & Espejo-Siles, R. (2025). Is Artificial Intelligence Use Related to Self-Control, Self-Esteem and Self-Efficacy Among University Students? *Education and Information Technologies*, *30*(2), 2507–2524. DOI: 10.1007/s10639-024-12906-6

Saltman, K. (2020). Artificial intelligence and the technological turn of public education privatization: In defence of democratic education. *London Review of Education*, *18*(2), 196–208. DOI: 10.14324/LRE.18.2.04

Salvani, S. (Director). (2020). Coded bias [Film]. 7th Empire Media; Thought-Matter Media.

Sanders, B., Zuckerman, K., Ash, J.S., Kopstick, A.J., Rivas Vazquez, L., Gorman, P. N. (2022). Early intervention referral information, transmission, and sources—A survey of state Part C Coordinators and Analysis of Referral Forms. *Journal of Developmental & Behavioral Pediatrics* *43*(3), 153-161, | DOI: DOI: 10.1097/DBP.0000000000001004

Sannino, A., Engeström, Y., & Lemos, M. (2018). Formative interventions for expansive learning and transformative agency. In *Cultural-historical activity theory approaches to design-based research* (pp. 113–147). Routledge. DOI: 10.4324/9780203703106-6

Sargent, J. M. (2024). Optimistic Realism in Higher Education: Strategies for Empowering Students in a Complex World (Doctoral dissertation, Idaho State University).

Sayers, D., Sousa-Silva, R., Höhn, S., Ahmedi, L., Allkivi-Metsoja, K., Anastasiou, D., ... & Yayilgan, S. Y. (2021). The Dawn of the Human-Machine Era: A forecast of new and emerging language technologies.

Schultz, B. D. (2018). *Spectacular things happen along the way: Lessons from an urban classroom*. Teachers College Press.

Schwartz, D., Tsang, J., & Blair, K. (2016). *The ABCs of how we learn: 26 scientifically proven approaches, how they work, and when to use them*. W W Norton & Co.

Seldon, A., & Abidoye, A. (2018). *The Fourth Education Revolution: Will Artificial Intelligence Liberate or Infantilize Learning?* UCL Institute of Education Press.

Selwyn, N. (2021). *Education and technology: Key issues and debates* (3rd ed.). Bloomsbury Academic.

Semel, A. (2019). An Untraditional Phenomenological Study of Teachers' Perceptions of Rhythmic Delivery of Classroom Commands during Transition Times (Doctoral dissertation, Grand Canyon University).

Sen, A. (1999). *Development as freedom*. Oxford University Press.

Seo, K., Tang, J., Roll, I., Fels, S., & Yoon, D. (2021). The Impact of Artificial Intelligence on Learner–Instructor Interaction in Online Learning. *International Journal of Educational Technology in Higher Education*, *18*(1), 1–23. DOI: 10.1186/s41239-021-00292-9 PMID: 34778540

Sethi, S. S., & Jain, K. (2024). AI Technologies for Social Emotional Learning: Recent Research and Future Directions. *Journal of Research in Innovative Teaching & Learning*, *17*(2), 213–225. DOI: 10.1108/JRIT-03-2024-0073

Setyaningsih, E., Asrori, M., Ngadiso, , Sumardi, , Zainnuri, H., & Hariyanti, Y. (2024). Exploring high school EFL teachers' experiences with Magic School AI in lesson planning. *Voices of English Language Education Society*, *8*(3). Advance online publication. DOI: 10.29408/veles.v8i3.27700

Seung, Y. (2024, June 10). The Impact of Artificial Intelligence on Cognitive Load—CIDDL. https://ciddl.org/the-impact-of-artificial-intelligence-on-cognitive-load/

Sewell, A., Anastasia, K., & Pugh, V. (2022). Universal Design for Learning as a Theory of Inclusive Practice for Use by Educational Psychologists. *Educational Psychology in Practice*, *38*(4), 364–378. DOI: 10.1080/02667363.2022.2111677

Shang, H., Sivaparthipan, C. B., & ThanjaiVadivel, . (2022). Interactive teaching using human-machine interaction for higher education systems. *Computers & Electrical Engineering*, *100*, 107811. DOI: 10.1016/j.compeleceng.2022.107811

Sheehan, T. (2023). Generative AI in education: Past, present, and future. *Educause Review*. https://er.educause.edu/articles/sponsored/2023/9/generative-ai-in-education-past-present-and-future

Shen, J. (2020). *The Innovation of Education in the Era of AI.*, DOI: 10.3390/proceedings2020047057

Shireesha, M., & Jeevan, J. (2024). The Role of Artificial Intelligence in Personalized Learning: A Pathway to Inclusive Education. Library of Progress-Library Science, Information Technology & Computer, 44(3).

Shonkoff, J. P., & Phillips, D. A. (Eds.). (2000). *From neurons to neighborhoods: The science of early childhood development.* National Academies Press., https://www.ncbi.nlm.nih.gov/books/NBK225562/

Silseth, K., & Erstad, O. (2018). Connecting to the outside: Cultural resources teachers use when contextualizing instruction. *Learning, Culture and Social Interaction, 17*, 56–68. DOI: 10.1016/j.lcsi.2017.12.002

Simhadri, N., & Swamy, T. N. V. R. (2023). Awareness among teaching on AI and ML applications based on fuzzy in education sector at USA. In Soft Computing. Springer Science+Business Media. https://doi.org/DOI: 10.1007/s00500-023-08329-z

Singer, N. (2023, June 8). New A.I. Chatbot Tutors Could Upend Student Learning. The New York Times. https://www.nytimes.com/2023/06/08/business/khan-ai-gpt-tutoring-bot.html

Singh, B., & Kaunert, C. (2024). Future of Digital Marketing: Hyper-Personalized Customer Dynamic Experience with AI-Based Predictive Models. In Revolutionizing the AI-Digital Landscape (pp. 189-203). Productivity Press.

Singh, A. (2024). The Future of Learning: AI-Driven Personalized Education. Available at *SSRN* 5076438. DOI: 10.56557/ajocr/2024/v9i49018

Slee, R. (2018). *Defining the Scope of Inclusive Education: Think Piece Prepared for the 2020 Global Education Monitoring Report, Inclusion and Education.* UNESCO.

Slimi, Z. (2023). *The Impact of Artificial Intelligence on Higher Education: An Empirical Study.* Retrieved from ERIC.

Smith, L. T. (1999). *Decolonizing methodologies: Research and indigenous peoples.* Zed Books.

Snow, C. E., Burns, M. S., & Griffin, P. (Eds.). (1998). *Preventing reading difficulties in young children.* National Academy Press.

Solove, D. J. (2020). *The privacy paradox: The impact of privacy concerns and privacy behavior.* Harvard University Press., DOI: 10.19044/ejes.v10no1a17

Sorrentino, P. (2018). The mystery of the digital natives' existence: Questioning the validity of the Prenskian metaphor. *First Monday*. Advance online publication. DOI: 10.5210/fm.v23i10.9434

Srinivasa, K. G., Kurni, M., & Saritha, K. (2022). Harnessing the Power of AI to Education. In *Learning, teaching, and assessment methods for contemporary learners: pedagogy for the digital generation* (pp. 311–342). Springer Nature Singapore. DOI: 10.1007/978-981-19-6734-4_13

Staff (2021, October 4). 'Howdy': Hackers Email Parents and Students After Allen ISD Refuses to Pay Ransom. NBC 5 Dallas-Fort Worth. https://www.nbcdfw.com/news/local/howdy-hackers-email-parents-and-students-after-allen-isd-refuses-to-pay-ransom/2758256/

Staff (2024, August 30). The state of AI: Who is leading AI adoption? eSchool News. https://www.eschoolnews.com/digital-learning/2024/08/30/the-state-of-ai-who-is-leading-ai-adoption/

Stanford Accelerator for Learning. (2025). The future is already here: AI and education in 2025. Retrieved on March 4, 2025, from https://acceleratelearning.stanford.edu/story/the-future-is-already-here-ai-and-education-in-2025/?form=MG0AV3

Steele, C. M. (1997). A threat in the air: How stereotypes shape intellectual identity and performance. *The American Psychologist*, *52*(6), 613–629. DOI: 10.1037/0003-066X.52.6.613 PMID: 9174398

Stelmach, A. (2025). The Development Of Artificial Intelligence And Its Ethical Implications. Retrieved on March 4, 2025, from https://www.forbes.com/councils/forbestechcouncil/2025/02/25/the-development-of-artificial-intelligence-and-its-ethical-implications/?form=MG0AV3

Stewart, M. (2021). Understanding learning: Theories and critique. In *University teaching in focus* (pp. 3–28). Routledge. DOI: 10.4324/9781003008330-2

Stone, P., Brooks, R., Brynjolfsson, E., Calo, R., Etzioni, O., Hager, G., Hirschberg, J., Kalyanakrishnan, S., Kamar, E., Kraus, S., Leyton-Brown, K., Parkes, D., Press, W., Saxenian, A., Shah, J., Tambe, M., & Teller, A. (2016, September). *Artificial intelligence and life in 2030.* One Hundred Year Study on Artificial Intelligence: Report of the 2015-2016 Study Panel, Stanford University. https://ai100.stanford.edu/2016-report

Stryker, C., & Kavlakoglu, E. (2024, August 9). *What is AI?* IBM. https://www.ibm.com/think/topics/artificial-intelligence

Sun, Y. (2023). Research on the Symbiotic and Reciprocal Relationship between Yellow River Culture and the Overall Environment in Moral Education during the New Era. *Pacific International Journal*, *6*(3), 129–133. DOI: 10.55014/pij.v6i3.426

Sweller, J. (2011). Cognitive load theory. In Mestre, J. P., & Ross, B. H. (Eds.), *The psychology of learning and motivation: Cognition in education* (pp. 37–76). Elsevier Academic Press., DOI: 10.1016/B978-0-12-387691-1.00002-8

Tabassum, A., Elmahjub, E., Padela, A. I., Zwitter, A., & Qadir, J. (2025). Generative AI and the Metaverse: A Scoping Review of Ethical and Legal Challenges. *IEEE Open Journal of the Computer Society*, *6*, 348–359. DOI: 10.1109/OJCS.2025.3536082

Tang, L., & Su, Y. S. (2024). Ethical implications and principles of using artificial intelligence models in the classroom: A systematic literature review.

TeachThough. (2014). A Useful Framework For Transparency In Education. TeachThough.com. Retrieved on March 4, 2025, from https://www.teachthought.com/education/transparency-in-education/?form=MG0AV3

Tedre, M., Toivonen, T., Kahila, J., Vartiainen, H., Valtonen, T., Jormanainen, I., & Pears, A. (2021). Teaching machine learning in K–12 classroom: Pedagogical and technological trajectories for artificial intelligence education. *IEEE Access : Practical Innovations, Open Solutions*, *9*, 110558–110572. DOI: 10.1109/ACCESS.2021.3097962

Texas Education Agency. (2022). *Texas prekindergarten guidelines: PK3 and PK4 comprehensive guide*. https://tea.texas.gov

Timbang, C., & Velasco, M. C. (2024). Digital Technology: Impact on Students' Learning Process, Social Interaction and Mental Well-Being. International Multidisciplinary Journal of Research for Innovation, Sustainability, and Excellence, 1(7), 247-258. https://risejournals.org/index.php/imjrise/article/view/585

Tomé, A., & Coelho, J. L. (2023). Physiotherapy Education in the Digital Era: A Roadmap of Educational Technologies for Allied Health Educators. In *Handbook of Research on Instructional Technologies in Health Education and Allied Disciplines*. IGI Global., DOI: 10.4018/978-1-6684-7164-7.ch002

Topali, P., Ortega-Arranz, A., Rodríguez-Triana, M. J., Er, E., Khalil, M., & Akçapınar, G. (2025). Designing human-centered learning analytics and artificial intelligence in education solutions: A systematic literature review. *Behaviour & Information Technology*, *44*(5), 1071–1098. DOI: 10.1080/0144929X.2024.2345295

Torraco, R. J. (2016). Writing Integrative Literature Reviews: Using the Past and Present to Explore the Future. *Human Resource Development Review, 15*(4), 404–428. DOI: 10.1177/1534484316671606

Trevarthen, C. (2001). Intrinsic motives for companionship in understanding: Their origin, development, and significance for infant mental health. *Infant Mental Health Journal, 22*(1-2), 95–131. DOI: 10.1002/1097-0355(200101/04)22:1<95::AID-IMHJ4>3.0.CO;2-6

Turkle, S. (2011). *Alone together: Why we expect more from technology and less from each other*. Basic Books.

U.S. Department of Education. (2019). *Individuals with Disabilities Education Act, Section 1414(d)(3): Individualized education programs—Development of IEP.* https://sites.ed.gov/idea/statute-chapter-33/subchapter-ii/1414/d/3

U.S. Department of Education. (2023). *Artificial Intelligence and the Future of Teaching and Learning: Insights and Recommendations*. Office of Educational Technology.

U.S. Department of Education. (n.d.). *Data Security: K-12 and Higher Education | Protecting Student Privacy*. Retrieved on March 4, 2025, from https://studentprivacy.ed.gov/data-security-k-12-and-higher-education

U.S. Department of Health & Human Services. (2025). *Head Start programs.* Head Start. https://headstart.gov

U.S. Department of State. (2020). National Artificial Intelligence Act of 2020. https://www.state.gov/artificial-intelligence/

UNESCO. (2020). Global Education Monitoring Report, 2020: Inclusion and Education: All Means All. *UNESCO*, 1-502. DOI: 10.54676/JJNK6989

Uneven Adoption of Artificial Intelligence Tools Among U.S. Teachers and Principals in the 2023–2024 School Year | RAND https://www.rand.org/pubs/research_reports/RRA134-25.html

United Nations. (1989). *Convention on the Rights of the Child*. UN General Assembly.

van Dijck, J. (2014). Datafication, dataism and dataveillance: Big Data between scientific paradigm and ideology. *Surveillance & Society, 12*(2), 197–208. DOI: 10.24908/ss.v12i2.4776

Venter, J., Coetzee, S. A., & Schmulian, A. (2024). Exploring the Use of Artificial Intelligence (AI) in the Delivery of Effective Feedback. *Assessment & Evaluation in Higher Education*, •••, 1–21. DOI: 10.1080/02602938.2024.2415649

Vincent-Lancrin, S., & Van der Vlies, R. (2020). Trustworthy artificial intelligence (AI) in education: Promises and challenges. OECD education working papers, (218), 0_1-17.

Vistorte, A. O. R., Deroncele-Acosta, A., Ayala, J. L. M., Barrasa, A., López-Granero, C., & Martí-González, M. (2024). Integrating Artificial Intelligence to Assess Emotions in Learning Environments: A Systematic Literature Review. *Frontiers in Psychology*, *15*, 1–13. DOI: 10.3389/fpsyg.2024.1387089 PMID: 38966729

Vygotsky, L. S. (1978). *Mind in Society: Development of Higher Psychological Processes*. Harvard University Press., DOI: 10.2307/j.ctvjf9vz4

Vygotsky, L. S. (1978). *Mind in society: The development of higher psychological processes*. Harvard University Press.

Vygotsky, L. S. (2004). Imagination and creativity in childhood. *Journal of Russian & East European Psychology*, *42*(1), 7–97. DOI: 10.1080/10610405.2004.11059210

Wang, S., Wang, F., Zhu, Z., Wang, J., & Tran, T. And Du, Z. (2024). AI in education: A systematic literature review. Expert Systems with Applications, 252, ISSN 0957-4174, https://doi.org/DOI: 10.1016/j.eswa.2024.124167

Wang, N., Xiao, W., & Su, Y.-S. (2024). Critical Analysis of the Technological Affordances, Challenges and Future Directions of Generative AI in Education: A Systematic Review. *Asia Pacific Journal of Education*, *44*(1), 139–155. DOI: 10.1080/02188791.2024.2305156

Wang, Y., Song, W., Tao, W., Liotta, A., Yang, D., Li, X., Gao, S., Sun, Y., Ge, W., Zhang, W., & Zhang, W. (2022). A systematic review on affective computing: Emotion models, databases, and recent advances. *Information Fusion*, *83*, 19–52. DOI: 10.1016/j.inffus.2022.03.009

Wartella, E., Rideout, V., Lauricella, A. R., & Connell, S. L. (2013). Parenting in the age of digital technology: A national survey. Northwestern University, Center on Media and Human Development.

Weiner, S., Lake, R., & Rosner, J. (2024, October). *AI is evolving, but teacher prep is lagging: A first look at teacher preparation program responses to AI*. Center on Reinventing Public Education. https://crpe.org

West, D. M. (2019). *Technology and privacy: The new landscape*. Brookings Institution Press.

West, S. M. (2019). Data protection in education: Ethical considerations and policy recommendations. *International Review of Education*, *65*(4), 547–562.

Whetstone, J. T. (2005). The Role of Ethics in Leadership: A Practical Model for Mindful Ethical Leadership. *Journal of Business Ethics*, *60*(1), 37–47.

Whitaker, T. (2020). *What great teachers do differently: Nineteen things that matter most*. Routledge. DOI: 10.4324/9780429325977

Wichita State University. (2025). The Impact of AI on Jobs and Education. Retrieved on March 3, 2025, https://www.wichita.edu/services/mrc/OIR/AI/jobimpacts.php?form=MG0AV3

Wiese, L. J., Patil, I., Schiff, D. S., & Magana, A. J. (2025). AI Ethics Education: A Systematic Literature Review. *Computers and Education: Artificial Intelligence*, *8*, 1–22. DOI: 10.1016/j.caeai.2025.100405

Williams, D. A. (2023). *Strategic diversity leadership: Activating change and transformation in higher education*. Routledge. DOI: 10.4324/9781003447122

Woolf, B. P. (2010). *Building Intelligent Interactive Tutors*. Elsevier.

Xiao, J., Bozkurt, A., Nichols, M., Pazurek, A., Stracke, C. M., Bai, J. Y. H., Farrow, R., Mulligan, D., Nerantzi, C., Sharma, R. C., Singh, L., Frumin, I., Swindell, A., Honeychurch, S., Bond, M., Dron, J., Moore, S., Leng, J., van Tryon, P. J. S., & Themeli, C. (2025). Venturing into the Unknown: Critical Insights into Grey Areas and Pioneering Future Directions in Educational Generative AI Research. *TechTrends*, *69*(3), 1–16. DOI: 10.1007/s11528-025-01060-6

Xie, Y., Huang, Y., Luo, W., Bai, Y., Qiu, Y., & Ouyang, Z. (2023). Design and Effects of the Teacher-Student Interaction Model in the Online Learning Spaces. *Journal of Computing in Higher Education*, *35*(1), 69–90. DOI: 10.1007/s12528-022-09348-9 PMID: 36618325

Yampolskiy, R. V. (2025). On Monitorability of AI. *AI and Ethics*, *5*(1), 689–707. DOI: 10.1007/s43681-024-00420-x

Yang, H. (2021). Explore How AI and VR Technology will Change the Development of Future Education. In Journal of Physics Conference Series (Vol. 1744, Issue 4, p. 42146). IOP Publishing. https://doi.org/DOI: 10.1088/1742-6596/1744/4/042146

Yang, S. J., Ogata, H., Matsui, T., & Chen, N. S. (2021). Human-centered artificial intelligence in education: Seeing the invisible through the visible. *Computers and Education: Artificial Intelligence*, *2*, 100008. DOI: 10.1016/j.caeai.2021.100008

Yan, L., Greiff, S., Teuber, Z., & Gašević, D. (2024). Promises and Challenges of Generative Artificial Intelligence for Human Learning. *Nature Human Behaviour*, *8*(10), 1839–1850. DOI: 10.1038/s41562-024-02004-5 PMID: 39438686

Yilmaz Can, D., & Durmus, C. (2024). From AI-generated lesson plans to the real-life classes: Explored by pre-service teachers. *10th International Conference on Higher Education Advances (HEAd'24)*, Valencia, June 18-21, 2024. https://doi.org/DOI: 10.4995/HEAd24.2024.17060

Yosso, T. J. (2005). Whose culture has capital? A critical race theory discussion of community cultural wealth. *Race, Ethnicity and Education*, *8*(1), 69–91. DOI: 10.1080/1361332052000341006

Yusuf, A., Pervin, N., Román-González, M., & Noor, N. M. (2024). Generative AI in Education and Research: A Systematic Mapping Review. *Review of Education*, *12*(2), e3489. DOI: 10.1002/rev3.3489

Zaman, B. (2023). Transforming Education Through AI, Benefits, Risks, and Ethical Considerations. *TechRxiv*. DOI: DOI: 10.36227/techrxiv.24231583.v1

Zawacki-Richter, O., Marín, V. I., Bond, M., & Gouverneur, F. (2019). Systematic review of research on artificial intelligence applications in higher education–where are the educators? *International Journal of Educational Technology in Higher Education*, *16*(1), 39. DOI: 10.1186/s41239-019-0171-0

Zhai, X., Chu, X., Chai, C. S., Jong, M. S., Starčič, A. I., Spector, M., Liu, J., Jing, Y., & Li, Y. (2021). A Review of AI (AI) in Education from 2010 to 2020 [Review of A Review of AI (AI) in Education from 2010 to 2020]. Complexity, 2021(1). Hindawi Publishing Corporation. DOI: 10.1155/2021/8812542

Zhang, A. (2025). Human Computer Interaction System for Teacher-Student Interaction Model Using Machine Learning. *International Journal of Human-Computer Interaction*, *41*(3), 1817–1828. DOI: 10.1080/10447318.2022.2115645

Zhao, J. (2025). The Role of Learners' AI Literacy and Resilience in Boosting Their Engagement and Motivation in AI-Based Settings: From an Achievement Goal Theory Perspective. *Learning and Motivation*, *91*, 1–11. DOI: 10.1016/j.lmot.2025.102152

Zhou, H., Lu, J., Huang, Y., & Chen, Y. (2021). Research on key Technology of Classroom Teaching Evaluation Based on AI. In Journal of Physics Conference Series (Vol. 1757, Issue 1, p. 12014). IOP Publishing. DOI: 10.1088/1742-6596/1757/1/012014

Zhu, B., Chau, K., & Mokmin, N. (2024). Optimizing cognitive load and learning adaptability with adaptive microlearning for in-service personnel. *Scientific Reports*, *14*(1), 25960. DOI: 10.1038/s41598-024-77122-1 PMID: 39472703

Zuboff, S. (2019). *The age of surveillance capitalism: The fight for a human future at the new frontier of power*. PublicAffairs.

Zukowski, J. (n.d.). How Gamification Can Motivate Students and Drive Results. Study.Com. https://teachinglicense.study.com/resources/how-gamification-motivates-students-drives-results.html

About The Contributors

Juan Araujo is professor and director of the School of Education at Texas Woman's University. He is a tenured professor in language and literacy with more than 22 years experience working with preservice and inservice teachers. He holds a PhD in Reading from University of North Texas, an MBE from Southern Methodist University, and a BS in Electrical Engineering with a minor in literature from New Jersey Institute of Technology. He has more than 10 edited texts, 25 + peer reviewed publications, and several funded grants relating to teacher education. He is editor of Literacy Research, and Instruction, and the Texas Association of Literacy Education journal.

Sharla Snider is Professor and Division Head of Early Childhood Education in the School of Education at Texas Woman's University. She holds a Doctor of Philosophy and Master of Arts in Early Childhood Education from Texas Woman's University and a Bachelor of Science in Elementary Education from the University of North Texas. Dr. Snider has served in various faculty and administrative roles, including former interim Chair of the Department of Literacy and Learning. She has published in peer-reviewed journals, presented at major conferences, and secured over $1 million in external funding from sources including the U.S. Department of Education and Intel Corporation. She teaches at all levels in early childhood education, technology integration, and research methods, including direction of doctoral work. Methodological expertise includes case study, ethnographic, narrative inquiry, and mixed methods research.

***

Rena Alasgarova is the Deputy Head of Secondary Academics at Baku-Oxford School and a leading voice at the intersection of education, ethics, and innovation. With a diverse academic background, including a Ph.D. in International Leadership and ongoing doctoral research in General Linguistics at Charles University in Prague, her work focuses on first language attrition, teacher development, and purposeful curriculum design. Dr. Alasgarova also teaches at ADA University, where she designed and leads Azerbaijan's first graduate course on the ethical and practical use of AI in education, equipping future educators to critically engage with emerging technologies in the classroom.

Aras Bozkurt is a researcher and faculty member at Anadolu University, Türkiye. With MA and Ph.D. degrees in Distance Education, Dr. Bozkurt's work focuses on empirical studies in areas such as distance education, online learning, networked learning, and educational technology. He applies critical theories like connectivism, rhizomatic learning, and heutagogy to his research. Dr. Bozkurt is also interested in emerging research paradigms, including social network analysis, sentiment analysis, and data mining. His studies also explore the integration of artificial intelligence technologies into educational processes, particularly in the context of human-machine interaction.

Jerry R. Burkett is an Assistant Professor of Educational Leadership. He has 23 years of public education experience on the elementary and secondary levels in Texas serving in various roles including teacher, principal, and district administrator. Dr. Burkett's experience includes work in Title I schools; community/parental involvement initiatives; implementing North Texas' first Science, Technology, Engineering, and Math (STEM) concept school on the elementary level; as well as incorporating partnership with corporations and universities into classroom. During his time at the University of North Texas at Dallas, he transformed the Educational Leadership program, aligning curriculum to national standards and developing a program that includes an emphasis on real-world experience from a practitioner focus. The program was also re-imagined allowing students to gain specialization in the administration of specialty schools and programs, such as STEM and Bilingual Education. In 2013 Dr. Burkett was selected as a member of the Phi Delta Kappa Emerging Leaders Class of 2013-14 and earned Dallas Baptist University's Distinguished Alumni Award. He resides in the Fort Worth area with his wife and son. He is active in coaching youth sports, running, weightlifting, and playing guitar.

Manuel B. Garcia is a professor of information technology and the founding director of the Educational Innovation and Technology Hub (EdITH) at FEU Institute of Technology, Manila, Philippines. He holds a Doctor of Information Technology degree from the University of the East and is currently pursuing a Doctor of Philosophy in Education at the University of the Philippines. His interdisciplinary research interests include topics that, individually or collectively, span the disciplines of education and information technology. He is a licensed professional teacher and a proud member of the National Research Council of the Philippines – an attached agency to the country's Department of Science and Technology (DOST-NRCP). Dr. Garcia is the first-ever recipient of the Ramon Dimacali Award for Information Technology, conferred by the Philippine Association for the Advancement of Science and Technology, and has been recognized as one of the World's Top 2% Scientists for 2023 and 2024 by Elsevier.

Mustafa Kayyali, an ardent advocate for excellence in higher education, driven by a relentless pursuit of quality, recognition, and innovation. My journey in academia started with a Master's in Quality Management and Evaluation in Higher Education from Universitat Oberta de Catalunya, followed by a Ph.D. in Quality Management from Azteca University. These academic pursuits have laid a strong foundation for my expertise in Accreditation, Quality Assurance, and Higher Education Rankings. As an entrepreneur, researcher, translator, and publisher, I am deeply involved in various facets of the academic world. My diverse interests encompass Management, Translation, Interpretation, and Academic consulting, contributing to a well-rounded understanding of the industry. Throughout my career, I have made significant contributions to academic literature, with more than 40 published papers and 30 book chapters to my name. Additionally, I take pride in having translated 6 books, bridging language gaps, and promoting knowledge exchange on a global scale. I am committed to fostering positive change in higher education and contributing to its continuous improvement.

Sara Kay Matthews is a Senior Instructor in the Margaret Ritchie School of Family and Consumer Sciences at the University of Idaho, where she teaches in the Early Childhood Development and Education division. With over two decades of experience in higher education and early childhood practice, Sara is deeply committed to preparing future educators through developmentally appropriate, evidence-based pedagogy. She earned her M.S. in Family and Consumer Sciences and her B.S. in Child, Family, and Consumer Sciences with a concentration in Child Development/Family Relations from the University of Idaho. Her professional interests include child development, parent-child relationships, early childhood curriculum design, and feeding practices in group care settings. A frequent presenter at national and regional conferences, Sara's recent work explores the integration of artificial intelligence in higher education and teacher preparation, with an emphasis on equity, ethical use, and critical thinking. Sara has authored training tools, developed innovative coursework, and actively participates in statewide early childhood initiatives. She is known for her thoughtful mentorship, engaging teaching style, and contributions to the professional development of early childhood educators.

Ahmed Hosny Saleh Metwally is an Assistant Professor in the Department of Educational Technology at Helwan University and a Visiting Researcher at the HCI Games Group, University of Waterloo. He obtained his Ph.D. from Northeast Normal University. His research focuses on gamification, gamified learning assignments, learning analytics, human-computer interaction, instructional design, artificial intelligence, the metaverse, and digital learning resources. Additionally, he serves as an Academic Editor for PLOS ONE and as an Editorial Board Member for the Educational Technology & Society journal. He is also a reviewer for numerous international SSCI journals, including Educational Technology & Society (ET&S), Computers & Education, The International Review of Research in Open and Distance Learning (IRRODL), and IEEE Access.

Chrissi Nerantzi (PFHEA, NTF, CATE) is a Professor in Creative and Open Education in the School of Education and a Senior Lead of the Knowledge Equity Network at the University of Leeds in the United Kingdom. Her research interests lie in creativity, open and boundary-crossing collaborative learning. Chrissi is a GO-GN alumna, the founder of the international open #creativeHE community, and has co-created many OERs and initiated a range of open professional development courses, networks, and communities that have been sustained over the years. She is the co-chair of the ICDE Open Education Network together with Dr. Rob Farrow from the Open University in the UK.

James Nixon is a Senior Lecturer and Programme Team Leader at Arden University. He has a broad range of experience teaching in higher education with UK and US institutions. His Ph.D. focuses on hauntological poetics and the legacy of Arthur Rimbaud. His current research interests include digital education practice and pedagogy, academic practice and misconduct, the effective use of AI for research purposes, and creative writing as a qualitative research method. James is a former Editor of the peer-reviewed journal of literary and cultural criticism GLITS-E, a Royal Holloway Emerging Writer Fellow, and a Writer-in-Residence at Phytology, Bethnal Green, London. His most recent work was published in The AI Literary Review.

Kingsley Ofosu-Ampong is a Lecturer of Information Systems at Heritage Christian University College, Ghana. He earned his Ph.D. in Information Systems from the University of Ghana. His research focuses on behavioral science and theories, artificial intelligence, technology-enhanced learning, and psychological needs in computing. Dr. Ofosu-Ampong's work has been published in outlets such as the Journal of Information Systems Education, Education and Information Technologies, Digital Business, and Digital Transformation and Society. He currently serves as the President of the Association for Information Systems Special Interest Group in Game Design and Research (AIS SIGGAME).

Jennifer Quong, PhD, is an Assistant Clinical Professor of Early Childhood Education at Texas Woman's University. Dr. Quong teaches undergraduate and graduate ECE courses online, hybrid, and face-to-face. In addition, she is the program director for the Bachelor's of Science in Early Childhood Education leading to PK-3 certification. Dr. Quong is creating articulation agreements between community colleges and universities. This work aims to develop streamlined pathways for early childhood educators to attain better compensation through higher education. In addition, Dr. Quong has been working with school districts to create partnerships for teachers and paraprofessionals to work towards their certifications. Dr. Quong's research interests include incorporating play-based learning back into the public school system, effective online teaching strategies, incorporating artificial intelligence into lesson planning and barriers in articulations between community colleges and universities. She has been a mentor for her state ECE quality rating system. She provides professional developments at the local, state and national levels. Dr. Quong began her comprehensive background in early childhood education by teaching in public education inclusion preschool classrooms. She transitioned to higher education at the community college level, where she led the Child Development Program.

Joshua Tabor is a Professor in the Department of Teacher Education in the College of Education at Texas Woman's University, specializing in effective online learning, AI in education, and gamification. With over two decades of experience in education, he brings a wealth of practical knowledge to his research and teaching. Dr. Tabor earned his doctorate from Texas A&M University and spent 18 years as a public school teacher, teaching AP Government and Economics and honing his skills in engaging students with complex material. Following his classroom tenure, Dr. Tabor served for six years as a digital learning specialist, where he guided teachers in integrating technology to enhance student engagement and learning outcomes. This experience informs his current research, which focuses on leveraging AI and gamification techniques to create more effective and engaging online learning environments. Dr. Tabor draws from popular culture and science fiction in his innovative teaching methodologies, effectively bridging the gap between academic content and students' interests. He is particularly focused on the emerging applications of AI in education and its potential to revolutionize both traditional and online classrooms. He currently serves as a co-chair of the artificial intelligence special interest group as a member of the Society for Information Technology and Teacher Education (SITE) and actively contributes to advancing the field of educational technology.

Tianchong Wang is a Lecturer in STEM in Innovative Education Futures at Flinders University's College of Education, Psychology and Social Work. He holds an EdD from the Chinese University of Hong Kong, an MSc from the University of Hong Kong, and a BA from Hong Kong Baptist University, along with various ICT qualifications. As a highly cited researcher with over 1400 citations and an h-index of 19, Tianchong's work centres on technology-enhanced learning and teaching, with a particular focus on Artificial Intelligence (AI) in Education. An advocate for the UN's SDG4, his research aims to enhance education equity, quality, and inclusiveness, foster positive change in learning environments, and empower educators and learners in underprivileged communities.

Serdar Yener currently works as an academic staff in Sinop University; a punctual individual with a proven track record of success and reliability in roles such as academic staff, researcher, project coordinator, and leader. He has participated in different organizations like UN, NATO, EU, academy as public affairs officer, academic staff, coordinator/director. After serving 19 years as army officer in Turkish Army, he has joined Sinop University /Turkey in 2016. He has carried out many projects under UN, EU, University in different areas. He worked as a public affairs officer under civil-military cooperation of NATO in Afghanistan in 2003. He contributed as coordinator of many social projects for the improvement of social life in Afghanistan. He has carried out many social projects in Lebanon under the umbrella of the UN. He got his PhD degree in Business and carried out many researches. He has more than 25 WOS/SCOPUS articles/books. He worked as Project Coordinator in employee issues, environment and marine litter-related projects.

Index

L

M

N

P

S

T

www.ingramcontent.com/pod-product-compliance
Lightning Source LLC
LaVergne TN
LVHW081527300926
849161LV00006B/1333

9798337360072